Books are to be

THE NEW PENGUIN BOOK OF

Scottish Verse

THE NEW PENGUIN BOOK OF

Scottish Verse

Edited by
ROBERT CRAWFORD
and MICK IMLAH

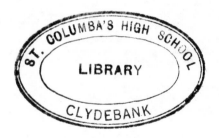

ALLEN LANE
THE PENGUIN PRESS

ALLEN LANE
THE PENGUIN PRESS

Published by the Penguin Group
Penguin Books Ltd, 27 Wrights Lane, London w8 5tz, England
Penguin Putnam Inc., 375 Hudson Street, New York, New York 10014, USA
Penguin Books Australia Ltd, Ringwood, Victoria, Australia
Penguin Books Canada Ltd, 10 Alcorn Avenue, Toronto, Ontario, Canada m4v 3b2
Penguin Books India (P) Ltd, 11, Community Centre, Panchsheel Park, New Delhi – 110 017, India
Penguin Books (NZ) Ltd, Private Bag 102902, NSMC, Auckland, New Zealand
Penguin Books (South Africa) (Pty) Ltd, 5 Watkins Street, Denver Ext 4, Johannesburg 2094, South Africa

Penguin Books Ltd, Registered Offices: Harmondsworth, Middlesex, England

First published 2000
1

Set in 10.5/13.25 pt PostScript Monotype Octavian
Typeset by Rowland Phototypesetting Ltd, Bury St Edmunds, Suffolk
Printed and bound in Great Britain by The Bath Press, Bath

A CIP catalogue record for this book is available from the British Library

ISBN 0–713–99238–7

Contents

Introduction

The story of Scottish poetry begins with a saint's hymn to creation. St Columba, an Irish immigrant who founded the famous monastery on Iona in 565 AD, was a Gaelic speaker who wrote in Latin, the international language of Christendom. His 'Altus Prosator' ('The Maker on High'), the organ-blast of praise which opens this anthology, is a masterpiece of innovative Latin verse, though it depicts a northern sea-world of whirlpools and voyages. The poem seeks to encompass the whole of creation, from the making of the world to the Day of Judgment – an ambition signalled by a structure whose stanzas begin in turn with each of the twenty-four letters, from A to Z, of the Roman alphabet.

Yet if Columba is the A of Scottish poetry, B is for Babel. Through the Dark Ages and the early Middle Ages, poetry was being written or spoken in half-a-dozen languages through the territories that make up modern Scotland. Gaelic, once the native tongue of most of Scotland as it was of Ireland, but these days confined to the Highlands and Western Isles, had an oral literature of bardic poetry going back to the second century AD. The oral poetry of the Pictish communities of the north-east has not been preserved. Welsh was spoken in Gallweddel (modern Galloway): the early Welsh poem, the *Gododdin* (*c.* 600 AD), deals with a war-band heading south from Din Eidyn (Edinburgh) to defend that region against invaders. (The name given to the other great Welsh bard, Taliesin, is related to that of the Gaelic bard, Ossian.) The earliest surviving form of the Old English poem 'The Dream of the Rood' (*c.* 700) is a fragment carved on a stone cross at Ruthwell in Dumfriesshire: Northumbrian Anglo-Saxon, from which the Scots language is derived, was spoken in south-eastern Scotland. Later, St Ronald (d. 1158) of Orkney, which was not annexed by Scotland until 1472, wrote elegant verse in Old Norse, while in Scotland's ecclesiastical centre, St Andrews, Guillaume le Clerc produced a sophisticated parody romance in Old French.

A recognizably national literature only began to emerge with the establishment of the Kingdom of Scotland, which grew through marriage and conquest during the eleventh century and survived determined English incursions in the thirteenth and fourteenth centuries. Independence was affirmed in what is now known as the Declaration of Arbroath (1320). This letter, sent to Pope John XXII by the nobility and clergy of Scotland, swore that 'so long as there shall be but one hundred of us remain alive, we will never consent to subject ourselves to the dominion of England' – an oath which held good for nearly 300 years. And in that time, while Gaelic held sway in its own territory, the Scots tongue was the language of poetry in the Scottish Lowlands.

The first considerable poems in Scots were patriotic epics. John Barbour's massive *The Bruce* (c. 1376) narrates, in rolling couplets, the career of King Robert I, whose forces defeated the English army at Bannockburn in 1314. Barbour's Bruce is a king of fashionable taste, who reads a French romance aloud to his officers; and the poem's varied delights include the halting of the army's progress so that a laundrywoman can give birth. But the most famous of the poem's 14,000 lines celebrate independence with the freshness and fervour of a nation escaping the colonial yoke:

> A! Fredome is a noble thing
> Fredome mays man to haiff liking.   *allows; contentment*
> Fredome all solace to man giffis,
> He levys at es that frely levys.   *lives; ease*

Beside Bruce in the gallery of the heroes of Scottish independence is the freedom-fighter William Wallace (d. 1305), celebrated in the *Wallace* of Blind Harry in the fifteenth century (and in the eighteenth by Robert Burns in his song 'Scots Wha Hae', set to an air supposed to have been played at the Battle of Bannockburn).

But this rugged nationalist poetry was suddenly succeeded by a court literature of universal scope and international stature. Blind Harry's contemporary Robert Henryson (c. 1420–c. 1490) was the eldest of the three great 'makars' whose works in this period – roughly equivalent to the lifetime of James IV (1473–1513) – epitomize the one unalloyed Golden Age in the whole turbulent course of Scottish poetry. In 'The Testament of Cresseid', Henryson (who is believed to have been a schoolmaster) picks up a tragic Classical myth where Geoffrey Chaucer's *Troilus and Criseyde* left it, and conducts his heroine, 'sumtyme countit the flour of Womanheid', to her leper's grave. To this bleak and gentle narrative, as to his comic animal fables, he appends a brief *moralitas*; but the feeling of the poem is all for humanity in 'distres', and Henryson's wry compassion informs and beautifies all he wrote. William Dunbar (c. 1460–c. 1520) was the most gifted poetical craftsman Scotland has ever produced: his range encompasses satire, the courtly love poem, bawdry, the dream allegory ('The Dance of the Sevin Deidly Synnis'), a 'flyting' with his fellow-poet Walter Kennedy, the superb music of his sacred poems ('Hale, Sterne Superne'), the trivial complaint ('On his heid-ake') and the desolate meditation on death. In all these modes his technical virtuosity is on proud display. The great achievement of Gavin Douglas (c.1474–1522) was in translation: his version, the *Eneados*, of Virgil's *Aeneid*; but in the extensive original Prologues to each of the twelve books of the epic, the Scots language appears, partly through the successful appropriation of terms from other languages in the manner of English prose writers eighty years later, as a richer and more flexible narrative medium than ever before or since.

'I se that makaris amang the laif / Playis heir ther pageant, syne gois to graif; / Sparit is nought ther faculté . . .' (Dunbar, 'The Lament for the Makars'). With the passing of its three exemplary practitioners, the prestige of Scots as a literary language went into steep decline. This is generally blamed on a sequence of three calamitous events: the Battle of Flodden (1513), the Reformation, and the Union of the Crowns (1603). At Flodden, James IV (at whose court Dunbar was the master among several professional poets) was slain by the English, along with the core of the Scottish nobility and an estimated 10,000 men in all. By the mid-century the Reformation had begun its crusade against a corrupt Church and disreputable arts: the procedure of the collection of verses known as the *Gude and Godlie Ballatis* (1567), which adapted secular songs by substituting the figure of Christ for the beloved, anticipates the long preoccupation of the mind of Scotland with ecclesiastical matters. Then in 1603, when the poet-king James VI became James I of England, his court moved as a body to London; after that, the absentee king ruled Scotland 'by his pen'.

James himself, and most of the so-called 'Castalian Band' of poets he gathered at court, including William Fowler and Robert Aytoun, wrote their verse in English. Other linguistic options were available. James's mother, Mary, Queen of Scots, wrote poems in French and Latin; William Drummond of Hawthornden, while writing mostly in mellifluous English, patented an extraordinary mixture of (mainly) Latin with Scots for his gleeful macaronic 'Polemo-Middinia'; while Drummond's contemporary, the Highlander Arthur Johnston, wrote poems about Donside in Latin while living in France. But of the leading poets of James VI's reign, only Alexander Montgomerie wrote principally in Scots; and in the century that followed, almost the only use of the native dialect in literature was in folk songs and ballads. This has been perceived as a defeat for the Scots language, its relegation to a supposedly lowlier artistic function; yet the anonymous 'folk' poets of the time used it to create a body of work that is among the great treasures of Scottish literature.

What are generally known as the Border ballads (though fine specimens came from other parts of Scotland, especially Aberdeenshire) date from the mid-sixteenth century to the beginning of the eighteenth. They were songs – 'made for singing', usually by women, 'an' no for reading', as Mrs Hogg, the mother of James, the 'Ettrick Shepherd', admonished Walter Scott, their principal collector. Their flinty narrative drive and shrewd sense of domestic hurt, their natural intensity, their strokes of the absurd and the unearthly, like the moment in 'The Battle of Otterburn' when Douglas turns from shouting at his page to remark,

> 'But I have dreamd a dreary dream,
>> Beyond the Isle of Sky;
> I saw a dead man win a fight,
>> And I think that man was I'

– these were admired abroad from the time of their first printing and, if it raises the status of the ballads to say so, their influence on Chatterton, Coleridge and Wordsworth was essential to the first phase of English Romanticism.

By the Union of the Parliaments in 1707, however, it was standard practice for any Lowland poet with a formal education to compose in English. For the Borderer James Thomson (1700–1748) the pursuit of a literary career entailed a move to London, where he wrote the seminal nature poem *The Seasons* (1726–30) and the song 'Rule, Britannia'. David Malloch, who followed Thomson south, assimilated to the point of trading his barbarian surname for the civilized 'Mallet'. These poets anticipate in verse Adam Smith's landmark assertion, in an Edinburgh lecture of 1751, that English was the language of the future for ambitious Scots.

At the same time as Scots literary culture was succumbing to the weight of English, a more deliberate onslaught was being waged on the Gaelic culture of the Highlands. After the defeat of the Jacobite Rising by the Hanoverian army at Culloden in 1746, proscriptive laws, military intimidation and (into the next century) the Clearances drove many Highlanders from their land and occupation. Yet Gaelic poetry was only refreshed by this calamity: the secret literature, as it came to be, of a cause apparently lost. The eighteenth century sees the established models of classical bardic verse (of which the main written repository is the Book of the Dean of Lismore, 1512–1542) being supplemented by new metres and subject-matter, and by poets outside the professional tradition. The greatest of all poets in Scottish Gaelic, Alasdair Mac Mhaighstir Alasdair (c. 1695–c. 1770), straddles the old and the new worlds of Highland experience. Deeply versed in the classical tradition, he can also experiment, using English borrowings (for example) with humour and dash. His greatest poem belongs to the post-Rising years: the 'Birlinn Chlann Raghnaill' ('Clanranald's Galley') adapts the conventions of praise poetry to a boat and crew fighting for survival in a storm that is as real as it is symbolic. Against this background, James Macpherson published (in 1760–1763) his purported translations of epic poetry in Gaelic relating to the third-century hero Fingal, as told by his son Ossian, which he claimed were still circulating in parts of the Highlands. The ecstatic reception accorded in Edinburgh and throughout Europe to the 'Ossian' poems – which, though based in part on authentic materials, were fabricated by Macpherson – has a touch of the *Dunciad* about it; yet the international appetite it revealed for an indigenous poetry was shortly to be satisfied from another quarter.

Allan Ramsay (1684–1758), father of the more famous painter of the same name, was responsible – as much in his collections of old Scottish poems as in his own verse – for the first considerable reaction in the eighteenth century against the grip of English on Scottish poetry. But it was in the work of Robert Fergusson (1750–1774) that such resistance began to be embodied in poems of high subtlety and originality, and sardonic point. Fergusson was an educated and versatile man, who found his subject-matter in, for instance, geometry as well as in the life of Edinburgh's streets. In his address 'To the Principal and Professors of the University of St Andrews, on their Superb Treat to Dr Samuel Johnson', he uses his own lexicographical awareness to twit the great dictionary-maker and proponent of Standard English. Johnson's definition of *oats* as 'A grain, which in England is generally given to horses, but in Scotland supports the people' provokes Fergusson to devise an oat-rich menu for the Doctor's visit; and the poem is in Scots.

The unfortunate Fergusson died too young (in Edinburgh's Bedlam, at twenty-four) to deliver much of a blow against the rule of English. But his lead was taken up by his younger contemporary and admirer, Robert Burns (1759–1796), a peasant farmer from Alloway in Ayrshire, whose first publication, *Poems, Chiefly in the Scottish Dialect* (Kilmarnock, 1786), was seized on by Edinburgh society and promptly established him in the popular consciousness as Scotland's national 'bard'. Burns's extraordinary fame at home and abroad – he has been translated into many languages – furnishes 'the one example in history', as the American essayist Emerson put it, 'of a language made classic through the genius of a single man'. (In fact, Burns wrote in various mixtures of Scots and English – his 'beastie' in 'To a Mouse' is 'timorous' – and poems at one end of the spectrum are modelled after William Shenstone.) In addition to the thirty-four poems of the Kilmarnock edition, Burns's 'genius' is variously evident in 'Holy Willie's Prayer', the finest and funniest example of his satirical 'priest-skelpin''; the exuberant 'cantata', *The Jolly Beggars*; a masterpiece of comic narrative, 'Tam o' Shanter'; and the hundreds of songs he either wrote or adapted.

Burns's techniques were simple; and, though his imaginative range was wide, the world he drew on was pronouncedly local. In the hands of a century of imitators, these characteristics stiffened into vices. It was as if Burns had involuntarily used up the last energies of Scots as a literary language. T. F. Henderson, whose *Scottish Vernacular Literature: A History* was published in 1898, mourned his subject as a thing of the past. In innumerable collections and compilations such as *The Poets of Ayrshire* (1890), the Scots language acts as a kind of anaesthetic, full of belittling or sweetening suffixes, the harmless progeny of Burns's 'beastie'. Hugh MacDiarmid wrote caustically about the 'doldrums' into which Scottish poetry had fallen after Burns's death: 'an apparently bottomless abyss of doggerel, moralistic rubbish, mawkish sentimentality and witless jocosity'. The conventional term of abuse for the verse of these generations is 'kailyard' (cabbage-patch), originally applied to a school of late Victorian fiction: and if the epithet has itself grown stale, it gives the flavour of what – with certain exceptions – presented itself as Scottish literature in the later nineteenth century: soft-headed, diminutive in scope and stubbornly rural.

Burns was six years old when, in the spring of 1765, James Watt took the fateful walk across Glasgow Green in which he suddenly seized on the principle of the expansion engine. In that moment a new world flashed into being, of iron and steam and smoke and sparks, whose hub was Glasgow herself: then a town of 30,000 people, a century later the Second City – and, in the coinage of Hector Bolitho, the 'Cancer' – of Empire. The way of life embodied in Burns's poems shrank smartly into the margins as industry took root. In 1800, 17 per cent of Scotland's population lived in towns of more than 10,000 inhabitants; in 1900, the figure was over 50 per cent. Where formerly the labouring Scot might be represented at the head of a plough or driving his herd, now he was crouched in the foundry or boilerhouse, whether in Lanark or some far outpost of the empire. The malaise of Scottish poetry in the nineteenth century was its general incapacity to register this shift in the national condition, to engage with the facts of the place and times it was made in.

The most powerful portrait in verse of the Scotsman at work in this period is not by a Scotsman at all. Rudyard Kipling's 'McAndrew's Hymn' (1893) is the monologue of 'the dour Scots engineer' on the *Mary Gloster*, 'the man they never knew', whose strong Calvinist pulse and propulsive engine-music carry an implicit criticism of an effete national poetic:

> Romance! Those first-class passengers they like it very well,
> Printed an' bound in little books; but why don't poets tell?
> I'm sick of all their quirks an' turns – the loves and doves they dream –
> Lord send a man like Robbie Burns to sing the Song o' Steam!
> To match with Scotia's noblest speech yon orchestra sublime
> Whaurto – uplifted like the Just – the tail-rods mark the time.

Since Burns, a crucial part of what Scotland has had to 'tell' has been Glasgow, her incredible slums and stupendous productivity; yet her output of imaginative literature was practically zero. In Alasdair Gray's epic novel *Lanark* (1981), one character observes that 'Imaginatively, Glasgow exists as a music-hall song and a few bad novels'. (The music-hall song is Will Fyffe's 'I Belong to Glasgow', whose real association is with alcohol.) For Hugh MacDiarmid, she was 'the great city that has never had / A single poet of the slightest consequence'. In fact, two poets of considerable interest, pioneers of writing about the new urban experience, were born in the mid-nineteenth century in the shadow of Glasgow, at Port Glasgow down the Clyde and at Barrhead, Renfrewshire, respectively: the second James Thomson ('BV', 1834–1882) and John Davidson (1857–1909). These, too, the region exported; each of them took his volatile west-coast temperament to London. Thomson, 150 years after his pastoral namesake, wrote his inconsolable *The City of Dreadful Night* there; Davidson, who had trained as a chemist, wrote poems of scientific curiosity ('Snow') as well as poems on the lot of suburban clerks, made up of what T. S. Eliot called (approvingly) 'dingy urban images':

> For here dwell those who must fulfil
> Dull tasks in uncongenial spheres,
> Who toil through dread of coming ill,
> And not with hope of happier years . . .
> ('A Northern Suburb')

In poetry of the first half of the twentieth century, Glasgow becomes blurrily synonymous with Hell. Poets from every other corner of the country used the name for its connotations of shame, horror or scorn. Edwin Muir came to Glasgow from Orkney when he was thirteen, and the shock of the contrast quivers through his whole career; the worst torture he can devise for his blind 'Milton' is the noise of Argyle Street at closing-time, 'the steely clamour known too well / on Saturday nights in every street in Hell'. MacDiarmid, raised in the pretty Border town of Langholm, angrily deplored the Glasgow phenomenon, most extensively in his 'Third Hymn to Lenin' ('The whole of Russia had no Hell like this'); the name sits sarcastically in the titles of half-a-dozen of his poems. The Western Islander Sorley MacLean sees city squalor as a pollution of the Gospels and the Gaelic way: (in his own translation) 'My eye is not on Calvary / nor on Bethlehem the Blessed, / but on a foul-smelling backland in Glasgow / where life rots as it grows . . .'

It was not until the late 1960s, and the coming of age (in the volume entitled *The Second Life*) of Edwin Morgan, that Glasgow had much of an identity in poems other than as a site of damnation. With his McAndrew-like embrace of modern technologies, Morgan associates urban renewal with personal regeneration, and in the debate between the tenement and the high-rise sides enthusiastically with the bulldozer:

> green May, and the slow great blocks rising
> under yellow tower cranes, concrete and glass and steel
> out of a dour rubble it was and barefoot children gone.
> ('The Second Life')

This is a poetry consciously 'getting real', attending to the ground beneath its feet, in a spirit Morgan revealed once in an interview: 'What an extraordinary thing to say that London is an unreal city! This is the kind of thing that really riles me about Eliot!'

In general, however, the health of Scottish poetry in the twentieth century was restored less by a transfusion of new subject-matter than by a rediscovery of linguistic resources – and by the timely arrival of its latest poet of outright genius.

The showpieces of the so-called 'Scots Renaissance' are three books written in Montrose by Hugh MacDiarmid (the pen-name of Christopher Murray Grieve, 1892–1978): two collections of lyrics, *Sangschaw* (1925) and *Penny Wheep* (1926), and the long poem *A Drunk Man Looks at the Thistle*, also published in 1926. MacDiarmid referred to the language of these successively as 'vernacular', 'braid Scots' and 'Lallans'; in fact it was synthetic, made up from usages in several Lowland dialects, supplemented by curiosities unearthed from John Jamieson's *Etymological Dictionary of the Scottish Language* (1808), and designed for express-ive utility. Some of the lyrics begin as demonstrations of single beautiful or suggestive words, of 'antrin things' – 'A watergaw wi' its chitterin' licht / Ayont the on-ding' is an indistinct type of rainbow, in a poem ('The Watergaw') which also features 'yow-trummle', cold weather after sheep-shearing; but their effect depends equally on the extraordinary strangeness of their images and perspectives. In 'Empty Vessel', for instance, the shape of a 'lass' singing to her vanished child is transformed in a dazzling religious conceit:

> The licht that bends owre a' thing
> Is less ta'en up wi't.

MacDiarmid's wonderful early poems seemed to invest the vernacular with un-limited new lyric and (in *A Drunk Man*) discursive potential. But no sooner was this apparent than their author moved restlessly on to a political and then to a philosophical mode of poetry; nor did their example convince all Scottish poets that the project was generally valid. Edwin Muir, whose poems speak bitterly of Burns and Walter Scott as 'sham bards of a sham nation', summarized his objection in *Scott and Scotland* (1936):

Scots has survived to our time as a language for simple poetry . . . all its other uses have lapsed, and it expresses therefore only a fragment of the Scottish mind. . . .Scotsmen feel in one language and think in another; . . . their emotions turn to the Scottish tongue, with all its associations of local sentiment, and their minds to a standard English which for them is almost bare of associations other than those of the classroom.

And elsewhere: 'Scottish dialect poetry is a regression to childhood, an escape from the responsibility of the whole reason to the simplicity and irresponsibility of the infant mind.' Such opinions earned Muir years of abuse from MacDiarmid. But the latter had already more or less abandoned his own use of 'Lallans', preferring to write in English – sometimes, as in the opening of 'On a Raised Beach', in a form of synthetic English – from 1934 onwards; and his explanation for the move (given in an interview of 1959) is only a milder restatement of Muir's position: 'even the revivified Scots that I had developed . . . wasn't sufficiently malleable for the expression of the whole range of modern intellectual and artistic interests . . . .'.

Yet the Scots Renaissance was neither a finite experiment nor a one-man show, for all that the freakishly dynamic MacDiarmid liked to figure himself as a 'minority o' ane' (that 'ane', of course, like his favourite Whitman, containing multitudes). Lesser poets, Charles Murray, Violet Jacob and Lewis Spence, had preceded him in their innovative use of Scots; and after his lead came the considerable achievements of William Soutar (1898–1943), Robert Garioch (1909–1981) and Sydney Goodsir Smith (1915–1975), who were selective in their response to what Garioch called his 'pulpit objurgations'. (For instance, Garioch's Second World War poem 'The Wire', noted by Douglas Dunn to have 'a virtually mediaeval poetic atmosphere', might seem to comply with MacDiarmid's injunction, 'Not Burns – Dunbar!' Yet else-where, in his poems of Edinburgh life, Garioch revisits the proscribed idiom – 'Auld Reekie no the same' – of Burns's literary begetter, Robert Fergusson.) MacDiarmid expanded the possibilities; but so did others. Above all, mingling the subjects of love and war like its historical antecedents, Sorley MacLean's volume *Dàin do Eimhir agus Dàin Eile* (1943) proved that a powerful contemporary poetry could be written in Gaelic, and this poetry only in Gaelic: an achievement comparable to MacDiarmid's in Scots two decades earlier, but against odds that were even longer. (Scotland currently has a population of around 5 million, of whom perhaps 70,000 speak Gaelic.)

Choice of language continued to be a live issue for poets through the second half of the twentieth century. A corps of Highland poets sustained the Gaelic revival, augmented by others, like Meg Bateman, who were not native speakers. W. N. Herbert appropriated MacDiarmid's dictionary Scots for generally playful ends. Tom Leonard presented quiet political satire through the use of 'an urban phonetic dialect':

> thi reason
> a talk wia
> BBC accent
> iz coz yi
> widny wahnt
> mi ti talk
> aboot thi
> trooth wia
> voice lik
> wanna yoo
> scruff.

Translation was once more a preoccupation, whether in practice or in poems (like Edwin Morgan's 'The First Men on Mercury') about the process. Yet language no longer seemed to cause poets ideological or practical anxiety. Most of the leading

Scottish poets of the 1970s, 1980s and 1990s – such as Norman MacCaig, Iain Crichton Smith, Douglas Dunn, Kathleen Jamie and Don Paterson – chose to write the bulk of their work in English. But this verse in English none the less declared itself, whether by setting or by some subtler trace of accent – variants of what Stevenson called the 'strong Scots accent of the mind' – to be wholly and contentedly Scottish.

What, then, across its range of languages, regions and traditions, are the common characteristics of Scottish poetry? The first is its weather. From the 'Altus Prosator' onwards, with its 'clouds showering wet winter', its 'floods' and 'blasts' and 'conduits utterly rich and as full as udders' (in Edwin Morgan's translation), bad weather has been not so much a theme as the element of Scottish poetry. Henryson sets out to write his *Testament* in 'ane doolie [miserable] sessoun', when 'Schouris of haill gart fra the north discend / That scant me fra the cauld I micht defend'. Dunbar's creative spirit sinks likewise to its work 'in to thir dirk and drublie dayis . . .'; Douglas has the same days, 'The tyme and sessoune bitter cold and paill, / Thai schort days that clerkis clepe brumaill' in the Prologue to the Seventh Book of his *Eneados*, glossed with relish as 'A eloquent description of wynter wyth hys grete stormes and tempestis'. (Four centuries later, in Edwin Muir's 'Scotland's Winter' or MacDiarmid's *To Circumjack Cencrastus* – 'the weary days', again, 'when it is scarce grey licht at noon' – winter is symbolic of political gloom or freezing-over.) The most famous of the Border ballads, 'Sir Patrick Spens', and the jewel of eighteenth-century Gaelic, the 'Birlinn Chlann Raghnaill' ('Clanranald's Galley'), are about storms at sea; the first-written and foremost of Thomson's *Seasons* is 'Winter'; while in Burns's most celebrated poem, Tam o' Shanter's adventures have the standard lashing backdrop:

> The wind blew as 'twad blawn its last;
> The rattling show'rs rose on the blast;
> The speedy gleams the darkness swallow'd;
> Loud, deep, and lang the thunder bellow'd . . .

This constant battering provokes at times a sort of desperate humour, as in the ballad 'Get Up and Bar the Door':

> The wind sae cauld blew south and north,
> And blew into the floor.

In such a context, when Alexander Hume sets out (in the 1590s) to record the sights and sounds of a summer's day in 'Of the Day Estivall', he is like one describing a miracle.

Yet Scottish poets had plenty of experience of milder climates. Indeed, before the

Union of 1603, they enjoyed closer contact with the continent of Europe, where many of them had some part of their education, than most of their English counterparts. National concerns co-existed naturally with a curiosity about the rest of the world. The principal matter of David Lindsay's verse is the condition of Scotland; but the other, outward view of his 'Dreme' has a relish of the sense of elsewhere and the naming of it:

> Secundlie, we considderit Africa,
> With mony fructfull famous regioun,
> As Ethiope, and Tripolitana,
> Zewges, quhare standis the tryumphant toun
> Off nobyll Cartage, that ciete of renoun;
> Garamantes, Nadabar, Libia,
> Getulia, and Maritania . . .

Perhaps as a result of its own multilingual background, Scottish poetry has been notably active in translation. Gavin Douglas's *Eneados* (c. 1513) was the first translation of a classical epic made in the British Isles, and was followed shortly by John Stewart's version of Ariosto's *Orlando Furioso*. Subsequent projects have taken forms as various as William Fowler's sixteenth-century versions of Petrarch's *Trionfi*, Walter Scott's adaptations of Romantic ballads by the German Gottfried Bürger (which were the starting-point of his own literary career), and Edwin Morgan's translations in the 1970s of Mayakovsky into Scots. One task of the Scots Renaissance, as Hugh MacDiarmid saw it, was to restore international standards and awareness to Scottish writing; in *A Drunk Man Looks at the Thistle* he inveighs against 'the dour provincial thought / that merks the Scottish breed', and presses for a way to make, out of distinctively local materials, a way of dealing with the universal:

> I wad ha'e Scotland to my eye
> Until I saw a timeless flame
> Tak' Auchtermuchty for a name,
> And kent that Ecclefechan stood
> As pairt o' an eternal mood.

As MacDiarmid knew, however, Scotland has often looked to her poets to help express a sense of nationhood: not least in his own century, when the movement in favour of devolution culminated, in 1999, in the establishment of a new parliament in Edinburgh. And nothing is finally more typical of Scottish poetry than its prejudice in Scotland's favour. This emerges successively in the pride of the early epics and of Gaelic poems in praise of clan and chieftain; in lamentations over the rhyming calamities, for Lowlands and Highlands, of Flodden and Culloden; and in poems celebrating the country's natural glories, of which Duncan Ban MacIntyre's 'Moladh Beinn Dobhrain' ('Ben Dorain', c. 1760) is a crowning example. Though his own politics were Unionist, Walter Scott collected and restored Scottish literary valuables in his *Minstrelsy of the Scottish Border* (1802), and his sense of the past could generate heat as well as archival dust; *The Lay of the Last Minstrel* has two of the most celebrated exclamations in Scottish poetry:

> Caledonia! Stern and wild,
> Meet nurse for a poetic child!

and

> Breathes there the man, with soul so dead,
> Who never to himself hath said,
>   This is my own, my native land!

And for all the trauma of the history it embodies – whether in poems written by the principals, such as Mary, Queen of Scots, and the Marquis of Montrose, or later about them, by Marion Angus ('Alas! Poor Queen') and William Aytoun – Scottish poetry radiates, to a degree unmatched by any other substantial national literature, a passionate love of country, a sense of joy in its belonging. Robert Louis Stevenson (1850–1894) maintained in his essay 'The Scot Abroad' that 'The happiest lot on earth is to be born a Scotsman':

You must pay for it in many ways. . . .But somehow life is warmer and closer; the hearth burns more redly; the lights of home shine softer on the rainy street; the very names, endeared in verse and music, cling nearer round our hearts.

– an outpouring which is outstandingly sentimental but also, so far as literature can test it, true. Stevenson, exiled to the South Seas by his poor health, is the suntanned laureate of all those Scots who left to work or live away: in a continuing tradition, he is himself a magician with 'endeared' place-names:

> The tropics vanish, and meseems that I,
> From Halkerside, from topmost Allermuir,
> Or steep Caerketton, dreaming gaze again.

But as the writer of some of the best poetry of childhood, Stevenson was a natural nostalgic. A surer proof of his patriotic superlatives is the case of Hugh MacDiarmid – scourge of the 'mawkish', a literary 'catfish' and 'volcano' as he saw himself: MacDiarmid, a Lowlander and a Communist, who still cannot contemplate the flower of the Jacobites without the poetic equivalent of bursting into tears:

> The rose of all the world is not for me.
> I want for my part
> Only the little white rose of Scotland
> That smells sharp and sweet — and breaks the heart.

In the end, the abrasive, exceptional MacDiarmid will be as proud as any to lie down, like his own 'Drunk Man', and be counted among the heroes and heroines, great and small, of Scottish history and Scottish poetry:

> The thistle rises and forever will,
> Getherin' the generations under't.
> This is the monument o' a' they were,
> And a' they hoped and wondered.

Editors' Note

The New Penguin Book of Scottish Verse aims to present a generous selection of the best poems written by those born or settled in Scotland, or, in the case of earlier work, coming out of the territory now known as Scotland. All the poems are published here in their original languages, with modern English verse translations. While recognizing that few if any readers will be able to read all the languages represented, it has been thought desirable to print the original text in every case and to offer only verse translations. Although the editors have thought it inappropriate to include their own verse, they have supplied new translations of older poems where no suitable version existed. Otherwise, in selecting poems for which translations are needed, the quality of the verse translations available has been a factor. Poems in Scots are glossed in English.

While the most reliable texts have been used throughout, there has been no attempt to standardize Scots or Gaelic orthography. Unlike (for instance) English, Scots does not exist as a standardized national or international language; indeed part of the pleasure or point of writing in Scots for some poets has been its orthographical fluidity. As a general rule, however, the distinctive form *Qu* has been retained and *Wh* not substituted, because it implies a significant difference of pronunciation and because readers will quickly get used to it, as they will to the *-is* plural ending.

The biographical notes are arranged chronologically by date of birth. They are placed at the back of the book so as not to intrude on the sequence of the poems.

The editors are grateful to Mr Ronald Black for assistance with Gaelic proof-reading, to Ms Jill Gamble for indexing, and to Dr Nicola Royan for providing much help with English-language glosses to the Scots poems; acknowledgement is also due for institutional support from the School of English, University of St Andrews, which aided the making of this anthology.

THE NEW PENGUIN BOOK OF
Scottish Verse

ST COLUMBA (521–597)

Altus Prosator

ALTUS prosator vetustus dierum et ingenitus
erat absque origine primordii et crepidine
est et erit in saecula saeculorum infinita
cui est unigenitus Christus et sanctus spiritus
coaeternus in gloria deitatis perpetua
non tres deos depromimus sed unum Deum dicimus
salva fidei in personis tribus gloriosissimis.

BONOS creavit angelos ordines et archangelos
principatum ac sedium potestatum virtutium
uti non esset bonitas otiosa ac majestas
trinitatis in omnibus largitatis muneribus
sed haberet caelestia in quibus privilegia
ostenderet magnopere possibili fatimine.

CAELI de regni apice stationis angelicae
claritate praefulgoris venustate speciminis
superbiendo ruerat Lucifer quem formaverat
apostataeque angeli eodem lapsu lugubri
auctoris cenodoxiae pervicacis invidiae
ceteris remanentibus in suis principatibus.

DRACO magnus taeterrimus terribilis et antiquus
qui fuit serpens lubricus sapientior omnibus
bestiis et animantibus terrae ferocioribus
tertiam partem siderum traxit secum in barathrum
locorum infernalium diversorumque carcerum
refugas veri luminis parasito praecipites.

EXCELSUS mundi machinam praevidens et harmoniam
caelum et terram fecerat mare aquas condiderat
herbarum quoque germina virgultorum arbuscula

The Maker on High

ANCIENT *exalted seed-scatterer whom time gave no progenitor:*
he knew no moment of creation in his primordial foundation
he is and will be all places in all time and all ages
with Christ his first-born only-born and the holy spirit co-borne
throughout the high eternity of glorious divinity:
three gods we do not promulgate one God we state and intimate
salvific faith victorious: three persons very glorious.

BENEVOLENCE *created angels and all the orders of archangels*
thrones and principalities powers virtues qualities
denying otiosity to the excellence and majesty
of the not-inactive trinity in all labours of bounty
when it mustered heavenly creatures whose well devised natures
received its lavish proffer through power-word for ever.

CAME *down from heaven summit down from angelic limit*
dazzling in his brilliance beauty's very likeness
Lucifer downfalling (once woke at heaven's calling)
apostate angels sharing the deadly downfaring
of the author of high arrogance and indurated enviousness
the rest still continuing safe in their dominions.

DAUNTINGLY *huge and horrible the dragon ancient and terrible*
known as the lubric serpent subtler in his element
than all the beasts and every fierce thing living earthly
dragged a third – so many – stars to his gehenna
down to infernal regions not devoid of dungeons
benighted ones hell's own parasite hurled headlong.

EXCELLENT *promethean armoury structuring world harmony*
had created earth and heaven and wet acres of ocean
also sprouting vegetation shrubs groves plantations

solem lunam ac sidera ignem ac necessaria
aves pisces et pecora bestias animalia
hominem demum regere protoplaustum praesagmine.

FACTIS simul sideribus aetheris luminaribus
conlaudaverunt angeli factura pro mirabili
immensae molis Dominum opificem caelestium
praeconio laudabili debito et immobili
concentuque egregio grates egerunt Domino
amore et arbitrio non naturae donario.

GRASSATIS primis duobus seductisque parentibus
secundo ruit diabolus cum suis satellitibus
quorum horrore vultuum sonoque volitantium
consternarentur homines metu territi fragiles
non valentes carnalibus haec intueri visibus
qui nunc ligantur fascibus ergastulorum nexibus.

HIC sublatus e medio deiectus est a Domino
cuius aeris spatium constipatur satellitum
globo invisibilium turbido perduellium
ne malis exemplaribus imbuti ac sceleribus
nullis unquam tegentibus saeptis ac parietibus
fornicarentur homines palam omnium oculis.

INVEHUNT nubes pontias ex fontibus brumalias
tribus profundioribus oceani dodrantibus
maris caeli climatibus caeruleis turbinibus
profuturas segitibus vineis et germinibus
agitatae flaminibus thesauris emergentibus
quique paludes marinas evacuant reciprocas.

KADUCA ac tyrannica mundique momentanea
regum praesentis gloria nutu Dei deposita
ecce gigantes gemere sub aquis magno ulcere
comprobantur incendio aduri ac supplicio
Cocytique Charybdibus strangulati turgentibus
Scyllis obtecti fluctibus eliduntur et scrupibus.

sun moon stars to ferry fire and all things necessary
birds fish and cattle and every animal imaginable
but lastly the second promethean the protoplast human being.

FAST upon the starry finishing the lights high shimmering
the angels convened and celebrated for the wonders just created
the Lord the only artificer of that enormous vault of matter
with loud and well judged voices unwavering in their praises
an unexampled symphony of gratitude and sympathy
sung not by force of nature but freely lovingly grateful.

GUILTY of assault and seduction of our parents in the garden
the devil has a second falling together with his followers
whose faces set in horror and wingbeats whistling hollow
would petrify frail creatures into stricken fearers
but what men perceive bodily must preclude luckily
those now bound and bundled in dungeons of the underworld.

HE Zabulus was driven by the Lord from mid heaven
and with him the airy spaces were choked like drains with faeces
as the turgid rump of rebels fell but fell invisible
in case the grossest villains became willy-nilly
with neither walls nor fences preventing curious glances
tempters to sin greatly openly emulatingly.

IRRIGATING clouds showering wet winter from sea-fountains
from floods of the abysses three-fourths down through fishes
up to the skyey purlieus in deep blue whirlpools
good rain then for cornfields vineyard-bloom and grain-yields
driven by blasts emerging from their airy treasuring
desiccating not the land-marches but the facing sea-marshes.

KINGS of the world we live in: their glories are uneven
brittle tyrannies disembodied by a frown from God's forehead:
giants too underwater groaning in great horror
forced to burn like torches cut by painful tortures
pounded in the millstones of underworld maelstroms
roughed rubbed out buried in a frenzy of flints and billows.

LIGATAS aquas nubibus frequenter cribrat Dominus
ut ne erumpant protinus simul ruptis obicibus
quarum uberioribus venis velut uberibus
pedetentim natantibus telli per tractus istius
gelidis ac ferventibus diversis in temporibus
usquam influunt flumina nunquam deficientia.

MAGNI Dei virtutibus appenditur dialibus
globus terrae et circulus abyssi magnae inditus
suffultu Dei iduma omnipotentis valida
columnis velut vectibus eundem sustenantibus
promontoriis et rupibus solidis fundaminibus
velut quibusdam basibus firmatus immobilibus.

NULLI videtur dubium in imis esse infernum
ubi habentur tenebrae vermes et dirae bestiae
ubi ignis sulphureus ardens flammis edacibus
ubi rugitus hominum fletus et stridor dentium
ubi Gehennae gemitus terribilis et antiquus
ubi ardor flammaticus sitis famisque horridus.

ORBEM infra ut legimus incolas esse novimus
quorum genu precario frequenter flectit Domino
quibusque impossibile librum scriptum revolvere
obsignatum signaculis septem de Christi monitis
quem idem resignaverat postquam victor exstiterat
explens sui praesagmina adventus prophetalia.

PLANTATUM a prooemio paradisum a Domino
legimus in primordio Genesis nobilissimo
cuius ex fonte flumina quattuor sunt manantia
cuius etiam florido lignum vitae in medio
cuius non cadunt folia gentibus salutifera
cuius inenarrabiles deliciae ac fertiles.

QUIS ad condictum Domini montem ascendit Sinai?
quis audivit tonitrua ultra modum sonantia
quis clangorem perstrepere inormitatis buccinae?

LETTING *the waters be sifted from where the clouds are lifted*
the Lord often prevented the flood he once attempted
leaving the conduits utterly full and rich as udders
slowly trickling and panning through the tracts of this planet
freezing if cold was called for warm in the cells of summer
keeping our rivers everywhere running forward for ever.

MAGISTERIAL *are his powers as the great God poises*
the earth ball encircled by the great deep so firmly
supported by an almighty robust nieve so tightly
that you would think pillar and column held it strong and solemn
the capes and cliffs stationed on solidest foundations
fixed uniquely in their place as if on immovable bases.

NO *one needs to show us: a hell lies deep below us*
where there is said to be darkness worms beasts carnage
where there are fires of sulphur burning to make us suffer
where men are gnashing roaring weeping wailing deploring
where groans mount from gehennas terrible never-ending
where parched and fiery horror feeds thirst and hunger.

OFTEN *on their knees at prayer are many said to be there*
under the earth books tell us they do not repel us
though they found it unavailing the scroll not unrolling
whose fixed seals were seven when Christ warning from heaven
unsealed it with the gesture of a resurrected victor
fulfilling the prophets' foreseeing of his coming and his decreeing.

PARADISE *was planted primally as God wanted*
we read in sublime verses entering into Genesis
its fountain's rich waters feed four flowing rivers
its heart abounds with flowers where the tree of life towers
with foliage never fading for the healing of the nations
and delights indescribable abundantly fruitful.

QUIZ *sacred Sinai: who is it has climbed so high?*
Who has heard the thunder-cracks vast in the sky-tracts?
Who has heard the enormous bullroaring of the war-horns?

quis quoque vidit fulgura in gyro coruscantia
quis lampades et iacula saxaque collidentia
praeter Israhelitici Moysen iudicem populi?

REGIS regum rectissimi prope est dies Domini
dies irae et vindictae tenebrarum et nebulae
diesque mirabilium tonitruorum fortium
dies quoque angustiae maeroris ac tristitiae
in quo cessabit mulierum amor ac desiderium
hominumque contentio mundi huius et cupido.

STANTES erimus pavidi ante tribunal Domini
reddemusque de omnibus rationem affectibus
videntes quoque posita ante obtutus crimina
librosque conscientiae patefactos in facie
in fletus amarissimos ac singultus erumpemus
subtracta necessaria operandi materia.

TUBA primi archangeli strepente admirabili
erumpent munitissima claustra ac poliandria
mundi praesentis frigora hominum liquescentia
undique conglobantibus ad compagines ossibus
animabus aethralibus eisdem obviantibus
rursumque redeuntibus debitis mansionibus.

VAGATUR ex climactere Orion caeli cardine
derelicto Virgilio astrorum splendidissimo
per metas Thetis ignoti orientalis circuli
girans certis ambagibus redit priscis reditibus
oriens post biennium Vesperugo in vesperum
sumpta in proplesmatibus tropicis intellectibus.

XRISTO de caelis Domino descendente celsissimo
praefulgebit clarissimum signum crucis et vexillum
tectisque luminaribus duobus principalibus
cadent in terram sidera ut fructus de ficulnea
eritque mundi spatium ut fornacis incendium
tunc in montium specubus abscondent se exercitus.

Who has seen the lightning flashing round the night-ring?
Who has seen javelins flambeaus a rock-face in shambles?
Only to Moses is this real only to the judge of Israel.

RUE *God's day arriving righteous high king's assizing*
dies irae day of the vindex day of cloud and day of cinders
day of the dumbfoundering day of great thundering
day of lamentation of anguish of confusion
with all the love and yearning of women unreturning
as all men's striving and lust for worldly living.

STANDING *in fear and trembling with divine judgement assembling*
we shall stammer what we expended before our life was ended
faced by rolling videos of our crimes however hideous
forced to read the pages of the conscience book of ages
we shall burst out into weeping sobbing bitter and unceasing
now that all means of action have tholed the last retraction.

THE *archangelic trumpet-blast is loud and great at every fastness*
the hardest vaults spring open the catacombs are broken
the dead of the world are thawing their cold rigor withdrawing
the bones are running and flying to the joints of the undying
their souls hurry to meet them and celestially to greet them
returning both together to be one not one another.

VAGRANT *Orion driven from the crucial hinge of heaven*
leaves the Pleiades receding most splendidly beneath him
tests the ocean boundaries the oriental quandaries
as Vesper circling steadily returns home readily
the rising Lucifer of the morning after two years mourning:
these things are to be taken as type and trope and token.

X SPIKES *and flashes like the Lord's cross marching*
down with him from heaven as the last sign is given
moonlight and sunlight are finally murdered
stars fall from dignity like fruits from a fig-tree
the world's whole surface burns like a furnace
armies are crouching in caves in the mountains.

YMNORUM cantionibus sedulo tinnientibus
tripudiis sanctis milibus angelorum vernantibus
quattuorque plenissimis animalibus oculis
cum viginti felicibus quattuor senioribus
coronas admittentibus agni Dei sub pedibus
laudatur tribus vicibus Trinitas aeternalibus.

ZELUS ignis furibundus consumet adversarios
nolentes Christum credere Deo a Patre venisse
nos vero evolabimus obviam ei protinus
et sic cum ipso erimus in diversis ordinibus
dignitatum pro meritis praemiorum perpetuis
permansuri in gloria a saeculis in saecula.

Yᴏᴜ *know then the singing of hymns finely ringing*
thousands of angels advancing spring up in sacred dances
quartet of beasts gaze from numberless eyes in praise
two dozen elders as happiness compels them
throw all their crowns down to the Lamb who surmounts them
'Holy holy holy' binds the eternal trinity.

Zᴀʙᴜʟᴜs *burns to ashes all those adversaries*
who deny that the Saviour was Son to the Father
but we shall fly to meet him and immediately greet him
and be with him in the dignity of all such diversity
as our deeds make deserved and we without swerve
shall live beyond history in the state of glory.

Translated from the Latin by Edwin Morgan

ANEIRIN (?6th century)

from *The Gododdin*

Mynog Gododdin traethiannor;
Mynog am ran cwyniador.
Rhag Eidyn, arial fflam, nid argor.
Ef dodes ei ddilys yng nghynnor;
Ef dodes rhag trin tewddor.
Yn arial ar ddywal disgynnwys.
Can llewes, porthes mawrbwys.
O osgordd Fynyddog ni ddiangwys
Namyn un, arf amddiffryt, amddiffwys.

*   *   *

Pan ym dyfydd
Lliaws pryder, pryderaf fraw.
Ffun yn ardeg
Arial rhedeg, ar hynt wylaw.
Cu cystuddiwn,
Cu caraswn, cellëig ffaw.
Ag Argoedwys,
Gwae gorddyfnwys i ymdduiliaw.
Ef da ddodes
Ar lluydd pwys ar lles rhiau,
Ar ddilyfn goed,
Ar ddilyw hoed, er cyfeddau.
Cyfedd wogant ef a'n dy-ddug ar dân adloyw
Ac ar groen gwyn [a gwin] gosgroyw.
Geraint rhag Dehau, gawr a ddoded,
Lluch gwyn, gwyn ddull ar yswyd.
Iôr ysbâr llary, iôr molud,
Mynud môr, göwn ei eisyllud,
Göwn i Geraint, hael fynog oeddud.

A lord of Gododdin will be praised in song;
A lordly patron will be lamented.
Before Eidyn, fierce flame, he will not return.
He set his picked men in the vanguard;
He set a stronghold at the front.
In full force he attacked a fierce foe.
Since he feasted, he bore great hardship.
Of Mynyddawg's war-band none escaped
Save one, blade-brandishing, dreadful.

*   *   *

When a crowd of cares
Comes on me, I brood on my fear.
Breath failing
As in running, at once I weep.
The dear one I mourn,
The dear one I'd loved, noble stag.
With Argoed's men,
Alas, he always took his place.
Well did he press
Against war-hosts, for rulers' good,
Against rough wood,
Against grief's flood, for the feasts.
He escorted us to a blazing fire
And to white fleece and sparkling wine.
Geraint from the south, the war-cry was raised,
Gleaming white, fair the look of his shield.
Gracious lord of the spear, praiseworthy lord,
The sea's benevolence, I know its nature,
I know Geraint: you were a bountiful prince.

Translated from the Welsh by Joseph P. Clancy

ANON. (?8th century)

The Dream of the Rood

Hwæt! ic swefna cyst secʒan wylle,
hwæt me ʒemætte to midre nihte,
syðþan reordberend reste wunedon.
Þuhte me, þæt ic ʒesawe syllicre treow
on lyft lædan leohte bewunden,
beama beorhtost: eall þæt beacen wæs
beʒoten mid ʒolde; ʒimmas stodon
faeʒere æt foldan sceatum, swylce þær fife wæron
uppe on þam eaxleʒespanne. Beheoldon þær enʒel dryhtnes ealle
faeʒere þurh forðʒesceaft: ne wæs ðær huru fracodes ʒealga,
ac hine þær beheoldon haliʒe gastas,
men ofer moldan ond eall þeos mære ʒesceaft.
Syllic wæs se siʒebeam ond ic synnum fah,
forwunded mid wommum. ʒeseah ic wuldres treow
wædum ʒeweorðode wynnum scinan,
ʒeʒyred mid golde, ʒimmas hæfdon
bewriʒene weorðlice wealdes treow:
hwæðre ic þurh þæt gold onʒytan meahte
earmra ærʒewin, þæt hit ærest ongan
swætan on þa swiðran healfe. Eall ic wæs mid sorʒum ʒedrefed.
Forht ic wæs for þære fæʒran ʒesyhðe; ʒeseah ic þæt fuse beacen
wendan wædum ond bleom: hwilum hit wæs mid wætan bestemed,
beswyled mid swates ganʒe, hwilum mid since ʒegyrwed.
Hwæðre ic þær licgende lanʒe hwile
beheold hreowceariʒ Hælendes treow,
oð ðæt ic ʒehyrde, þæt hit hleoðrode;
ongan ða word sprecan wudu selesta:
'Þæt wæs ʒeara iu (ic þæt ʒyta ʒeman),
þæt ic wæs aheawen holtes on ende,
astyred of stefne minum. ʒenaman me ðær stranʒe feondas,
ʒeworhton him þær to wæfersyne, heton me heora wergas hebban;
bæron me ðær beornas on eaxlum, oð ðæt hie me on beorg asetton,
ʒefæstnodon me þær feondas ʒenoʒe. ʒeseah ic þa Frean mancynnes
efstan elne mycle þæt he me wolde on ʒestigan.

The Dream of the Rood

Listen! Hear how I dreamed a great dream
After midnight while most men slept.
It seemed I saw the tree of glory
Held high in heaven, haloed with light,
Blazing as a beacon. Every bough was
Brilliantly golden; gleaming jewels
Girdled earth's surface – five shone also
Ranged at right-angles – and crowds of angels
All through the universe viewed it with awe,
No gangsters' gallows. High, holy spirits
Marvelled with men and all of mighty creation.
    That symbol was sacred, and I was stained
With sinful scars. I saw glory's tree
Shawled with light, joyfully shining;
Gems had clothed those forest branches,
Yet through gold's glint I still could glimpse
Tokens of torture, of that first time
Blood ran from its right side. Writhing,
I dreaded my dream. The shifting symbol
Changed colours and coating; once, wet with blood,
It stood in gore; once, again, it glittered with treasure.
    I lay a long time, anxiously looking
At the Saviour's tree, till that best of branches
Suddenly started to speak:
    'Years, years ago, I remember it yet,
They cut me down at the edge of a copse,
Wrenched, uprooted me. Devils removed me,
Put me on show as their jailbirds' gibbet.
Men shouldered me, shifted me, set me up
Fixed on a hill where foes enough fastened me.
I looked on the Lord then, Man of mankind,
In his hero's hurry to climb high upon me.
I dared not go against God's word,
Bow down or break, although I saw

Þær ic þa ne dorste ofer Dryhtnes word
buʒan oððe berstan, þa ic bifian ʒeseah
eorðan sceatas: ealle ic mihte
feondas ʒefyllan, hwæðre ic fæste stod.
Onʒyrede hine þa ʒeonʒ hæleð (þæt wæs God ælmihtiʒ)
stranʒ ond stiðmod; ʒestah he on ʒealgan heanne
modiʒ on manigra ʒesyhðe, þa he wolde mancyn lysan.
Bifode ic, þa me se beorn ymbclypte: ne dorste ic hwæðre buʒan to eorðan,
feallan to foldan sceatum: ac ic sceolde fæste standan.
Rod wæs ic ærered: ahof ic ricne cyning,
heofona hlaford; hyldan me ne dorste.
Þurhdrifan hi me mid deorcan næʒlum, on me syndon þa dolʒ ʒesiene,
opene inwidhlemmas: ne dorste ic hira næniʒum sceððan.
Bysmeredon hie unc butu ætgædere. Eall ic wæs mid blode bestemed,
beʒoten of þæs guman sidan, siððan he hæfde his ʒast onsended.
Feala ic on þam beorge ʒebiden hæbbe
wraðra wyrda: ʒeseah ic weruda God
þearle þenian: þystro hæfdon
bewriʒen mid wolcnum Wealdendes hræw,
scirne sciman; sceadu forðeode,
wann under wolcnum. Weop eal ʒesceaft,
cwiðdon cyninʒes fyll: Crist wæs on rode.
Hwæðere þær fuse feorran cwoman
to þam æðelinge: ic þæt eall beheold.
Sare ic wæs mid sorgum ʒedrefed, hnaʒ ic hwæðre þam secʒum to handa
eaðmod elne mycle. Genamon hie þær ælmihtiʒne God,
ahofon hine of ðam hefian wite; forleton me þa hilderincas
standan steame bedrifenne: eall ic wæs mid strælum forwundod.
Aledon hie ðær limweriʒne, ʒestodon him æt his lices heafdum,
beheoldon hie ðær heofenes dryhten ond he hine ðær hwile reste
meðe æfter ðam miclan ʒewinne. Ongunnon him þa moldern wyrcan
beornas on banan ʒesyhðe, curfon hie ðæt of beorhtan stane,
ʒesetton hie ðæron sigora wealdend. Ongunnon him þa sorhleoð galan
earme on þa æfentide, þa hie woldon eft siðian
meðe fram þam mæran þeodne: reste he ðær mæte weorode.
Hwæðere we ðær reotende gode hwile
stodon on staðole; siððan . . . up ʒewat
hilderinca: hræw colode,
fæʒer feorgbold. þa us man fyllan ongan

Earth's surface shaking. I could have flattened
All of those fiends; instead, I stood still.
Then the young hero who was King of Heaven,
Strong and steadfast, stripped for battle,
Climbed the high gallows, his constant courage
Clear in his mission to redeem mankind.
I flinched when he touched me, but dared not fall
Or stoop to the soil. I had to stand.
Created a cross, I carried the King,
The stars' strong Lord. I dared not bow.
They drove in dark nails, deep, cruel wounds
Are in me still, I could not stop them.
They cursed us both. I was black with blood
Sprung from His side once he sent His Soul on its way.
On that hill I held out in horror,
Saw Heaven's Ruler ceaselessly racked;
Low clouds lessened the Light of Lights,
God's corpse; darkness cut in
Black under cumulus, creation wept,
Crying for the King's death, Christ on his wooden cross.
Yet keen men came from far up-country,
Walking to the King. I kept watch.

 Though scarred with sorrow, I stooped to their hands,
Totally humble. There they held God,
Hefted him from his hard trials, left me
Shot through with arrows, standing streaming with blood.
They laid him down, weary, stood at his head
Just looking at God; tired out after his torments,
He took time to rest. They started to hew
Out of bright stone in sight of his slayers
The strong Saviour's tomb. They sang,
Sobbed, and sang in that sorry gloaming,
Saddened to go again, leaving behind
The lonely Lord laid there. Then we three crosses
Witnessed and wept; a wail went up
From warrior comrades; the corpse,
Seat of the soul, grew cold.
Suddenly someone started to axe us

ealle to eorðan: þæt wæs egeslic wyrd!

Bedealf us man on deopan seaþe: hwæðre me ðær dryhtnes þegnas,

freondas ʒefrunon; . . . . . .

gyredon me golde ond seolfre.

Nu ðu miht ʒehyran, hæleð min se leofa,

þæt ic bealuwara weorc ʒebiden hæbbe,

sarra sorʒa. Is nu sæl cumen,

þæt me weorðiað wide ond side

menn ofer moldan ond eall þeos mære ʒesceaft

ʒebiddaþ him to þyssum beacne. On me bearn Godes

þrowode hwile; forþan ic þrymfæst nu

hlifiʒe under heofenum ond ic hælan mæʒ

æʒhwylcne anra, þara þe him bið eʒesa to me:

iu ic wæs ʒeworden wita heardost,

leodum laðost, ær þan ic him lifes weʒ

rihtne ʒerymde reordberendum.

Hwæt! me þa ʒeweorðode wuldres ealdor

ofer holmwudu, heofonrices weard,

swylce swa he his modor eac Marian sylfe

ælmihtiʒ God for ealle menn

ʒeweorðode ofer eall wifa cynn.

Nu ic þe hate, hæleð min se leofa,

þæt ðu þas ʒesyhðe secʒe mannum:

onwreoh wordum, þæt hit is wuldres beam.

se ðe ælmihtiʒ God on þrowode

for mancynnes maneʒum synnum

ond Adomes ealdʒewyrhtum.

Deað he þær byriʒde: hwæðere eft dryhten aras

mid his miclan mihte mannum to helpe.

He ða on heofenas astaʒ; hider eft fundaþ

on þysne middanʒeard mancynn secan

on domdæʒe Dryhten sylfa,

ælmihtiʒ God ond his englas mid,

þæt he þonne wile deman, se ah domes ʒeweald,

anra ʒehwylcum, swa he him ærur her

on þyssum lænum life ʒeearnaþ:

ne mæʒ þær æniʒ unforht wesan

for þam worde, þe se Wealdend cwyð!

Frineð he for þære mæniʒe, hwær se man sie,

se ðe for Dryhtnes naman deaðes wolde

Flat to the field. The three crosses crashed.
God's friends, His servants, found me buried,
Dumped in a deep pit. They decorated me
With silver and gold.

                        Hear now, friend,
How I tholed the work of the wicked,
Tearings and torments. The time has come
When worshippers honour me far and wide
Across all countries, throughout creation
Men pray to this sign. On me God's Son
Suffered; for that I am set up high
Shining in heaven, and I can heal
Any person who fears me in faith.
Once I was taken for toughest torture,
Monstrous to men, before I opened
The right road for people on earth.
God in His glory, the sky's Guard, gave me
To tower above trees, as He made in grace
His mother also, Mary herself,
Much more marvellous in all men's minds
Than the rest of the race of women.

   My friend, you must obey your vision.
Work out in words, tell people this dream
Of the tree of glory against which God
Suffered for mankind's many sins
And the ancient evil of Adam.
He dined on death there, but rose up Lord,
Hero and helper, he climbed into heaven
From where He'll descend on the Day of Judgement,
Almighty God, the Lord with good angels,
The mighty Maker, to search out mankind,
Judging each as each on earth
Deserved in this life unlasting.
None on that day can hear without dread
God's voice. In front of great crowds
He will ask for the man who might be willing
To brave bitter death as Christ did on those beams.
People will fear Him, few have considered
What to begin to say to the Saviour.

biteres onbyriʒan, swa he ær on ðam beame dyde:
ac hie þonne forhtiað ond fea þencaþ,
hwæt hie to Criste cweðan onʒinnen.
Ne þearf ðær þonne æniʒ unforht wesan,
þe him ær in breostum bereð beacna selest;
ac ðurh ða rode sceal rice ʒesecan
of eorðweʒe æʒhwylc sawl,
seo þe mid Wealdende wunian þenceð.ˈ
Gebæd ic me þa to þan beame bliðe mode
elne mycle, þær ic ana wæs
mæte werede: wæs modsefa
afysed on forðweʒe; feala ealra ʒebad
langunghwila. Is me nu lifes hyht,
þæt ic þone siʒebeam secan mote
ana oftor þonne ealle men
well weorþian: me is willa to ðam
mycel on mode ond min mundbyrd is
ʒeriht to þære rode. Nah ic ricra feala
freonda on foldan, ac hie forð heonon
ʒewiton of worulde dreamum, sohton him wuldres cyning,
lifiaþ nu on heofenum mid heahfædere,
wuniaþ on wuldre ond ic wene me
daʒa ʒehwylce, hwænne me dryhtnes rod,
þe ic her on eorðan ær sceawode,
on þysson lænan life ʒefetiʒe
ond me þonne ʒebrinʒe, þær is blis mycel,
dream on heofonum, þær is Dryhtnes folc
ʒeseted to symle, þær is singal blis;
ond he þonne asette, þær ic syþþan mot
wunian on wuldre, well mid þam halʒum
dreames brucan. Si me Dryhten freond,
se ðe her on eorþan ær þrowode
on þam ʒealʒtreowe for guman synnum.
He us onlysde ond us lif forgeaf,
heofonlicne ham. Hiht wæs ʒeniwad
mid bledum ond mid blisse, þam þe þær bryne þolodan.
Se Sunu wæs sigorfæst on þam siðfate,
mihtiʒ ond spedig, þa he mid maniʒeo com,
gasta weorode on Godes rice

He who on earth has carried the crucifix
Bright in his breast, that best of symbols,
Need not cower then; God shall greet
All who come through the cross to their homes in heaven,
Every soul from the earth.'
   My heart grew happy when I heard that cross.
I lay alone, my spirit longing,
Urging my soul on its journey.
Now, more than all, I live my life
Hoping to see that tree of glory
And worship it well. My will
Spurs my spirit; yon cross protects me.
My strong friends are few. They have gone away
From the wealth of this world in search of God,
Living now with the high Lord of heaven.
Every day I expect that moment
When the cross of the King I caught sight of on earth
Will fetch me far from this fleeting state
To bring me where true glory blossoms
Joyfully in heaven, where the host of God
Banquets in bliss forever;
Then he shall set me to stay in splendour,
Housed with the holy in the hall of my Lord.
Hero, who here in the past knew horror
On earth on the criminal's cross,
Be my friend, God, who gave us our lives,
Redeemer who gave us homes in heaven.
New hope came with bountiful blessings
For those who before knew nothing but burning.
Mighty and masterful, coming with massed
Hosts of the holy to the house of God,
The one almighty Son was sure

anwealda ælmihtiȝ enȝlum to blisse
ond eallum ðam halȝum, þam þe on heofonum ær
wunedon on wuldre, þa heora wealdend cwom,
ælmihtiȝ God, þær his eðel wæs.

Of victory then, elating the angels
And all of those who had in heaven
Places in glory when their Prince was coming,
The Lord God almighty, home.

Translated from the Old English by Robert Crawford

MUGRÓN, ABBOT OF IONA (d. 980)

Cros Chríst

Cros Chríst tarsin ngnúisse,
   tarsin gclúais fon cóirse.
Cros Chríst tarsin súilse.
   Cros Chríst tarsin sróinse.

Cros Chríst tarsin mbélsa.
   Cros Chríst tarsin cráessa.
Cros Chríst tarsin cúlsa.
   Cros Chríst tarsin táebsa.

Cros Chríst tarsin mbroinnse
   (is amlaid as chuimse).
Cros Chríst tarsin tairrse.
   Cros Chríst tarsin ndruimse.

Cros Chríst tar mo láma
   óm gúaillib com basa.
Cros Chríst tar mo lesa.
   Cros Chríst tar mo chasa.

Cros Chríst lem ar m'agaid.
   Cros Chríst lem im degaid.
Cros Chríst fri cach ndoraid
   eitir fán is telaig.

Cros Chríst sair frim einech
   Cros Chríst síar fri fuined.
Tes, túaid cen nach n-anad,
   cros Chríst cen nach fuirech.

Cros Chríst tar mo déta
   nám-tháir bét ná bine.
Cros Chríst tar mo gaile.
   Cros Chríst tar mo chride.

Christ's Cross

Christ's cross across this face,
across the ear like this,
Christ's cross across this eye,
Christ's cross across this nose.

Christ's cross across this mouth.
Christ's cross across this throat.
Christ's cross across this back.
Christ's cross across this side.

Christ's cross cross this stomach,
(like this it is just fine).
Christ's cross across this gut,
Christ's cross across this spine.

Christ's cross across my arms
from my shoulders to my hands.
Christ's cross across my thighs.
Christ's cross across my legs.

Christ's cross with me before.
Christ's cross with me behind.
Christ's cross against each trouble
both on hillock and in glen.

Christ's cross east towards my face,
Christ's cross west towards sunset.
South and north, ceaselessly,
Christ's cross without delay.

Christ's cross across my teeth
lest to me come harm or hurt.
Christ's cross cross my stomach.
Christ's cross across my heart.

Cros Chríst súas fri fithnim.
  Cros Chríst sís fri talmain.
Ní thí olc ná urbaid
  dom chorp ná dom anmain.

Cros Chríst tar mo ṡuide.
  Cros Chríst tar mo lige.
Cros Chríst mo bríg uile
  co roisem Ríg nime.

Cros Chríst tar mo muintir.
  Cros Chríst tar mo thempal.
Cros Chríst isin altar.
  Cros Chríst isin chentar.

O mullach mo baitse
  co ingin mo choise,
a Chríst, ar cach ngábad
  for snádad do chroise.

Co laithe mo báisse,
  ría ndol isin n-úirse,
cen ainis do-bérsa
  crois Críst tarsin ngnúisse.

Christ's cross up to heaven's span.
Christ's cross down to earth.
Let no evil or harm
come to my body or soul.

Christ's cross cross my sitting,
Christ's cross cross my lying.
Christ's cross, my whole power
till we reach heaven's King.

Christ's cross across my church,
across my community.
Christ's cross in the next world.
Christ's cross in the present-day.

From the tip of my head
to the nail of my foot,
Christ, against each peril
the shelter of your cross.

Till the day of my death,
before going in this clay,
joyfully I will make
Christ's cross across my face.

Translated from the Gaelic by Thomas Owen Clancy

ANON. (12th century)

Arann

Arann na n-oigheadh n-iomdha,
   tadhall fairrge re a formna;
oiléan i mbearntar buidhne,
   druimne i ndeargthar gaoi gorma.

Ard ós a muir a mullach,
   caomh a luibh, tearc a tonnach;
oiléan gorm groigheach gleannach,
   corr bheannach dhoireach dhrongach.

Oighe baotha ar a beannaibh,
   mónainn mhaotha ina mongaibh,
uisge uar ina haibhnibh,
   meas ar a dairghibh donnaibh.

Míolchoin ghéara agus gadhair,
   sméara is airne dubh droighin,
dlúth a froigh ris na feadhaibh,
   doimh ag deabhaidh 'na doiribh.

Díoghlaim chorcra ar a cairrgibh,
   féar gan lochta ar a leargaibh,
ós a creagaibh caon cumhdaigh,
   surdghail laogh, bric ag beadhgaigh.

Mín a magh, méith a muca,
   suairc a guirt (sgéal is creite),
cna for bharraibh a fiodhcholl,
   seóladh na siothlong seice.

Aoibhinn dóibh ó thig soineann,
   bric fá bhruachaibh a habhann;
freagraid faoilinn 'má fionnall;
   aoibhinn gach ionam Arann!

Arran

Arran of the many deer,
    ocean touching its shoulders;
island where troops are ruined,
    ridge where blue spears are blooded.

High above the sea its summit,
    dear its green growth, rare its bogland;
blue island of glens, of horses,
    of peaked mountains, oaks and armies.

Frisky deer on its mountains,
    moist bogberries in its thickets,
cold waters in its rivers,
    acorns on its brown oak-trees.

Hunting dogs and keen greyhounds,
    brambles, sloes of dark blackthorn;
close against the woods its dwellings;
    stags sparring in its oak-groves.

Purple lichen from its rocks,
    faultless grass on its greenswards;
on its crags, a shielding cloak;
    fawns capering, trout leaping.

Smooth its plain, well-fed its swine,
    glad its fields – believe the story! –
nuts upon its hazels' tops,
    the sailing of longships past it.

Fine for them when good weather comes –
    trout beneath its river banks;
gulls reply round its white cliff –
    fine at all times is Arran.

Translated from the Gaelic by Thomas Owen Clancy

EARL ROGNVALD KALI (ST RONALD OF ORKNEY) (d. 1158)

Tarl em'k ǫrr at efla,
íþróttir kann'k níu,
týni'k trauðla rúnum,
tíð er mér bók ok smíðir,
skríða kann'k á skíðum,
skýt'k ok rœ'k, svá't nýtir,
hvárt tveggja kann'k hyggja
harpslǫtt ok bragóþttu.

The Attributes of a Gentleman

Chess I'm eager to play,
nine skills I know,
I scarcely forget runes,
book and handicrafts are my custom,
I can glide on skis,
I shoot and row as will serve,
I know how to consider
both harp-playing and poetry.

Translated from the Old Norse by Paul Bibire

GUILLAUME LE CLERC (WILLIAM MALVEISIN, BISHOP OF ST ANDREWS) (d. 1238)

from *Fergus*

Fergus a trait le bonne espee.
Li serpens vient gole baee
Comme vis dïables saillant,
Et les dens ensanble estrangnant.
N'est nus hom, se il l'esgardast,
Que illuques remaindre osast,
Fors cil ki illuec l'atendi
Qui ot le cuer preu et hardi.
Nus contre lui estre ne doit.
Li serpens li saut a esploit;
De la coe grant cop li donne
Si que li escus en resonne.
Mais il est mauvais a quasser.
Fergus vole contre un piler,
Si se hurte par tel aïr
Qu'a poi ne li estuet partir
Le cuer del ventre par angoisse.
Li serpens debrise et defroisse
L'arbré u li escus pendoit;
Plus menüement se tornoit
Que ne fesist une culuevre.
A Fergus desplot molt ceste uevre
Et saciés que molt li anuie.
Uns autres fust mis a la fuie;
Mais mius velt morir a honnor
Que vivre et faire deshonnor
Et que li tornast a reproce.
Li sans li saut parmi la boche

from *Fergus of Galloway: Knight of King Arthur*

Fergus attempts to make off with the Shield of Dunottar

. . . When Fergus drew his favourite blade,
The dragon froze – her jaws splayed,
Pretending to be petrified,
So the doomed knight might look inside
That broiling maw of filth and fire –
Then shut it, with a hiss of ire.

No man in such a pass would choose
To wait and see what he might lose;
None but Sir Fergus, who possessed
The stoutest heart in the South-West.
So there he crouched, at the serpent's whim,
Who turned and slapped her tail at him,

Which made him glad he'd seized the shield;
For though it cracked, it did not yield,
And kept him, for the moment, sound;
But when he tried to stand his ground
He found his boots were treading water,
And as he cartwheeled through Dunottar

He struck a wall with such a crack
His ribs were crushed against his back,
And all his senses so displaced
He thought he heard a burning taste.
The dragon, meanwhile, paused, and wept
At the cradle where her shield had slept,

Et par orelles et par le nés
Que tos en est ensanglentés.
Et quant il aperçut le sanc
Qui li arousse l'auberc blanc
Lors a tel dol, a poi ne font.
La targe lieve contremont,
Si fiert, iriés comme lion,
Del branc le serpent a bandon
Sor le hance qu'ot hirechie,
Que en travers li a trenchie
La teste et le col a moitié.
Qui or li donnasi tot en fié
D'Engleterre la signorie
N'eüst il la disme partie
De grant joie ne de leece.

As if in a Highland melodrama.
Fergus cursed through fractured armour.
His only comfort where he lay,
That chevalier of Galloway,
Was joining, since he hadn't fled,
The ranks of the heroic dead.

For so much blood had spouted out
Of his face from the first round of the bout
That when his eyes fell on the hue
Of the tunic he had put on blue,
He almost fainted in distress
At the ruined state of his warrior dress.

Instead, provoked by the red rag,
He sprang up like a cornered stag
And lashed out with his wounded pride
At the tough scales of the serpent's hide: —
Then slicing up at the shocked head,
Severed the neck and dropped her dead.

Now, had you asked him to disown
His day's work, for the English throne
Or a long drink from our Saviour's Cup,
He would have told you to shut up,
So pleased was he to sniff the air
As Fergus of Galloway — Dragon-Slayer!

Translated from the Old French by Mick Imlah

MUIREADHACH ALBANACH Ó DÁLAIGH

(*fl.* 1200–1224)

M'anam do sgar riomsa a-raoir

M'anam do sgar riomsa a-raoir,
    calann ghlan dob ionnsa i n-uaigh;
rugadh bruinne maordha mín
    is aonbhla lín uime uainn.

Do tógbhadh sgath aobhdha fhionn
    a-mach ar an bhfaongha bhfann:
laogh mo chridhise do chrom,
    craobh throm an tighise thall.

M'aonar a-nocht damhsa, a Dhé,
    olc an saoghal camsa ad-chí:
dob álainn trom an taoibh naoi
    do bhaoi sonn a-raoir, a Rí.

Truagh leam an leabasa thiar,
    mo pheall seadasa dhá snámh;
tárramair corp seada saor
    is folt claon, a leaba, id lár.

Do bhí duine go ndreich moill
    ina luighe ar leith mo phill;
gan bharamhail acht bláth cuill
    don sgáth duinn bhanamhail bhinn.

Maol Mheadha na malach ndonn
    mo dhabhach mheadha a-raon rom;
mo chridhe an sgáth do sgar riom,
    bláth mhionn arna car do chrom.

Elegy on Mael Mhedha, his Wife

My soul parted from me last night.
  In the grave, a pure dear body.
A kind, refined soul was taken
  from me, a linen shroud about her.

A fair white flower has been plucked
  from the weak and tumbled stalk.
The love of my heart is bent,
  the heavy stem of yon house.

Tonight I am alone, God.
  Bad is this bent world you see.
Dear was the young body's weight
  who was here last night, my King.

Wretched I find yonder bed,
  my long blanket set a-swim:
I've seen a body, fine, long,
  with curled hair, bed, in your midst.

There was a soft-gazed woman
  lay on one side of my bed;
none like her but the hazel's flower,
  that dark shadow, womanly, sweet.

Mael Mhedha of the dark brows,
  my cask of mead at my side;
my heart, the shadow split from me,
  flowers' crown, planted, now bowed down.

Táinig an chlí as ar gcuing,
   agus dí ráinig mar roinn:
corp idir dá aisil inn
   ar dtocht don fhinn mhaisigh mhoill.

Leath mo throigheadh, leath mo thaobh,
   a dreach mar an droighean bán,
níor dhísle neach dhí ná dhún,
   leath mo shúl í, leath mo lámh.

Leath mo chuirp an choinneal naoi;
   's guirt riom do roinneadh, a Rí:
agá labhra is meirtneach mé –
   dob é ceirtleath m'anma í.

Mo chéadghrádh a dearc mhall mhór,
   déadbhán agus cam a cliabh:
nochar bhean a colann caomh
   ná a taobh ré fear romham riamh.

Fiche bliadhna inne ar-aon,
   fá binne gach bliadhna ar nglór,
go rug éinleanabh déag dhún,
   an ghéag úr mhéirleabhar mhór.

Gé tú, nocha n-oilim ann,
   ó do thoirinn ar gcnú chorr;
ar sgaradh dár roghrádh rom,
   falamh lom an domhnán donn.

Ón ló do sáidheadh cleath corr
   im theach nochar ráidheadh rum –
ní thug aoighe d'ortha ann
   dá barr naoidhe dhorcha dhunn.

A dhaoine, ná coisgidh damh;
   faoidhe ré cloistin ní col;
táinig luinnchreach lom 'nar dteagh –
   an bhruithneach gheal donn ar ndol.

My body's gone from my grip
  and has fallen to her share;
my body's splintered in two,
  since she's gone, soft, fine and fair.

One of my feet she was, one side –
  like the whitethorn was her face –
our goods were never 'hers' and 'mine' –
  one of my hands, one of my eyes.

Half my body, that young candle –
  it's harsh, what I've been dealt, Lord.
I'm weary speaking of it:
  she was half my very soul.

My first love, her great soft eye;
  ivory-white and curved her breast;
neither her fair flesh nor her side
  lay near another man but me.

We were twenty years together.
  Our speech grew sweeter each year.
She bore me eleven children,
  the tall young long-fingered tree.

Though I am, I do not thrive
  since my proud hazel-nut fell.
Since my great love parted from me,
  the dark world's empty and bare.

Since the day a stout post was fixed
  for my house, it's not been said:
no house-guest has put a charm
  on her fresh brown shadowy head.

People, do not restrain me.
  The sound of weeping's no sin.
Fierce bare ruin's come to our house:
  the warm bright brown-haired one's gone.

Is é rug uan í 'na ghrúg,
   Rí na sluagh is Rí na ród;
beag an cion do chúl na ngéag
   a héag ó a fior go húr óg.

Ionmhain lámh bhog do bhí sonn,
   a Rí na gclog is na gceall:
ach! an lámh nachar logh mionn,
   crádh liom gan a cor fám cheann.

In his anger, He's taken her,
  the King of hosts and of roads.
Small the sin of the branched hair:
  she died; her husband's fresh and young.

Dear the soft hand which was here,
  King of the churches and bells.
Och! that hand never swore false oath.
  Sore, that it's not under my head.

Translated from the Gaelic by Thomas Owen Clancy

ANON. (*c.* 1300)

Qwhen Alexander our kynge was dede

Qwhen Alexander our kynge was dede,
That Scotlande lede in lauche and le,   *lived; law; protection*
Away was sons of alle and brede,   *abundance; ale; bread*
   Off wyne and wax, of gamyn and gle.   *play; pleasure*
Our golde was changit in to lede.   *lead*
   Christ, borne in virgynyte,
Succoure Scotlande, and ramede,   *cure*
   That stade is in perplexite.   *stood*

JOHN BARBOUR (c. 1320–1395)

from *The Bruce*

from *Book I: In praise of Freedom*

A! Fredome is a noble thing	
Fredome mays man to haiff liking.	*allows; contentment*
Fredome all solace to man giffis,	
He levys at es that frely levys.	*lives; ease*
A noble hart may haiff nane es	
Na ellys nocht that may him ples	
Gyff fredome failyhe, for fre liking	*without freedom*
Is yharnyt our all other thing.	*desired; over*
Na he that ay has levyt fre	
May nocht knaw weill the propyrté	
The angyr na the wrechyt dome	*condition*
That is couplyt to foule thyrldome,	*thralldom*
Bot gyff he had assayit it.	
Than all perquer he suld it wyt,	*perfectly; know*
And suld think fredome mar to prys	*more; prize*
Than all the gold in warld that is.	
Thus contrar thingis evermar	
Discoveryngis off the tother ar,	
And he that thryll is has nocht his.	*in thrall*
All that he has enbandounyt is	
Till hys lord quhatever he be.	
Yheyt has he nocht sa mekill fre	*yet*
As fre wyll to leyve or do	
That at his hart hym drawis to.	*which*

from *Book XVI: Bruce in Ireland halts his army at Limerick so that a laundrywoman may give birth*

Syne went thai southwart in the land	*then*
And rycht till Lynrike held thar way	*Limerick*
That is the southmaist toun perfay	*indeed*
That in Irland may fundyn be.	*found*
Thar lay thai dayis twa or thre	

And buskyt syne agayn to far,   *got ready; go*
And quhen that thai all redy war
The king has hard a woman cry,   *heard*
He askyt quhat that wes in hy.   *happening*
'It is the laynder, schyr,' said ane,   *laundress; sir*
'That hyr child-ill rycht now has tane   *[gone into labour]*
And mon leve now behind us her,   *must stay; here*
Tharfor scho makys yone ivill cher.'   *unhappy cry*
The king said, 'Certis, it war pité
That scho in that poynt left suld be,
For certis I trow thar is no man
That he ne will rew a woman than.'   *pity; [in such a case]*
His ost all thar arestyt he   *host; stopped*
And gert a tent sone stentit be   *pitched*
And gert hyr gang in hastily,   *made her go in quickly*
And other wemen to be hyr by.
Quhill scho wes deliver he bad   *while she gave birth he stayed*
And syne furth on his wayis raid,
And how scho furth suld caryit be
Or ever he furth fur ordanyt he.   *before*
This wes a full gret curtasy
That swilk a king and sa mychty   *such*
Gert his men dwell on this maner   *made*
Bot for a pouer lauender.   *poor*

KING JAMES I (1394–1437)

from *The Kingis Quair*

Heigh in the hevynnis figure circulere
The rody sterres twynklyng as the fyre;   *bright*
And in Aquary, Citherea the clere,   *clear*
Rynsid hir tressis like the goldin wyre,   *washed*
That late tofore in fair and fresche aryre
Through Capricorn heved hir hornis bright,   *lifted*
North northward approchit the mydnyght, –

Quhen as I lay in bed allone waking,   *when*
New partit out of slepe a lyte tofore,   *having slept a little earlier*
Fell me to mynd of many diuerse thing –
Of this and that – can I noght say quharfore,   *why*
Bot slepe for craft in erth myght I no more.   *[by any means]*
For quhich, as tho, coude I no better wyle   *which; therefore; know*
Bot toke a boke to rede apon a quhile.   *while*

Of quhich the name is clepit properly   *called*
Boece (efter him that was the compiloure),
Schewing the counsele of Philosophye,
Compilit by that noble senatoure
Of Rome, quhilom that was the warldis floure,   *formerly; flower of the world*
And from estate by Fortune a quhile
Foriugit was to pouert in exile: *condemned; poverty*

And thereto, here, this worthy lord and clerk
His metir suete, full of moralitee,   *metre*
His flourit pen so fair he set awerk,   *eloquent*
Discryving first of his prosperitee,   *writing*
And out of that his infelicitee;
And than how he, in his poetly report,
In philosophy can him to confort.   *[found comfort]*

*   *   *

Me thoght that thus all sodeynly a lyght
In at the wyndow come quhare that I lent,
Of quhich the chamber wyndow schone full bryght,
And all my body so it hath ouerwent
That of my sicht the vertew hale iblent;   *blinded*
And that withall a voce vnto me saide:
'I bring thee confort and hele, be noght affrayde.'   *health*

And furth anon it passit sodeynly   *away; at once*
Quhere it come in, the ryght way ageyne;
And sone, me thoght, furth at the dure in hye   *in haste*
I went my weye, nas nothing me ageyne, –   *[there was nothing against me]*
And hastily by bothe the armes tueyne
I was araisit vp into the air,
Clippit in a cloude of cristall clere and fair,   *embraced*

Ascending vpward ay fro spere to spere   *sphere*
Through air and water and the hote fyre
Till that I come vnto the circle clere
Of Signifer, quhare fair, bryght, and schire   *clear*
The signis schone, – and in the glade empire   *glad*
Of blisfull Venus ane caryit now   *[I am carried]*
So sudaynly, almost I wist noght how.

Of quhich the place quhen I com there nye   *near*
Was all, me thoght, of cristall stonis wroght.
And to the port I liftit was in hye,   *gate*
Quhare sodaynly (as quho sais, 'at a thoght')   *as they say*
It opnyt, and I was anon inbroght
Within a chamber large, rowm, and fair: *spacious*
And there I fand of peple grete repair.   *[a great many]*

This is to seyne, that present in that place
Me thoght I sawe of euery nacioun
Loueris that endit thair lyfis space   *life's term*
In lovis seruice, mony a mylioun.
Of quhois chancis maid is mencioun   *whose*
In diuerse bukis (quho thame list to se),   *who; wishes*
And therfore here thair namys lat I be.

The quhois auenture and grete labour   *adventure*
Aboue their hedis writin there I fand –
This is to seyne, martris and confessour   *martyrs*
Ech in his stage, and his make in his hand,   *mate*
And therwithall, thir peple sawe I stand
With mony a solempit contenance,
After as lufe thame lykit to auance.   *promote*

Of gude folkis that fair in lufe befill   *befell*
There saw I sitt in order by thame one
With hedis hore, and with thame stude Gude Will   *grey*
To talk and play; and after that anon
Besyde thame and next there saw I gone
Curage amang the fresche folkis yong,   *desire*
And with thame playit full merily and song.

And in ane-othir stage endlong the wall,   *another; along*
There saw I stand in capis wyde and lang   *capes*
A full grete nowmer; bot thair hudis all   *number*
(Wist I noght quhy) atour thair eyen hang,   *know; over*
And ay to thame come Repentance amang
And maid thame chere, degysit in his wede;   *entertained; dressed; clothing*
And dounward efter that yit I tuke hede.

Ryght ouerthwert the chamber was there drawe   *across; drawn*
A trevesse thin and quhite, all of plesance,   *curtain*
The quhich behynd, standing there I sawe
A warld of folk, and by thair contenance
Thair hertis semyt full of displesance,   *unhappiness*
With billis in thair handis, of one assent,   *petitions*
Vnto the Iuge thair playntis to present.   *complaints*

ROBERT HENRYSON (c.1420–c.1490)

The Two Mice

Esope, myne authour, makis mentioun   *Aesop*
Of twa myis, and thay wer sisteris deir,
Of quham the eldest duelt in ane borous toun;   *whom; burgh*
The uther wynnit uponland weill neir,   *dwelt; [in the country]*
Soliter, quhyle under busk, quhyle under breir,   *alone; sometimes; bush; briar*
Quhilis in the corne, in uther mennis skaith,   *men's harm*
As owtlawis dois, and levit on hir waith.   *lived; plunder*

This rurall mous into the wynter tyde   *time*
Had hunger, cauld, and tholit grit distres;   *endured*
The uther mous, that in the burgh can byde,   *lived*
Was gild brother and made ane fre burges,   *guild; citizen of the burgh*
Toll-fre als, but custum mair or les,   *tax-free; [exempt from large and small dues]*
And fredome had to ga quhairever scho list
Amang the cheis in ark, and meill in kist.   *cheese; container; meal; chest*

Ane tyme quhen scho wes full and unfutesair,   *not footsore*
Scho tuke in mynd hir sister uponland,
And langit sair to heir of hir weilfair,
To se quhat lyfe scho led under the wand.   *branch*
Bairfute, allone, with pykestaf in hir hand,
As pure pylgryme scho passit owt off town
To seik hir sister, baith oure daill and down.

Furth mony wilsum wayis can scho walk,   *across; wild*
Throw mosse and mure, throw bankis, busk, and breir,   *bog; moor*
Fra fur to fur, cryand fra balk to balk,   *furrow; ridge*
'Cum furth to me, my awin sister deir!
Cry peip anis!' With that the mous culd heir   *once*
And knew hir voce, as kinnisman will do   *kinsfolk*
Be verray kynd, and furth scho come hir to.   *[naturally]*

The hartlie joy, Lord God, geve ye had sene   *heartfelt; if*
Beis kithit quhen that thir sisteris met,   *[is shown]*
And grit kyndnes wes schawin thame betuene,   *showing*
For quhylis thay leuch, and quhylis for joy thay gret,   *sometimes; laughed; wept*
Quhyle kissit sweit, quhylis in armis plet;   *embraced*
Ane thus thay fure quhill soberit wes their mude;   *behaved; until; sobered*
Syne fute for fute unto the chalmer yude.   *then; [keeping pace together]; chamber; went*

As I hard say, it was ane sober wane,   *heard; humble dwelling*
Off fog and farne full misterlyk wes maid,   *moss and fern; poverty*
Ane sillie scheill under ane erdfast stane,   *simple hovel under a stone fixed in the earth*
Off quhilk the entres wes not hie nor braid;   *which; entrance; neither high nor broad*
And in the samin thay went, but mair abaid,   *[without further delay]*
Withoutin fyre or candill birnand bricht,   *burning brightly*
For comonly sic pykeris luffis not lycht.   *[such thieves do not love light]*

Quhen thay wer lugit thus, thir sely myse,   *lodged; simple*
The youngest sister into hir butterie hyid,   *larder; hastened*
And brocht furth nuttis and peis, insteid off spyce;   *brought out; peas*
Giff this wes gude fair, I do it on thame besyde.   *good fare; [I leave it to those here]*
This burges mous prompit forth in pryde,   *town mouse; burst out*
And said, 'Sister, is this your dayly fude?'   *food*
'Quhy not,' quod scho, 'is not this meit richt gude?'   *why; said; food*

'Na, be my saull, I think it bot ane scorne.'   *soul; insult*
'Madame,' quod scho, 'ye be the mair to blame.
My mother sayd, sister, quhen we wer borne,
That I and ye lay baith within ane wame;   *one womb*
I keip the rate and custome off my dame,   *standard; mother*
And off my syre, levand in povertie,   *father; living*
For landis have we nane in propertie.'   *possession*

'My fair sister,' quod scho, 'have me excusit –
This rude dyat and I can not accord.   *rough diet*
To tender meit my stomok is ay usit,   *delicate food; accustomed*
Forquhy I fair als weill as ony lord.   *because; fare*
Thir wydderit peis and nuttis, or thay be bord,   *withered; before; pierced*
Will brek my teith and mak my wame full sklender,   *break; teeth; stomach; thin*
Quhilk usit wes before to meitis tender.'

'Weil, weil, sister,' quod the rurall mous,
'Geve it pleis yow, sic thing as ye se heir,   *if; please; such; here*
Baith meit and dreink, harberie and hous,   *lodging*
Sal be your awin, will ye remane al yeir.   *
Ye sall it have wyth blyith and hartlie cheir,   *happy; heartfelt; attitude*
And that suld mak the maissis that ar rude,   *dishes; rustic*
Amang freindis, richt tender, and wonder gude.   *extremely*

'Quhat plesure is in the feistis delicate,   *dainty feasts*
The quhilkis ar gevin with ane glowmand brow?   *which are given; frowning*
Ane gentill hart is better recreate   *noble; refreshed*
With blyith visage, than seith to him ane kow.   *[than if a whole cow were cooked for him]*
Ane modicum is mair for till allow,   *[small portion]; to praise*
Swa that gude will be kerver at the dais,   *provided that; carver; high table*
Than thrawin vult and mony spycit mais.'   *twisted face; many spiced dishes*

For all hir mery exhortatioun,
This burges mous had littill will to sing,
Bot hevilie scho kest hir browis doun   *sorrowfully; cast; eyebrows*
For all the daynteis that scho culd hir bring;   *[the country mouse] brought her*
Yit at the last scho said, halff in hething,   *scorn*
'Sister, this victuall and your royall feist   *food*
May weill suffice unto ane rurall beist.

'Lat be this hole and cum into my place: *leave*
I sall to yow schaw, be experience,   *by*
My Gude Friday is better nor your Pace,   *Good Friday (fast); than Easter (feast)*
My dische likingis is worth your haill expence.   *leavings; whole expenditure*
I have housis anew off grit defence;   *[in plenty]; security*
Off cat nor fall-trap I have na dreid.'   *mouse-trap; fear*
'I grant,' quod scho, and on togidder thay yeid.   *went*

In skugry ay, throw rankest gers and corne,   *secrecy; thickest grass*
And under cowert prevelie couth thay creip;   *cover; stealthily; crept*
The eldest wes the gyde and went beforne,
The younger to hir wayis tuke gude keip.   *[paid close attention]*

* *[shall be your own, even if you wish to remain here all year]*

On nicht thay ran and on the day can sleip,   *by night; slept*
Quhill in the morning, or the laverok sang,   *until; before; lark*
Thay fand the town, and in blythlie couth gang.   *came to; merrily [went in]*

Not fer fra thyne unto ane worthie wane,   *[not far from there]; dwelling*
This burges brocht thame sone quhare thay suld be.   *quickly*
Withowt 'God speid' thair herberie wes tane   *[without ceremony]; lodging*
Into ane spence with vittell grit plentie: *pantry; food in abundance*
Baith cheis and butter upon thair skelfis hie,   *high shelves*
And flesche and fische aneuch, baith fresche and salt,
And sekkis full off grotis, meill, and malt.   *sacks; oats; meal*

Efter, quhen thay disposit wer to dyne,
Withowtin grace, thay wesche and went to meit,   *saying grace; washed; to their food*
With all coursis that cukis culd devyne,   *cooks; devise*
Muttoun and beif, strikin in tailyeis greit.   *carved in big slices*
Ane lordis fair thus couth thay counterfeit   *[style of eating]; imitated*
Except ane thing: thay drank the watter cleir
Insteid off wyne; bot yit thay maid gude cheir.   *[enjoyed themselves]*

With blyith upcast and merie countenance,   *[pleasant taunting]*
The eldest sister sperit at hir gest   *asked; guest*
Giff that scho be ressone fand difference   *[with good reason]*
Betuix that chalmer and hir sarie nest.   *wretched*
'Ye, dame,' quod scho, 'how lang will this lest?'   *yes*
'For evermair, I wait, and langer to.'   *expect*
'Giff it be swa, ye ar at eis,' quod scho.   *so; in comfort*

Till eik thair cheir ane subcharge furth scho brocht –   *
Ane plait off grottis, and ane disch full off meill;   *plate of oats*
Thraf-caikkis als I trow scho spairit nocht   *oatcakes also; believe; did not spare*
Aboundantlie about hir for to deill,   *serve*
And mane full fyne scho brocht insteid off geill,   *white bread; jelly*
And ane quhyte candill owt off ane coffer stall   *white; chest; stole*
Insteid off spyce, to gust thair mouth withall.   *[add relish to]*

[to increase their entertainment she brought out an extra course]

This maid thay merie, quhill thay micht na mair,   *thus; [until they could no more]*
And 'Haill, Yule, haill!' cryit upon hie.   *loudly*
Yit efter joy oftymes cummis cair,   *often comes sorrow*
And troubill efter grit prosperitie.
Thus as thay sat in all thair jolitie,
The spenser come with keyis in his hand,   *steward came*
Oppinnit the dure, and thame at denner fand.   *opened the door; dinner; found*

Thay taryit not to wesche, as I suppose,   *did not wait to wash*
Bot on to ga, quha micht formest win.   *off they went; [who might be the first]*
The burges had ane hole, and in scho gois;
Hir sister had na hole to hyde hir in.
To se that selie mous, it wes grit sin;   *wretched; pity*
So desolate and will off ane gude reid;   *bewildered; plan*
For verray dreid scho fell in swoun neir deid.   *sheer; almost dead*

Bot, as God wald, it fell ane happie cace: *willed; [there befell a fortunate chance]*
The spenser had na laser for to byde,   *leisure; stay*
Nowther to seik nor serche, to sker nor chace, *neither; seek nor search; frighten nor chase*
Bot on he went, and left the dure up wyde.   *door; [open]*
The bald burges his passage weill hes spyde;   *bold*
Out off hir hole scho come and cryit on hie,
'How fair ye, sister? Cry peip, quhairever ye be!'

This rurall mous lay flatling on the ground,   *flat*
And for the deith scho wes full sair dredand,   *was sorely fearing death*
For till hir hart straik mony wofull stound;   *to her heart struck; pang*
As in ane fever scho trimbillit, fute and hand.   *trembled, foot*
And quhan hir sister in sic ply hir fand,   *when; plight*
For verray pietie scho began to greit,   *pity; weep*
Syne confort hir with wordis hunny-sweit.   *then; comforted; sweet as honey*

'Quhy ly ye thus? Ryse up, my sister deir!
Cum to your meit; this perrell is overpast.'
The uther answerit with hevie cheir,   *sorrowfully*
'I may not eit, sa sair I am agast!   *eat*
I had lever thir fourty dayis fast   *rather; these*
With watter-caill, and to gnaw benis or peis,   *cabbage soup*
Than all your feist in this dreid and diseis.'   *distress*

With fair tretie yit scho gart hir upryse,   *entreaty; caused her to get up*
And to the burde thay went and togidder sat.   *table; together*
And scantlie had thay drunkin anis or twyse,   *scarcely; once*
Quhen in come Gib Hunter, our jolie cat,   *Gilbert (a tomcat)*
And bad 'God speid.' The burges up with that,   *'Good day'; leapt up*
And till hir hole scho fled as fyre of flint;   *fire from a flint*
Bawdronis the uther be the bak hes hint.   *[Scottish name for a cat]; seized*

Fra fute to fute he kest hir to and fra,   *tossed*
Quhylis up, quhylis down, als cant as ony kid.   *brisk; kid*
Quhylis wald he lat hir rin under the stra;   *run; straw*
Quhylis wald he wink, and play with hir buk-heid;   *blindman's buff*
Thus to the selie mous grit pane he did;
Quhill at the last throw fortune and gude hap,   *good luck*
Betwix ane dosor and the wall scho crap.   *[wall-hanging]; crept*

And up in haist behind the parraling   *tapestry*
Scho clam so hie that Gilbert micht not get hir,   *climbed*
Syne be the cluke thair craftelie can hing   *claw; hung there*
Till he wes gane; hir cheir wes all the better.   *gone; spirit*
Syne doun scho lap quhen thair wes nane to let hir,   *leapt; hinder*
And to the burges mous loud can scho cry,   *did*
'Fairweill, sister, thy feist heir I defy!   *renounce*

'Thy mangerie is mingit all with cair;   *banquet; mixed*
Thy guse is gude, thy gansell sour as gall;   *[garlic sauce]*
The subcharge off thy service is bot sair;   *extra course; only; sorrow*
Sa sall thow find heir-efterwart ma fall.   *hereafter; [may befall]*
I thank yone courtyne and yone perpall wall   *curtain; partition*
Off my defence now fra yone crewell beist.
Almichtie God keip me fra sic ane feist.   *keep*

'Wer I into the kith that I come fra,   *[if I were in the land I came from]*
For weill nor wo I suld never cum agane.'   *[anything in the world]; return here*
With that scho tuke hir leif and furth can ga,   *leave; went off*
Quhylis throw the corne, and quhylis throw the plane.   *plain*
Quhen scho wes furth and fre scho wes full fane,   *away; glad*
And merilie markit unto the mure;   *went*
I can not tell how eftirwart scho fure,   *fared*

Bot I hard say scho passit to hir den,   *heard*
Als warme as woll, suppose it wes not greit,   *wool; even though; big*
Full beinly stuffit, baith but and ben,   *
Off beinis and nuttis, peis, ry, and quheit;   *wheat*
Quhenever scho list scho had aneuch to eit,   *whenever; wished; enough*
In quyet and eis withoutin ony dreid,
Bot to hir sisteris feist na mair scho yeid.   *went*

Moralitas

Freindis, heir may ye find, and ye will tak heid,   *if*
Into this fabill ane gude moralitie:
As fitchis myngit ar with nobill seid,   *weeds; mixed; seed*
Swa intermellit is adversitie   *intermixed*
With eirdlie joy, swa that na estate is frie   *earthly; rank; free*
Without trubill and sum vexatioun,   *trouble*
And namelie thay quhilk clymmis up maist hie,   *[especially those who climb]; most*
That ar not content with small possessioun.   *possessions*

Blissed be sempill lyfe withoutin dreid;   *blessed*
Blissed be sober feist in quietie.   *moderate; quietness*
Quha hes aneuch, of na mair hes he neid,   *whoever*
Thocht it be littill into quantatie.   *though*
Grit aboundance and blind prosperitie
Oftymes makis ane evill conclusioun;
The sweitest lyfe, thairfoir, in this cuntrie,
Is sickernes with small possessioun.   *security*

O wantoun man, that usis for to feid   *wanton; is accustomed*
Thy wambe, and makis it a god to be;   *belly*
Luke to thyself, I warne the weill, but dreid.   *[without doubt]*
The cat cummis, and to the mous hes ee;   *eye*
Quhat vaillis than thy feist and royaltie,   *avails*
With dreidfull hart and tribulatioun?
Best thing in eird, thairfor, I say for me,   *earth*
Is blyithnes in hart, with small possessioun.   *happiness*

* *[very cosily furnished, both in the outer and inner parts]*

Thy awin fyre, freind, thocht it be bot ane gleid, *own; even if; ember*
It warmis weill, and is worth gold to the; *thee*
And Solomon sayis, gif that thow will reid, *read*
'Under the hevin I can not better be
Than ay be blyith and leif in honestie.' *ever; live*
Quhairfoir I may conclude be this ressoun: *wherefore; statement*
Of eirthly joy it beiris maist degré, *[holds the highest place]*
Blyithnes in hart, with small possessioun.

The Testament of Cresseid

Ane doolie sessoun to ane cairfull dyte *dismal season; sorrowful poem*
Suld correspond and be equivalent: *should conform*
Richt sa it wes quhen I began to wryte *just so it was when*
This tragedie – the wedder richt fervent, *weather; [eerily intense]*
Quhen Aries, in middis of the lent, *middle of spring*
Schouris of haill gart fra the north discend, *[caused showers of hail to fall from the north]*
That scant me fra the cauld I micht defend. *[so that I could scarcely ward off the cold]*

Yit nevertheles within myne oratur *oratory*
I stude, quhen Titan had his bemis bricht *stood; [the sun]; bright beams*
Withdrawin doun and sylit under cure, *concealed; cover*
And fair Venus, the bewtie of the nicht,
Uprais and set unto the west full richt *rose up; straight*
Hir goldin face, in oppositioun *[astronomical] opposition*
Of god Phebus, direct discending doun. *[the sun]; directly*

Throwout the glas hir bemis brast sa fair *through; window; burst*
That I micht se on everie syde me by; *could see; around me*
The northin wind had purifyit the air *northern*
And sched the mistie cloudis fra the sky; *scattered*
The froist freisit, the blastis bitterly *frost became icy*
Fra Pole Artick come quhisling loud and schill, *North Pole; whistling; shrill*
And causit me remufe aganis my will. *move away; against*

For I traistit that Venus, luifis quene, *trusted; [love's queen]*
To quhome sum tyme I hecht obedience, *whom; vowed*
My faidit hart of lufe scho wald mak grene, *faded; love; she would make green*
And therupon with humbill reverence

I thocht to pray hir hie magnificence;   *thought*
Bot for greit cald as than I lattit was,   *because of the great cold; at that time; prevented*
And in my chalmer to the fyre can pas.   *chamber; went*

Thocht lufe be hait, yit in ane man of age   *though; hot; an older man*
It kendillis nocht sa sone as in youtheid,   *kindles; not so soon; youth*
Of quhome the blude is flowing in ane rage;   *blood*
And in the auld the curage doif and deid,   *desire; dull; dead*
Of quhilk the fyre outward is best remeid: *which; outer; remedy*
To help be phisike quhair that nature faillit   *by medicine; where nature has failed*
I am expert, for baith I have assaillit.   *I have tried both*

I mend the fyre and beikit me about,   *put fuel on; warmed myself*
Than tuik ane drink, my spreitis to comfort,   *took; spirits*
And armit me weill fra the cauld thairout.   *against the cold outside*
To cut the winter nicht and mak it schort   *cut short*
I tuik ane quair – and left all uther sport –   *book; other diversion*
Writtin be worthie Chaucer glorious,
Of fair Creisseid and worthie Troylus.

And thair I fand, efter that Diomeid   *found; after*
Ressavit had that lady bricht of hew,   *received; bright complexion*
How Troilus neir out of wit abraid   *almost; mind; went*
And weipit soir with visage paill of hew;   *wept bitterly*
For quhilk wanhope his teiris can renew,   *despair; tears burst out again*
Quhill esperance rejoisit him agane: *until hope gladdened him*
Thus quhyle in joy he levit, quhyle in pane.   *now; distress*

Of hir behest he had greit comforting,   *promise*
Traisting to Troy that scho suld mak retour,   *trusting; should return*
Quhilk he desyrit maist of eirdly thing,   *desired; most of any earthly thing*
Forquhy scho was his only paramour.   *because*
Bot quhen he saw passit baith day and hour   *passed*
Of hir ganecome, than sorrow can oppres   *return; oppressed*
His wofull hart in cair and hevines.   *grieving; misery; melancholy*

Of his distres me neidis nocht reheirs,   *I need not recount*
For worthie Chauceir in the samin buik,   *same book*
In gudelie termis and in joly veirs,   *fine verse*
Compylit hes his cairis, quha will luik.   *[has described his sorrows]; [if anyone wishes to look]*

To brek my sleip ane uther quair I tuik,   *break; sleep; another book*
In quhilk I fand the fatall destenie   *found; fated destiny*
Of fair Cresseid, that endit wretchitlie.

Quha wait gif all that Chauceir wrait was trew? *who knows if; wrote; true*
Nor I wait nocht gif this narratioun
Be authoreist, or fenyeit of the new   *has authority; is newly imagined*
Be sum poeit, throw his inventioun   *[poetic] invention*
Maid to report the lamentatioun   *relate*
And wofull end of this lustie Creisseid,   *beautiful*
And quhat distres scho thoillit, and quhat deid. *what; suffered; death*

Quhen Diomeid had all his appetyte,
And mair, fulfillit of this fair ladie,   *more; satisfied*
Upon ane uther he set his haill delyte,   *whole desire*
And send to hir ane lybell of repudie, *sent; [formal document of rejection]*
And hir excludit fra his companie.   *banished*
Than desolait scho walkit up and doun,   *abandoned*
And sum men sayis, into the court, commoun. *in; promiscuous woman*

O fair Creisseid, the flour and A per se   *flower; paragon*
Of Troy and Grece, how was thow fortunait   *destined*
To change in filth all thy feminitie,
And be with fleschelie lust sa maculait,   *fleshly; defiled*
And go amang the Greikis air and lait,   *Greeks; early and late*
Sa giglotlike takand thy foull plesance! *wantonly; [taking pleasure]*
I have pietie thow suld fall sic mischance! *pity; experience; such misfortune*

Yit nevertheless, quhat ever men deme or say   *judge*
In scornefull langage of thy brukkilnes,   *frailty*
I sall excuse als far furth as I may   *as far*
Thy womanheid, thy wisdome and fairnes,
The quhilk fortoun hes put to sic distres   *fortune*
As hir pleisit, and nathing throw the gilt *pleased her; not at all; guilt*
Of the, throw wickit langage to be spilt!   *thee; wicked; injured*

This fair lady, in this wyse destitute   *manner*
Of all comfort and consolatioun,
Richt privelie, but fellowschip or refute, *secretly; without protection*
Disagysit passit far out of the toun   *disguised; went*

Ane myle or twa, unto ane mansioun   *two*
Beildit full gay, quhair hir father Calchas   *built handsomely; where*
Quhilk than amang the Greikis dwelland was.   *dwelling*

Quhen he hir saw, the caus he can inquyre   *inquired*
Of hir cumming; scho said, siching full soir,   *sighing bitterly*
'Fra Diomeid had gottin his desyre   *after*
He wox werie and wald of me no moir.'   *grew weary; would; more*
Quod Calchas, 'Douchter, weip thow not thairfoir;   *said; daughter; weep*
Peraventure all cummis for the best.   *perhaps*
Welcum to me; thow art full deir ane gest!'   *very dear guest*

This auld Calchas, efter the law was tho,   *[in accordance with]; [in those days]*
Wes keiper of the tempill as ane preist   *priest*
In quhilk Venus and hir sone Cupido   *son; Cupid*
War honourit, and his chalmer was thame neist;   *private room; next to them*
To quhilk Cresseid, with baill aneuch in breist,   *misery enough; breast*
Usit to pas, hir prayeris for to say,   *was accustomed*
Quhill at the last, upon ane solempne day,   *until; solemn*

As custome was, the pepill far and neir   *people*
Befoir the none unto the tempill went   *before noon*
With sacrifice, devoit in thair maneir;   *devout; manner*
Bot still Cresseid, hevie in hir intent,   *sorrowful; mind*
Into the kirk wald not hir self present,   *church*
For giving of the pepill ony deming   *for fear of; suspicion*
Of hir expuls fra Diomeid the king;   *expulsion*

Bot past into ane secreit orature,   *went; oratory*
Quhair scho micht weip hir wofull desteny.
Behind hir bak scho cloisit fast the dure   *closed*
And on hir kneis bair fell doun in hy;   *in haste*
Upon Venus and Cupide angerly   *angrily*
Scho cryit out, and said on this same wyse: *very manner*
'Allace, that ever I maid yow sacrifice!

'Ye gave me anis ane devine responsaill   *once; response*
That I suld be the flour of luif in Troy;   *flower of love*
Now am I maid ane unworthie outwaill,   *outcast*
And all in cair translatit is my joy.

Quha sall me gyde? Quha sall me now convoy,   *protect*
Sen I fra Diomeid and nobill Troylus   *since*
Am clene excludit, as abject odious?   *an outcast*

'O fals Cupide, is nane to wyte bot thow   *none; blame*
And thy mother, of lufe the blind goddes!   *love*
Ye causit me alwayis understand and trow   *believe*
The seid of lufe was sawin in my face,   *sown*
And ay grew grene throw your supplie and grace.   *ever; help and favour*
Bot now, allace, that seid with froist is slane,   *frost*
And I fra luifferis left, and all forlane.'   *lovers; abandoned*

Quhen this was said, doun in ane extasie,   *trance*
Ravischit in spreit, intill ane dreame scho fell,   *ravished; spirit; into*
And be apperance hard, quhair scho did ly,   *apparently heard*
Cupide the king ringand ane silver bell,   *ringing*
Quhilk men micht heir fra hevin unto hell;   *hear*
At quhais sound befoir Cupide appeiris   *whose; appears*
The sevin planetis, discending fra thair spheiris;   *planets; spheres*

Quhilk hes power of all thing generabill,   *have; generating*
To reull and steir be thair greit influence   *rule; govern by their great [planetary] influence*
Wedder and wind, and coursis variabill.   *weather; movements*
And first of all Saturne gave his sentence,   *judgement*
Quhilk gave to Cupide litill reverence,   *respect*
Bot as ane busteous churle on his maneir   *rough churl*
Come crabitlie with auster luik and cheir.   *came ill-naturedly; austere look and expression*

His face fronsit, his lyre was lyke the leid,   *wrinkled face; lead*
His teith chatterit and cheverit with the chin,   *teeth; shivered*
His ene drowpit, how sonkin in his heid,   *eyes drooped; sunken; head*
Out of his nois the meldrop fast can rin,   *nose; [drop of mucus]; ran*
With lippis bla and cheikis leine and thin;   *bluish lips and lean cheeks*
The ice-schoklis that fra his hair doun hang   *icicles; hung*
Was wonder greit, and as ane speir als lang.   *

were wondrously large, and as long as a spear

Atovir his belt his lyart lokkis lay   *down over; grey hair*
Felterit unfair, ovirfret with froistis hoir,   *matted unattractively, covered in hoar frost*
His garmound and his gyte full gay of gray,   *garments; mantle*
His widderit weid fra him the wind out woir,   *withered clothes; carried out*
Ane busteous bow within his hand he boir,   *cruel; bore*
Under his girdill ane flasche of felloun flanis   *girdle; sheaf of deadly arrows*
Fedderit with ice and heidit with hailstanis.   *feathered; headed; hailstones*

Than Juppiter, richt fair and amiabill,   *very beautiful; friendly*
God of the starnis in the firmament   *stars*
And nureis to all thing generabill;   *nurse*
Fra his father Saturne far different,
With burelie face and browis bricht and brent;   *handsome; forehead fair and smooth*
Upon his heid ane garland wonder gay
Of flouris fair, as it had bene in May.   *flowers; as if it had been*

His voice was cleir, as cristall wer his ene,
As goldin wyre sa glitterand was his hair,   *glittering*
His garmound and his gyte full gay of grene   *mantle*
With goldin listis gilt on everie gair;   *edgings; gore*
Ane burelie brand about his middill bair,   *strong sword; bore*
In his richt hand he had ane groundin speir,   *right; sharpened spear*
Of his father the wraith fra us to weir.   *wrath; [ward off]*

Nixt efter him come Mars the god of ire,   *came*
Of strife, debait, and all dissensioun,   *contention*
To chide and fecht, als feirs as ony fyre,   *dispute; fight; as fierce*
In hard harnes, hewmound, and habirgeoun,   *armour; helmet; mailcoat*
And on his hanche ane roustie fell fachioun,   *haunch; rusty cruel sword*
And in his hand he had ane roustie sword,
Wrything his face with mony angrie word.   *twisting*

Schaikand his sword, befoir Cupide he come,   *shaking*
With reid visage and grislie glowrand ene,   *red; staring*
And at his mouth ane bullar stude of fome,   *bubble; stood; foam*
Lyke to ane bair quhetting his tuskis kene;   *boar; whetting; sharp*
Richt tuilyeour lyke, but temperance in tene,   *brawler-like; [intemperate in anger]*
Ane horne he blew with mony bosteous brag,   *violent blast*
Quhilk all this warld with weir hes maid to wag.   *war; shake*

Than fair Phebus, lanterne and lamp of licht,
Of man and beist, baith frute and flourisching,   *blossom*
Tender nureis, and banischer of nicht,   *nurse*
And of the warld causing, be his moving
And influence, lyfe in all eirdlie thing,   *earthly*
Without comfort of quhome, of force, to nocht   *whose; [necessarily]*
Must all ga die that in this warld is wrocht.

As king royall he raid upon his chair,   *rode; chariot*
The quhilk Phaeton gydit sum tyme unricht;   *which; guided once astray*
The brichtnes of his face quhen it was bair   *uncovered*
Nane micht behald for peirsing of his sicht;   *[fear of his piercing stare]*
This goldin cart with fyrie bemis bricht
Four yokkit steidis full different of hew   *yoked steeds; colour*
But bait or tyring throw the spheiris drew.   *[without cease or tiring]*

The first was soyr, with mane als reid as rois,   *sorrel; rose*
Callit Eoye, into the orient;   *Eous*
The secund steid to name hecht Ethios,   *was called Ethous*
Quhitlie and paill, and sum deill ascendent;   *whitish and pale; [rising up somewhat]*
The thrid Peros, richt hait and richt fervent;   *third Pyrois; hot and burning*
The feird was blak, and callit Philogie,   *fourth; Philogeus*
Quhilk rollis Phebus doun into the sey.   *rolled; sea*

Venus was thair present, that goddes gay,
Hir sonnis querrell for to defend, and mak   *son's cause*
Hir awin complaint, cled in ane nyce array,   *own; clad; strange*
The ane half grene, the uther half sabill blak,
Quhyte hair as gold, kemmit and sched abak;   *combed; parted backwards*
Bot in hir face semit greit variance,   *seemed; changefulness*
Quhyles perfyte treuth and quhyles inconstance.   *sometimes; fidelity*

Under smyling scho was dissimulait,   *deceitful*
Provocative with blenkis amorous,   *glances*
And suddanely changit and alterait,   *altered*
Angrie as ony serpent vennemous,
Richt pungitive with wordis odious;   *stinging*
Thus variant scho was, quha list tak keip: *whoever wished to take heed*
With ane eye lauch, and with the uther weip,   *laughed; wept*

In taikning that all fleschelie paramour,   *token*
Quhilk Venus hes in reull and governance,   *rule*
I sum tyme sweit, sum tyme bitter and sour,   *sweet*
Richt unstabill and full of variance,
Mingit with cairfull joy and fals plesance,   *mixed*
Now hait, now cauld, now blyith, now full of wo,
Now grene as leif, now widderit and ago.   *withered; gone*

With buik in hand than come Mercurius,   *Mercury*
Richt eloquent and full of rethorie,   *rhetoric*
With polite termis and delicious,
With pen and ink to report all reddie,   *ready to record*
Setting sangis and singand merilie;   *composing songs*
His hude was reid, heklit atovir his croun,   *fringed*
Lyke to ane poeit of the auld fassoun.   *manner*

Boxis he bair with fyne electuairis,   *medicines*
And sugerit syropis for digestioun,
Spycis belangand to the pothecairis,
With mony hailsum sweit confectioun;   *wholesome*
Doctour in phisick, cled in ane skarlot goun,   *scarlet*
And furrit weill – as sic ane aucht to be –   *well-furred*
Honest and gude, and not ane word culd lie.

Nixt efter him come lady Cynthia,
The last of all and swiftest in hir spheir;
Of colour blak, buskit with hornis twa,   *dressed*
And in the nicht scho listis best appeir;   *likes*
Haw as the leid, of colour nathing cleir,   *pale; lead; [with no apparent colouring]*
For all hir licht scho borrowis at hir brother   *from*
Titan, for of hirself scho hes nane uther.   *the sun*

Hir gyte was gray and full of spottis blak,   *mantle*
And on hir breist ane churle paintit full evin   *peasant; [precisely]*
Beirand ane bunche of thornis on his bak,   *carrying*
Quhilk for his thift micht clim na nar the hevin.   *theft; [could climb no nearer]*
Thus quhen thay gadderit war, thir goddes sevin,   *gathered; were*
Mercurius thay cheisit with ane assent   *chose*
To be foirspeikar in the parliament.   *speaker*

Quha had bene thair and liken for to heir   *if anyone; desirous*
His facound toung and termis exquisite,   *eloquent*
Of rethorick the prettick he micht leir,   *practice; learn*
In breif sermone ane pregnant sentence wryte.
Befoir Cupide veiling his cap a-lyte,   *doffing; [a little]*
Speiris the caus of that vocatioun,   *asks*
And he anone schew his intentioun.   *quickly; revealed; charge*

'Lo,' quod Cupide, 'quha will blaspheme the name
Of his awin god, outher in word or deid,   *whether; deed*
To all goddis he dois baith lak and schame,   *insult*
And suld have bitter panis to his meid;   *punishments; recompense*
I say this by yone wretchit Cresseid,
The quhilk throw me was sum tyme flour of lufe,   *who; through*
Me and my mother starklie can reprufe,

'Saying of hir greit infelicitie   *misfortune*
I was the caus, and my mother Venus,
Ane blind goddes hir cald, that micht not se,   *called; see*
With sclander and defame injurious.   *slander; defamation*
Thus hir leving unclene and lecherous   *living*
Scho wald retorte in me and my mother,   *[throw back on]*
To quhome I schew my grace abone all uther.   *showed; above*

'And sen ye ar all sevin deificait,   *deified*
Participant of devyne sapience,   *sharing in*
This greit injure done to our hie estait   *injury; high rank*
Me think with pane we suld mak recompence;   *it seems to me; punishment*
Was never to goddes done sic violence.
As weill for yow as for myself I say:
Thairfoir ga help to revenge, I yow pray!'   *go and help*

Mercurius to Cupide gave answeir
And said, 'Schir King, my counsall is that ye
Refer yow to the hiest planeit heir
And tak to him the lawest of degré,   *add; lowest*
The pane of Cresseid for to modifie –   *pain; determine*
As God Saturne, with him tak Cynthia.'
'I am content', quod he, 'to tak thay twa.'   *those two*

Than thus proceidit Saturne and the Mone   *proceeded; Moon*
Quhen thay the mater rypelie had degest: *[fully considered]*
For the dispyte to Cupide scho had done   *injury*
And to Venus, oppin and manifest,   *open*
In all hir lyfe with pane to be opprest,
And torment sair with seiknes incurabill,   *tormented sorely*
And to all lovers be abhominabill.

This duleful sentence Saturne tuik on hand,   *doleful; [took charge of]*
And passit doun quhair cairfull Cresseid lay,   *sorrowful*
And on hir heid he laid ane frostie wand.   *head*
Than lawfullie on this wyse can he say: *
'Thy greit fairnes and all thy bewtie gay,
Thy wantoun blude, and eik thy goldin hair,   *also*
Heir I exclude fra the for evermair.   *banish*

'I change thy mirth into melancholy,
Quhilk is the mother of all pensivenes;
Thy moisture and thy heit in cald and dry;   *heat*
Thyne insolence, thy play and wantones   *arrogance*
To greit diseis; thy pomp and thy riches   *distress*
In mortall neid; and greit penuritie   *penury*
Thow suffer sall, and as ane beggar die.'

O cruell Saturne, fraward and angrie,   *perverse*
Hard is thy dome and to malitious!   *judgement*
On fair Cresseid quhy hes thow na mercie,
Quhilk was sa sweit, gentill and amorous?
Withdraw thy sentence and be gracious –
As thow was never; sa schawis throw thy deid,   †
Ane wraikfull sentence gevin on fair Cresseid.   *vindictive*

Than Cynthia, quhen Saturne past away,
Out of hir sait discendit doun belyve,   *seat; swiftly*
And red ane bill on Cresseid quhair scho lay,   *[read a formal document]*
Contening this sentence diffinityve:

* *[in accordance with legal proceedings he spoke thus]*
† *[as you never have been; so much is evident from your deed]*

'Fra heit of bodie I the now depryve,   *of bodily heat*
And to thy seiknes sall be na recure   *for; no cure*
Bot in dolour thy dayis to indure.

'Thy cristall ene minglit with blude I mak,
Thy voice sa cleir, unplesand, hoir and hace,   *rough; hoarse*
Thy lustie lyre ovirspred with spottis blak,   *beautiful skin; covered*
And lumpis haw appeirand in thy face: *lumpis; livid*
Quhair thow cummis, ilk man sall fle the place. *wherever you go*
This sall thow go begging fra hous to hous   *thus*
With cop and clapper lyke ane lazarous.'   *cup; rattle; leper*

This doolie dreame, this uglye visioun   *dismal*
Brocht to ane end, Cresseid fra it awoik,   *brought*
And all that court and convocatioun
Vanischit away. Than rais scho up and tuik   *rose*
Ane poleist glas, and hir schaddow culd luik; *mirror; [observed her reflection]*
And quhen scho saw hir face sa deformait,
Gif scho in hart was wa aneuch, God wait!   *sorry enough; knows*

Weiping full sair, 'Lo, quhat it is', quod sche,
'With fraward langage for to mufe and steir   *fractious; provoke; stir*
Our craibit goddis; and sa is sene on me!   *ill-tempered; so*
My blaspheming now have I bocht full deir;   *paid for most dearly*
All eirdlie joy and mirth I set areir.   *[put in the past]*
Allace, this day! allace, this wofull tyde   *time*
Quhen I began with my goddis for to chyde!'   *quarrel*

Be this was said, ane chyld come fra the hall   *when; child*
To warne Cresseid the supper was reddy;
First knokkit at the dure, and syne culd call,   *then called out*
'Madame, your father biddis yow cum in hy: *[quickly]*
He hes merwell sa lang on grouf ye ly,   *marvelled; prostrate*
And sayis your beedes bene to lang sum deill; *prayers; [are too long]*
The goddis wait all your intent full weill.'   *know*

Quod scho, 'Fair chyld, ga to my father deir,
And pray him cum to speik with me anone.'   *at once*
And sa he did, and said, 'Douchter, quhat cheir?'
'Allace!' quod scho, 'Father, my mirth is gone!'

'How sa?' quod he; and scho can all expone,   *explained*
As I have tauld, the vengeance and the wraik   *revenge*
For hir trespas Cupide on hir culd tak.   *[had taken]*

He luikit on hir uglye lipper face,
The quhylk befor was quhite as lillie flour;
Wringand his handis, oftymes he said, allace
That he had levit to se that wofull hour!
For he knew weill that thair was na succour
To hir seiknes, and that dowblit his pane;
Thus was thair cair aneuch betuix thame twane.   *sorrow; [the two of them]*

Quhen thay togidder murnit had full lang,   *lamented*
Quod Cresseid: 'Father, I wald not be kend;   *recognized*
Thairfoir in secreit wyse ye let me gang   *[disguised]*
Unto yone spitall at the tounis end,   *[leper-house]*
And thidder sum meit for cheritie me send   *thither; food; charity*
To leif upon, for all mirth in this eird   *live; earth*
Is fra me gane – sic is my wickit weird!'   *fate*

Than in ane mantill and ane baver hat,   *cloak; beaver-skin*
With cop and clapper, wonder prively,   *cup and rattle; secretly*
He opnit ane secreit yet, and out thairat   *opened; gate; therefrom*
Convoyit hir, that na man suld espy,   *escorted; so that*
Unto ane village half ane myle thairby;   *from there*
Delyverit hir in at the spittaill hous,   *delivered*
And daylie sent hir part of his almous.   *alms*

Sum knew hir weill, and sum had na knawledge
Of hir becaus scho was sa deformait,   *deformed*
With bylis blak ovirspred in hir visage,   *boils; covered*
And hir fair colour faidit and alterait.   *faded; changed*
Yit thay presumit, for hir hie regrait   *because of her great lamentation*
And still murning, scho was of nobill kin;   *constant moaning*
With better will thairfoir they tuik hir in.

The day passit and Phebus went to rest,
The cloudis blak overheled all the sky.   *covered over*
God wait gif Cresseid was ane sorrowfull gest,
Seing that uncouth fair and harbery!   *seeing; unfamiliar; lodging*

But meit or drink scho dressit hir to ly   *without food; [prepared herself]*
In ane dark corner of the hous allone,
And on this wyse, weiping, scho maid hir mone: *lament*

'O sop of sorrow, sonkin into cair!   *sunk*
O cative Creisseid! For now and ever mair   *wretched*
Gane is thy joy and all thy mirth in eird;   *gone*
Of all blyithnes now art thou blaiknit bair;   *[made pale and bare]*
Thair is na salve may saif or sound thy sair!   *remedy; cure; suffering*
Fell is thy fortoun, wickit is thy weird,   *cruel; fortune; evil; fate*
Thy blys is baneist, and thy baill on breird!   *banished; misery; [widespread]*
Under the eirth, God gif I gravin wer,   *grant; buried*
Quhair nane of Grece nor yit of Troy micht heird!   *[could hear it]*

'Quhair is thy chalmer wantounlie besene,   *[luxuriously furnished]*
With burely bed and bankouris browderit bene?   *
Spycis and wyne to thy collatioun,
The cowpis all of gold and silver schene,   *goblets; shining*
The sweitmeitis servit in plaittis clene   *sweetmeats; elegant dishes*
With saipheron sals of ane gude sessoun?   *saffron sauce; good seasoning*
Thy gay garmentis with mony gudely goun,
Thy plesand lawn pinnit with goldin prene?   *linen; pinned; brooch*
All is areir, thy greit royall renoun!   *[in the past]*

'Quhair is thy garding with thir greissis gay   *garden; plants*
And fresche flowris, quhilk the quene Floray   *Flora*
Had paintit plesandly in everie pane,   *part*
Quhair thou was wont full merilye in May
To walk and tak the dew be it was day,   *[as soon as]*
And heir the merle and mawis mony ane,   *hear; blackbird; thrush*
With ladyis fair in carrolling to gane,   *singing; go*
And se the royall rinkis in thair ray,   *knights; array*
In garmentis gay garnischit on everie grane?   *decorated; detail*

'Thy greit triumphand fame and hie honour,
Quhair thou was callit of eirdlye wichtis flour,   *[the flower of earthly creatures]*
All is decayit, thy weird is welterit so;   *overturned*
Thy hie estait is turnit in darknes dour;

* *handsome; [covers for seats]; [finely embroidered]*

This lipper ludge tak for thy burelie bour,   *lepers' lodge; bower*
And for thy bed tak now ane bunche of stro,   *straw*
For waillit wyne and meitis thou had tho   *choice; food*
Tak mowlit breid, peirrie and ceder sour: *mouldy; perry; cider*
Bot cop and clapper now is all ago.   *except for; gone*

'My cleir voice and courtlie carrolling,
Quhair I was wont with ladyis for to sing,
Is rawk as ruik, full hiddeous, hoir and hace;   *raucous as a rook; grating; hoarse*
My plesand port, all utheris precelling,   *bearing; excelling*
Of lustines I was hald maist conding –   *beauty; [to have the most]*
Now is deformit the figour of my face;
To luik on it na leid now lyking hes.   *[no person now has pleasure]*
Sowpit in syte, I say with sair siching,   *sunk; sorrow; sighing*
Ludgeit amang the lipper leid, "Allace!"   *lodged; leper-folk*

'O ladyis fair of Troy and Grece, attend
My miserie, quhilk nane may comprehend,
My frivoll fortoun, my infelicitie,   *fickle*
My greit mischeif, quhilk na man can amend.   *distress*
Be war in tyme, approchis neir the end,   *beware*
And in your mynd ane mirrour mak of me:
As I am now, peradventure that ye   *perhaps*
For all your micht may cum to that same end,
Or ellis war, gif ony war may be.   *else worse*

'Nocht is your fairnes bot ane faiding flour,
Nocht is your famous laud and hie honour   *glory*
Bot wind inflat in uther mennis eiris;   *blown*
Your roising reid to rotting sall retour;   *rosy-redness*
Exempill mak of me in your memour,   *memory*
Quhilk of sic thingis wofull witnes beiris.
All welth in eird, away as wind it weiris;   *[passes]*
Be war thairfoir, approchis neir the hour:
Fortoun is fikkill quhen scho beginnis and steiris!'   *moves*

Thus chydand with hir drerie destenye,   *miserable*
Weiping scho woik the nicht fra end to end;   *[stayed awake]*
Bot all in vane – hir dule, hir cairfull cry,
Micht not remeid nor yit hir murning mend.   *remit*

Ane lipper lady rais and till hir wend,   *rose; went to her*
And said: 'Quhy spurnis thow aganis the wall   *beat*
To sla thyself and mend nathing at all?   *slay*

'Sen thy weiping dowbillis bot thy wo,   *since; only doubles*
I counsall the mak vertew of ane neid; *thee; to make a virtue of necessity*
Go leir to clap thy clapper to and fro,   *learn*
And leif efter the law of lipper leid.'
Thair was na buit, bot furth with thame scho yeid   *help; then; went*
Fra place to place, quhill cauld and hounger sair   *until*
Compellit hir to be ane rank beggair.

That samin tyme, of Troy the garnisoun,   *same; garrison*
Quhilk had to chiftane worthie Troylus,   *as chieftain*
Throw jeopardie of weir had strikken doun   *opportunity of war*
Knichtis of Grece in number mervellous;
With greit tryumphe and laude victorious   *glory*
Agane to Troy richt royallie thay raid
The way quhair Cresseid with the lipper baid.   *dwelt*

Seing that companie, all with ane stevin   *one voice*
Thay gaif ane cry, and schuik coppis gude speid; *gave; shook; bowls; at once*
Said: 'Worthie lordis, for Goddis lufe of hevin,
To us lipper part of your almous deid!'   *give; alms*
Than to thair cry nobill Troylus tuik heid,
Having pietie, neir by the place can pas   *pity; passed*
Quhair Cresseid sat, not witting quhat scho was.   *knowing who*

Than upon him scho kest up baith hir ene –   *cast*
And with ane blenk it come into his thocht
That he sumtime hir face befoir had sene.
Bot scho was in sic plye he knew hir nocht;   *plight*
Yit than hir luik into his mynd it brocht
The sweit visage and amorous blenking
Of fair Cresseid, sumtyme his awin darling.

Na wonder was, suppois in mynd that he   *if*
Tuik hir figure sa sone – and lo, now quhy: *[responded to her]*
The idole of ane thing in cace may be   *image; [by chance]*
Sa deip imprentit in the fantasy   *imagination*

That it deludis the wittis outwardly,
And sa appeiris in forme and lyke estait   *the same state*
Within the mynd as it was figurait.   *as it was fixed in the mind*

Ane spark of lufe than till his hart culd spring   *to; sprang*
And kendlit all his bodie in ane fyre:
With hait fewir, ane sweit and trimbling   *hot fever; sweat*
Him tuik, quhill he was reddie to expyre;
To beir his scheild his breist began to tyre;
Within ane quhyle he changit mony hew,   *[turned many colours]*
And nevertheles not ane ane uther knew.   *[still]*

For knichtlie pietie and memoriall   *piety; [in memory]*
Of fair Cresseid, ane gyrdill can he tak,   *girdle; took*
Ane purs of gold, and mony gay jowall,   *jewels*
And in the skirt of Cresseid doun can swak;   *flung*
Than raid away and not ane word he spak,
Pensive in hart, quhill he come to the toun,   *until*
And for greit cair oftsyis almaist fell doun.   *often*

The lipper folk to Cresseid than can draw   *approached*
To se the equall distributioun
Of the almous, bot quhen the gold thay saw,
Ilkane to uther prevelie can roun,   *each to the other; [whispered]*
And said; 'Yone lord hes mair affectioun,
However it be, unto yone lazarous   *that leper*
Than to us all; we knaw be his almous.'   *[know that by]*

'Quhat lord is yone,' quod scho, 'have ye na feill,   *idea*
Hes done to us so greit humanitie?'   *kindness*
'Yes,' quod a lipper man, 'I knaw him weill;
Schir Troylus it is, gentill and fre.'
Quhen Cresseid understude that it was he,
Stiffer than steill thair stert ane bitter stound   *steel; pain*
Throwout hir hart, and fell doun to the ground.

Quhen scho ovircome, with siching sair and sad,   *revived; sighing*
With mony cairfull cry and cald ochane: *cold; moan*
'Now is my breist with stormie stoundis stad,   *oppressed*
Wrappit in wo, ane wretch full will of wane!'   *wrapped; [destitute]*

Than swounit scho oft or scho culd refrane,   *swooned; before she could stop*
And ever in hir swouning cryit scho thus;
'O fals Cresseid and trew knicht Troylus!

'Thy lufe, thy lawtie, and thy gentilnes   *loyalty; nobility*
I countit small in my prosperitie,   *[reckoned little]*
Sa elevait I was in wantones,   *raised up*
And clam upon the fickill quheill sa hie.   *climbed so high on the fickle wheel [of Fortune]*
All faith and lufe I promissit to the
Was in the self fickill and frivolous: *itself*
O fals Cresseid and trew knicht Troilus!

'For lufe of me thow keipt gude continence,   *[maintained self-restraint]*
Honest and chaist in conversatioun;
Of all wemen protectour and defence
Thou was, and helpit thair opinioun;   *reputation*
My mynd in fleschelie foull affectioun
Was inclynit to lustis lecherous:
Fy, fals Cresseid! O trew knicht Troylus!

'Lovers be war and tak gude heid about
Quhome that ye lufe, for quhome ye suffer paine.
I lat yow wit, thair is richt few thairout   *let; know; few; about*
Quhome ye may traist to have trew lufe agane;   *trust; [love you truly in return]*
Preif quhen ye will, your labour is in vaine.   *test*
Thairfoir I reid ye tak thame as ye find,   *advise; [when you find them]*
For thay ar sad as widdercok in wind.   *steadfast; weathercock*

'Becaus I knaw the greit unstabilnes,
Brukkill as glas, into my self, I say,   *fragile; [of my own self]*
Traisting in uther als greit unfaithfulnes,   *[expecting in others the same great infidelity]*
Als unconstant, and als untrew of fay —   *faith*
Thocht sum be trew, I wait richt few ar thay;   *though*
Quha findis treuth, lat him his lady ruse!   *whoever finds fidelity; praise*
Nane but myself as now I will accuse.'   *[from now]*

Quhen this was said, with paper scho sat doun,
And on this maneir maid hir testament: *in*
'Heir I beteiche my corps and carioun   *commit; corpse; carrion*
With wormis and with taidis to be rent;   *toads; [torn apart]*

My cop and clapper, and myne ornament,
And all my gold the lipper folk sall have
Quhen I am deid, to burie me in grave.

'This royall ring set with this rubie reid,   *[as love-token]*
Quhilk Troylus in drowrie to me send,   *leave*
To him agane I leif it quhen I am deid,   *sorrowful; death; known*
To mak my cairfull deid unto him kend.
Thus I conclude schortlie, and mak ane end:
My spreit I leif to Diane, quhair scho dwellis,   *Diana*
To walk with hir in waist woddis and wellis.   *wild woods; springs*

'O Diomeid, thou hes baith broche and belt   *brooch*
Quhilk Troylus gave me in takning   *token*
Of his trew lufe!' and with that word scho swelt.   *died*
And sone ane lipper man tuik of the ring,
Syne buryt hir withouttin tarying;
To Troylus furthwith the ring he bair,   *bore*
And of Cresseid the deith he can declair.   *[told]*

Quhen he had hard hir greit infirmitie,
Hir legacie and lamentatioun,
And how scho endit in sic povertie,
He swelt for wo and fell doun in ane swoun;   *fainted*
For greit sorrow his hart to brist was boun;   *burst; ready*
Siching full sadlie, said, 'I can no moir –
Scho was untrew and wo is me thairfoir.'

Sum said he maid ane tomb of merbell gray,   *marble*
And wrait hir name and superscriptioun,   *wrote*
And laid it on hir grave quhair that scho lay,
In goldin letteris, conteining this ressoun: *statement*
'Lo, fair ladyis! Cresseid of Troyis toun,
Sumtyme countit the flour of womanheid,
Under this stane, lait lipper, lyis deid.'   *[of late]*

Now, worthie wemen, in this ballet schort,   *poem*
Maid for your worschip and instructioun,
Of cheritie, I monische and exhort,   *admonish*
Ming not your lufe with fals deceptioun.   *corrupt*

Beir in your mynd this schort conclusioun
Of fair Cresseid, as I have said befoir.
Sen scho is deid, I speik of hir no moir.   *since she is dead*

from *Orpheus and Eurydice*

Syne nethir-mare he went quhare Pluto was   *further down; where*
And Proserpine, and thiderward he drewe,
Ay playand on his harp as he coud pas;   *[went on]*
Till at the last Erudices he knewe,
Lene and dedelike, pitouse and pale of hewe,   *pitiful*
Rycht warsch and wan, and walowit as a wede,   *sickly; withered*
Hir lily lyre was lyke unto the lede.   *skin; lead*

Quod he: 'My lady lele and my delyte,   *true*
Full wa is me to se yow changit thus.   *sorry*
Quhare is thy rude as rose, wyth chekis quhite?   *complexion; white*
Thy cristall eyne with blenkis amorouse?   *eyes; loving glances*
Thi lippis rede to kis diliciouse?'
Quod scho, 'As now, I dar noucht tell, perfay,   *she; just now; in truth*
Bot ye sall wit the cause ane othir day.'   *know*

Quod Pluto, 'Sir, thouch scho be like ane elf,   *though*
Thare is na cause to plenye, and forquhy?   *complain; why*
Scho fure als wele dayly as did myself,   *[has fared as well]*
Or king Herode for all his chevalry.
It is langour that puttis hir in sik ply;   *grief; such; plight*
Were scho at hame in hir contree of Trace,   *Thrace*
Scho wald refete full sone in fax and face.'   *would recover; very soon; hair*

Than Orpheus before Pluto sat doun,
And in his handis quhite his harp can ta,   *white hands; took*
And playit mony suete proporcion,   *sweet harmonies*
With base tonys in ypodorica,   *low notes; hypodorian mode*
With gemilling in yperlydica;   *[doubling in hyperlydian mode]*
Till at the last, for reuth and grete pitee   *compassion*
Thay wepit sore that coud hym here and see.

Than Proserpyne and Pluto bad hym as   *ask*
His warison, and he wald ask rycht noucht   *reward; [nothing at all]*
Bot licence wyth his wyf away to pas   *permission; go*
Till his contree, that he so fer had soucht.   *to; far; sought*
Quod Proserpyne: 'Sen I hir hidir broucht,   *[Since I brought her here]*
We sall noucht part bot wyth condicion.'   *[except with a stipulation]*
Quod he: 'Thareto I mak promission.'   *to that; promise*

'Erudices than be the hand thou tak,
And pas thy way, bot underneth this payne: *under; penalty*
Gyf thou turnis, or blenkis behind thy bak,   *if*
We sall hir have forevir till hell agayn.'
Thouch this was hard, yit Orpheus was fayn,   *willing*
And on thai went, talkand of play and sport,   *talking*
Quhill thay almaist come to the utter port.   *until; outer gate*

Thus Orpheus, wyth inwart lufe replete,   *filled with inner love*
So blyndit was in grete affection,
Pensif apon his wyf and lady suete,
Remembrit noucht his hard condicion.
Quhat will ye more? In schort conclusion,
He blent bakward and Pluto come anone,   *looked; at once*
And unto hell agayn with hir is gone.

Allace, it was rycht grete hertsare for to here   *painful; hear*
Of Orpheus the weping and the wo,
Quhen that his wyf, quhilk he had bocht so dere,   *redeemed; dearly*
Bot for a luke sa sone was hynt hym fro.   *just; so soon; torn*
Flatlyngis he fell and mycht no forthir go,   *prostrate*
And lay a quhile in suoun and extasy;   *swoon; trance*
Quhen he ourcome, thus out on lufe can cry: *recovered; cried*

'Quhat art thou lufe? How sall I the dyffyne?   *describe*
Bitter and suete, cruel and merciable;   *merciful*
Plesand to sum, til othir playnt and pyne;   *pleasant; lamentation; suffering*
To sum constant, till othir variabil.
Hard is thy law, thi bandis unbrekable;
Quha servis the, thouch he be newir sa trewe,   *whoever serves; never*
Perchance sum tyme he sall have cause to rewe!   *rue*

'Now fynd I wele this proverbe trew,' quod he,
' "Hert is on the hurd, and hand is on the sore;   *heart; treasure*
Quhare lufe gois, on forse turnis the ee."   *[where love goes]; [eye must turn]*
I am expert, and wo is me tharfore;
Bot for a luke my lady is forlore.'   *lost*
Thus chydand on with lufe, our burn and bent,   *complaining; over stream and field*
A wofull wedow hamewart is he went . . .   *widower; homewards*

BLIND HARRY (c. 1450–1493)

from *The Actis and Deidis of the Illustere and Vailyeand Campioun
Schir William Wallace, Knicht of Ellerslie*

The Sevint Buik, Lines 1029–92

In Abyrdeyn he gert a consaill cry,	*had a council called*
Trew Scottis men suld semble hastely.	*assemble*
Till Cowper he raid to wesy that abbay;	*Coupar; inspect*
The Inglis abbot fra thine was fled away.	
Bischop Synclar, with out langar abaid,	*delay*
Met thaim at Glammys, syne furth with thaim he raid.	*them; Glamis; then*
In till Breichyn thai lugyt all that nycht;	*Brechin*
Syne on the morn Wallace gert graith thaim rycht,	*[had them equipped]*
Displayed on breid the baner off Scotland	*[openly]*
In gud aray, with noble men at hand;	
Gert playnly cry, that sawfte suld be nayne	*saved; none*
Off Sotheroun blud, quhar thai mycht be ourtayn.	*overtaken*
In playne battaill throuch out the Mernys thai rid.	
The Inglismen, at durst thaim nocht abid,	*dared not stay*
Befor the ost full ferdly furth thai fle	*very afraid; flee*
Till Dwnottar, a snuk within the se.	*to Dunottar; promontory*
Na ferrar thai mycht wyn out off the land.	*further*
Thai semblit thar quhill thai war iiij thousand;	*gathered; 4,000*
To the kyrk rane, wend gyrth for till haiff tayne,	*went; sanctuary*
The laiff ramaynd apon the roch off stayne.	*rest*
The byschope than began tretty to ma	*make*
Thair lyffis to get, out off the land to ga.	*go*
Bot thai war rad, and durst nocht weill affy;	*fearful*
Wallace in fyr gert set all haistely,	*[set all on fire]*
Brynt wp the kyrk, and all that was tharin,	*therein*
Atour the roch the laiff ran with gret dyn.	*around*
Sum hang on craggis rycht dulfully to de,	*miserably*
Sum lap, sum fell, sum floteryt in the se.	*leapt; floundered*
Na Sotheroun on lyff was lewyt in that hauld,	*[was allowed to live]; refuge*
And thaim with in thai brynt in powdir cauld.	*ashes*
Quhen this was done, feill fell on kneis doun,	*many*
At the byschop askit absolutioun.	*from*

Than Wallace lewch, said; 'I forgiff yow all; *laughed*
Ar ye wer men, rapentis for sa small? *warriors; repentant; little*
Thai rewid nocht ws in to the toun off Ayr; *rued; us; of*
Our trew barrownis quhen that thai hangyt thar.'

Till Abyrdeyn than haistely thai pass,
Quhar Inglismen besyly flittand was. *busily fleeing*
A hundreth schippys, that ruthyr bur and ayr, *[had rudder and oars]*
To turss thair gud, in hawyn was lyand thar. *carry; goods; harbour*
Bot Wallace ost come on thaim sodeynlye; *[Wallace's army]*
Thar chapyt nane off all that gret menyhe; *escaped*
Bot feill serwandis, in thaim lewyt nane. *except mere servants*
At ane eb se the Scottis is on thaim gayne; *ebb-tide*
Tuk out the ger, syne set the schippys in fyr;
The men on land thai bertynyt bayne and lyr. *hacked; flesh*
Yeid nane away bot preistis, wyffis and barnys; *went; children*
Maid thai debait, thai chapyt nocht but harmys. *defence; [unharmed]*
In to Bowchane Wallace maid him to ryd, *Buchan*
Quhar lord Bewmound was ordand for to bid. *stay*
Erll he was maid bot off schort tyme befor;
He brukit it nocht for all his bustous schor. *enjoyed; boisterous demeanour*
Quhen he wyst weill that Wallace cummand was, *coming*
He left the land, and couth to Slanys pass;
And syne be schip in Ingland fled agayne.
Wallace raid throw the northland in to playne.
At Crummade feill Inglismen thai slew.
The worthi Scottis till hym thus couth persew.
Raturnd agayne, and come till Abirdeyn,
With his blith ost, apon the Lammess ewyn; *Lammas even*
Stablyt the land, as him thocht best suld be.
Syne with ane ost he passit to Dunde,
Gert set a sege about the castell strang. *besieged*
I leyff thaim thar, and forthir we will gang. *leave; further*

AITHBHREAC INGHEAN CORCADAIL (*fl.* 1460s)

A phaidrín do dhúisg mo dhéar

A phaidrín do dhúisg mo dhéar,
   ionmhain méar do bhitheadh ort;
ionmhain cridhe fáilteach fial
   'gá raibhe riamh gus a nocht.

Dá éag is tuirseach atáim,
   an lámh má mbítheá gach n-uair,
nach cluinim a beith i gclí
   agus nach bhfaicim í uaim.

Mo chridhe-se is tinn atá
   ó theacht go crích an lá dhúinn;
ba ghoirid do éist ré ghlóir,
   ré h-agallaimh an óig úir.

Béal asa ndob aobhdha glór,
   dhéantaidhe a ghó is gach tír:
leómhan Muile na múr ngeal,
   seabhag Íle na magh mín.

Fear ba ghéar meabhair ar dhán,
   ó nach deachaidh dámh gan díol;
taoiseach deigh-einigh suairc séimh,
   agá bhfaightí méin mheic ríogh.

Dámh ag teacht ó Dhún an Óir
   is dámh ón Bhóinn go a fholt fiar:
minic thánaig iad fá theist,
   ní mionca ná leis a riar.

O rosary that recalled my tear

O rosary that recalled my tear,
dear was the finger in my sight,
that touched you once, beloved the heart
of him who owned you till tonight.

I grieve the death of him whose hand
you did entwine each hour of prayer;
my grief that it is lifeless now
and I no longer see it there.

My heart is sick, the day has reached
its end for us two, brief the span
that I was given to enjoy
the converse of this goodly man.

Lips whose speech made pleasant sound,
in every land beguiling all,
hawk of Islay of smooth plains,
lion of Mull of the white wall.

His memory for songs was keen,
no poet left him without fee,
nobly generous, courteous, calm,
of princely character was he.

Poets came from Dún an Óir,
and from the Boyne, to him whose hair
was all in curls, drawn by his fame;
to each he gave a generous share.

Seabhag seangglan Sléibhe Gaoil,
   fear do chuir a chaoin ré cléir;
dreagan Leódhuis na learg ngeal,
   éigne Sanais na sreabh séimh.

A h-éagmhais aon duine a mháin
   im aonar atáim dá éis,
gan chluiche, gan chomhrádh caoin,
   gan ábhacht, gan aoibh i gcéill.

Gan duine ris dtig mo mhiann
   ar sliocht na Niall ó Niall óg;
gan mhuirn gan mheadhair ag mnáibh,
   gan aoibhneas an dáin im dhóigh.

Mar thá Giodha an fhuinn mhín,
   Dún Suibhne do-chím gan cheól,
faithche longphuirt na bhfear bhfial:
   aithmhéala na Niall a n-eól.

Cúis ar lúthgháire má seach,
   gusa mbímis ag teacht mall:
's nach fuilngim a nois, mo nuar,
   a fhaicinn uam ar gach ard.

Má bhrisis, a Mheic Dhé bhí,
   ar bagaide na dtrí gcnó,
fa fíor do ghabhais ar ngiall:
   do bhainis an trian ba mhó.

Cnú mhullaigh a mogaill féin
   bhaineadh do Chloinn Néill go nua:
is tric roighne na bhfear bhfial
   go leabaidh na Niall a nuas.

An rogha fá deireadh díbh
   's é thug gan mo bhrígh an sgéal:
do sgar riom mo leathchuing rúin,
   a phaidrín do dhúisg mo dhéar.

Slim handsome hawk of Sliabh Gaoil,*
who satisfied the clergy's hopes,
salmon of Sanas of quiet stream,
dragon of Lewis of sun-drenched slopes.

Bereft of this man, all alone
I live, and take no part in play,
enjoy no kindly talk, nor mirth,
now that his smiles have gone away.

Niall Og is dead; none of his clan
can hold my interest for long;
the ladies droop, their mirth is stilled,
I cannot hope for joy in song.

Gigha of smooth soil is bereft,
no need of music Dùn Suibhne feels,
the grass grows green round the heroes' fort;
they know the sorrow of the MacNeills.

The fort that brought us mirth, each time
we made our way there; now the sight
of it is more than I can bear
as I look on it from each height.

If Thou, Son of the living God,
hast breached the cluster on the tree,
Thou hast taken from us our choicest nut,
and plucked the greatest of the three.

The topmost nut of the bunch is plucked,
Clan Neill has newly lost its head:
often the best of the generous men
descends to the MacNeills' last bed.

His death, the finest of them all,
has sapped my strength, and cost me dear,
taking away my darling spouse,
O rosary that recalled my tear.

* In Knapdale, where Dùn Suibhne (Castle Sween) is situated.

Is briste mo chridhe im chlí,
   agus bídh nó go dtí m'éag,
ar éis an abhradh dhuibh úir,
   a phaidrín do dhúisg mo dhéar.
                              A phaidrín.

Muire mháthair, muime an Ríogh,
   go robh 'gam dhíon ar gach séad,
's a Mac do chruthuigh gach dúil,
   a phaidrín do dhúisg mo dhéar.

My heart is broken in my breast,
and will not heal till death, I fear,
now that the dark-eyed one is dead,
O rosary that recalled my tear.

May Mary Mother, the King's nurse,
guard each path I follow here,
and may Her Son watch over me,
O rosary that recalled my tear.

Translated from the Gaelic by Derick Thomson

WILLIAM DUNBAR (c.1460–c.1520)

Hale, Sterne Superne

Hale, sterne superne, hale, in eterne,	*hail; star [on high]; eternity*
In Godis sicht to schyne!	*God's sight; shine*
Lucerne in derne for to discerne,	*lantern; darkness; by which to see*
Be glory and grace devyne!	*by*
Hodiern, modern, sempitern,	*[for this day and this age and forever]*
Angelicall regyne,	*queen of angels*
Our tern inferne for to dispern,	*darkness; hellish; disperse*
Helpe, rialest rosyne.	*most royal rose*
Ave Maria, gracia plena:	
Haile, fresche floure femynyne;	
Yerne us guberne, virgin matern,	*diligently; govern; mother*
Of reuth baith rute and ryne.	*pity; root; bark*

Haile, yhyng benyng fresche flurising,	*young; benign*
Haile, Alphais habitakle!	*[Alpha's dwelling-place]*
Thy dyng ofspring maid us to syng	*worthy; made*
Befor his tabernakle.	
All thing maling we doune thring	*malign; thrust down*
Be sicht of his signakle,	*sign*
Quhilk king us bring unto his ryng	*which*
Fro dethis dirk umbrakle.	*shadow*
Ave Maria, gracia plena:	
Haile, moder and maide but makle;	*mother; without stain*
Bricht syng, gladyng our languissing	*bright sign, making glad our sorrow*
Be micht of thi mirakle.	*power; miracle*

Haile, bricht be sicht in hevyn on hicht,	*by*
Haile, day-sterne orientale!	
Our licht most richt in clud of nycht,	
Our dirknes for to scale.	*scatter*
Hale, wicht in ficht, puttar to flicht	*brave; flight*
Of fendis in battale!	*fiends*
Haile, plicht but sicht, hale, mekle of mycht,	*anchor unseen; great in might*
Haile, glorius virgin, hale!	

Ave Maria, gracia plena:
  Haile, gentill nychttingale,
Way stricht, cler dicht, to wilsome wicht   *
  That irke bene in travale.   *are weary from travelling*

Hale, qwene serene, hale, most amene,   *kindly*
  Haile, hevinlie hie emprys!   *empress*
Haile, schene, unseyne with carnale eyne,   *beautiful one*
  Haile, ros of paradys!   *rose*
Haile, clene bedene ay till conteyne,   *wholly pure; ever to continue*
  Haile, fair fresche floure-de-lyce,   *fleur-de-lys*
Haile, grene daseyne, haile fro the splene,   *fresh daisy; heart*
  Of Jesu genitrice!   *begetter*
    Ave Maria, gracia plena:
  Thow baire the prince of prys,   *bore; glory*
Our teyne to meyne and ga betweyne,   *affliction; mend*
  As humile oratrice.   *human intercessor*

Haile, more decore than of before   *beautiful*
  And swetar be sic sevyne!   *seven times sweeter*
Our glore forlore for to restore   *glory lost*
  Sen thow art quene of hevyn.   *since*
Memore of sore, stern in aurore,   *mindful of grief; dawn*
  Lovit with angellis stevyne,   *voices*
Implore, adore, thow indeflore,   *unspoilt*
  To mak our oddis evyne!
    Ave Maria, gracia plena:
  With lovingis lowde ellevyn   *praises; eleven*
Quhill store and hore my youth devore, *adversity; old age; devour*
  Thy name I sall ay nevyne.   *pronounce*

Empryce of prys, imperatrice,
  Bricht polist precious stane,   *polished; stone*
Victrice of vyce, hie genitrice   *conqueress*
  Of Jesu lord soverayne,
Our wys pavys fro enemys   *wise shield*
  Agane the feyndis trayne,   *against the fiend's tricks*
Oratrice, mediatrice, salvatrice,
  To God gret suffragane!   *assistant*

* *straight path, clearly marked, for wandering beings*

Ave Maria, gracia plena:
Haile, sterne meridiane,   *midday-star*
Spyce, flour-de-lice of paradys,
That baire the gloryus grayne.   *seed*

Imperiall wall, place palestrall   *magnificent palace*
Of peirles pulcritud,
Tryumphale hall, hie trone regall
Of Godis celsitud!   *God's majesty*
Hospitall riall, the lord of all   *refuge; royal*
Thy closet did include,   *chamber; enclose*
Bricht ball cristall, ros virginall,   *globe*
Fulfillit of angell fude.   *filled with the food of angels*
    Ave Maria, gracia plena:
Thy birth has with his blude   *blood*
Fra fall mortall originall   *[the Fall]*
Us raunsound on the rude.   *ransomed; cross*

Done is a Battell on the Dragon Blak

Done is a battell on the dragon blak;   *against*
Our campioun Chryst confoundit hes his force;   *champion*
The yettis of hell ar brokin with a crak,   *gates*
The signe triumphall rasit of the croce.   *raised; cross*
The divillis trymmillis with hiddous voce,   *devils tremble; hideous voice*
The saulis ar borrowit and to the bliss can go,   *souls; redeemed*
Chryst with his blud our ransonis dois indoce: *blood; ransoms; endorse*
Surrexit Dominus de sepulchro.   *The Lord is risen from the tomb*

Dungin is the deidly dragon Lucifer,   *beaten; deadly*
The crewall serpent with the mortall stang,   *cruel; sting*
The auld kene tegir with his teith on char   *fierce tiger; teeth bared*
Quhilk in a wait hes lyne for us so lang,   *which; ambush; lain*
Thinking to grip us in his clowis strang.   *strong claws*
The mercifull lord wald nocht that it wer so;   *did not wish it so*
He maid him for to felye of that fang: *capture; prey*
Surrexit Dominus de sepulchro.

He for our saik that sufferit to be slane *sake; [allowed himself]; slain*
And lyk a lamb in sacrifice wes dicht *made ready*
Is lyk a lyone rissin up agane
And as gyane raxit him on hicht. *giant raised himself on high*
Sprungin is Aurora radius and bricht; *risen; radiant*
On loft is gone the glorius Appollo; *[above has]*
The blisfull day depairtit fro the nycht:
Surrexit Dominus de sepulchro.

The grit victour agane is rissin on hicht *great*
That for our querrell to the deth wes woundit. *cause*
The sone that wox all paill now schynis bricht, *waxed*
And, dirknes clerit, our fayth is now refoundit.
The knell of mercy fra the hevin is soundit,
The Cristin ar deliverit of thair wo; *Christians*
The Jowis and thair errour ar confoundit: *Jews*
Surrexit Dominus de sepulchro.

The fo is chasit, the battell is done ceis; *put to flight; [at an end]*
The presone brokin, the jevellouris fleit and flemit; *prison; gaolers; fled and frightened*
The weir is gon, confermit is the peis, *war*
The fetteris lowsit and the dungeoun temit; *fetters loosed; emptied*
The ransoun maid, the presoneris redemit; *prisoners redeemed*
The feild is win, ourcumin is the fo, *won; overcome*
Dispulit of the tresur that he yemit: *despoiled; treasure; guarded*
Surrexit Dominus de sepulchro.

from *The Flyting of Dunbar and Kennedy*

Dunbar attacks his rival

Iersche brybour baird, vyle beggar with thy brattis, *Gaelic vagabond bard; torn clothes*
  Cuntbittin crawdoun Kennedy, coward of kynd; *cunt-bitten; poxed; [by nature]*
Evill-farit and dryit as Densmen on the rattis, *ill-favoured; withered; Danes; wheels*
  Lyk as the gleddis had on thy gulesnowt dynd; *as if; kites; [yellow nose]; dined*
  Mismaid monstour, ilk mone owt of thy mynd, *[mad once a month]*

Renunce, rebald, thy rymyng; thow bot royis; *renounce, rascal; [you only talk nonsense]*
   Thy trechour tung hes tane ane heland strynd — *
Ane lawland ers wald mak a bettir noyis. *a Lowland arse*

Revin, raggit ruke, and full of rebaldrie, *raven; rook; ribaldry*
   Scarth fra scorpione, scaldit in scurrilitie, *monster born from a scorpion; scalded*
I se the haltane in thy harlotrie *I see thee arrogant in your rascality*
   And into uthir science no thing slie, *[skilled in no other learning]*
   Of every vertew void, as men may sie;
Quytclame clergie and cleik to the ane club, *[renounce clerkly learning]; grab*
   Ane baird blasphemar in brybrie ay to be; *bard; larceny*
For wit and woisdome ane wisp fra the may rub. *[one strand of straw]*

Thow speiris, dastard, gif I dar with the fecht: *ask; if; fight*
   Ye! dagone dowbart, thairof haif thow no dowt. *yes; misshapen; fool*
Quhairevir we meit, thairto my hand I hecht *[I give my word]*
   To red thy rebald rymyng with a rowt. *get rid of; blow*
   Throw all Bretane it sal be blawing owt *throughout Britain*
How that thow, poysonit pelour, gat thy paikis; *poisonous; robber; thrashing*
   With ane doig-leich I schepe to gar the schowt, *dog-leash; intend; make you shout*
And nowther to the tak knyfe, swerd nor aix . . . *[and not to take to you]*

     *   *   *

Thow callis the rethory with thy goldin lippis — *yourself; [a rhetorician]*
   Na, glowrand, gaipand fule, thow art begyld. *no; staring; gaping; deceived*
Thow art bot gluntoch, with thy giltin hippis, *[a hairy Highlander]; yellow hips*
   That for thy lounry mony a leisch hes fyld. *knavery; leash; defiled*
   Wan-visaged widdefow, out of thy wit gane wyld, *gallows-bird*
Laithly and lowsy, als lauchtane as ane leik: *loathsome; livid; leek*
   Sen thow with wirschep wald sa fane be styld — *since; honour; designated*
Haill, soverane senyeour! Thy bawis hingis throw thy breik. *balls; breeches*

Forworthin fule, of all the warld reffuse, *deformed; rejected*
   Quhat ferly is, thocht thow rejoys to flyte? *wonder; [that you enjoy abuse]*
Sic eloquence as thay in Erschry use, *Irishry [the Highlands]*
   In sic is sett thy thraward appetyte. *perverse*

      * *treacherous tongue; [has caught a Highland accent]*

Thow hes full littill feill of fair indyte: *understanding; composition*
I tak on me ane pair of Lowthiane hippis *[vow]; Lothian*
  Sall fairer Inglis mak, and mair parfyte, *English*
Than thow can blabbar with thy Carrik lippis. *blabber; Carrick*

Bettir thow ganis to leid ane doig to skomer, *[you are more suited]; shit*
  Pynit pykpuris pelour, than with thy maister pingill. *skinny; cutpurse; [to strive]*
Thow lay full prydles in the peis this somer *without pride; peas; summer*
  And fane at evin for to bring hame a single, *glad; evening; [straw]*
  Syne rubb it at ane uthir auld wyfis ingle: *then; old wife's; hole*
Bot now in winter for purteth thow art traikit – *poverty; worn-out*
  Thow hes na breik to latt thy bellokis gyngill; *breeches; stop; bollocks; jingle*
Beg the ane bratt for, baird, thow sall go naikit. *[beg yourself a cloak, bard, or]*

Lene larbar loungeour, lowsy in lisk and lonye; *lean; impotent idler; groin; loin*
  Fy, skolderit skyn, thow art bot skyre and skrumple; *

For he that rostit Lawrance had thy grunye, *roasted; [St Lawrence]; snout*
  And he that hid sanct Johnis ene with ane wimple, *[St John's]; eyes*
  And he that dang sanct Augustyne with ane rumple *beat; [St Augustine]; fishtail*
Thy fowll front had, and he that Bartilmo flaid. *face; [St Bartholomew]; flayed*
  The gallowis gaipis eftir thy graceles gruntill, *[gape for]; features*
As thow wald for ane haggeis, hungry gled . . . *haggis; kite*

    *   *   *

Ersche katherene, with thy polk breik and rilling, *Gaelic reiver; [bag]; [rough shoes]*
  Thow and thy quene, as gredy gleddis ye gang *wench; kites*
With polkis to mylne and beggis baith meill and schilling. †
  Thair is bot lys and lang nailis yow amang; *lice*
Fowll heggirbald, for henis thus will ye hang; *rascal; [theft of hens]*
Thow hes ane perrellus face to play with lambis; *dangerous*
  Ane thowsand kiddis, wer thay in faldis full strang, *kids; [secure fields]*
Thy lymmerfull luke wald fle thame and thair damis. *villainous; [make flee]; dams*

Intill ane glen thow hes, owt of repair, *in; has; [away from society]*
  Ane laithly luge that wes the lippir menis. *horrible; hut; leper men's*
With the ane sowtaris wyfe off blis als bair, *shoemaker's; [as miserable as you]*
  And lyk twa stalkaris steilis in cokis and henis – *stalkers; steal; cocks*

* scorched skin; creased; wrinkled*
† bags; mill; beg; oatmeal; [husks]

Thow plukkis the pultré and scho pullis of the penis.　　*poultry; [plucks the feathers]*
All Karrik cryis, 'God gif this dowsy be drownd!'　　*Carrick; grant; fool*
　　And quhen thow heiris ane guse cry in the glenis,　　*when; hear; goose*
Thow thinkis it swetar than sacryne bell of sound.　　*sacring*

Thow lazarus, thow laithly lene tramort,　　*Lazarus; putrefying; carcass*
　　To all the warld thow may example be
To luk upoun thy gryslie peteous port;　　*piteous; appearance*
　　For hiddowis, haw and holkit is thyne ee,　　*hideous; livid; hollow; eye*
　　Thy cheik-bane bair, and blaiknit is thy ble;　　*cheek-bone; pallid; complexion*
Thy choip, thy choll, garris men for to leif chest;　　*jaw; jowl; makes; live; chastely*
　　Thy gane it garris us think that we mon de:　　*[ugly face]; must die*
　　I conjure the, thow hungert heland gaist . . .　　*hungry Highland ghost*

　　　*　　*　　*

Thow held the burch lang with ane borrowit goun　　*[stayed in town]*
　　And ane cap rowsy, barkit all with sweit,　　*slimy; encrusted; sweat*
And quhen the laidis saw the sa lyk a loun,　　*boys; fool*
　　Thay bickerit the with mony bae and bleit:　　*assailed; [cries of 'baa']*
　　Now upaland thow leivis on rubbit quheit;　　*[in the country]; stolen wheat*
Oft for ane caus thy burdclaith neidis no spredding,　　*tablecloth*
　　For thow hes nowthir for to drink nor eit,　　*neither*
Bot lyk ane berdles baird that had no bedding.　　*beardless bard*

Strait Gibbonis air that nevir ourstred ane hors,　　*mean; [heir of Gibbon]; sat on*
　　Bla berfute berne, in bair tyme wes thow borne;　　*blue; barefoot; fellow; [impoverished]*
Thow bringis the Carrik clay to Edinburgh cors,　　*[market-cross]*
　　Upoun thy botingis hobland, hard as horne;　　*boots; hobbling*
　　Stra wispis hingis owt quhair that the wattis ar worne.　　*wisps of straw; welts*
Cum thow agane to skar us with thy strais,　　*[if you come]; scare; straws*
　　We sall gar scale our sculis all the to scorne,　　*disperse; schools*
And stane the up the calsay quhair thow gais.　　*stone; [paved street]*

Off Edinburch the boyis as beis out thrawis　　*of; like bees; [pour out]*
　　And cryis owt, 'Hay! heir cumis our awin queir clerk!'　　*queer; scholar*
Than fleis thow lyk ane howlat chest with crawis,　　*[you fly away]; owl; chased by crows*
　　Quhill all the brachattis at thy botingis dois bark.　　*hounds; boots*

Than carlingis cryis, 'Keip curches in the merk —	*old women; handkerchiefs; [hidden]*
Our gallowis gaipis — lo! quhair ane greceles gais!'	*[ill-favoured one]*
Ane uthir sayis, 'I se him want ane sark —	*[he lacks a shirt]*
I reid yow, cummer, tak in your lynning clais!'	*advise; gossip; linen clothes*

Than rynis thow doun the gait with gild of boyis,	*run; street; clamour*
And all the toun tykis hingand in thy heilis;	*dogs; hanging; heels*
Of laidis and lownis thair rysis sic ane noyis	*boys; rogues*
Quhill runsyis rynis away with cairt and quheilis,	*horses; cart; wheels*
And caiger aviris castis bayth coillis and creilis,	*[pedlar's horses]; coals; creels*
For rerd of the and rattling of thy butis.	*[your uproar]; boots*
Fische-wyvis cryis, 'Fy!' and castis doun skillis and skeilis,	*fishwives; baskets; tubs*
Sum claschis the, sum cloddis the on the cutis.	*strike; pelt; ankles*

Loun lyk Mahoun, be boun me till obey,	*[Mahomet-like]; bound*
Theif, or in greif mischeif sall the betyd!	*sorrow; befall*
Cry grace, tykis face, or I the chece and fley;	*[dog-face]; will chase and scare*
Oule, rare and yowle — I sall defowll thy pryd!	*owl; shriek; howl; [trample on]*
Peilit gled, baith fed and bred of bichis syd,	*defeathered; kite; bitch's side*
And lyk ane tyk, purspyk — quhat man settis by the?	*pickpocket; [regards]*
Forflittin, countbittin, beschittin, barkit hyd,	*
Clym-ledder, fyle tedder, foule edder: I defy the!	†

Mauch muttoun, byt buttoun, peilit gluttoun, air to Hilhous,	‡
Rank beggar, ostir-dregar, flay-fleggar in the flet,	§
Chittirlilling, ruch rilling, lik-schilling in the milhous,	¶
Baird rehator, theif of nator, fals tratour, feyindis gett,	‖

* *[flyted-out]; cunt-bitten; shit-covered; tanned hide*
† *[gallows-fodder]; [fouler of the hangman's rope]; adder*
‡ *[maggoty mutton]; [button-biter]; destitute; [heir to Hillhouse]*
§ *oyster-dredger; flea-frightener; hall*
¶ *chitterling; [rough hide shoe]; husk; millhouse*
‖ *knavish; [by nature]; [offspring of a fiend]*

Filling of tauch, rak-sauch — cry crauch, thow art oursett!   *
Muttoun-dryver, girnall-ryver, yadswyvar — fowll fell the!   †
   Herretyk, lunatyk, purspyk, carlingis pet,   heretic; [old woman's fart]
Rottin crok, dirtin dok — cry cok, or I sall quell the!   ‡

* lump of tallow; gallows-bird; [give up]

† sheep-driver; [grain-thief]; [mare-fucker]; [a curse on you]

‡ [old ewe]; [dirty arse]; [give up]; destroy

The Dance of the Sevin Deidly Synnis

Off Februar the fyiftene nycht,   fifteenth
Full lang befoir the dayis lycht,   well before
   I lay in till a trance;
And then I saw baith hevin and hell:
Me thocht, amangis the feyndis fell,   cruel
   Mahoun gart cry ane dance   Mahomet; [made happen]
Off schrewis that wer nevir schrevin,   shrews; shriven
Aganis the feist of Fasternis evin   [Shrove Tuesday]
   To mak thair observance;
He bad gallandis ga graith a gyis,   prepare a play
And kast up gamountis in the skyis,   dances
   That last came out of France.

'Lat se,' quod he, 'Now quha begynnis;'   who
With that the fowll Sevin Deidly Synnis
   Begowth to leip at anis.   began; at once
And first of all in dance wes Pryd,
With hair wyld bak and bonet on syd,   pulled
   Lyk to mak waistie wanis;   [make waste poor dwellings]
And round abowt him, as a quheill,   wheel
Hang ail in rumpillis to the heill   pleats; heel
   His kethat for the nanis: garment; purpose
Mony prowd trumpour with him trippit,   trumpeter
Throw skaldand fyre ay as thay skippit   scalding
   Thay gyrnd with hiddous granis.   moaned; groans

Heilie harlottis on hawtane wyis	*proud strumpets; haughty*
Come in with mony sindrie gyis,	*[different steps]*
Bot yit luche nevir Mahoun.	*laughed*
Quhill preistis come in with bair schevin nekkis,	*shaven*
Than all the feyndis lewche and maid gekkis,	*laughed; gestures*
Blak Belly and Bawsy Brown.	*[names for devils]*
Than Yre come in with sturt and stryfe;	*Anger; quarrelling*
His hand wes ay upoun his knyfe,	
He brandeist lyk a beir:	*swaggered; bear*
Bostaris, braggaris, and barganeris,	*boasters; quarrellers*
Eftir him passit in to pairis,	*[in groups]*
All bodin in feir of weir;	*[dressed ready for war]*
In jakkis, and stryppis and bonettis of steill,	*jackets*
Thair leggis wer chenyeit to the heill,	*chainmailed*
Frawart wes thair affeir:	*contrary; appearance*
Sum upoun udir with brandis beft,	*swords; struck*
Sum jaggit uthiris to the heft,	*stabbed*
With knyvis that scherp cowd scheir.	*[could cut sharply]*
Nixt in the dance followit Invy,	*Envy*
Fild full of feid and fellony,	*hostility*
Hid malyce and dispyte;	*hidden*
For pryvie hatrent that tratour trymlit.	*private; hatred; traitor; trembled*
Him followit mony freik dissymlit,	*[men in disguise]*
With fenyeit wirdis quhyte;	*[false soft words]*
And flattereris in to menis facis;	
And bakbyttaris in secreit places,	*backbiters*
To ley that had delyte;	*lie*
And rownaris of fals lesingis;	*whisperers; slanders*
Allace! that courtis of noble kingis	
Of thame can nevir be quyte.	*quit*
Nixt him in dans come Cuvatyce,	*Covetousness*
Rute of all evill and grund of vyce,	
That nevir cowd be content;	*could*
Catyvis, wrechis, and ockeraris,	*caitiffs; usurers*
Hud-pykis, hurdaris, and gadderaris,	*misers; hoarders; gatherers*
All with that warlo went:	*monster*

Out of thair throttis thay schot on udder   *vomited on others*
Hett moltin gold, me thocht a fudder,   *cartload*
   As fyreflawcht maist fervent;   *lightning*
Ay as thay tomit thame of schot,   *emptied*
Feyndis fild thame new up to the thrott
   With gold of allkin prent.   *[all sorts]*

Syne Sweirnes, at the secound bidding,   *then; Slothfulness*
Come lyk a sow out of a midding,   *midden*
   Full slepy wes his grunyie: *snout*
Mony sweir bumbard belly huddroun,   *[fat-bellied gluttons]*
Mony slute daw and slepy duddroun,   *[slatternly sluts]; [slovenly person]*
   Him servit ay with sounyie;   *delay*
He drew thame furth in till a chenyie,   *chain*
And Belliall, with a brydill renyie,   *Belial; rein*
   Evir lascht thame on the lunyie: *[their arses]*
In dance thay war so slaw of feit,
Thay gaif thame in the fyre a heit,
   And maid thame quicker of counyie.   *motion*

Than Lichery, that lathly cors,   *Lechery; loathsome; body*
Come berand lyk a bagit hors,   *neighing; [well-hung stallion]*
   And Ydilnes did him leid;   *Idleness*
Thair wes with him ane ugly sort,   *band*
And mony stynkand fowll tramort,   *stinking; bodies*
   That had in syn bene deid.   *[died in sin]*
Quhen thay wer entrit in the dance,
Thay wer full strenge of countenance,
   Lyk turkas birnand reid;   *pincers; burning*
All led thay uthir by the tersis,   *each; penises*
Suppois thay fycket with thair ersis,   *even if; squirmed*
   It mycht be na remeid.   *relief*

Than the fowll monstir Glutteny,   *Gluttony*
Off wame unsasiable and gredy,   *belly; insatiable*
   To dance he did him dres:
Him followit mony fowll drunckart,
With can and collep, cop and quart,   *[drinking vessels]*
   In surffet and exces;

Full mony a waistles wallydrag,   *fat scruffbag*
With wamis unweildable, did furth wag,   *unmanageable*
   In creische that did incres;   *blubber*
'Drynk!' ay thay cryit, with mony a gaip,   *gawp*
The feyndis gaif thame hait leid to laip,   *hot lead*
   Thair lovery wes na les.   *portion*

Na menstrallis playit to thame but dowt,   *[for sure]*
For glemen thair wer haldin owt,   *[entertainers were barred there]*
   Be day and eik by nycht;
Except a menstrall that slew a man,   *[except for any]*
Swa till his heretage he wan,   *[attained his destiny]*
   And entirt be breif of richt.   *[by legal right]*

Than cryd Mahoun for a Heleand padyane;   *Highland pageant*
Syne ran a feynd to feche Makfadyane,   *[MacFadyen – stock Highlander]*
   Far northwart in a nuke;
Be he the correnoch had done schout,   *[by the time]; lament*
Erschemen so gadderit him abowt,   *[Highlanders]*
   In Hell grit rowme thay tuke.
Thae tarmegantis, with tag and tatter,   *savages*
Full lowd in Ersche begowth to clatter,   *[Gaelic]*
   And rowp lyk revin and ruke: *croak; raven; rook*
The Devill sa devit wes with thair yell,   *deafened*
That in the depest pot of hell
   He smorit thame with smuke.   *smothered*

I That in Heill Wes and Gladnes

The Lament for the Makars

I that in heill wes and gladnes   *health*
Am trublit now with gret seiknes
And feblit with infermité:
Timor mortis conturbat me.   *[the fear of death disturbs me]*

Our plesance heir is all vane glory;   *joy*
This fals warld is bot transitory,
The flesch is brukle, the fend is sle: *fragile; cunning*
Timor mortis conturbat me.

The stait of man dois change and vary;
Now sound, now seik, now blith, now sary,   *wretched*
Now dansand mery, now like to dee:
Timor mortis conturbat me.

No stait in erd heir standis sickir;   *earth; secure*
As with the wynd wavis the wickir   *willow*
Wavis this warldis vanité:
Timor mortis conturbat me.

Onto the ded gois all estatis,   *[into death]*
Princis, prelotis and potestatis,   *prelates; lords*
Baith riche and pur of al degré:
Timor mortis conturbat me.

He takis the knychtis into feild,   *[battlefield]*
Anarmyt undir helme and scheild;   *armed*
Victour he is at all mellé: *combat*
Timor mortis conturbat me.

That strang unmercifull tyrand
Takis on the moderis breist sowkand   *mother's; sucking*
The bab full of benignité: *baby; grace*
Timor mortis conturbat me.

He takis the campion in the stour,   *champion; battle*
The capitane closit in the tour,   *enclosed*
The lady in bour full of bewté:
Timor mortis conturbat me.

He sparis no lord for his piscence,   *strength*
Na clerk for his intelligence;   *scholar*
His awfull strak may no man fle:
Timor mortis conturbat me.

Art-magicianis and astrologgis,
Rethoris, logicianis, and theologgis –
Thame helpis no conclusionis sle: *cunning*
Timor mortis conturbat me.

In medicyne the most practicianis,   *best practitioners*
Lechis, surrigianis, and phisicianis,   *doctors*
Thameself fra ded may not supplé: *deliver*
Timor mortis conturbat me.

I se that makaris amang the laif   *poets; [rest of us]*
Playis heir ther pageant, syne gois to graif;
Sparit is nought ther faculté: *profession*
Timor mortis conturbat me.

He has done petuously devour
The noble Chaucer of makaris flour,
The monk of Bery, and Gower, all thre: *[John Lydgate]*
Timor mortis conturbat me.

The gud Syr Hew of Eglintoun,
And eik Heryot, and Wyntoun   *also*
He has tane out of this cuntré:
Timor mortis conturbat me.

That scorpion fell has done infek   *cruel; poisoned*
Maister Johne Clerk and James Afflek
Fra balat-making and trigidé:
Timor mortis conturbat me.

Holland and Barbour he has berevit;   *snatched away*
Allace that he nought with us levit   *left*
Schir Mungo Lokert of the Le: *Sir*
Timor mortis conturbat me.

Clerk of Tranent eik he has tane
That maid the anteris of Gawane;   *adventures*
Schir Gilbert Hay endit has he:
Timor mortis conturbat me.

He has Blind Hary and Sandy Traill
Slane with his schour of mortall haill,
Quhilk Patrik Johnestoun myght nought fle:
Timor mortis conturbat me.

He has reft Merseir his endite,   *taken away; writing*
That did in luf so lifly write,   *vividly*
So schort, so quyk, of sentence hie: *concise; [noble substance]*
Timor mortis conturbat me.

He has tane Roull of Aberdene,
And gentill Roull of Corstorphin –
Two bettir fallowis did no man se:
Timor mortis conturbat me.

In Dunfermelyne he has done roune
With Maister Robert Henrisoun;
Schir Johne the Ros enbrast has he: *embraced*
Timor mortis conturbat me.

And he has now tane last of aw,
Gud gentill Stobo and Quintyne Schaw   *[John Reid of Stobo]*
Of quham all wichtis has peté: *persons*
Timor mortis conturbat me.

Gud Maister Walter Kennedy
In poynt of dede lyis veraly –   *[on the point of]*
Gret reuth it wer that he suld de: *pity*
Timor mortis conturbat me.

Sen he has all my brether tane,
He will naught lat me lif alane;
On forse I man his nyxt pray be: *[inevitably]; prey*
Timor mortis conturbat me.

Sen for the ded remeid is none   *since; remedy*
Best is that we for dede dispone,   *prepare*
Eftir our deid that lif may we:
Timor mortis conturbat me.

ANON. (*c.* 1490–1510)

Christis Kirk on the Grene

Was nevir in Scotland hard nor sene	*heard; seen*
Sic dansing nor deray,	*such; disturbance*
Nowthir at Falkland on the grene	*neither*
Nor Peblis at the play,	
As wes of wowaris, as I wene,	*wooers; imagine*
At Christ Kirk on ane day.	
Thair come our kitteis weschin clene	*[young girls]; washed*
In thair new kirtillis of gray,	*gowns*
Full gay,	
At Christis Kirk of the grene.	

To dans thir damysellis thame dicht,	*those damsels; [prepared themselves]*
Thir lassis licht of laitis,	*light of manners*
Thair gluvis wes of the raffell rycht,	*[roedeer-skin]*
Thair schone wes of the straitis;	*shoes; [woollen cloth]*
Thair kirtillis wer of lynkome licht,	*linen*
Weill prest with mony plaitis.	*pleats*
Thay wer so nyss quhen men thame nicht	*giddy; approached*
Thay squeilit lyk ony gaitis,	*goats*
So loud,	
At Christis Kirk of the grene that day.	

Of all thir madynis myld as meid	*mead*
Wes nane so gympt as Gillie;	*neat*
As ony ross hir rude wes reid,	*cheek*
Hir lyre wes lyk the lillie;	*complexion*
Fow yellow yellow wes hir heid,	*full*
Bot scho of lufe wes sillie;	*[by love]; made silly*
Thocht all hir kin had sworn hir deid	*though*
Scho wald haif bot sweit Willie	*only*
Allone,	
At Christis Kirk of the grene.	

Scho skornit Jok and skraipit at him,	*scoffed*
And murionit him with mokkis;	*grimaced at him*

He wald haif luvit, scho wald nocht lat him,   *hair*
 For all his yallow loikkis:
He chereist hir, scho bad ga chat him;   *cherished; [bade him go hang]*
 Scho compt him nocht twa clokkis;   *counted; beetles*
So schamefully his schort gown set him,   *fitted*
 His lymmis wes lyk twa rokkis,   *legs; poles*
   Scho said,
 At Christis Kirk of the grene.

Thome Lular wes thair menstrall meit;   *fit*
 O Lord! as he coud lanss;   *leap*
He playit so schill, and sang so sweit   *tunefully*
 Quhill Towsy tuke a transs.   *trance*
Auld lychtfute thair he did forleit,   *['lightfoot' dances]; forsake*
 And counterfutit Franss;   *[imitated the French]*
He use him self as man discreit   *behaved*
 And up tuke moreiss danss,   *Morris*
   Full loud,
 At Christis Kirk of the grene.

Than Stevin come stoppand in with stendis;   *stepping; strides*
 No rynk mycht him arreist.   *man*
Platfute he bobbit up with bendis;   *['flatfoot' dance]; leaps*
 For Mald he maid requiest.
He lap quhill he lay on his lendis;   *jumped until; buttocks*
 Bot rysand he wes preist   *rising; ready*
Quhill that he oistit at bath the endis   *until; coughed; both*
 For honour of the feist,
   That day,
 At Christis Kirk of the grene.

Syne Robene Roy begowth to revell,   *then; began*
 And Dowie till him druggit;   *to; dragged*
'Lat be,' quod Jok; and cawd him javell   *rascal*
And be the taill him tuggit.   *by*
The kensy cleikit to the cavell,   *scoundrel; grasped; ruffian*
 Bot Lord! than gif thay luggit,   *if; grabbed; ears*
Thai partit thair play thane with a nevell,   *separated; then; blow*
 God wait gif hair wes ruggit   *knows; pulled*
   Betwix thame,
 At Christis Kirk of the grene.

Ane bent a bow, sic sturt coud steir him;   *anger; moved*
   Grit skayth wesd to haif skard him;   *[harm it was]; scared*
He chesit a flane as did affeir him,   *chose; arrow; suit*
   The toder said 'Dirdum Dardum'.   *other; ['Big Deal']*
Throw baith the cheikis he thocht to cheir him,   *through; pierce*
   Or throw the erss haif chard him;   *[to have pierced]*
Bot be ane akerbraid it come nocht neir him,   *[acre's breadth]*
   I can nocht tell quhat mard him,   *prevented*
      Thair
   At Christis Kirk of the grene.

With that a freynd of his cryd 'Fy!'
   And up ane arrow drew;
He forgit it so fowriously   *bent*
   The bow in flenders flew.   *splinters*
Sa wes the will of God, trow I,
   For had the tre bene trew,   *wood*
Men said that kend his archery   *knew*
   That he had slane anew,   *enough*
      That day,
   At Christis Kirk of the grene.

Ane hasty hensure callit Hary,   *swaggerer*
   Quha wes ane archer heynd,   *skilful*
Titt up a taikle withowttin tary,   *took; tackle; delay*
   That torment so him teynd.   *enraged*
I wait nocht quhidder his hand coud vary,   *whether; waver*
   Or the man wes his freynd,
For he eschaipit throu michtis of Mary   *powers*
   As man that no ill meynd,   *meant*
      Bot gud,
   At Christis Kirk of the grene.

Than Lowry as ane lyon lap,
   And sone a flane coud fedder;   *feather*
He hecht to perss him at the pap,   *swore; breast*
   Thair on to wed a weddir.   *wager; [castrated ram]*
He hit him on the wame a wap,   *belly; blow*
   It buft lyk ony bledder;   *puffed; bladder*

Bot swa his fortoun wes and hap   *luck*
  His doublet wes maid of ledder,   *leather*
    And saift him,   *saved*
  At Christis Kirk of the grene.

The baff so boustuousle abasit him   *blow; violently; felled*
  To the erd he duschit down;   *crashed*
The tother for dreid he preissit him   *[busied himself]*
  And fled out of the town.
The wyffis come furth and up thay paisit him   *women; lifted*
  And fand lyff in the loun;   *found; fellow*
And with thre routis thay raisit him,   *shouts; revived*
  And coverit him of swoune.   *recovered; swoon*
    Agane,
  At Christis Kirk of the grene.

A yaip yung man that stude him neist   *eager*
  Lowsd of a schot with yre;   *loosed off; anger*
He ettlit the bern in at the breist;   *[aimed at]; man*
  The bolt flew owr the byre.   *cowshed*
Ane cryit 'Fy! he had slane a preist
  A myll beyond ane myre';   *mile; bog*
Than bow and bag fra him he keist   *quiver*
  And fled as ferss as fyre   *fast*
    Of flynt,
  At Christis Kirk of the grene.

With forkis and flailis thay lait grit flappis,   *blows*
  And flang togiddir lyk friggis;   *[good fellows]*
With bowgaris of barnis thay beft blew kappis   *rafters; beat; caps*
  Quhill thay of bernis maid briggis.   *[made bridges of men]*
The reird raiss rudly with the rappis,   *uproar; rose; blows*
  Quhen rungis wes layd on riggis;   *cudgels; backs*
The wyffis come furth with cryis and clappis,
  'Lo quhair my lyking liggis!'   *love; lies*
    Quod thay   *said*
  At Christ Kirk of the grene.

Thay girnit and lait gird with granis, — *grimaced; [struck blows]; groans*
    Ilk gossep uder grevit; — *each; [vexed the other]*
Sum straik with stingis, sum gadderit stanis, — *poles*
    Sum fled and evill eschewit; — *avoided*
The menstrall wan within twa wanis, — *hid; dwellings*
    That day full weill he previt. — *proved*
For he come hame with unbirsed banis, — *unbruised bones*
    Quhair fechtaris wer mischevit — *fighters; injured*
        For evir,
    At Christis Kirk of the grene.

Heich Hucheoun, with a hissill ryss, — *tall; hazel branch*
    To red can throu thame rummill; — *separate; scram*
He mudlet thame down lyk ony myss, — *knocked; mice*
    He wes no baty bummill. — *[feeble type]*
Thocht he wes wicht he wes nocht wyss — *strong*
    With sic jangleris to jummill, — *wranglers; meddle*
For fra his thowme thay dang a sklyss, — *thumb; struck; slice*
    Quhill he cryd 'Barla fummyll! — *until; ['Enough!']*
        I am slane,'
    At Christis Kirk of the grene.

Quhen that he saw his blude so reid,
    To fle micht no man lat him; — *flee; prevent*
He wend it bene for auld done feid, — *thought; feud*
    The far sarar it set him. — *[more sorely]; afflicted*
He gart his feit defend his heid, — *made*
    He thocht ane cryd, 'Haif at him!' — *have*
Quhill he wes past out of all pleid — *strife*
    He suld bene swift that gat him — *[would have been]*
        Throu speid,
    At Christis Kirk of the grene.

The toun sowtar in greif wes bowdin, — *shoemaker; anger; swollen*
    His wyfe hang in his waist; — *at*
His body wes with blud all browdin, — *stained*
    He granit lyk ony gaist. — *groaned; ghost*

Hir glitterand hair that wes full goldin
   So hard in lufe him lest *tied*
That for hir saik he wes nocht yoldin, *[unbeaten]*
   Sevin myll quhill he wes chest, *chased*
      And mair,
   At Christis Kirk of the grene.

The millar wes of manly mak;
   To meit him wes na mowis; *joke*
Thair durst nocht ten cum him to tak.
   So nowit he thair nowis. *knocked; heads*
The buschment haill about him brak *[whole ambush]*
   And bikkerit him with bowis. *attacked*
Syne tratourly behind his bak *then; treacherously*
   Thay hewit him on the howiss *hacked; calves*
      Behind,
   At Christis Kirk of the grene.

Twa that wes heidmen of the heird *two; headmen; herd*
   Ran upoun utheris lyk rammis;
Than followit feymen rycht on affeird. *[doomed men]; unafraid*
   Bet on with barrow trammis. *beat; shafts*
Bot quhair thair gobbis wes ungeird *mouths; unprotected*
   Thay gat upoun the gammis. *[got blows]; gums*
Quhill bludy berkit wes thair beird *clotted*
   As thay had wirreit lammis, *mangled; lambs*
      Maist lyk,
   At Christ Kirk of the grene that day.

The wyvis kest up ane hiddouss yell *hideous*
   Quhen all thir yunkeris yokkit; *[those young men]; [set to it]*
Als ferss as ony fyrflaught fell *[flash of lightning]*
   Freikis to the feild thay flokkit; *[stout fellows]*
Tha cairlis with clubbis coud uder quell, *men; eachother; quelled*
   Quhill blud at breistis out bokkit; *spurted*
So rudly range the Commoun bell,
   Quhill all the stepill rokkit *steeple*
      For reird, *noise*
   At Christis Kirk of the grene.

Quhen thay had berit lyk baitit bulis,   *roared; bated bulls*
 And branewod brynt in bailis, *madmen; burned; bonfires*
Thay wer als meik as ony mulis   *meek; mules*
 That mangit wer with mailis.   *[worn out]; burdens*
For fantness tha forfochin fulis   *faintness; exhausted*
 Fell down lyk flawchtir failis, *[turfs cut with spades]*
And freschmen come in and held thair dulis, *ground*
 And dang thame down in dailis *knocked; heaps*
   Be dene,   *soon*
 At Christ Kirk of the grene.

Quhen all wes done, Dik with ane aix
 Come furth to fell a fidder.   *cartload*
Quod he, 'Quhair ar yone hangit smaix *mean wretches*
 Rycht now wald slane my bruder?' *[would have]*
His wyfe bade him, 'Ga hame, gud glaikis!' *fool*
 And sa did Meg his muder.
He turnd and gaif thame bayth thair paikis, *[a blow]*
 For he durst ding nane udir, *strike no other*
   For feir,
 At Christ Kirk of the grene that day.

GAVIN DOUGLAS, BISHOP OF DUNKELD
(c. 1474–1522)

from *Eneados*

The Proloug of the Sevynt Buik

As brycht Phebus, schene souerane, hevynnis e,	*fair; eye*
The opposit held of his chymmis hie,	*[took the opposite]; [high mansions]*
Cleir schynand bemys, and goldin symmeris hew,	*summer's*
In lattoun colour altering haill of new;	*brass; entirely new*
Kithing no syng of heyt be his visage,	*showing; sign; by*
So neir approchit he his wynter staige;	
Redy he was to entir the thrid morne	
In cloudy skyis vndir Capricorne.	
All thocht he be the hart and lamp of hevin,	*although*
Forfeblit wolx his lemand giltly lewyne,	*[enfeebled waxed]; [shining golden light]*
Throw the declyning of his large round speir.	*sphere*
The frosty regioun ringis of the yeir,	*season; reigns*
The tyme and sessoune bitter cald and paill,	
Thai schort days that clerkis clepe brumaill;	*call; wintry*
Quhen brym blastis of the northyne art	*fierce; from; quarter*
Ourquhelmit had Neptunus in his cart,	*chariot*
And all to schaik the levis of the treis,	
The rageand storm ourwalterand wally seis;	*[rolling over swollen seas]*
Reveris ran reid on spait with watteir broune,	
And burnis hurlis all thair bankis downe,	*streams*
And landbrist rumland rudely wyth sic beir,	*surf rumbling; racket*
So loud ne rummist wyld lioun or beir.	*never; roared; bear*
Fludis monstreis, sic as meirswyne or quhailis,	*dolphins; whales*
For the tempest law in the deip devallyis.	*[dive low in the deep]*
Mars occident, retrograide in his speir,	*[in the west]; sphere*
Provocand stryff, regnit as lord that yer;	
Rany Orioune wyth his stormy face	
Bewalit of the schipman by his rays;	*blew away [from his course]*
Frawart Saturne, chill of complexioune,	*perverse*
Throw quhais aspect derth and infectioune	
Bene causit oft, and mortale pestilens,	
Went progressiue the greis of his ascens;	*advancing; degrees*

And lusty Hebe, Junois douchtir gay,	
Stud spulyeit of hir office and array.	
The soill ysowpit into wattir wak,	*soaked; boggy*
The firmament ourkest with rokis blak,	*clouds*
The ground fadyt, and fauch wolx all the feildis,	*yellow-brown*
Montayne toppis sleikit wyth snaw ourheildis,	*smoothed; [snow-covers]*
On raggit rolkis of hard harsk quhyne stane,	*harsh crags; whinstone*
With frosyne frontis cauld clynty clewis schane;	*surfaces; stony cliffs shone*
Bewtie wes lost, and barrand schew the landis,	*bare showed*
With frostis haire ourfret the feildis standis.	*hoar frost; covered*
Soure bittir bubbis, and the schowris snell,	*sore; squalls; biting*
Semyt on the sward ane similitude of hell,	*turf*
Reducyng to our mynd, in every steid,	*place*
Goustly schaddois of eild and grisly deid,	*[old age]; death*
Thik drumly scuggis dirknit so the hevyne.	*gloomy clouds*
Dym skyis oft furth warpit feirfull levyne,	*threw; lightning*
Flaggis of fyir, and mony felloun flawe,	*flashes; fearful squall*
Scharp soppis of sleit, and of the snypand snawe.	*showers*
The dowy dichis war all donk and wait,	*dismal ditches; dark; wet*
The law vaille flodderit all wyth spait,	*spate*
The plane stretis and every hie way	*level*
Full of fluschis, doubbis, myre and clay.	*marshes; [muddy pools]*
Laggerit leys wallowit farnys schewe,	*mired pastures; shrivelled ferns*
Broune muris kithit thair wysnit mossy hewe,	*moors; showed wizened*
Bank, bra, and boddum blanschit wolx and bair;	*lowland; [grew blanched and bare]*
For gurll weddir growyt bestis haire;	*stormy; shuddered*
The wynd maid wayfe the reid weyd on the dyk,	*wave; weed*
Bedovin in donkis deyp was every syk;	*sunk; bogs; stream*
Our craggis, and the front of rochis seyre,	*over; sheer*
Hang gret isch schoklis lang as ony spere;	*[icicles]*
The grund stude barrand, widderit, dosk and gray,	*barren; gloomy*
Herbis, flouris, and gersis wallowit away;	*grasses; withered*
Woddis, forestis, wyth nakyt bewis blout,	*boughs; bare*
Stud strypyt of thair weyd in every hout.	*clothes; copse*
So bustuysly Boreas his bugill blew,	*stridently*
The deyr full dern dovne in the dalis drew;	*deer; secretly; down*
Smal byrdis, flokand throw thik ronnis thrang,	*[dense branches]*
In chyrmyng and with cheping changit thair sang,	*chirping*
Sekand hidlis and hirnys thaim to hyde	*[nooks and crannies]*
Fra feirfull thudis of the tempestuus tyde.	*blasts*

The wattir lynnis routtis, and every lynde   *[waterfalls]; roar; lime-tree*
Quhyslyt and brayt of the swouchand wynde.   *rasped; moaning*
Puire laboraris and byssy husband men
Went wayt and wery draglyt in the fen;   *wet; bedraggled*
The silly scheip and thair lytill hyrd gromis   *[shepherd boys]*
Lurkis vndir le of bankis, wodys, and bromys;   *[broom bushes]*
And uthir dantit gretar bestial,   *domestic; bigger beasts*
Within thair stabillis sesyt into stall,   *tethered*
Sic as mulis, horsis, oxin and ky,   *cows*
Fed tuskit baris, and fat swyne in sty,   *boars*
Sustenit war by mannis gouernance
On hervist and on symmeris purviance.   *provision*
Widequhair with fors so Eolus schouttis schyll   *everywhere; shrill*
In this congelyt sessioune scharp and chyll,   *frozen*
The callour air, penetrative and puire,   *fresh; pure*
Dasyng the bluide in every creature,   *numbing*
Maid seik warm stovis, and beyne fyris hoyt,   *pleasant*
In double garmont cled and wyly coyt,   *undercoat*
Wyth mychty drink, and meytis confortive,   *[comforting food]*
Agayne the storme wyntre for to strive.

   Repaterit weill, and by the chymnay beykyt,   *refreshed; warmed*
At evin be tyme dovne a bed I me streikit,   *stretched*
Warpit my heid, kest on claythis thrinfauld,   *wrapped; bedclothes; threefold*
For till expell the perrellus peirsand cauld.   *piercing*
I crocit me, syne bownit for to sleip,   *[crossed myself]; prepared*
Quhair, lemand throw the glas, I did tak keip   *gleaming; [observe]*
Latonia, the lang irksum nycht;   *[the Moon]*
Hir subtell blenkis sched and wattry lycht,   *glances*
Full hie wp quhyrlyt in hir regioune,   *whirled*
Till Phebus rycht in oppositioune,
Into the Crab hir propir mansioune draw,
Haldand the hycht allthocht the son went law.   *although; sun; low*
Hornit Hebawde, quhilk clepe we the nycht owle,   *call*
Within hir caverne hard I schout and yowle;   *heard*
Laithlie of forme, wyth crukit camschow beik,   *ugly; crooked; deformed; beak*
Vgsum to heir was hir wyld elriche screik: *horrible; weird*
The wyld geis claking eik by nychtis tyde   *geese; honking; also; night-time*
Attoure the citie fleand hard I glyde.   *[out over]; flying; heard*

   On slummyr I slaid full sad, and slepit sownd   *into slumber; slid*
Quhill the oryent wpwart gan rebound.

Phebus crownit byrd, the nychtis orloger,   *[the cockerel]; time-keeper*
Clappand his wyngis thryse had crawin cleir.
Approching neir the greiking of the day,   *dawn*
Wythin my bed I waikynnit quhair I lay,
So fast declinis Synthea the mone,
And kais keklis on the ruiff abone.   *jackdaws; cackle*
Palamedes byrdis crouping in the sky,   *[cranes]; croaking*
Fleand on randoune schapin lik ane Y,   *[in formation]*
And as ane trumpat rang thair vocis soun,
Quhais cryis bene pronosticatioun   *forecast*
Off wyndy blastis and ventositeis.   *gales*
Fast by my chalmir, in heych wysnit treis,   *chamber; wizened*
The soir gled quhislis loud wyth mony ane pew,   *red kite*
Quhairby the day was dawin weil I knew;
Bad beit the fyire, and the candill alycht,   *[ordered the fire made]*
Syne blissit me, and, in my wedis dycht   *[blessed myself]; dressed*
Ane schot wyndo vnschet a lytill on char,   *[hinged window]; opened; ajar*
Persawit the mornyng bla, wan, and har,   *perceived; bleak; grey*
Wyth cloudy gum and rak ourquhelmyt the air,   *mist; fog*
The sulye stythlie, hasart, rowch and hair,   *soil; stiff; grey; rough; hoary*
Branchis brattlyng, and blayknit schew the brays,   *rattling; braes*
With hyrstis harsk of waggand wyndilstrays;   *ridges; harsh; wandering; dry stalks*
The dew droppis congelyt on stibyll and rynd,   *stubble; bark*
And scharp hailstanis, mortfundit of kynd,   *[petrified by nature]*
Hoppand on the thak and on the causay by.   *thatch; causeway*
The schot I clossit and drew inwart in hy,   *window; [quickly]*
Chiverand for cauld, the sessoun was so snell;   *shivering; bitter*
Schup wyth hait flambe to fleme the fresyng fell.   *attempted; flame; expel; [cruel cold]*
   And, as I bownit me to the fyre me by,   *[took myself]*
Bayth wp and downe the hous I did aspy;
And seand Virgill on ane lettrune stand,   *lectern*
To writ anone I hynt ane pen in hand,   *[at once]; took*
For tyll performe the poet grave and sad,   *complete [the translation]*
Quham sa fer furth, or than, begun I had;   *so long ago*
And wolx ennoyit sum deyll in my hart,   *[grew somewhat annoyed]*
Thair restit vncompleittit so gret ane part.
And til myself I said: 'In guid effect,   *earnest*
Thow man draw furth, the yok lyis on thi nek.'
Wythin my mynd compasing thocht I so,   *planning*
Na thing is done quhill ocht remanis to do.   *[while anything]*

For byssines, quhilk occurrit on cace,   *despite business; [by chance]*
Ourvoluit I this volume, lay ane space;   *turned over; [made time]*
And, thocht I wery was, me lyst nocht tyre,   *though; [I did not wish to tire]*
Full laith to leve our werk, swa in the myre,   *loth; [so bogged down]*
Or yit to stynt for byttir storme or rane:
Heyr I assayit to yok our pleuch agane: *tried; yoke; plough*
And, as I culd, with afauld diligence,   *single-minded*
This nixt buike following of profund sentence   *substance*
Has thus begoune in the chyll wyntir cauld,
Quhen frostis days ourfret bayth fyrth and fauld.   *embroider; wood; fold*

Explicit tristis prologus   *[The sad prologue ends]*

The Proloug of the Twelt Buik

Dyonea, nycht hyrd, and wach of day,   *[Venus]; herd; watch*
The starnis chasit of the hevin away,   *stars*
Dame Cynthea dovn rolling in the see,   *[the Moon]*
And Venus lost the bewte of hir e,   *eye*
Fleand eschamyt within Cylenyus cave;   *fleeing ashamed; [the house of Mercury]*
Mars onbydrew, for all his grundin glave,   *[drew away]; sharpened sword*
Nor frawart Saturn, from his mortall speyr,   *perverse; sphere*
Durst langar in the firmament appeir,
Bot stall abak yond in his regioun far
Behynd the circulat warld of Jupiter;
Nycthemyne, affrayit of the lycht,   *[the Night Owl]*
Went vndir covert, for gone was the nycht;   *[into hiding]*
As fresch Aurora, to mychty Tythone spous,   *[Titan]*
Ischit of hir safron bed and evir hous,   *left; ivory*
In crammysin cled and granit violat,   *crimson; clad; [dyed cloth]*
With sanguyne cape, the selvage purpurat,   *blood-red; border; purple*
Onschot the windois of hyr large hall,   *opened*
Spred all wyth rosys, and full of balm ryall,
And eik the hevinly portis crystallyne   *also; gates*
Vpwarpis braid, the warld to illumyn.   *flung wide*
The twinkling stremowris of the orient   *streamers*
Sched purpour sprangis with gold and asure ment,   *bands; azure; mixed*
Persand the sabill barmkyn nocturnall,   *piercing; battlements*
Bet doun the skyis clowdy mantill wall: *ramparts*

Eous the steid, with ruby harnis reid,   *[one of the horses of the sun]*

Abuf the seyis lyftis furth his heid,   *seas*

Of cullour soyr, and sum deill brovn as berry,   *sorrel*

For to alichtyn and glaid our emyspery,   *[light up]; gladden; hemisphere*

The flambe owtbrastyng at his neys thyrlys;   *[nostrils]*

Sa fast Phaeton wyth the quhip him quhirlys,   *whirls*

To roll Apollo his faderis goldin chair,   *chariot*

That schrowdyth all the hevynnis and the ayr;

Quhill schortly, with the blesand torch of day,   *blessing*

Abilyeit in his lemand fresch array,   *dressed; shining*

Furth of hys palyce ryall ischyt Phebus,   *issued*

Wyth goldin crovn and vissage gloryus,

Crysp haris, brycht as chrysolite or topace,   *topaz*

For quhais hew mycht nane behald his face,   *whose*

The fyry sparkis brastyng fra his ene,

To purge the ayr, and gylt the tendyr grene,

Defundand from hys sege etheriall   *[pouring down]; seat*

Glaid influent aspectis celicall.   *[influence of heavenly aspects]*

Before his regale hie magnificens

Mysty vapour vpspringand, sweit as sens,   *incense*

In smoky soppis of donk dewis wak,   *clouds; [dank watery dews]*

Moich hailsum stovis ourheildand the slak;   *

The aureat fanys of hys trone souerane   *[golden vanes]; throne*

With glytrand glans ourspred the occiane,   *flashes; ocean*

The large fludis lemand all of lycht

Bot with a blenk of his supernale sycht.   *[with but a blink]; heavenly*

For to behald, it was a gloir to se

The stabillit wyndis and the cawmyt see,   *calmed; settled*

The soft sessoun, the firmament serene,   *spell*

The downe illumynat air, and fyrth amene;   *tranquil; pleasant estuary*

The syluer scalyt fyschis on the greit   *gravel*

Ourthwort cleir stremis sprynkland for the heyt,   *[all around]*

Wyth fynnis schynand brovn as synopar,   *cinnabar*

And chyssell talis, stowrand heyr and thar;   *chiselled; rushing*

The new cullour alychtnyng all the landis,

Forgane thir stannyris schane the beryall strandis,   †

Quhill the reflex of the diurnal bemis   *reflection; daily*

The bene bonkis kest ful of variant glemis,   *pleasant; banks*

* *[moist wholesome vapours blanketing the valley]*

† *[against the modesty of the shingle; the beryl banks]*

And lusty Flora did hyr blomis spreid	
Vnder the feit of Phebus sulyart steid;	*dazzling*
The swardit soyll enbrovd wyth selcouth hewis	*turfed; embroidered; rare*
Wod and forest obumbrat with thar bewis,	*shaded; boughs*
Quhois blissfull branchis, porturat on the grund,	*portrayed*
With schaddois schene schew rochis rubycund:	*shining; rocks; reddish*
Towris, turattis, kyrnellis, pynnaclis hie	*battlements*
Of kirkis, castellis, and ilke fair cite,	*every*
Stude payntit, euery fyall, fane, and stage,	*[round tower]; weather vane*
Apon the plane grund, by thar awin vmbrage.	*own shadows*
Of Eolus north blastis havand no dreyd,	
The sulye spred hyr braid bosum on breid,	*soil; abroad*
Zephyrus confortabill inspiratioun	*breathing*
For till ressaue law in hyr barm adoun;	*[low down on her bosom]*
The cornis croppis and the beris new brerd	*[row-grown barley]*
Wyth glaidsum garmond revesting the erd;	*reclothing*
So thik the plantis sprang in euery pece,	
The feyldis ferleis of thar fructuus flece;	*[marvel at]; fruitful; fleece*
Byssy dame Ceres, and provd Pryapus,	
Reiosyng of the planis plenteus,	*rejoicing*
Plenyst sa plesand and maist propirly,	*stocked*
By natur nurist wondir nobilly.	*nourished*
On the fertill skyrt lappis of the ground	*folds*
Streking on breid ondyr the cirkill rovnd,	*[spread out]*
The variant vestur of the venust vaill	*[peaceful valley]*
Schrowdis the scherald fur, and euery faill	*[new-mown furrow]; sward*
Ourfret with fulyeis of figuris full diuers,	*leaves; [various shapes]*
The spray bysprent with spryngand sproutis dispers;	*spotted; sprouting; shoots*
For callour humour on the dewy nycht,	*fresh; moisture*
Rendryng sum place the gers pilis thar hycht	*[blades of grass]*
Als far as catal, the lang symmeris day,	*as; cattle*
Had in thar pastur eyt and knyp away;	
And blisfull blossummis in the blomyt yard	*bloom-filled*
Submittis thar hedis in the yong sonnis salfgard;	*bend; charge*
Ive levis rank ourspred the barmkin wall,	*ivy; vigorous; battlement*
The blomyt hawthorn cled his pikis all;	*dressed; thorns*
Furth of fresch burgionis the wyne grapis ȝing	*full; buds*
Endlang the treilyeis dyd on twystis hing.	*along; trellis; tendrils*
The lowkyt buttonis on the gemmyt treis	*closed; buds; gemmed*
Ourspredand leyvis of naturis tapestreis;	

Soft gresy verdour eftir balmy schowris
On curland stalkis smyling to thar flowris;
Behaldand thame sa mony diuers hew,   *beholding*
Sum pers, sum paill, sum burnet, and sum blew,   *dark blue; brown*
Sum grece, sum gowlis, sum purpour, sum sangwane,   *grey; scarlet; purple; blood-red*
Blanchit or brovne, fawch yallow mony ane,   *tawny*
Sum hevynly cullorit in celestiall gre,   *degree*
Sum wattry hewit as the haw wally see,   *bluish stormy sea*
And sum depart in freklys red and quhyte,   *[varied in colour]; freckles*
Sum brycht as gold with aureat levis lyte.   *little*
The dasy dyd on breid hir crownell smaill,   *[opened up]; coronet*
And euery flour onlappit in the daill;   *unfolded*
In battill gyrs burgionys the banwart wyld,   *[thick grass]; burgeons; banewort*
The clavyr, catcluke, and the cammamyld;   *clover; trefoil; camomile*
The flour delice furth spred his hevinly hew,   *[fleur-de-lys]*
Flour dammes, and columby blank and blew;   *[primula]; columbine; white*
Seyr downis smaill on dent de lion sprang,   *many; [dandelions]*
The ying grene blomyt straberry levis amang;
Gymp gerraflouris thar royn levys vnschet,   *graceful gillyflowers; roan; opened*
Fresch prymros, and the purpour violet;
The roys knoppis, tetand furth thar heyd,   *[rosebuds]; peeking*
Gan chyp, and kyth thar vermel lippis red,   *split; reveal; vermilion*
Crysp scarlet levis sum scheddand, baith attanis   *[at once]*
Kest fragrant smell amyd from goldin granis;
Hevinly lylleis, with lokerand toppis quhyte,   *curling*
Oppynnit and schew thar creistis redymyte,   *ornate*
The balmy vapour from thar sylkyn croppis
Distylland hailsum sugurat hunny droppis,
And syluer schakaris gan fra levis hyng,   *danglers*
Wyth crystal sprayngis on the verdour ying;   *streaks*
The plane pulderyt with semely settis sovnd,   *powdered; shoots*
Bedyit full of dewy peirlis rovnd,   *soaked*
So that ilk burgioun, syon, herb, and flour,   *bud; branch*
Wolx all enbalmyt of the fresch liquour,   *grew*
And bathit hait did in dulce humouris fleit,   *[bathed heat]; [sweet moistures]; [made flee]*
Quharof the beis wrocht thar hunny sweit,   *bees*
By michty Phebus operatiounis,
In sappy subtell exalatiounis.
Forgane the cummyn of this prince potent,   *against*
Redolent odour vp from rutis sprent,   *leapt*

Hailsum of smell as ony spicery,
Tryakle, droggis, or electuary,   *medicine; syrup*
Seroppis, sewane, sugour, and synamome,   *spice; cinnamon*
Precyus invnctment, salve, or fragrant pome,   *ointment; pomander*
Aromatik gummis, or any fyne potioun,
Must, myr, aloes, or confectioun;   *musk; myrrh*
Ane paradice it semyt to draw neyr
Thyr galyart gardyngis and ilke greyn herbere.   *gallant; flowerbed*
Maist amyabill walxis the amerant medis: *grew; [emerald meadows]*
Swannys swouchis throw owt the rysp and redis,   *rustle; sedge*
Our al thir lowys and the fludis gray   *lochs*
Seyrsand by kynd a place quhar thai suld lay: *seeking; [instinctively]*
Phebus red fowle hys corall creist can steyr,   *stir*
Oft streking furth hys hekkyll, crawand cleir,   *hackle; crowing*
Amyd the wortis and the rutys gent   *plants; roots; delicate*
Pykland his meyt in alleis quhar he went,   *pecking; food; alleys*
Hys wifis, Toppa and Pertelok, hym by,
As byrd al tyme that hantis bygamy: *practises*
The payntit povne, pasand with plomys gym,   *painted; peacock; [neat plumes]*
Kest vp his taill, a provd plesand quheil rym,   *wheel-rim*
Yschrowdyt in hys fedramme brycht and schene,   *feathers*
Schapand the prent of Argus hundreth ene: *showing; [the like]*
Amang the brounis of the olyve twestis   *twigs; branches*
Seyr small fowlis wirkand crafty nestis,   *many*
Endlang the hedgeis thyk, and on rank akis,   *along; oaks*
Ilk byrd reiosyng with thar myrthfull makis.   *each; mates*
In corneris and cleir fenystaris of glas   *windows*
Full byssely Aragne wevand was,   *[the spider]*
To knit hyr nettis and hir wobbys sle,   *cunning webs*
Tharwith to caucht the myghe and littill fle: *midge*
So dusty puldyr vpstowris in euery streyt,   *powder; [stirs up]*
Quhill corby gaspyt for the fervent heyt.   *until; the crow*
Vnder the bewys beyn in lusty valis,   *[pleasant boughs]; delightful*
Within fermans and parkis cloys of palys,   *farms; [enclosed fields]*
The bustuus bukkis rakis furth on raw;   *bold bucks trot; row*
Heyrdis of hertis throw the thyk wod schaw,   *harts; appear*
Baith the brokettis, and with brayd burnyst tyndis;   *[two-year-old stags]; tines*
The sprutlyt calvys sowkand the reid hyndis,   *spotted; sucking; hinds*
The yong fownis followand the dun dayis,   *fawns; does*
Kyddis skippand throw ronnis eftir rayis.   *thickets; roe deer*

In lyssouris and on leys litill lammis   *pastures; leas*
Full tait and trig socht bletand to thar dammis.   *nimble; neat; sought; bleating*
Tydy ky lowys, veilys by thame rynnis;   *plump cattle low; calves*
All snog and slekyt worth thir bestis skynnis.   *smooth; sleek*
On salt stremis wolx Doryda and Thetis,   *[sea-goddesses]*
By rynnand strandis Nymphis and Naedes,   *streams*
Syk as we clepe wenchis and damysellis,   *call*
In gresy gravis wandrand by spring wellis,   *grassy; groves*
Of blomyt branchis and flowris quhite and rede
Plettand thar lusty chaiplettis for thar hede;   *plaiting; pretty; garlands*
Sum sing sangis, dansis ledys, and rovndis,   *[choral rounds]; [lead dances]; [ring dances]*
Wyth vocis schill, quhill all the daill resovndis;   *shrill*
Quharso thai walk into thar caraling,   *singing*
For amorus lays doith all the rochis ryng.   *rocks*
Ane sang, *The schip salis our the salt fame,*
Will bring thir merchandis and my lemman hame;   *lover*
Sum other singis, *I will be blyth and lycht,*
Myne hart is lent apon sa gudly wycht.   *[given to]; person*
And thochtfull luffaris rowmys to and fro,
To leis thar pane, and plene thar joly wo;   *lose; bewail*
Eftyr thar gys, now syngand, now in sorow,   *guise*
With hartis pensyve, the lang symmeris morow: *morning*
Sum ballettis lyst endyte of his lady,   *songs; [seek to write]*
Sum levis in hoip, and sum aluterly   *hope; utterly*
Disparyt is, and sa quyte owt of grace,
His purgatory he fyndis in euery place.
To pleis his luife sum thocht to flat and fene,   *flatter; feign*
Sum to hant bawdry and onlesum mene;   *practise; [unlawful conduct]*
Sum rownys to hys fallow, thame betwene,   *whisper*
Hys mery stouth and pastans lait yistrene.   *trick; pastimes; [of the previous day]*
Smyland sayis ane, I couth in previte   *could; [privately]*
Schaw the a bowrd. Ha, quhat be that? quod he;   *jest*
Quhat thing? That moste be secret sayd the tother.
Gude Lord! mysbeleif ye your verray brother?   *mistrust*
Na, neuyr a deill, bot harkis quhat I wald;
Thou mon be prevy: lo, my hand vphald.   *[must be discreet]*
Than sal thou walk at evin: quod he, quhiddyr?
In sik a place heyr west, we bayth togiddyr,
Quhar scho so freschly sang this hyndir nycht;   *last*
Do chois the ane, and I sal quynch the lycht.   *quench*

I sal be thar I hope, quod he, and lewch;   *laughed*
Ga, now I knaw the mater weill enewch.
Thus oft dywulgat is this schamefull play,   *divulged*
Na thyng according to our hailsum May,
Bot rathyr contagius and infective,
And repugnant that sessoun nutrytive,   *nourishing*
Quhen new curage kytlis all gentill hartis,   *kindles*
Seand throu kynd ilk thyng springis and revertis.   *naturally; springs; sprouts*
Dame naturis menstralis, on that other part,   *minstrels*
Thayr blyssfull bay entonyng euery art,   *birdsong; making tuneful; place*
To beyt thar amouris of thar nychtis baill,   *prepare; [lovers]; heartache*
The merll, the mavys, and the nychtingale,   *blackbird; song-thrush*
With mery notis myrthfully furth brest,
Enforsing thame quha mycht do clynk it best.   *urging; sing*
The cowschet crowdis and pirkis on the rys,   *wood-pigeon; perches; twigs*
The styrlyng changis diuers stevynnys nys,   *starling; wanton notes*
The sparrow chyrmis in the wallis clyft,   *chirps; cleft*
Goldspynk and lyntquhyte fordynnand the lyft;   *goldfinch; finch; deafening; sky*
The gukgo galis, and so quytteris the quaill,   *cuckoo calls; twitters; quail*
Quhill ryveris rerdyt, schawis, and euery vaill,   *echo; woods*
And tender twystis trymlyt on the treis,   *twigs*
For byrdis sang and bemyng of the beis.   *buzzing; bees*
In wrablis dulce of hevynly armonyis   *[sweet warblings]*
The larkis, lowd releschand in the skyis,   *carolling*
Lovys thar lege with tonys curyus,   *praise; liege; notes*
Baith to dame Natur, and the fresch Venus,
Rendryng hie lawdis in thar obseruance,   *praises*
Quhais suguryt throtis mayd glayd hartis dans,   *whose sugared throats*
And al small fowlys singis on the spray:
   Welcum the lord of lycht, and lamp of day,
Welcum fostyr of tendir herbys grene,   *patron*
Welcum quyknar of florist flowris schene,   *quickener; flourished; bright*
Welcum support of euery rute and vane,
Welcum confort of alkynd fruyt and grane,
Welcum the byrdis beyld apon the breyr,   *shelter*
Welcum maister and rewlar of the yeyr,
Welcum weilfar of husbandis at the plewis,   *farmers; ploughs*
Welcum reparar of woddis, treis, and bewis,   *boughs*
Welcum depayntar of the blomyt medis,   *painter; blooming meadows*
Welcum the lyfe of euery thing that spredis,

Welcum stourour of alkynd bestiall, *keeper*
Welcum be thi brycht bemys, glading all,
Welcum celestiall myrrour and aspy, *observer*
Attechyng all that hantis sluggardy! *reproving; practise; laziness*
    And with this word, in chalmer quhair I lay,
The nynt morow of fresche temperat May, *ninth day*
On fut I sprent into my bayr sark, *leaped; shirt*
Wilfull for till compleyt my langsum wark
Twichand the lattyr buke of Dan Virgill, *concerning*
Quhilk me had tareyt al to lang a quhile; *delayed*
And to behald the cummyng of this kyng, *[the sun]*
That was sa welcum tyll all warldly thyng, *[most welcome of all]*
With sic tryumphe and pompos curage glayd *glided*
Than of his souerane chymmis, as is sayd, *from; mansions*
Newly arissyn in hys estayt ryall,
That, by hys hew, but orleger or dyall, *[without timekeeper or sundial]*
I knew it was past four houris of day,
And thocht I wald na langar ly in May
Les Phebus suld me losanger attaynt: *[call me sluggard]*
For Progne had, or than, sung hyr complaynt, *Procne*
And eik hir dreidful systir Philomene *also*
Hir lais endit, and in woddis grene *songs; compose*
Hyd hir selvin, eschamyt of hyr chance; *ashamed; fate*
And Esacus completis his pennance *[Cormorant]*
In riveris, fludis, and on euery laik:
And Peristera byddis luffaris awaik; *[Dove]*
Do serve my lady Venus heyr wyth me,
Lern thus to mak your obseruance, quod sche,
Into myne hartis ladeis sweit presens
Behaldis how I beinge, and do reuerens. *bow*
Hir nek scho wrinklis, trasing mony fold,
With plomis glitterand, asur apon gold, *plumes; azure*
Rendring a cullour betwix grene and blew,
In purpour glans of hevinly variant hew; *flash*
I meyn our awin native bird, gentill dow,
Syngand in hyr kynd, *I come hidder to wou;* *woo*
So pryklyng hyr grene curage for to crowd
In amorus voce and wowar soundis lowd, *amorous*
That, for the dynning of hir wanton cry, *sounding*
I irkyt of my bed, and mycht nocht ly, *wearied*

Bot gan me blys, syne in my wedis dres,   *[blessed myself]; then; clothes*
And, for it was ayr morow, or tyme of mes,   *[early morning]; [before Mass]*
I hynt a scriptour and my pen furth tuike,   *found pen-case*
Syne thus begouth of Virgill the twelt buike.   *began; twelfth*

    Explicit scitus prologus;   *[Here ends the skilful prologue]*
    Quhairof the authour sais thus:

The lusty crafty preambill, perll of May   *delightful; 'Pearl of May'*
I the entitill, crownit quhill domisday;   *[to be praised till domesday]*
And al wyth gold, in syng of stayt ryall,   *sign*
Most beyn illumnit thi letteris capital.   *must be illuminated*

SIR DAVID LINDSAY (1490–1555)

from *The Dreme of Schir Dauid Lyndesay*

The Deuisioun of the Eirth

Then, certanlye, scho tuke me be the hand,
And said: my sone, cum on thy wayis with me.
And so scho gart me cleirly vnderstand   *made*
How that the eirth trypartit wes in thre,
In Affrik, Europe, and Assie;
Efter the myndis of the Cosmographouris,
That is to say, the warldis Discriptouris.

First, Asia contenis in the Orient,
And is, weill, more than baith the vther twane.
Affrik and Ewrope, in the Occident,
And ar deuydit be ane sey, certane,   *divided; sea*
And that is callit the see Mediterane,
Quhilk at the strait of Marrok hes entre,   *entry*
That is betuix Spanye and Barbarie.

Towart the southwest lyis Affrica;
And, in the northwest, Europa doith stand;
And all the est contenis Asia:
On this wyse is deuydit the ferme land.   *[continental]*
It war mekle to me to tak on hand   *much*
Thir regionis to declare in speciall;
Yit, sall I schaw thare names in generall.

In mony diuers famous Regionis
Is deuydit this part of Asia,
Weill planesit with Cieteis, towris, and townis: *set out*
The gret Ynde, and Mesopotamia,
Penthapolis, Egypt, and Seria,
Capadocia, Seres, and Armenye,
Babilone, Caldia, Perth, and Arabye,

Sedone, Iudea, and Palestina,
Euer, Sethea, Tyir, and Galelie,
Hiberia, Bactria, and Phelestina,
Hircanea, Compagena, and Samarie.
In lytill Asia standis Galathie,
Pamphilia, Isaria, and Leid,
Regia, Arathusa, Assiria, and Meid.

Secundlie, we considderit Africa,
With mony fructfull famous regioun,
As Ethiope, and Tripolitana,
Zewges, quhare standis the tryumphant toun
Off nobyll Cartage, that ciete of renoun;
Garamantes, Nadabar, Libia,
Getulia, and Maritania,

Futhensis, Numedie, and Thingetane:
Off Affrick thir ar the principall.
Than Ewrope we considderit, in certane,
Quhose Regionis schortlie rehers I sall.
Foure principallis I fynd abone thame all,
Quhilkis ar Spanye, Italie, and France,
Quhose Subregionis wer mekle tyll auance: *tell*

Nether Scithia, Trace, and Garmanie,
Thusia, Histria, and Panonia,
Denmark, Gotland, Grunland, and Almanie,
Pole, Hungarie, Boeme, Norica, Rethia,
Teutonia, and mony diuers ma.
And was in foure deuidit Italie,
Tuskane, Ethuria, Naiplis, and Champanye;

And subdeuydit sindry vther wayis,
As Lumbardie, Ueneis, and vther ma,
Calaber, Romanie, and Ianewayis.
In Grece, Eperus, and Dalmatica,
Tessalie, Athica, and Illeria,
Achaya, Boetia, and Macedone,
Archadie, Pierie, and Lacedone.

And France we sawe deuydit in to thre,
Belgica, Rethia, and Aquitane,
And subdeuydit in Flanderis, Picardie,
Normandie, Gasconye, Burguinye, & Bretane,
And vtheris diuers Duchereis, in certane,
The quhilkis wer to lang for to declare;
Quharefor, of thame as now I speik na mare.

In Spanye lyis Castelye and Arrogone,
Nauerne, Galice, Portigall, and Garnate.
Than sawe we famous Ylis mony one,   *Isles*
Quhilks in the Occiane sey was situate.
Thame to discryue my wyt wes desolate;
Off Cosmographie I am nocht exparte,   *expert*
For I did neuer study in that arte.

Yit I sall sum of thare names declare,
As Madagascar, Gardes, and Taprobane,
And vtheris diuers Ylis gude and fair,
Situate in to the sey Mediterrane,
As Syper, Candie, Corsica, and Sardane,
Crete, Abidos, Thoes, Cecilia,
Tapsone, Eolie, and mony vther ma.

Quho wald at lenth heir the Discriptioun
Off euerilk Yle, als weill as the ferme land,
And properteis of euerilk Regioun,
To study and to reid man tak on hand,
And the attentike werkis vnderstand,
Off Plenius, and worthy Tholomie,   *[Ptolemy]*
Quhilks war exparte in to Cosmographie.

Thare sall thay fynd the names and properteis
Off euery Yle, and of ilke Regioun.
Than I inquirit of eirthly Paradyce,
Off the quhilk Adam tynt Possessioun.
Than schew scho me the Situatioun   *showed*
Off that precelland place, full of delyte,
Quhose properteis wer lang for to Indyte.

A N O N . from *The Book of the Dean of Lismore (1512–1542)*

A Ughdar so Oiséan

Is fada anocht i nOil Finn,
    fada linn an oidhche aréir;
an lá andiu giodh fada dhamh,
    do ba leór fad an laoi andé.

Fada liom gach lá dhá dtig;
    ní mar sin do cleachtaoi dúinn,
gan deabhaidh gan déanamh creach,
    gan bheith ag foghlaim chleas lúidh.

Gan aonach gan cheól gan chruit,
    gan bhronnadh cruidh gan gníomh greagh,
gan díoladh ollamhan dh'ór,
    bheith gan fhidhchill gan ól fleadh.

Gan chion ar suirghe ná ar seilg, –
    an dá cheird ris an raibh m'úidh, –
gan dul i gcliathaibh ná i gcath,
    uchán ach is deireadh dúinn.

Gan bhreith ar eilid ná ar fiadh,
    ní h-amhlaidh sin budh mhian linn,
gan luadh ar coinbheirt ná ar coin:
    is fada anocht i nOil Finn.

Gan earradh gaisgidh do ghnáth,
    gan imirt mar dob ál linn,
gan snámh dhár laochraidh ar loch:
    is fada anocht i nOil Finn.

Don t-saoghal mar atá mé,
    is truagh, a Dhé, mar tá sinn!
im aonar ag tarraing chloch:
    is fada anocht i nOil Finn.

The Author of this is Ossian

The night in Elphin goes slow,
slowly too last night went by;
although I felt today long,
longer still was yesterday.

Each day that comes wearies me;
this is not how we once were,
no fighting now and no raids,
no learning of agile feats.

No meetings, music or harps,
no cattle gifts, horsemen's deeds,
no paying the poets with gold,
no chess, no feasting or drink.

No love for courting or hunt –
two ploys to which I was prone –
no battle-array or fight,
alas, a poor way to end.

No catching of hind or deer,
not how I wanted to be,
no talk of dogs and their feats:
the night in Elphin goes slow.

No war-gear ever again,
nor playing of games we loved,
nor heroes swimming the loch:
the night in Elphin is long.

Alas for my worldly plight,
I'm wretched, O God, as I am,
alone, and gathering stones:
the night in Elphin is long.

Deireadh na Féine fuair nós,
    is mé Oiséan mór mac Finn,
ag éisdeacht ré gothaibh clog:
    is fada anocht i nOil Finn.

Faigh, a Phádraig, dhúinn ó Dhia
    fios an ionaidh i mbia sinn;
go saorthar m'anam roimh locht:
    is fada anocht i nOil Finn.

The last of the famous Fian,
great Ossian, the son of Fionn,
listening to baying of bells:
the night in Elphin is long.

Find out, O Patrick, from God
word of the place I'll be in;
may my soul be saved from harm:
it's a long night in Elphin.

Translated from the Gaelic by Derick Thomson

GEORGE BUCHANAN (1506–1582)

Ad Henricum Scotorum Regem

Caltha suos nusquam vultus a sole reflectit,
　illo oriente patens, illo abeunte latens:
nos quoque pendemus de te, sol noster, ad omnes
　expositi rerum te subeunte vices.

To Henry Darnley, King of Scots*

The marigold nowhere turns from the sun.
Opening at dawn, it closes in the dusk.
We too depend on you, our sun. To all
Your turns of fortune we are left exposed.

Translated from the Latin by Robert Crawford

* *Husband of Mary, Queen of Scots, he was murdered in 1567*

from *The Gude and Godlie Ballatis (1567 edition)*
Compiled and collected by the brothers W E D D E R B U R N —
J A M E S (d.1553), J O H N (d.1556), and R O B E R T (d.1557)

With huntis vp

With huntis vp, with huntis vp,
  It is now perfite day,   *perfect*
Jesus, our King, is gaine in hunting,
  Quha lykis to speid thay may.   *succeed*

Ane cursit Fox lay hid in Rox,   *rocks*
  This lang and mony ane day,
Deuoring scheip, quhill he mycht creip,
  Nane mycht him schaip away.   *scare*

It did him gude to laip the blude
  Of yung and tender lambis,   *young*
Nane culd he mis, for all was his,
  The yung anis with thair dammis.

The hunter is Christ, that huntis in haist,
  The hundis ar Peter and Paull,   *hounds*
The Paip is the Fox, Rome is the Rox,
  That rubbis vs on the gall.

That creull beist, he neuer ceist,   *ceased*
  Be his vsurpit power,   *by*
Under dispens, to get our penneis,   *dispensation*
  Our Saulis to deuoir.   *Souls*

Quha culd deuise sic merchandis,   *who*
  As he had thair to sell,
Onles it war proude Lucifer,   *unless*
  The greit maister of hell.

He had to sell the Tantonie bell,   *[St Anthony's bell]*
    And Pardonis thairin was,
Remissioun of sinnis, in auld scheip skinnis,
    Our Saulis to bring from grace.

With bullis of leid, quhyte wax and reid,   *[papal bulls]; lead*
    And vther quhylis with grene,
Closit in ane box, this vsit the Fox,   *closed*
    Sic peltrie was neuer sene.   *trash*

With dispensationis and obligationis,
    According to his Law,
He wald dispence, for money from hence,   *arrange*
    With thame he neuer saw.

To curs and ban the sempill pure man,   *simple; poor*
    That had nocht to flé the paine,   *escape*
Bot quhen he had payit all to ane myit,   *mite*
    He mon be absoluit than.   *[might be absolved]*

To sum, God wot, he gaif tot quot,   *gave; [as much as was needed]*
    And vther sum pluralitie,
Bot first with penneis, he mon dispens,   *pence; [must pay]*
    Or ellis it will nocht be.

Kingis to marie, and sum to tarie,   *delay*
    Sic is his power and mycht,
Quha that hes gold, with him will he hold,
    Thoct it be contrair all rycht.   *although; [goes against]*

O blissit Peter, the Fox is ane lier,
    Thow knawis weill it is nocht sa,
Quhill at the last, he salbe downe cast,
    His peltrie, Pardonis, and all.

God send euerie Preist ane wyfe

God send euerie Preist ane wyfe,
And euerie Nunne ane man,
That thay mycht leue that haly lyfe,   *live*
As first the Kirk began.

Sanct Peter, quhome nane can reprufe,
His lyfe in Mariage led:
All guide Preistis, quhome God did lufe,
Thair maryit wyffis had.

Greit causis than, I grant, had thay
Fra wyffis to refraine:
Bot greiter causis haif thay may,
Now wyffis to wed againe.

For than suld nocht sa mony hure   *whores*
Be vp and downe this land:
Nor zit sa mony beggeris pure,   *yet; poor*
In Kirk and mercat stand.   *market-place*

And nocht sa mekle bastard seid,   *much; seed*
Throw out this cuntrie sawin: *sown*
Nor gude men vncouth fry suld feid,   *strange children*
And all the suith war knawin.   *if; truth*

Sen Christis law, and commoun law,   *since*
And Doctouris will admit,
That Preistis in that zock suld draw,   *yoke*
Quha dar say contrair it?

ALEXANDER SCOTT (c. 1515–1583)

from Ane New Yeir Gift to the Quene Mary, quhen scho come first Hame, 1562

WELCUM, illustrat Ladye, and oure Quene!
Welcum, oure lyone with the Floure-delyce! *[fleur-de-lys]*
Welcum, oure thrissill with the Lorane grene! *thistle; Lorraine*
Welcum, oure rubent roiss vpoun the ryce! *ruby; rose; twig*
Welcum, oure jem and joyfull genetryce! *[mother]*
Welcum, oure beill of Albion to beir! *shelter*
Welcum, oure plesand Princes maist of pryce!
God gif the grace aganis this guid new yeir.

This guid new yeir, we hoip, with grace of God,
Salbe of peax, traquillitie, and rest; *shall be; peace*
This yeir sall rycht and ressone rewle the rod,
Quhilk sa lang seasoun hes bene soir supprest;
This yeir ferme faith sall frelie be confest,
And all erronius questionis put areir; *behind*
To laboure that this lyfe amang ws lest
God gife the grace aganis this guid new yeir.

Heirfore addres the dewlie to decoir *adorn*
And rewle thy regne with hie magnificence;
Begin at God to gar sett furth his gloir,
And of his gospell gett experience;
Caus his trew Kirk be had in reuerence; *cause; reverence*
So sall thy name and fame spred far and neir:
Now, this thy dett to do with diligence, *duty*
God gif the grace aganis this guid new yeir.

Hence, heart

Hence heart, with her that must depart,
And hald thee with thy sovereign,
For I had lever want ane heart *rather*
Nor have the heart that does me pain.

Therefore go, with thy luve remain,
And lat me live thus unmolest:
And see that thou come not again,
But bide with her thou luvis best.

Sen sho that I have servit lang
Is to depairt so suddenly,
Address thee now, for thou sall gang   *shall; go*
And bear thy lady company.
Fra sho be gone, heartless am I,   *since*
For why? thou art with her possest.
Therefore, my heart, go hence in hie,   *haste*
And bide with her thou luvis best.

Though this belappit body here   *beleaguered*
Be bound to servitude and thrall,
My faithful heart is free inteir
And mind to serve my lady at all.
Wald God that I were perigal   *worthy*
Under that redolent rose to rest.
Yet at the least, my heart, thou sall
Abide with her thou luvis best.

Sen in your garth the lily white   *garden*
May not remain amang the lave,   *rest*
Adieu, the flour of hail delight,   *all*
Adieu the succor that may me save,
Adieu the fragrant balm suave,   *sweet*
And lamp of ladies lustiest.   *most beautiful*
My faithful heart sho sall it have
To bide with her it luvis best.

Deplore, ye ladies clear of hue,
Her absence, sen sho must depart,
And specially ye luvars true,
That woundit been with luvis dart:
For some of you sall want ane heart
As weil as I. Therefore at last
Do go with mine, with mind inwart,
And bide with her thou luvis best.

Return thee, heart

Return thee, heart, hamewart again,
And bide where thou was wont to be;
Thou art ane fool to suffer pain
For luve of her that luves not thee.
My heart, lat be sic fantasy;
Luve nane bot as they make thee cause;   *but*
And lat her seek ane heart for thee,
For feind a crum of thee sho fawis.   *[hardly]; crumb; cares*

To what effect should thou be thrall
But thank, sen thou has thy free will?
My heart, be not sa bestial,
Bot knaw who does thee good or ill;
Remain with me and tarry still,
And see wha playis best their pawis,   *part*
And lat fillok ga fling her fill,   *[the girl]*
For feind a crum of thee sho fawis.

Thocht sho be fair I will not feignie;
Sho is the kind of others ma;
For why there is a fellon many,
That seemis good, and are not sa.
My heart, take nowder pain nor wa,
For Meg, for Meriory, or yet Mawis,
Bot be thou glaid and lat her ga,
For feind a crum of thee sho fawis.

Because I find sho took in ill,
At her departing thou make na care;
Bot all beguiled, go where sho will,
Be shrew the heart that mane makis mair.
My heart, be merry late and air,
This is the final end and clause,
And let her fallow ane filly fair,
For feind a crum of thee sho fawis.

To luve unluvit

To luve unluvit it is ane pain:
For sho that is my sovereign,
Some wanton man so he has set her,
That I can get no luve again,
Bot breaks my heart, and nocht the better.

When that I went with that sweet may,   *maid*
To dance, to sing, to sport and play,
And oft times in my armis plet her;   *embraced*
I do now mourn both nicht and day,
And breaks my heart, and nocht the better.

Where I was wont to see her go
Richt trimly passand to and fro,
With comely smilis when that I met her:
And now I live in pain and woe,
And breaks my heart, and nocht the better.

Whattan ane glaikit fool am I   *stupid*
To slay myself with melancholy,
Sen weil I ken I may nocht get her.
Or what suld be the cause, and why,
To break my heart, and nocht the better?

My heart, sen thou may nocht her please,
Adieu, as good luve comes as gais,
Go choose ane odder and forget her: *[another]*
God give him dolor and disease,
That breaks their heart and nocht the better.

SIR THOMAS MAITLAND (1522–c.1572)

Sir Thomas Maitland's Satyr upon Sir Niel Laing

Canker'd, cursed creature, crabbed, corbit kittle,	*crooked whelp*
Buntin-ars'd, beugle-back'd, bodied like a beetle;	*plump-arsed; crookbacked*
Sarie shitten, shell-padock, ill shapen shit,	*badly; tortoise*
Kid-bearded gennet, all alike great:	*mare*
Fiddle-douped, flindrikin, fart of a man,	*scraggy-bummed; twit*
Wa worth the, wanwordie, wanshapen wran!	*[woe on you]; unworthy; misshapen; wren*

MRS MACGREGOR OF GLENSTRAE (*fl.* 1570)

Cumha Ghriogair MhicGhriogair Ghlinn Sréith

Moch madainn air latha Lùnasd'
Bha mi sùgradh mar ri m'ghràdh,
Ach mun tàinig meadhon latha
Bha mo chridhe air a chràdh.

Ochain, ochain, ochain uiridh
  Is goirt mo chridhe, laoigh,
Ochain, ochain, ochain uiridh
  Cha chluinn t'athair ar caoidh.

Mallachd aig maithibh is aig càirdean
Rinn mo chràdh air an-dòigh,
Thàinig gun fhios air mo ghràdh-sa
Is a thug fo smachd e le foill.

Nam biodh dà fhear dheug d'a chinneadh
Is mo Ghriogair air an ceann,
Cha bhiodh mo shùil a' sileadh dheur,
No mo leanabh féin gun dàimh.

Chuir iad a cheann air ploc daraich,
Is dhòirt iad fhuil mu làr:
Na'm biodh agamsa an sin cupan,
Dh'òlainn dìth mo shàth.

Is truagh nach robh m'athair an galar,
Agus Cailean Liath am plàigh,
Ged bhiodh nighean an Ruadhanaich
Suathadh bas is làmh.

Chuirinn Cailean Liath fo ghlasaibh,
Is Donnchadh Dubh an làimh;
Is gach Caimbeulach th' ann am Bealach
Gu giùlan nan glas-làmh.

Lament for MacGregor of Glenstrae

One morning of August
I was dallying with my love,
but before the moon was shining
my heart had learned to grieve.

Ochone, ochone my little one   alas
    my heart is deathly sore.
Ochone, ochone my little one
    your father cannot hear.

A curse on my family and friends
who brought me to this plight,
who stole upon my love by stealth
and killed him by deceit.

If there were twelve of his people
and Gregor at their head,
my eyes would not be tearful,
nor my child's father dead.

They placed his head on an oak stump
and let his blood fall:
if I had had a cup there
I'd have drunk it all.

May sickness kill my father
and Colin die of the plague,   [Colin Campbell of Glenorchy]
and the daughter of the Red-haired one   [his wife, daughter of Lord Ruthven]
suffer grief's fatigue.

White Colin I would lock in jail,
Black Duncan I'd arrest;   [eldest son of Colin Campbell]
and every Campbell now in Balloch
I'd padlock by the wrist.

Ràinig mise réidhlean Bhealaich,
Is cha d'fhuair mi ann tàmh:
Cha d'fhàg mi ròin de m'fhalt gun tarraing
No craiceann air mo làimh.

Is truagh nach robh mi an riochd na h-uiseig,
Spionnadh Ghriogair ann mo làimh:
Is i a' chlach a b'àirde anns a' chaisteal
A' chlach a b'fhaisge do'n bhlàr.

Is ged tha mi gun ùbhlan agam
Is ùbhlan uile aig càch,
Is ann tha m' ubhal cùbhraidh grinn
Is cùl a chinn ri làr.

Ged tha mnathan chàich aig baile
'Nan laighe is 'nan cadal sàmh,
Is ann bhios mise aig bruaich mo leapa
A' bualadh mo dhà làimh.

Is mór a b'annsa bhith aig Griogair
Air feadh coille is fraoich,
Na bhith aig Baran crìon na Dalach
An taigh cloiche is aoil.

Is mór a b'annsa bhith aig Griogair
Cur a' chruidh do'n ghleann,
Na bhith aig Baran crìon na Dalach
Ag òl air fìon is air leann.

Is mór a b'annsa bhith aig Griogair
Fo bhrata ruibeach ròin,
Na bhith aig Baran crìon na Dalach
A' giùlan sìoda is sròil.

Ged a bhiodh ann cur is cathadh
Is latha nan seachd sìon,
Gheibheadh Griogair dhòmh-sa cragan
'S an caidlimid fo dhìon.

When I reached the fields of Balloch,
there was no peace to be found:
I tore each hair from my head
and the skin from my hand.

If only I were in the lark's shape,
with Gregor's strength in my hand:
the highest stone in the castle
would be nearest to the ground.

And though I have no apples left
when other apples are entire,
my fragrant complete apple
has his head on the bare floor.

When other wives are sleeping soft
by husbands without wounds,
I'll be at my bed's edge
beating my two hands.

Better to be with Gregor
in the wood of wild rain,
than with the withered Baron
in his house of lime and stone.

Better to be with Gregor
driving cattle to the glen,
than with the withered Baron
drunk on beer and wine.

Better to be with Gregor
beneath the warm seal's skin,
than with the withered Baron
wearing silk and satin.

Though there would be hail and snow,
day of the seven showers,
Gregor would find me shelter
to sleep from the storm's force.

Ba hu, ba hu, àsrain bhig,
   Cha'n 'eil thu fhathast ach tlàth:
Is eagal leam nach tig an latha
   Gun dìol thu t'athair gu bràth.

O lullaby my little child
  you are yet but small:
I fear the day will never come
  when you'll destroy them all.

Translated from the Gaelic by Iain Crichton Smith

MARY, QUEEN OF SCOTS (1542–1587)

from *Sonnets to Bothwell*

IX

Pour luy aussi ie iette mainte larme.
Premier quand il se fist de ce corps possesseur,
Duquel alors il n'auoit pas le coeur.
Puis me donna vn autre dur alarme,
Quand il versa de son sang mainte dragme,
Dont de grief il me vint lesser doleur,
Qui m'en pensa oster la vie, & frayeur
De perdre las le seul rampar qui m'arme.
Pour luy depuis iay mesprisé l'honneur
Ce qui nous peut seul pouruoir de bonheur.
Pour luy i'ay hazardé grandeur & conscience.
Pour luy tous mes parentz i'ay quité, & amis,
Et tous autres respectz sont apart mis,
Brief de vous seul ie cerche l'alliance.

O Domine Deus!

(said to have been composed on the morning of her execution, 1587)

O Domine Deus! speravi in Te:
O care mi Jesu! nunc libera me,
In durà catenà, in miserà poenà, desidero te;
Languendo, gemendo, et genu flectendo,
Adoro, imploro, ut liberes me!

For him also I powrit out mony teiris,
First quhen he maid himself possessor of this body,
Of the quhilk then he had not the hart.   which
Efter he did geue me one uther hard charge,
Quhen he bled of his blude great quantitie,
Through the great sorrow of the quhilk came to me that dolour,
That almost caryit away my life, and the feire
To lese the onely strength that armit me.   lose
For him since I haif despisit honour,
The thing onely that bringeth felicitie.
For him I have hazardit greitnes and conscience,
For him I have forsaken all kin and frendes,
And set aside all uther respectes,
Schortly, I seke the aliance of yow onely.

Translated anonymously

My Lord and My God, I have hoped in Thee:
O Jesu, sweet Saviour, now liberate me!
I have languished for Thee in afflictions and chains,
Through long years of anguish and bodily pains.
Adoring, imploring, on humbly bowed knee,
I crave of thy mercy to liberate me.

Translated from the Latin by Agnes Strickland

NIALL MÓR MACMHUIRICH (c. 1550–c. 1615)

Soraidh slán don oidhche a-réir

Soraidh slán don oidhche a-réir,
    fada géar ag dul ar ccúl;
dá ndáiltí mo chur i ccroich,
    is truagh nách í a-nocht a tús.

Atáid dias is tigh-se a-nocht
    ar nách ceileann, rosg a rún;
gion go bhfuilid béal re béal
    is géar géar silleadh a súl.

Tocht an ní chuireas an chiall
    ar shilleadh díochra na súl;
cá feirrde an tocht do-ní an béal –
    sgéal do-ní an rosg ar a rún.

Uch, ní léigid lucht na mbréag
    smid tar mo bhéal, a rosg mall;
tuig an ní-se adeir mo shúil
    is tú insan chúil úd thall.

'Cúinnibh dhúinn an oidhche a-nocht,
    truagh gan sinn mar so go bráth;
ná léig an mhaidean is-teach –
    éirigh 's cuir a-mach an lá.'

Uch, a Mhuire, a bhuime sheang,
    ós tú is ceann ar gach cléir,
tárthaigh agus gabh mo lámh –
    soraidh slán don oidhche a-réir.

Farewell for ever to last night

Farewell for ever to last night;
swift though it passed, its joy remains:
though I were hanged for my share in it
I'd live it over tonight again.

There are two in this house tonight
whose eyes give their secrets away:
though they are not lip to lip
eager is the eyes' play.

The eyes' swift glances must give all
the tale their prisoned lips would tell;
the eyes have kept no secret here,
lips' silence is of no avail.

Those who would make my true words false
have sealed my lips, O languid eye;
but in your corner, out of reach,
understand what my eyes say:

'Keep the memory of this night,
let there be no change till doom;
do not let the morning in:
throw out the cold day from the room.'

Mother Mary, of fostering grace,
since poets look to you for light,
save me now, and take my hand –
farewell for ever to last night.

Translated from the Gaelic by Derick Thomson

ALEXANDER MONTGOMERIE (c. 1555–1598)

Ane Dreame

I dreamit ane dreame, o that my dreame wer trew!
   Me thocht my maistris to my chalmer came,   *mistress; chamber*
And with hir harmeles handis the cowrteingis drew,   *curtains*
And sueitlie callit on me be my name: *sweetly*
'Art ye on sleip,' quod sche, 'o fy for schame!
   Haue ye nocht tauld that luifaris takis no rest?'   *learned*
Me thocht I ansuerit, 'trew it is, my dame,
   I sleip nocht, so your luif dois me molest.'
With that me thocht hir nicht-gowne of sche cuist,   *cast*
   Liftit the claiths and lichtit in my armis;   *bedclothes*
Hir Rosie lippis me thocht on me sche thirst,
   And said, 'may this nocht stanche yow of your harmes!'   *relieve*
'Mercy, madame,' me thocht I menit to say,
Bot quhen I walkennit, alace, sche was away.

Sonet

Thocht Polibus, pisander, and with them,
   Antinous, with monie wowaris, than   *wooers*
Did preis for to suppryse, and bring to schame,   *press*
   Penellope, in absence of hir man,
Yit sche remanit chast as sche began,
   To tyme Ulisses happinit to cum hame;
That nane of thais as yit, do quhat thai can,
   Lang saxtene yeiris dowcht to defyle hir fame.   *managed*
Ewin so, most sueit, discreit, and mansueit muse,   *gentle*
   Remember on your yoldin sirviture: *given; servitude*
Thoill nane your blaseme bewtie to abuse,   *let; blossoming*
   Thocht thai vith leing lippis wald yow allure;
Bot sen my lyffe dois on your luife depend;
In trew luiff with Penellope contend.

The Royall Palice of the Heichest Hewin

The royall palice of the heichest hewin,   *heaven*
   the staitlie fornace of the sterrie round,
the loftie wolt of wandring planettis sewin,   *vault*
   the air, the fyre, the wattir, and the ground —
suppois of thais the science be profound,
   surppassing far our gros and sillie sens,
The pregnant spreittis yit of the leirnit hes fund,   *spirits; learned*
   by age, by tyme, and lang experience,
Thair pitche, thair powir, and Inflwence,
   the cowrs of natwre and hir mowingis all;
Sa that we neid nocht now be in suspence
   off erthelie thingis, nor yit celestiall;
Bot onlie of this monstwre luif we dout,
quhais craftie cowrs no cwning can find out.

ALEXANDER HUME (c. 1556–1609)

Of the Day Estivall

O perfite light, quhilk schaid away   *separated*
The darkenes from the light,
And set a ruler ou'r the day,
Ane uther ou'r the night:

Thy glorie when the day foorth flies
Mair vively dois appeare   *vividly*
Nor at midday unto our eyes   *than*
The shining sun is cleare.

The shaddow of the earth anon
Remooves and drawes by,
Sine in the east, when it is gon,   *then*
Appeares a clearer sky:

Quhilk sunne perceaves the little larks,   *which; soon*
The lapwing and the snyp,   *snipe*
And tunes their sangs like Natures clarks,
Ou'r midow, mure and stryp.   *meadow; stream*

Bot everie bais'd nocturnall beast   *frightened*
Na langer may abide;
They hy away, baith maist and least,   *hurry*
Them selves in house to hide.

They dread the day, fra thay it see,   *when*
And from the sight of men
To saits and covars fast they flee,   *dens; coverts*
And lyons to their den.

Oure hemisphere is poleist clein,   *polished*
And lightened more and more,
While everie thing be clearely sein,   *until*
Quhilk seemed dim before;

Except the glistering astres bright,   *stars*
Which all the night were cleere,
Offusked with a greater light   *obscured*
Na langer dois appeare.

The golden globe incontinent   *immediately*
Sets up his shining head,
And ou'r the earth and firmament
Displayes his beims abroad.   *abroad*

For joy the birds with boulden throts,   *swollen*
Agains his visage shein,   *against; shining*
Takes up their kindelie musicke nots   *natural; notes*
In woods and gardens grein.

Up braids the carefull husbandman,   *rises*
His cornes and vines to see,
And everie tymous artisan,   *early*
In buith worke busilie.   *booth*

The pastor quits the slouthfull sleepe   *shepherd*
And passis forth with speede,
His little camow-nosed sheepe   *snub-nosed*
And rowtting kie to feede.   *lowing; cattle*

The passenger from perrels sure   *traveller*
Gangs gladly foorth the way;
Breife, everie living creature   *[in brief]*
Takes comfort of the day.

The subtile, mottie rayons light   *moted; beams*
At rifts thay are in wonne,   *[enter]*
The glansing thains and vitre bright   *fanes; glass*
Resplends against the sunne.   *[shines back]*

The dew upon the tender crops,
Lyke pearles white and round
Or like to melted silver drops,
Refreshes all the ground.

The mystie rocke, the clouds of raine,
From tops of mountaines skails,   *evaporates*
Cleare are the highest hils and plaine,
The vapors takes the vails.

Begaried is the saphire pend   *ornamented; vault*
With spraings of skarlet hew,   *streaks*
And preciously from end till end
Damasked white and blew.

The ample heaven of fabrik sure
In cleannes dois surpas
The chrystall and the silver pure,
Or clearest poleist glas.

The time sa tranquill is and still,
That nawhere sall ye find,
Saife on ane high and barren hill,   *except*
Ane aire of peeping wind.

All trees and simples, great and small,   *herbs*
That balmie leife do beir,
Nor thay were painted on a wall,   *than if*
Na mair they move or steir.   *stir*

Calme is the deepe and purpour se,   *purple*
Yee, smuther nor the sand: *indeed; smoother than*
The wals that woltring wont to be   *waves; tossing*
Are stable like the land.

Sa silent is the cessile air,   *yielding*
That every cry and call,
The hils and dails and forrest fair
Againe repeates them all.

The rivers fresh, the callor streames,   *cool*
Ou'r rockes can softlie rin,
The water cleare like chrystall seames,
And makes a pleasant din.

The fields and earthly superfice   *surface*
With verdure greene is spread,
And naturallie, but artifice,   *without*
In partie coulors cled.   *many; clad*

The flurishes and fragrant flowres,   *blossoms*
Throw Phoebus fostring heit,
Refresht with dew and silver showres,
Casts up ane odor sweit.

The clogged, busie, bumming beis,   *laden; humming*
That never thinks to drowne,
On flowers and flourishes of treis
Collects their liquor browne.

The sunne maist like a speedie post   *messenger*
With ardent course ascends,
The beautie of the heavenly host
Up to our zenith tends;

Nocht guided be na Phaeton
Nor trained in a chyre,   *driven; chariot*
Bot be the high and haly On,
Quhilk dois allwhere impire.   *govern*

The burning beims downe from his face
Sa fervently can beat,
That man and beast now seekes a place
To save them fra the heat.

The brethles flocks drawes to the shade
And frechure of their fald,   *freshness*
The startling nolt, as they were made, *[stampeding cattle]; mad*
Runnes to the rivers cald.

The heards beneath some leaffie trie,   *shepherds*
Amids the flowers they lie,
The stabill ships upon the sey
Tends up their sails to drie.   *stretch*

The hart, the hynd, and fallow deare
Are tapisht at their rest,   *crouching*
The foules and birdes that made the beare   *noise*
Prepares their prettie nest.

The rayons dures descending downe   *strong*
All kindlis in a gleid,   *[live coal]*
In cittie nor in borroughstowne   *burgh*
May nane set foorth their heid.

Back from the blew paymented whun   *[whinstone pavement]*
And from ilk plaister wall
The hote reflexing of the sun   *reflection*
Inflams the aire and all.

The labowrers that timellie raise,
All wearie, faint and weake,
For heate downe to their houses gaise,   *go*
Noone meate and sleepe to take.   *[midday meal]*

The callowr wine in cave is sought,   *cellar*
Mens brothing breists to cule;   *sweating; cool*
The water cald and cleare is brought,
And sallets steipt in ule.   *salads; oil*

Sume plucks the honie plowm and peare,   *honey; plum*
The cherrie and the pesche,   *peach*
Sume likes the reymand London beare,   *foaming*
The bodie to refresh.

Forth of their skepps some raging bees   *hives*
Lyes out and will not cast,   *[settle outside]; swarm*
Some uther swarmes hyves on the trees,
In knots togidder fast.   *clusters*

The corbeis and the kekling kais   *crows; cackling jackdaws*
May scarce the heate abide,
Halks prunyeis on the sunnie brais   *hawks; preen*
And wedders back and side.   *weather*

With gilted eyes and open wings   *gilded*
The cock his courage shawes,
With claps of joy his breast he dings,   *strikes*
And twentie times he crawes.

The dow with whisling wings sa blew   *dove*
The winds can fast collect,
Hir pourpour pennes turnes mony hew,   *feathers*
Against the sunne direct.

Now noone is went, gaine is mid-day,   *noon; gone*
The heat dois slake at last,
The sunne descends downe west away,
Fra three of clock be past.

A little cule of braithing wind   *[cool breeze]*
Now softly can arise,
The warks throw heate that lay behind
Now men may enterprise.

Furth fairis the flocks to seeke their fude
On everie hill and plaine,
Ilk labourer, as he thinks gude,
Steppes to his turne againe.

The rayons of the sunne, we see,
Diminish in their strength,
The schad of everie towre and tree   *shadow*
Extended is in length.

Great is the calme, for everiequhair
The wind is sitten downe,   *settled*
The reik thrawes right up in the air   *smoke*
From everie towre and towne.

Their firdoning the bony birds   *warbling*
In banks they do begin,
With pipes of reides the jolie hirds   *shepherds*
Halds up the mirrie din.

The maveis and the philomeen,   *thrush; nightingale*
The stirling whissilles lowd,   *starling*
The cuschetts on the branches green   *wood-pigeons*
Full quietly they crowd.   *coo*

The gloming comes, the day is spent,   *dusk*
The sun goes out of sight,
And painted is the occident
With pourpour sanguine bright.

The skarlet nor the golden threid,
Who would their beawtie trie,
Are nathing like the colour reid
And beautie of the sky.

Our west horizon circuler,
Fra time the sunne be set,
Is all with rubies (as it wer)
Or rosis reid ou'rfret.   *embroidered*

What pleasour were to walke and see,
Endlang a river cleare,   *along*
The perfite forme of everie tree
Within the deepe appeare!

The salmon out of cruifs and creils   *cruives; creels*
Up hailed into skowts,   *pulled; [flat-bottomed boats]*
The bels and circles on the weills,   *bubbles; pools*
Throw lowpping of the trouts.   *leaping*

O, then it were a seemely thing,
While all is still and calme,
The praise of God to play and sing,
With cornet and with shalme.   *shawm*

Bot now the hirds with mony schout
Cals uther be their name:
'Ga, Billie, turne our gude about,   *[livestock]*
Now time is to go hame.'

With bellie fow the beastes belive   *full; quickly*
Are turned fra the corne,
Quhilk soberly they hameward drive,
With pipe and lilting horne.

Throw all the land great is the gild   *clamour*
Of rustik folk that crie,
Of bleiting sheepe fra they be fild,
Of calves and rowting ky.

All labourers drawes hame at even,
And can till uther say,
Thankes to the gracious God of heaven,
Quhilk send this summer day.   *sent*

WILLIAM FOWLER (1560–1612)

from *The Tarantula of Loue*

Upon this firthe, as on the sees of love,
my beaten bark, with waltring wawes tost sore,   *weltering*
to the bright fyre her wandring course dothe move,
imagining I see the on the schore:
thy words, the Mapp and cairt is, O my glore,
thy eyes, the ey attractiue calamite,   *always*
thy winks, the tuinkling stars which I adore,
the pointed compass ar thy proper feite,
the rudder is my reason vndiscreit,
the airs my greiffs, the reas my piteous plaint,   *sail-yards*
the ancar doubt, the suits sowre sueit,
the schip my half deade harte through mad Intent,
the see my teares, my sighs the whirling wynde,
which makes me seik the heaven I can not fynd.

Sonet. In Orknay

Upon the utmost corners of the warld,
and on the borders of this massive round,
quhaire fates and fortoune hither hes me harld,
I doe deplore my greiffs upon this ground;
and seing roring seis from roks rebound
by ebbs and streames of contrair routing tyds,
and phebus chariot in there wawes ly dround,   *waves*
quha equallye now night and day devyds,
I cal to mynde the storms my thoughts abyds,
which euer wax and never dois decress,
for nights of dole dayes Ioys ay ever hyds,
and in there vayle doith al my weill suppress: *vale*
so this I see, quhaire ever I remove,
I chainge bot sees, but can not chainge my love.

MARK ALEXANDER BOYD (1563–1601)

Venus and Cupid

Frae bank to bank, frae wood to wood I rin
Owrhailit with my feeble fantasie,   *overwhelmed*
Like til a leaf that fallis from a tree,
Or til a reed owrblawin with the wind.
Twa gods guides me: the ane of them is blin,
Yea, and a bairn brocht up in vanitie;
The nixt a wife ingenerit of the sea
And lichter nor a dauphin with her fin.   *lighter than; dolphin*

Unhappie is the man for evermair
That tills the sand and sawis in the air;
But twice unhappier is he, I lairn,
That feedis in his hairt a mad desire,
And follows on a woman throu the fire,
Led by a blin, and teachit by a bairn.

SIR ROBERT AYTOUN (1570–1638)

Sonnet: On the River Tweed

Faire famous flood, which sometyme did devyde,
But now conjoynes, two Diadems in one,
Suspend thy pace and some more softly slyde,
Since wee have made the Trinchman of our mone, *thee; spokesman; complaint*
And since non's left but thy report alone
To show the world our Captaines last farewell
That courtesye I know when wee are gon
Perhapps your Lord the Sea will it reveale,
And you againe the same will not conceale,
But straight proclaim't through all his bremish bounds, *raging*
Till his high tydes these flowing tydeings tell
And soe will send them with his murmering sounds
 To that Religious place whose stately walls
 Does keepe the heart which all our hearts inthralls.

Upon Mr Thomas Murrays fall

The other night from Court returning late,
Tyr'd with attendance, out of love with state,
I mett a boy who ask't if he should goe
A long to light mee home, I told him noe.
Yet he did vrge the darkness of the night,
The foulness of the way requir'd a light.
Its true, good boy, quoth I, yet thou mayst be
More vsefull to some other then to mee.
I cannot miss my way, but they that take
The way from whence I came, have neede to make
 A light there guide, for I dare boldly say
 Its ten to one, but they shall lose there way.

What Meanes this Strangeness

What meanes this Strangeness now of late
   Since tyme doth truth approve?
Such distance may well stand with State,
   It cannot stand with love.
Its either cunning or distrust
   That doth such wayes allow,
The first is base, the last's vnjust,
   Let neither blemish you.
If you intend to draw mee on,
   You over act your part,
And if you meane to send me gon,
   You neede not halfe this Art.
Speake but the word, or doe but cast
   A looke which seemes to frowne,
I'le give you all the love that's past,
   The rest shall be my owne.
And such a faire and Efald way   *equal*
   On both sides none can blame,
Since every one is bound to play
   The fairest of his game.

ANONYMOUS BALLADS

Sir Patrick Spens

The king sits in Dumfermline town,
    Drinking the blude-red wine:
'O whare will I get a skeely skipper,   *skilful*
    To sail this new ship of mine ?'

O up and spake an eldern knight,
    Sat at the king's right knee:
'Sir Patrick Spens is the best sailor
    That ever saild the sea.'

Our king has written a braid letter,   *broad*
    And seald it with his hand,
And sent it to Sir Patrick Spens,
    Was walking on the strand.

'To Noroway, to Noroway,
    To Noroway oer the faem: *foam*
The king's daughter of Noroway,
    'Tis thou maun bring her hame.'   *must*

The first word that Sir Patrick read,
    Sae loud, loud laughed he;
The neist word that Sir Patrick read,   *next*
    The tear blinded his ee.

'O wha is this has done this deed,
    And tauld the king o me,
To send us out at this time of the year
    To sail upon the sea ?

'Be it wind, be it weet, be it hail, be it sleet,
    Our ship must sail the faem;
The king's daughter of Noroway,
    'Tis we must fetch her hame.'

They hoysed their sails on Monenday morn,
    Wi a' the speed they may;
They hae landed in Noroway,
    Upon a Wodensday.

They hadna been a week, a week
    In Noroway but twae,
When that the lords o Noroway
    Began aloud to say:

'Ye Scottishmen spend a' our king's goud,   *gold*
    And a' our queenis fee!'   *possessions*
'Ye lie, ye lie, ye liars loud,
    Fu loud I hear ye lie!

'For I brought as much white monie   *silver*
    As gane my men and me,
And I brought a half-fou o gude red goud
    Out oer the sea wi me.

'Make ready, make ready, my merrymen a',
    Our gude ship sails the morn:'
'Now, ever alake! my master dear,
    I fear a deadly storm!

'I saw the new moon late yestreen,
    Wi the auld moon in her arm;
And if we gang to sea, master,
    I fear we'll come to harm.'

They hadna sailed a league, a league,
    A league but barely three,
When the lift grew dark, and the wind blew loud,   *sky*
    And gurly grew the sea.   *stormy*

The ankers brak, and the topmasts lap,   *flew*
    It was sic a deadly storm,
And the waves came oer the broken ship,
    Till a' her sides were torn.

'O where will I get a gude sailor,
   To take my helm in hand,
Till I get up to the tall topmast,
   To see if I can spy land?'

'O here am I, a sailor gude,
   To take the helm in hand,
Till you go up to the tall topmast;
   But I fear you'll neer spy land.'

He hadna gane a step, a step,
   A step but barely ane,
When a bout flew out of our goodly ship,   *bung*
   And the salt sea it came in.

'Gae fetch a web o the silken claith,
   Another o the twine,
And wap them into our ship's side,   *weave*
   And letna the sea come in.'

They fetched a web o the silken claith,
   Another o the twine,
And they wapped them roun that gude ship's side,
   But still the sea came in.

O laith, laith were our gude Scots lords
   To weet their cork-heeld shoon;
But lang or a' the play was playd,
   They wat their hats aboon.

And mony was the feather-bed
   That flattered on the faem,
And mony was the gude lord's son
   That never mair cam hame.

The ladyes wrang their fingers white,
   The maidens tore their hair,
A' for the sake of their true loves,
   For them they'll see na mair.

O lang, lang may the ladyes sit,
    Wi their fans into their hand,
Before they see Sir Patrick Spens
    Come sailing to the strand.

And lang, lang may the maidens sit,
    Wi their goud kaims in their hair,
A' waiting for their ain dear loves,
    For them they'll see na mair.

O forty miles off Aberdeen
    'Tis fifty fathoms deep,
And there lies gude Sir Patrick Spens,
    Wi the Scots lords at his feet.

The Battle of Otterburn

It fell about the Lammas tide,
    When the muir-men win their hay,   *moor-men*
The doughty Douglas bound him to ride
    Into England, to drive a prey.

He chose the Gordons and the Græmes,
    With them the Lindesays, lights and gay;
But the Jardines wald not with him ride,
    And they rue it to this day.

And he has burnd the dales of Tyne,
    And part of Bambrough shire,
And three good towers on Reidswire fells,
    He left them all on fire.

And he marchd up to Newcastle,
    And rode it round about:
'O wha 's the lord of this castle?
    Or wha 's the lady o't?'

But up spake proud Lord Percy then,
    And O but he spake hie!
I am the lord of this castle,
    My wife's the lady gay.

'If thou'rt the lord of this castle,
    Sae weel it pleases me,
For, ere I cross the Border fells,
    The tane of us shall die.'   *one*

He took a lang spear in his hand,
    Shod with the metal free,
And for to meet the Douglas there
    He rode right furiouslie.

But O how pale his lady lookd,
    Frae aff the castle-wa,
When down before the Scottish spear
    She saw proud Percy fa.

'Had we twa been upon the green,
    And never an eye to see,
I wad hae had you, flesh and fell;
    But your sword sall gae wi me.'   *shall*

'But gae ye up to Otterbourne,
    And, wait there dayis three,
And, if I come not ere three dayis end,
    A fause knight ca ye me.'

'The Otterbourne's a bonnie burn;
    'Tis pleasant there to be;
But there is nought at Otterbourne
    To feed my men and me.

'The deer rins wild on hill and dale,
    The birds fly wild from tree to tree;
But there is neither bread nor kale   *food*
    To fend my men and me.

'Yet I will stay at Otterbourne,
    Where you shall welcome be;
And, if ye come not at three dayis end,
    A fause lord I'll ca thee.'

'Thither will I come,' proud Percy said,
    'By the might of Our Ladye;'
'There will I bide thee,' said the Douglas,   *wait for*
    'My troth I plight to thee.'

They lighted high on Otterbourne,
    Upon the bent sae brown;   *[coarse grass]*
They lighted high on Otterbourne,
    And threw their pallions down.   *tents*

And he that had a bonnie boy,
    Sent out his horse to grass;
And he that had not a bonnie boy,
    His ain servant he was.

But up then spake a little page,
    Before the peep of dawn:
'O waken ye, waken ye, my good lord,
    For Percy's hard at hand.'

'Ye lie, ye lie, ye liar loud!
    Sae loud I hear ye lie:
For Percy had not men yestreen
    To dight my men and me.   *face*

'But I have dreamd a dreary dream,
    Beyond the Isle of Sky;
I saw a dead man win a fight,
    And I think that man was I.'

He belted on his guid braid sword,
    And to the field he ran,
But he forgot the helmet good,
    That should have kept his brain.

When Percy wi the Douglas met,
   I wat he was fu fain;
They swakked their swords, till sair they swat,
   And the blood ran down like rain.

pleased
struck; sweated

But Percy with his good broad sword,
   That could so sharply wound,
Has wounded Douglas on the brow,
   Till he fell to the ground.

Then he calld on his little foot-page,
   And said, Run speedilie,
And fetch my ain dear sister's son,
   Sir Hugh Montgomery.

'My nephew good,' the Douglas said,
   'What recks the death of ane!
Last night I dreamd a dreary dream,
   And I ken the day's thy ain.

'My wound is deep; I fain would sleep;
   Take thou the vanguard of the three,
And hide me by the braken-bush,
   That grows on yonder lilye lee.

bracken bush
[pretty meadow]

'O bury me by the braken-bush,
   Beneath the blooming brier;
Let never living mortal ken
   That ere a kindly Scot lies here.'

He lifted up that noble lord,
   Wi the saut tear in his ee;
He hid him in the braken-bush,
   That his merrie men might not see.

salt

The moon was clear, the day drew near,
   The spears in flinders flew,
But mony a gallant Englishman
   Ere day the Scotsmen slew.

splinters

The Gordons good, in English blood
   They steepd their hose and shoon;
The Lindsays flew like fire about,
   Till all the fray was done.

The Percy and Montgomery met,
   That either of other were fain;
They swapped swords, and they twa swat,
   And aye the blood ran down between.

each of them eager [to fight] the other
smote

'Now yield thee, yield thee, Percy,' he said.
   'Or else I vow I'll lay thee low!'
'To whom must I yield,' quoth Earl Percy,
   'Now that I see it must be so?'

'Thou shalt not yield to lord nor loun,
   Nor yet shalt thou yield to me;
But yield thee to the braken-bush,
   That grows upon yon lilye lee.'

'I will not yield to a braken-bush,
   Nor yet will I yield to a brier;
But I would yield to Earl Douglas,
   Or Sir Hugh the Montgomery, if he were here.'

As soon as he knew it was Montgomery,
   He struck his sword's point in the gronde;
The Montgomery was a courteous knight,
   And quickly took him by the honde.

This deed was done at the Otterbourne,
   About the breaking of the day;
Earl Douglas was buried at the braken-bush,
   And the Percy led captive away.

Edom O'Gordon

It fell about the Martinmas,
   When the wind blew schrile and cauld,   *shrill*
Said Edom o Gordon to his men,
   'We maun draw to a hald.   *[seek shelter]*

'And what an a hald sall we draw to,
   My merry men and me?
We will gae to the house of the Rhodes,
   To see that fair lady.'

She had nae sooner busket her sell,   *dressed herself*
   Nor putten on her gown,
Till Edom o Gordon and his men
   Were round about the town.

They had nae sooner sitten down,
   Nor sooner said the grace,
Till Edom o Gordon and his men
   Were closed about the place.

The lady ran up to her tower-head,
   As fast as she could drie,   *do*
To see if by her fair speeches
   She could with him agree.

As soon he saw the lady fair,
   And hir yates all locked fast,
He fell into a rage of wrath,
   And his heart was aghast.

'Cum down to me, ye lady fair,
   Cum down to me; let's see;
This night ye's ly by my ain side,
   The morn my bride sall be.'

'I winnae cum down, ye fals Gordon,
    I winnae cum down to thee;
I winnae forsake my ane dear lord,
    That is sae far frae me.'

'Gi up your house, ye fair lady,
    Gi up your house to me,
Or I will burn yoursel therein,   *and also*
    Bot and your babies three.'

'I winnae gie up, you fals Gordon,
    To nae sik traitor as thee,
Tho you should burn mysel therein,
    Bot and my babies three.'

'Set fire to the house,' quoth fals Gordon,
    'Sin better may nae bee;
And I will burn hersel therein,
    Bot and her babies three.'

'And ein wae worth ye, Jock my man!   *[may you be sorry]*
    I paid ye weil your fee;
Why pow ye out my ground-wa-stane,   *pull; foundation-stone*
    Lets in the reek to me?   *smoke*

'And ein wae worth ye, Jock my man!
    For I paid you weil your hire;
Why pow ye out my ground-wa-stane,
    To me lets in the fire?'

'Ye paid me weil my hire, lady,
    Ye paid me weil my fee,
But now I'm Edom of Gordon's man,
    Maun either do or die.'

O then bespake her youngest son,
    Sat on the nurses knee,
'Dear mother, gie owre your house,' he says,
    'For the reek it worries me.'   *smoke*

'I winnae gie up my house, my dear,
    To nae sik traitor as he;
Cum weil, cum wae, my jewels fair,
    Ye maun tak share wi me.'   *must*

O then bespake her dochter dear,
    She was baith jimp and sma;   *slender*
'O row me in a pair o shiets,
    And tow me owre the wa.'

They rowd her in a pair of shiets,
    And towd her owre the wa,
But on the point of Edom's speir
    She got a deadly fa.

O bonny, bonny was hir mouth,
    And chirry were her cheiks,
And clear, clear was hir yellow hair,
    Whereon the reid bluid dreips!

Then wi his speir he turnd hir owr;
    O gin hir face was wan!   *if*
He said, You are the first that eer
    I wist alive again.   *wished*

He turned his owr and owr again;
    O gin hir skin was whyte!
He said, I might ha spard thy life
    To been some mans delyte.

'Busk and boon, my merry men all,   *[get ready]*
    For ill dooms I do guess;
I cannae luik in that bonny face,
    As it lyes on the grass.'

'Them luiks to freits, my master deir,   *frets*
    Then freits will follow them;
Let it neir be said brave Edom o Gordon
    Was daunted with a dame.'

O then he spied hir ain deir lord,
    As he came owr the lee;
He saw his castle in a fire,
    As far as he could see.

'Put on, put on, my mighty men,   *press on*
    As fast as ye can drie!
For he that's hindmost of my men
    Sall neir get guid o me.'

And some they raid, and some they ran,
    Fu fast out-owr the plain,
But lang, lang eer he coud get up
    They were a' deid and slain.

But mony were the mudie men   *bold*
    Lay gasping on the grien;
For o fifty men that Edom brought out
    There were but five ged heme.

And mony were the mudie men
    Lay gasping on the grien,
And mony were the fair ladys
    Lay lemanless at heme.   *loverless*

And round and round the waes he went,   *walls*
    Their ashes for to view;
At last into the flames he flew,
    And bad the world adieu.

The Wife of Usher's Well

There lived a wife at Usher's Well,
    And a wealthy wife was she;
She had three stout and stalwart sons,
    And sent them oer the sea.

They hadna been a week from her,
   A week but barely ane,
Whan word came to the carline wife   *old*
   That her three sons were gane.

They hadna been a week from her,
   A week but barely three,
Whan word came to the carlin wife
   That her sons she'd never see.

'I wish the wind may never cease,
   Nor fashes in the flood,   *troubles*
Till my three sons come hame to me,
   In earthly flesh and blood.'

It fell about the Martinmass,
   When nights are lang and mirk,   *dark*
The carlin wife's three sons came hame,
   And their hats were o the birk.   *birch*

It neither grew in syke nor ditch,   *rill*
   Nor yet in ony sheugh;   *hollow*
But at the gates o Paradise.
   That birk grew fair eneugh.

      *   *   *

'Blow up the fire, my maidens,
   Bring water from the well;
For a' my house shall feast this night,
   Since my three sons are weil'

And she has made to them a bed,
   She's made it large and wide,
And she's taen her mantle her about,
   Sat down at the bed-side.

      *   *   *

Up then crew the red, red cock,
    And up and crew the gray;
The eldest to the youngest said,
    'Tis time we were away.

The cock he hadna crawd but once,
    And clappd his wings at a',
When the youngest to the eldest said,
    Brother, we must awa.

'The cock doth craw, the day doth daw,
    The channerin worm doth chide;   *grumbling*
Gin we be mist out o our place,
    A sair pain we maun bide.   *must*

'Fare ye weel, my mother dear!
    Fareweel to barn and byre!
And fare ye weel, the bonny lass
    That kindles my mother's fire!'

The Great Silkie of Sule Skerry   *seal*

I am a man, upo da land,   *the*
    I am a selkie i da sea;
An whin I'm far fa every strand
    My dwelling is in Shöol Skerry.

An eartly nourris sits and sings,   *nurse*
    And aye she sings, Ba, lily wean!   *pretty child*
Little ken I my bairnis father,
    Far less the land that he staps in.

Then ane arose at her bed-fit,   *[the foot of her bed]*
    An a grumly guest I'm sure was he: *sullen*
'Here am I, thy bairnis father,
    Although that I be not comelie.

'I am a man, upo the lan,
   An I am a silkie in the sea;
And when I'm far and far frae lan,
   My dwelling is in Sule Skerrie.'

'It was na weel,' quo the maiden fair,
   'It was na weel, indeed,' quo she,
'That the Great Silkie of Sule Skerrie
   Suld hae come and aught a bairn to me.' *given*

Now he has taen a purse of goud, *gold*
   And he has pat it upo her knee,
Sayin, Gie to me my little young son,
   An tak thee up thy nourris-fee. *nurse's wages*

An it sall come to pass on a simmer's day,
   When the sin shines het on evera stane,
That I will tak my little young son,
   An teach him for to swim the faem. *foam*

An thu sall marry a proud gunner,
   An a proud gunner I'm sure he'll be,
An the very first schot that ere he schoots, *ever*
   He'll schoot baith my young son and me.

Get Up and Bar the Door

It fell about the Martinmas time,
   And a gay time it was then,
When our goodwife got puddings to make,
   And she's boil'd them in the pan.

The wind sae cauld blew south and north,
   And blew into the floor:
Quoth our goodman, to our goodwife,
   'Gae out and bar the door.'

'My hand is in my hussy'f skap,   *housewifery*
    Goodman, as ye may see,
An it shou'd nae be barr'd this hundred year,   *if*
    It's no be barr'd for me.'

They made a paction 'tween them twa,
    They made it firm and sure;
That the first word whae'er shou'd speak,
    Shou'd rise and bar the door.

Then by there came two gentlemen,
    At twelve o'clock at night,
And they could neither see house nor hall,
    Nor coal nor candle light.

'Now, whether is this a rich man's house,
    Or whether is it a poor?'
But ne'er a word wad ane o'them speak,
    For barring of the door.

And first they ate the white puddings,
    And then they ate the black;
Tho' muckle thought the goodwife to hersel,
    Yet ne'er a word she spake.

Then said the one unto the other,
    'Here, man, tak ye my knife,
Do ye tak aff the auld man's beard,
    And I'll kiss the goodwife.'

'But there's nae water in the house,
    And what shall we do than?'
'What ails ye at the pudding broo,   *water*
    That boils into the pan?'

O up then started our goodman,
    An angry man was he;
'Will ye kiss my wife before my een,
    And scad me wi' pudding bree?'   *scald*

Then up and started our goodwife,
   Gied three skips on the floor;
'Goodman, you've spoken the foremost word,
   Get up and bar the door.'

Clerk Saunders

Clerk Saunders and may Margaret   *maid*
   Walked ower yon garden green;
And sad and heavy was the love
   That fell thir twa between.   *these*

'A bed, a bed,' Clerk Saunders said,
   'A bed for you and me!'
'Fye na, fye na,' said may Margaret,
   'Till anes we married be.   *once*

'For in may come my seven bauld brothers,
   Wi' torches burning bright;
They'll say – "We hae but ae sister,
   And behold she's wi' a knight!"'

'Then take the sword frae my scabbard,
   And slowly lift the pin;   *latch*
And you may swear, and safe your aith,
   Ye never let Clerk Saunders in.

'And take a napkin in your hand,
   And tie up baith your bonny een;   *eyes*
And you may swear, and safe your aith,
   Ye saw me na since late yestreen.'

It was about the midnight hour,
   When they asleep were laid,
When in and came her seven brothers,
   Wi' torches burning red.

When in and came her seven brothers,
  Wi' torches burning bright;
They said, 'We hae but ae sister,
  And behold her lying with a knight!'

Then out and spake the first o' them,
  'I bear the sword shall gar him die!'   *make*
And out and spake the second o' them,
  'His father has nae mair than he!'

And out and spake the third o' them,
  'I wot that they are lovers dear!'
And out and spake the fourth o' them,
  'They hae been in love this mony a year!'

Then out and spake the fifth o' them,
  'It were great sin true love to twain!'
And out and spake the sixth o' them,
  'It were shame to slay a sleeping man!'

Then up and gat the seventh o' them,
  And never a word spake he;
But he has striped his bright brown brand   *thrust*
  Out through Clerk Saunders' fair bodye.

Clerk Saunders he started, and Margaret she turn'd
  Into his arms as asleep she lay;
And sad and silent was the night
  That was atween thir twae.

And they lay still and sleeped sound,
  Until the day began to daw;
And kindly to him she did say,
  'It is time, true love, you were awa.'

But he lay still, and sleeped sound,
  Albeit the sun began to sheen;
She looked atween her and the wa',
  And dull and drowsie were his een.

Then in and came her father dear,
    Said – 'Let a' your mourning be:
I'll carry the dead corpse to the clay,
    And I'll come back and comfort thee.'

'Comfort weel your seven sons,
    For comforted will I never be:
I ween 'twas neither knave nor loon   *[low-born boy]*
    Was in the bower last night wi' me.'

The clinking bell gaed through the town,
    To carry the dead corse to the clay;
And Clerk Saunders stood at may Margaret's window,
    I wot, an hour before the day.

'Are ye sleeping, Margaret?' he says,
    'Or are ye waking presentlie?
Give me my faith and troth again,
    I wot, true love, I gied to thee.'

'Your faith and troth ye sall never get,
    Nor our true love sall never twin,
Until ye come within my bower,
    And kiss me cheik and chin.'

'My mouth it is full cold, Margaret,
    It has the smell, now, of the ground;
And if I kiss thy comely mouth,
    Thy days of life will not be lang.

'O, cocks are crowing a merry midnight,
    I wot the wild fowls are boding day;
Give me my faith and troth again,
    And let me fare me on my way.'

'Thy faith and troth thou sall na get,
    And our true love sall never twin,
Until ye tell what comes of women,
    I wot, who die in strong traivelling?'   *suffering*

'Their beds are made in the heavens high,
　　Down at the foot of our good Lord's knee,
Weel set about wi' gillyflowers;
　　I wot sweet company for to see.

'O cocks are crowing a merry midnight,
　　I wot the wild fowl are boding day;
The psalms of heaven will soon be sung,
　　And I, ere now, will be miss'd away.'

Then she has ta'en a crystal wand,
　　And she has stroken her troth thereon;　　　　　　*struck*
She has given it him out at the shot-window,　　　　*hinged window*
　　Wi' mony a sad sigh, and heavy groan.

'I thank ye, Marg'ret; I thank ye, Marg'ret;
　　And aye I thank ye heartilie;
Gin ever the dead come for the quick,　　　　　　　　*if*
　　Be sure, Marg'ret, I'll come for thee.'

In hosen and shoon, and gown alone,　　　　　　　　*shoes*
　　She climb'd the wall, and follow'd him,
Until she came to the green forest,
　　And there she lost the sight o' him.

'Is there ony room at your head, Saunders?
　　Is there ony room at your feet?
Or ony room at your side, Saunders,
　　Where fain, fain, I wad sleep?'

'There's nae room at my head, Marg'ret,
　　There's nae room at my feet;
My bed it is full lowly now:
　　Amang the hungry worms I sleep.

'Cauld mould is my covering now,
　　But and my winding-sheet;　　　　　　　　　　　*and also*
The dew it falls nae sooner down,
　　Than my resting place is weet.

'But plait a wand o' bonnie birk,   *birch*
 And lay it on my breast;
And shed a tear upon my grave,
 And wish my saul gude rest.

'And fair Marg'ret, and rare Marg'ret,
 And Marg'ret o' veritie,   *truth*
Gin e'er ye love another man,
 Ne'er love him as ye did me.'

Then up and crew the milk-white cock,
 And up and crew the grey;
Her lover vanish'd in the air,
 And she gaed weeping away.

Thomas Rymer

True Thomas lay on Huntlie bank,
 A ferlie he spied wi' his ee.   *marvel*
And there he saw a lady bright,
 Come riding down by the Eildon Tree.

Her shirt was o the grass-green silk,
 Her mantle o the velvet fyne,
At ilka tett of her horse's mane   *every strand*
 Hang fifty siller bells and nine.

True Thomas, he pulld aff his cap,
 And louted low down to his knee: *bent*
'All hail, thou mighty Queen of Heaven!
 For thy peer on earth I never did see.'

'O no, O no, Thomas,' she said,
 'That name does not belang to me;
I am but the queen of fair Elfland,
 That am hither come to visit thee.

'Harp and carp, Thomas,' she said,   *play and sing*
   'Harp and carp along wi me,
And if ye dare to kiss my lips,
   Sure of your bodie I will be.'

'Betide me weal, betide me woe,
   That weird shall never daunton me;'   *fate*
Syne he has kissed her rosy lips,
   All underneath the Eildon Tree.

'Now, ye maun go wi me,' she said,   *must*
   'True Thomas, ye maun go wi me,
And ye maun serve me seven years,
   Thro weal or woe, as may chance to be.'

She mounted on her milk-white steed,
   She's taen True Thomas up behind,
And aye wheneer her bridle rung,
   The steed flew swifter than the wind.

O they rade on, and farther on –
   The steed gaed swifter than the wind –
Untill they reached a desart wide,
   And living land was left behind.

'Light down, light down, now, True Thomas,
   And lean your head upon my knee;
Abide and rest a little space,
   And I will shew you ferlies three.   *wonders*

'O see ye not yon narrow road,
   So thick beset with thorns and briers?
That is the path of righteousness,
   Tho after it but few enquires.

'And see not ye that braid braid road,
   That lies across that lily leven?   *meadow*
That is the path of wickedness,
   Tho some call it the road to heaven.

'And see not ye that bonny road,
  That winds about the fernie brae?
That is the road to fair Elfland,
  Where thou and I this night maun gae.

'But, Thomas, ye maun hold your tongue,
  Whatever ye may hear or see,
For, if you speak word in Elflyn land,
  Ye 'll neer get back to your ain countrie.'

O they rade on, and farther on,
  And they waded thro rivers aboon the knee,
And they saw neither sun nor moon,
  But they heard the roaring of the sea.

It was mirk mirk night, and there was nae stern light,   *dark; star*
  And they waded thro red blude to the knee;
For a' the blude that's shed on earth
  Rins thro the springs o that countrie.

Syne they came on to a garden green,
  And she pu'd an apple frae a tree:
'Take this for thy wages, True Thomas,
  It will give the tongue that can never lie.'

'My tongue is mine ain,' True Thomas said;
  'A gudely gift ye wad gie to me!
I neither dought to buy nor sell,   *fear*
  At fair or tryst where I may be.

'I dought neither speak to prince or peer,
  Nor ask of grace from fair ladye:'
'Now hold thy peace,' the lady said,
  'For as I say, so must it be.'

He has gotten a coat of the even cloth,
  And a pair of shoes of velvet green,
And till seven years were gane and past
  True Thomas on earth was never seen.

The Wee Cooper of Fife

There was a wee cooper who lived in Fife,
   Nickity, nackity, noo, noo, noo,
And he has gotten a gentle wife.
   Hey Willie Wallacky, how John Dougall,
   Alane, quo Rushety, roue, roue, roue.

She wadna bake, nor she wadna brew,
For the spoiling o her comely hue.

She wadna card, nor she wadna spin,   *weave*
For the shaming o her gentle kin.

She wadna wash, nor she wadna wring,
For the spoiling o her gouden ring.

The cooper's awa to his woo-pack   *woolpack*
And has laid a sheep-skin on his wife's back.

'It's I'll no thrash ye, for your proud kin,
But I will thrash my ain sheep-skin.'

'Oh, I will bake, and I will brew,
And never mair think on my comely hue.

'Oh, I will card, and I will spin,
And never mair think on my gentle kin.

'Oh, I will wash, and I will wring,
And never mair think on my gouden ring.'

A' ye wha hae gotten a gentle wife
Send ye for the wee cooper o Fife.

Mary Hamilton

Word's gane to the kitchen,
    And word's gane to the ha,
That Marie Hamilton gangs wi bairn   *carries the child*
    To the hichest Stewart of a'.

He's courted her in the kitchen,
    He's courted her in the ha,
He's courted her in the laigh cellar,   *low*
    And that was warst of a'.

She's tyed it in her apron
    And she 's thrown it in the sea:
Says, Sink ye, swim ye, bonny wee babe!
    You'l neer get mair o me.

Down then cam the auld queen,
    Goud tassels tying her hair: *gold*
'O Marie, where's the bonny wee babe
    That I heard greet sae sair?'

'There never was a babe intill my room,
    As little designs to be;
It was but a touch o my sair side,
    Come oer my fair bodie.'

'O Marie, put on your robes o black,
    Or else your robes o brown,
For ye maun gang wi me the night,   *must*
    To see fair Edinbro town.'

'I winna put on my robes o black,
    Nor yet my robes o brown;
But I'll put on my robes o white,
    To shine through Edinbro town.'

When she gaed up the Cannogate,
    She laughd loud laughters three;
But whan she cam down the Cannogate
    The tear blinded her ee.

When she gaed up the Parliament stair,
    The heel cam aff her shee;   *shoe*
And lang or she cam down again   *before*
    She was condemnd to dee.   *die*

When she cam down the Cannogate,
    The Cannogate sae free,
Many a ladie lookd oer her window,
    Weeping for this ladie.

'Ye need nae weep for me,' she says,
    'Ye need nae weep for me;
For had I not slain mine own sweet babe,
    This death I wadna dee.

'Bring me a bottle of wine,' she says,
    'The best that eer ye hae,
That I may drink to my weil-wishers,
    And they may drink to me.

'Here's a health to the jolly sailors,
    That sail upon the main;
Let them never let on to my father and mother
    But what I'm coming hame.

'Here's a health to the jolly sailors,
    That sail upon the sea;
Let them never let on to my father and mother
    That I cam here to dee.

'Oh little did my mother think,
    The day she cradled me,
What lands I was to travel through,
    What death I was to dee.

'Oh little did my father think,
     The day he held up me,
What lands I was to travel through,
     What death I was to dee.

'Last night I washd the queen's feet,
     And gently laid her down;
And a' the thanks I've gotten the nicht
     To be hangd in Edinbro town!

'Last nicht there was four Maries,
     The nicht there'll be but three;
There was Marie Seton, and Marie Beton,
     And Marie Carmichael, and me.'

Bonny Barbara Allan

It was in and about the Martinmas time,
     When the green leaves were a falling,
That Sir John Graeme, in the West Country,
     Fell in love with Barbara Allan.

He sent his men down through the town,
     To the place where she was dwelling:
'O haste and come to my master dear,
     Gin ye be Barbara Allan.'   *if*

O hooly, hooly rose she up,   *slowly*
     To the place where he was lying,
And when she drew the curtain by,
     'Young man, I think you're dying.'

'O it's I'm sick, and very, very sick,
     And 'tis a' for Barbara Allan:'
'O the better for me ye's never be,
     Tho your heart's blood were a spilling.

'O dinna ye mind, young man,' said she,
   'When ye was in the tavern a drinking,
That ye made the healths gae round and round,
   And slighted Barbara Allan?'

He turnd his face unto the wall,
   And death was with him dealing:
'Adieu, adieu, my dear friends all,
   And be kind to Barbara Allan.'

And slowly, slowly raise she up,
   And slowly, slowly left him,
And sighing said, she coud not stay,
   Since death of life had reft him.   *stolen*

She had not gane a mile but twa,
   When she heard the dead-bell ringing,
And every jow that the dead-bell geid,   *toll*
   It cry'd, Woe to Barbara Allan!

'O mother, mother, make my bed!
   O make it saft and narrow!
Since my love died for me to-day,
   I'll die for him to-morrow.'

The Twa Corbies

As I was walking all alane,
I heard twa corbies making a mane;   *moan*
The tane unto the t'other say,
'Where sall we gang and dine to-day?'

'In behint yon auld fail dyke,   *turf-wall*
I wot there lies a new slain knight;
And naebody kens that he lies there,
But his hawk, his hound, and lady fair.

'His hound is to the hunting gane,
His hawk to fetch the wild-fowl hame,
His lady's ta'en another mate,
So we may mak our dinner sweet.

'Ye'll sit on his white hause-bane,   *collar-bone*
And I'll pike out his bonny blue een;
Wi ae lock o his gowden hair   *golden*
We'll theek our nest when it grows bare.   *thatch*

'Mony a one for him makes mane,
But nane sall ken where he is gane;   *shall know*
Oer his white banes, when they are bare,
The wind sall blaw for evermair.'

ANON. from *The Bannatyne Manuscript, writtin in tyme of pest (1568)*

How the first Helandman of god was maid of Ane hors turd in argylle as is said

God and sanct petir was gangand be the way	
Heiche vp in ardgyle quhair thair gait lay	*Argyll; [where their direction led them]*
Sanct petir said to god in a sport word	
Can ye not mak a heilandman of this hors tourd	
God turnd owre the hors turd with his pykit staff	*[walking-staff]*
And vp start a helandman blak as ony draff	*brewer's grain*
Qwod god to the helandman quhair wilt thow now	*said*
I will doun in the lawland lord / and thair steill a kow	
And thow steill A cow cairle thair thay will hang the	*churl*
Quattrack lord of that ffor anis mon I die	*what harm; once; must*
God than he lewch and owre the dyk lap	*laughed; leapt*
and owt of his scheith his gowlly owtgatt	*sheath; knife*
Sanct petir socht this gowly fast vp & doun	
yit cowld not find it in all that braid rownn	*space*
Now qwod god heir a marvell how can this be	*said*
That I sowld want my gowly And we heir bot thre	*should*
Humff qwod the helandman and turnd him abowt	
And at his plaid nuk the guly fell owt	*from the fold of his plaid*
Ffy qwod sanct petir thow will nevir do weill	*Fie*
And thow bot new maid sa sone gais to steill	*[newly made so soon goes]*
Vmff qwod the helandman & swere be yon kirk	*[I swear by yon Kirk]*
Sa lang as I may geir gett to steill / will I nevir wirk	*things*

WILLIAM DRUMMOND OF HAWTHORNDEN
(1585–1649)

Sonnet

Sleepe, Silence Child, sweet Father of soft Rest,
Prince whose Approach Peace to all Mortalls brings,
Indifferent Host to Shepheards and to Kings,
Sole Comforter of Minds with Griefe opprest.
Loe, by thy charming Rod all breathing things
Lie slumbring, with forgetfulnesse possest,
And yet o're me to spred thy drowsie Wings
Thou spares (alas) who cannot be thy Guest.
Since I am thine, O come, but with that Face
To inward Light which thou art wont to show,
With fained Solace ease a true felt Woe,
Or if deafe God thou doe denie that Grace,
    Come as thou wilt, and what thou wilt bequeath,
    I long to kisse the Image of my Death.

The Angels for the Natiuitie of our Lord

Rvnne (Sheepheards) run where Bethleme blest appeares,
Wee bring the best of newes, bee not dismay'd,
A Sauiour there is borne, more olde than yeares,
Admidst Heauens rolling hights this Earth who stay'd;
In a poore Cotage Inn'd, a Virgine Maide
A weakling did him beare, who all vpbeares,
There is hee poorelie swadl'd, in Manger lai'd,
To whom too narrow Swadlings are our Spheares:
Runne (Sheepheards) runne, and solemnize his Birth,
This is that Night, no, Day growne great with Blisse,
In which the power of Sathan broken is,
In Heauen bee glorie, Peace vnto the Earth.
    Thus singing through the Aire the Angels swame,
    And Cope of Starres re-echoed the same.

The Oister

With open shells in seas, on heauenly due
A shining oister lushiouslie doth feed,
And then the Birth of that ætheriall seed
Shows, when conceau'd, if skies lookt darke or blew:
Soe doe my thoughts (celestiall twins) of you,
At whose aspect they first beginne & breed,
When they are borne to light demonstrat true,
If yee then smyld, or lowr'd in murning weed.
Pearles then are framd orient, faire in forme,
In their conception if the heauens looke cleare;
But if it thunder, or menace a storme,
They sadlie darke and wannish doe appeare:
    Right so my thoughts are, so my notes do change,
    Sweet if yee smyle, & hoarse if yee looke strange.

All Changeth

The angrye winds not ay
Doe cuffe the roring deep,
And though Heauens often weep
Yet doe they smyle for joy when com'd is May,
Frosts doe not euer kill the pleasant flowres,
And loue hath sweets when gone are all the sowres.
This said a shepheard closing in his armes
His Deare, who blusht to feele loues new alarmes.

Polemo-Middinia inter Vitarvam et Nebernam

Nymphae quae colitis highissima monta *Fifaea*,
Seu vos *Pittenwema* tenent seu *Crelia* crofta,
Sive *Anstraea* domus, ubi nat haddocus in undis,
Codlineusque ingens, & fleucca & sketta pererrant
Per costam, et scopulis lobster mony-footus in udis
Creepat, & in mediis ludit whitenius undis;
Et vos skipperii, soliti qui per mare breddum
Valde procul lanchare foris, iterumque redire,
Linquite scellatas bottas shippasque picatas,
Whistlantesque simul fechtam memorate bloodaeam,
Fechtam terribilem, quam marvellaverit omnis
Banda Deum, & Nympharum Cockelshelleatarum,
Maia ubi sheepifeda atque ubi solgoosifera *Bassa*
Suellant in pelago, cum Sol boottatus *Edenum*
Postabat radiis madidis & shouribus atris.
Quo viso, ad fechtae noisam cecidere volucres,
Ad terram cecidere grues, plish plashque dedere
Sol-goosi in pelago prope littora *Bruntiliana*;
Sea-sutor obstupuit, summique in margine saxi
Scartavit praelustre caput, wingasque flapavit;
Quodque magis, alte volitans heronius ipse
Ingeminans clig clag shyttavit in undis.
Namque in principio (storiam tellabimus omnem)
Muckrellium ingentem turbam *Vitarva* per agros
Nebernae marchare fecit, & dixit ad illos:
Ite hodie armati greppis, dryvate caballos
Crofta per & agros *Nebernae*, transque fenestras:
Quod si forte ipsa *Neberna* venerit extra,
Warrantabo omnes, & vos bene defendebo.
Hic aderant *Geordie Akinhedius*, & little *Johnus*,
Et *Jamie Richaeus*, & stout *Michael Hendersonus*,
Qui jolly tryppas ante alios dansare solebat,
Et bobbare bene, & lassas kissare bonaeas;
Duncan Oliphantus valde stalvartus, & ejus
Filius eldestus joly boyus, atque *Oldmoudus*,
Qui pleugham longo gaddo dryvare solebat,
Et *Rob Gib* wantonus homo, atque *Oliver Hutchin*,

The Midden-Battle between Lady Scotstarvit and the Mistress of Newbarns

Ye nymphs who cultivate the highest mountains of Fife,
Or if you hold farms at Pittenween or at Crail,
Or have your home at Anstruther, where the haddock swims in the waves,
And the huge codling, and the fluke and skate wander
Along the coast, and in the rocks the many-footed lobster in the wet
Creeps, and in the midst of the waves the whiting plays;
And ye skippers, who are accustomed through the broad sea
Very far away to launch forth, and to come back again,
Leave your shell-like boats and ships covered with pitch,
And whistling at the same time call to mind the bloody fight,
The terrible fight, at which will marvel all
The band of the Gods, and of the nymphs of the cockleshells,
Where the sheep-feeding Isle of May and where the solan-goose-bearing Bass Rock
Rise in the sea at the same time that the Sun in boots to Edinburgh
Was sending wet rays and stormy showers.
At which sight, at the noise of the fight birds fell,
To earth fell cranes, and 'plish plash' solan geese
Gave themselves up in the sea near the shore of Burntisland;
The cormorant was stupified, and on the edge of the highest rock
Scratched his very illustrious head, and flapped his wings;
And something more: the heron itself flying high
Increasingly shat 'clig clag' into the waves.
For in the beginning (we shall tell the whole story)
The lady of Scotstarvit made a large disorderly crowd of dungbasket carriers
To march through the fields of Newbarns, and she said to them:
'Today go armed with pronged forks, drive horses
Through the farm and fields of Newbarns, and past the windows:
But if by chance the lady of Newbarns herself will come outside,
I warrant you all, and I will protect you well.'
Here were present Geordie Akinhead, and little John,
And Jamie Richy, and stout Michael Henderson,
Who was accustomed to dance jolly capers before the others,
And to bob up and down well, and to kiss the bonny lasses;
Duncan Oliphant very stalwart, and his
Eldest son, a jolly boy, and also Oldmouth [sagacious in speech],
Who the plough was accustomed to drive with a long stick,
And Rob Gib, the wanton fellow, and also Oliver Hutchin,

Et plouky-fac'd Wattis Stranq, atque inkne'd Alshinder Atkin,
Et *Willie Dick* heavi-arstus homo, pigerrimus omnium,
Valde lethus pugnare, sed hunc Corn-greivus heros
Nout-headdum vocavit, & illum forcit ad arma.
In super hic aderant *Tom Tailor & Tom Nicolsonus,*
Et *Tamie Gilchristus,* & fool *Jockie Robinsonus,*
Andrew Alshinderus, & *Jamie Thomsonus,* & alter
(Heu pudet, ignoro nomen) slaveri-beardus homo,
Qui pottas dightabat, & assam jecerat extra.
Denique prae reliquis *Geordium* affatur, & inquit,
Geordie, mi formanne, inter stoutissimus omnes,
Huc ades, & crooksaddeliis, heghemisque, creilisque,
Brechimmisque simul cunctos armato jumentos;
Amblentemque meam naiggam, fattumque magistri
Curserem, & reliquos trottantes simul averos,
In cartis yockato omnes, extrahito muckam
Crofta per & agros *Nebernae* transque fenestras,
Quod si forte ipsa *Neberna* contra loquatur,
In sidis tu pone manus, et dicito, *fart, iade.*
Nec mora, formannus cunctos flankavit averos,
Workmannosque ad workam omnes vocavit, & illi
Extemplo cartas bene fillavere gigantes:
Whistlavere viri, workhorsosque ordine swieros
Drivavere omnes, donec iterumque iterumque
Fartavere omnes, & sic turba horrida mustrat,
Haud aliter quam si cum multis *Spinola* trouppis
Proudus ad *Ostendam* marchasset fortiter urbem.
Interea ipse ante alios piperlaius heros
Praecedens, magnam gestans cum burdine pyppam,
Incipit *Harlaei* cunctis sonare Batellum.
Tunc *Neberna* furens, foras ipsa egressa vidensque
Muck-creilleos transire viam, valde angria facta,
Haud tulit affrontam tantam, verum, agmine facto
Convocat extemplo horsboyos atque ladaeos,
Jackmannum, hyremannos, pleughdryv'sters atque pleughmannos,
Tumblentesque simul ricoso ex kitchine boyos,
Hunc qui gruelias scivit bene lickere plettas,
Hunc qui dirtiferas tersit cum dishcloute dishas;
Et saltpannifumos, & widebricatos fisheros,
Hellaeosque etiam salteros eduxit ab antris
Coalheughos nigri grinnantes more divelli;

And pimply-faced Wattie Strang, and knock-kneed Alexander Atkin,
And Willie Dick, the heavy-arsed man, the laziest of all,
Very loath to fight, but this foreman hero
Called him a blockhead, and forced him to fight.
In addition here were Tom Tailor and Tom Nicolson,
And Tamie Gilchrist, and the fool Jockie Robinson,
Andrew Alexander, and Jamie Thomson, and another
(Alas, it is a shame, I do not know his name) slobbery-bearded man,
Who wiped the pots, and threw out the ashes.
At last in front of the rest Geordie is spoken to, and she says,
'Geordie, my foreman, the stoutest of all,
Come hither, and with crook-saddles, and hames, and creels,
And horse-collars, and at the same time prepare all the beasts of burden for battle;
And my ambling nag, and the master's fat
Racer, and at the same time, the remaining trotting cart-horses;
To carts harness them all, draw out the dung
Through the farms and fields of Newbarns and past the windows;
But if by chance the lady of Newbarns herself speaks against it,
You place your hand on your hip and say, "Fart, you jade!"'
Without delay, the foreman harnessed all of the cart-horses
And called all of the workmen to work, and they
Immediately filled well the gigantic carts;
The men whistled, and with the lazy workhorses set in order
They drove off all of them, until again and again
They all farted, and such a terrible uproar is displayed,
Exactly as if Spinola with many troops
The proud man marched bravely to the city of Ostend.
Meanwhile, the same bagpiping hero before the others
Went ahead, carrying as a burden the great pipes,
He began to play the 'Battle of Harlaw', for everyone.
Then the lady of Newbarns, raging, and having come out herself, seeing
The dung baskets cross the road, became very angry;
Not at all did she tolerate so great an affront; in truth, she a throng does
Call together immediately of horseboys and laddies [servants],
The retainer, hired men, plough drivers and ploughmen,
And at the same time boys tumbling out of the smoky kitchen,
This one who knew well how to lick gruel from the plates,
That one who wiped off the dirty dishes with a dishtowel;
And smoky salt-panners, and wide-breeked fishermen,
And hellions once saltmen she led out from caves,
Coalhewers grinning in the way of the wicked devil;

Life-guardamque sibi saevas vocat improba lassas
Magaeam magis doctam milkare cowaeas,
Et doctam sweeppare fleuras, & sternere beddas,
Quaeque novit spinare, & longas ducere threedas;
Nansaeam claves bene quae keepaverate omnes,
Yellantemque *Elpen*, & longo bardo *Anapellam*,
Fartantemque simul *Gyllam*, gliedamque *Ketaeam*
Egregie indutam blacco caput suttie clutto,
Mammaeamque etiam vetulam, quae sciverat aptè
Infantum teneras blande oscularier arsas,
Quaeque lanam cardare solet olifingria *Beattie*.
Tum vero hungraeos ventres *Neberna* gruelis
Farsit, & guttas rasuinibus implet amaris,
Postea newbarmae ingentem dedit omnibus haustum:
Staggravere omnes, grandesque ad sidera riftos
Barmifumi attollunt, & sic ad praelia marchant.
Nec mora, marchavit foras longo ordine turma,
Ipsa prior *Neberna* suis stout facta ribauldis,
Roustaeam manibus gestans furibunda goulaeam,
Tandem muckcreilios vocat ad pellmellia fleidos.
Ite, ait, uglei felloes, si quis modo posthac
Muckifer has nostras tenet crossare fenestras,
Juro ego quod ejus longum extrahabo thrapellum,
Et totam rivabo faciem, luggasque gulaeo hoc
Ex capite cuttabo ferox, totumque videbo
Heart-blooddum fluere in terram. Sic verba finivit.
Obstupuit *Vitarva* diu dirtfleyda, sed inde
Couragium accipiens, muckcreilleos ordine cunctos
Middini in medio faciem turnare coegit.
O qualem primo fleuram gustasses in ipso
Batalli onsetto! pugnat muckcreillius heros
Fortiter, & muckam per posteriora cadentem
In creillis shoollare ardet: sic dirta volavit.
O qualis feire fairie fuit, si forte vidisses
Pypantes arsas, & flavo sanguine breickas
Dripantes, hominumque heartas ad praelia fantas!
O qualis hurlie burlie fuit! namque alteri nemo
Ne vel foot-breddum yerdae yeeldare volebat:
Stout erant ambo quidem, valdeque hard-hearta caterva.
Tum vero è medio mukdryv'ster prosilit unus,
Gallantaeus homo, & greppam minatur in ipsam

And she boldly calls to her the lifeguard and the wild girls:
Maggie who was well instructed to milk the cows,
And taught to sweep the floors and make the beds,
And who knew how to spin and draw out long threads;
Nancy who had kept all the keys well,
And yelling Elpen, and Anabel, with the long beard [?],
And quick-farting Gill, and squint-eyed Katie
Excellently dressed with her black head in a sooty rag,
And Mammie, already somewhat old, who had known appropriately
How to kiss tenderly the soft arses of children,
As well as greasy-fingered Bettie who is used to carding the wool.
Then indeed the hungry bellies the lady of Newbarns with gruel
Stuffed full and filled up their guts with bitter [unripe] grapes,
Afterwards, she gave to all a huge draught of new beer:
All of them were staggered, and great belches to the stars
They sent up, inflamed with beer, and so they march to battle.
Without delay, the throng marched forth in a long line,
The lady of Newbarns herself first, strengthened by her clowns,
Carrying furiously in her hands a rusty gully [large knife],
At last she calls to the dungbasketers who were frightened and in utter confusion
'Go,' she says, 'You ugly fellows. If in the future
Any dungcarrier even tries to cross past our windows,
I swear that I shall cut out his long throat
And tear up his whole face, and his ears with this gully
I shall cut ferociously from his head, and I shall see all
Of his heart's blood flow into the earth.' So she finished speaking.
The lady of Scotstarvit was stupified and frightened shitless for a long while, but
Taking courage, the whole of the dungcarts in line
In the middle of the dung heap she forced to turn in a fashion.
O what a smell you would have experienced in the very first
Onset of battle! The dungbasket hero fights
Bravely, and falling dung next in order
He is eager to shovel in basketfuls; so the shit flew.
O what an angry tumult there was! If by chance you had seen
The piping arses, and the breeks with yellow blood
Dripping, and the faint hearts of men in the fight!
O what a hurly burly there was! For no one or other
Was willing to yield a single footbreadth of ground;
Both sides indeed were stout, and very hard-hearted troops.
Then in truth out of the midst springs one muckdriver,
A gallant man, and threatens with his pitchfork

Nebernam, quoniam misere scaldaverat omnes,
Dirtavitque totam petticottam gutture thicko,
Perlineasque ejus skirtas, silkamque gownaeam,
Vasquineamque rubram mucksherdo begariavit.
Sed tamen ille fuit valde faint-heartus, & ivit
Valde procul, metuens shottum woundumque profundum;
At non valde procul fuerat revengda, sed illum
Extemplo *Gyllaea* ferox invasit, & ejus
In faciem girnavit atrox, & tigrida facta,
Bublentem grippans bardum, sic dixit ad illum:
Vade domum, filthaea nequam, aut te interficiabo.
Tum cum Herculeo magnum fecit Gilliwyppum,
Ingentemque manu sherdam levavit, & omnem
Gallentey hominis gash-beardum besmiriavit.
Sume tibi hoc (inquit) sneezing valde operativum
Pro praemio, swingere, tuo. Tum denique fleido
Ingentem Gilliwamphra dedit, validamque nevellam,
Ingeminatque iterum, donec bis fecerit ignem
Ambobus fugere ex oculis: sic *Gylla* triumphat.
Obstupuit bumbasedus homo, backumque repente
Turnavit veluti nasus bloodasset, & *O fy!*
Ter quater exclamat, & O quam saepe nizavit!
Disjuniumque omnem evomuit valde hungrius homo
Lausavitque supra & infra, miserabile visu,
Et luggas necko imponens, sic cucurrit absens,
Non audens gimpare iterum, ne worsa tulisset.
Haec *Vitarva* videns, yellavit turpia verba,
Et *fy, fy!* exclamat, prope nunc victoria losta est.
Elatisque hippis magno cum murmure fartum
Barytonum emisit, veluti Monsmegga cracasset:
Tum vero quaccare hostes, flightamque repente
Sumpserunt, retrospexit *Jackmannus*, & ipse
Sheepheadus metuit sonitumque ictumque buleti.
Quod si King Spanius, *Philippus* nomine, septem
Consimiles hisce habuisset forte canones
Batterare *Sluissam*, *Sluissam* dingasset in assam;
Aut si tot magnus *Ludovicus* forte dedisset
Ingentes fartas ad moenia *Montalbana*,
Ipsam continuo tounam dingasset in yerdam.
Exit Corngreivus, wracco omnia tendere videns,
Consiliumque meum si non accipitis, inquit,

The lady of Newbarns herself, since she had scolded all of them violently,
And he soiled all of her petticoat with thick mud,
And her skirts trimmed with perlin [lace], and her silk gown,
And her red petticoat was bespattered with pieces of cow dung.
But for all that he was very faint-hearted, and went
Very far off, fearing a shot and a deep wound;
But at least not long after she [Neberna] was avenged, for that man
The fierce Gill assailed immediately and in his face
She snarled horribly and looked like a tigress;
Gripping his snotty beard, she spoke to him thus:
'Go home, you filthy good-for-nothing, or else I shall kill you.'
Then, when like Hercules she struck a great hard blow,
She lifted up in her hand a huge patch of cow-dung and all of
The protruding beard of the gallant man she besmeared.
'Take upon yourself,' (she said) 'this very effective snuff
For your reward, you rascal.' Then at last to the frightened one
She gave a tremendous blow, and a powerful blow,
And redoubled again, until twice she made fire
To escape from both his eyes: in this way Gill is victorious.
The bewildered man was stupified, and suddenly backwards
He turned just as if his nose had been bloodied, and 'O fy!'
Three, four times he exclaims, and O how often he sneezed [snorted?]!
And he vomited up his whole breakfast and the very hungry man
Let loose above and below, a miserable sight,
And putting his ears to his neck he ran away in such a fashion,
Not daring to scoff for a second time, and he would not suffer worse.
Seeing this, the mistress of Scotstarvit yelled filthy words,
And 'fy, fy!' she exclaims, 'Now the victory is nearly lost.'
And from elevated hips with a massive murmur a baritone fart
She let fly, such as would have cracked Mons Meg:
Thereupon truly the enemies quaked, and suddenly to flight
They took; the retainer looked back, and that same
Sheepheaded man was afraid of the sounds and the blows of a bullet.
And if by chance the Spanish King, by the name of Philip, seven
Exactly equal cannons had made to open their mouths
To batter Sluys, he would have smashed Sluys to ashes;
Or if great Louis had given by chance so many
Enormous farts to the fortifications of Montauban,
That same town he would have instantly smashed to the ground.
The foreman left, seeing everything covered with debris;
'And if you do not accept my advice,' she [Gill] said,

Formosas scartabo facies, & vos wirriabo.
Sed needlo per seustram broddatus, inque privatas
Partes stobbatus, greittans, lookansque grivatè,
Barlafumle clamat, & dixit, *O Deus, O God!*
Quid multis? Sic fraya fuit, sic guisa peracta est,
Una nec interea spillata est dropa cruoris.

'I shall scratch your beautiful faces, and I shall strangle you.'
But pierced with a needle by the seamstress, and in private
Parts stabbed, weeping, and looking aggrieved,
He cried, 'Truce,' and said 'O God, O God!'
What further? In this way the fray ended, in this way the affair was acted out,
Nevertheless, not one drop of blood was spilled.

Translated from the macaronic Latin by Allan H. MacLaine

ARTHUR JOHNSTON (1587–1641)

from *Ad Robertum Baronium*

Adspice, Gadiacis quod misi tristis ab undis.
  Baroni, plenum rusticitatis opus.
Urbe procul, parvus, nec sat fecundus agellus
  Est mihi, saxosis asper ubique iugis.
Hic ego, qui Musis olim Phoeboque litavi,
  Devotus Cereri praedia bobus aro.
Curvus humum spectans, interdum pone iuvencos
  Sector, et impresso vomere findo solum.
Interdum stimulo, nec raro vocibus, utor,
  Et stupidum numeros discere cogo pecus.
Nunc subigo rastris, nunc terram crate fatigo,
  Horrida nunc duro tesqua bidente domo.
Hic manus exossat lapidosa novalia, lymphis
  Hic rigat inductis, hic scrobe siccat humum.
Saepe flagellatae lassant mihi brachia fruges,
  Ambo fatigantur saepe ligone pedes.
Ipse lutum nudus furca versare tricorni
  Cogor, et immundo spargere rura fimo.
Vere novo videas mandantem semina sulcis:
  Arva sub Arcturi sidere falce meto.
Pars messis torrenda focis, frangendaque saxo est,
  Pars mihi flumineis mersa domatur aquis.
Aestibus in mediis, hiemis memor, ignibus apta
  Pabula suffossa quaerere cogor humo.
Viscera dum rimor terrae, prope conspicor umbras,
  Ignotum nec me Manibus esse reor.
Ingeminant curae, ceu tempestate coorta,
  Cum prior urgetur fluctibus unda novis.
Vix intempesta clauduntur lumina nocte,
  Excitor, ut cecinit nuncia lucis avis.

To Robert Baron

Dear Doctor Baron, Aberdeen,
Read this, my mudstained, gloomy work
Sent from a burn that feeds the Don.
Out on my croft, far out of town,
Among rough, stony, worn-out fields,
Ex-poet, and ex-learned man,
I plough my furrow with dour beasts.
Bent double, eyes glued to the clods,
I trek behind my oxen's lines,
Goading them on or chanting verse,
Teaching the ox boustrophedon.

Sometimes I hoe and hoe the marl,
Sometimes I harrow it to death,
Or jab it. With my writing hand
I haul the stones from new-ploughed fields
Then, maybe, irrigate the land,
Or drain it with a shallow pit.
Both arms ache with threshing crops,
Both feet are just about done in.
Stripped off, I fork muck with a graip,
Then spread dung on the heavy soil.
Arcturus winks. I scythe my crops.

Some of the harvest's scorched, ground down,
Some of it's in the Gadie burn.
Through the hot summer I prepare
For snow, cutting and banking peat.
Excavating the earth's bowels
I just about see spooks and think
The dead peer back. What makes it worse,
As when a storm first hits and then
Wave after wave pounds in, my head's
Just touched the pillow in pitch dark
When I'm awoken by the lark.

Pellibus hirsutis humeros involvo pedesque:
  Rapa famem pellit, fluminis unda sitim.
Mille modis pereo; nil infelicius, uno
  Me miserabilius nil gravis Orcus habet.
Me mea nunc genitrix, et quae dedit ubera nutrix,
  Horreret: vultu terreor ipse meo.
Non ego sum, quod eram: foedantur pulvere cani,
  Ora situ turpi, crura pedesque luto.
Obstipum caput est, et adunco suetus aratro
  Semper humi figo lumina, more bovis.

My overalls are shaggy pelts.
Breakfast's a turnip once again,
The Gadie burn to wash it down.
I'm dying in a thousand ways —
The Underworld might cheer me up —
So lonely, scared the mirror shows
Not who I was. Teeth like a dog's,
Hair dandruff-white, boils on my lips,
I take my stand knee-deep in shite,
Bowed-down, too harnessed to the plough,
Downcast, the beast I have become.

Translated from the Latin by Robert Crawford

JAMES GRAHAM, MARQUIS OF MONTROSE
(1612–1650)

On Himself, upon hearing what was his Sentence

Let them bestow on ev'ry Airth a Limb;   *part*
Open all my Veins, that I may swim
To Thee my Saviour, in that Crimson Lake;
Then place my purboil'd Head upon a Stake;
Scatter my Ashes, throw them in the Air:
Lord (since Thou know'st where all these Atoms are)
I'm hopeful, once Thou'lt recollect my Dust,
And confident Thou'lt raise me with the Just.

FRANCIS SEMPILL OF BELTREES (c.1616–1682)

Maggie Lauder

Wha wadna be in love
   Wi' bonnie Maggie Lauder?
A piper met her gaun to Fife,
   And spier'd what was't they ca'd her: *asked*
Richt scornfully she answered him,
   Begone, you hallanshaker!   *tramp*
Jog on your gate, you bladderskate!   *way; windbag*
   My name is Maggie Lauder.

Maggie! quoth he; and, by my bags,
   I'm fidgin' fain to see thee!   *excited*
Sit doun by me, my bonnie bird;
   In troth I winna steer thee;   *interfere with*
For I'm a piper to my trade;
   My name is Rob the Ranter:
The lasses loup as they were daft,   *jump*
   When I blaw up my chanter.   *pipe*

Piper, quo Meg, hae ye your bags,   *said*
   Or is your drone in order?
If ye be Rob, I've heard o' you;
   Live you upo' the Border?
The lasses a', baith far and near,
   Have heard o' Rob the Ranter;
I'll shake my foot wi' richt gude will,
   Gif ye'll blaw up your chanter.

Then to his bags he flew wi' speed;
   About the drone he twisted:
Meg up and wallop'd ower the green;
   For brawly could she frisk it!
Weel done! quo he. Play up! quo she.
   Weel bobb'd! quo Rob the Ranter;   *danced*
It's worth my while to play, indeed,
   When I hae sic a dancer!

Weel hae ye play'd your part! quo Meg;
   Your cheeks are like the crimson!
There's nane in Scotland plays sae weel,
   Sin' we lost Habbie Simson.   *[famous piper]*
I've lived in Fife, baith maid and wife,
   This ten years and a quarter:
Gin ye should come to Anster Fair,
   Spier ye for Maggie Lauder.

from *The Banishment of Poverty by His Royal Highness James Duke of Albany*

Pox fa that pultron Povertie,   *befall; poltroon*
Wae worth the time that I him saw;
Sen first he laid his fang on me,
Myself from him I dought ne'er draw.   *could*

His wink to me has been a law.
He haunts me like a penny-dog;
Of him I stand far greater aw
Than pupill does of pedagogue.

The first time that he met with me,
Was at a clachan in the west;   *village*
Its name I trow Kilbarchan be,
Where Habbie's drones blew many a blast;   *[Habbie Simson, famous piper]*

There we shook hands, cauld be his cast;   *lot*
An ill dead may that custron die;   *death; vagabond*
For there he gripped me full fast,
When first I fell in cautionrie.   *suretyship*

Yet I had hopes to be reliev'd,
And fre'ed from that foul laidly lown;   *rascal*
Fernzier, when Whiggs were ill mischiev'd,   *the preceding year*
And forc'd to fling their weapons down,

When we chased them from Glasgow town,
I with that swinger thought to grapple;   *bankrupt*
But when Indemnity came down,
The laydron pow'd me by the thrapple.   *waster; pulled; neck*

But yet in hopes of some relief,
A rade I made to Arinfrew,   *daft expedition*
Where they did bravely buff my beef,   *[beat me up]*
And made my body black and blew.

MÀIRI NIGHEAN ALASDAIR RUAIDH/
MARY MACLEOD (c. 1616–c. 1706)

Tuireadh

A rinn Màiri nighean Alasdair Ruaidh goirid an déis a fàgail an Sgarbaigh.

Hóireann ó ho bhì ó
Hóireann ó ho bhì ó
Hóireann ó ho bhì ó
Ri hóireann ó o hao o!

Is muladach mì, hì ó
   Hóireann ó ho bhì ó
O cheann seachdain, hì ó
   Ro hóireann ó o hao o,

Is mi an eilean gun
Fhiar gun fhasgadh.

Ma dh'fhaodas mi
Théid mi dhachaigh;

Nì mi an t-iomramh
Mar as fhasa,

Do Uilbhinnis
A' chruidh chaisfhinn,

Far an d'fhuair mi
Gu h-òg m'altrum,

Air bainne chìoch
Nam ban basgheal,

Thall aig Fionnghail
Dhuinn nighean Lachainn,

Blue Song

(made by Mary, daughter of Red Alasdair, soon after she was left in Scarba)

Hoireann o

I am sad
since a week ago

Left on this island,
no grass, no shelter.

If I could
I'd get back home,

Making the journey
rightaway

To Ullinish
of white-hoofed cattle

Where I grew up,
a little girl

Breast-fed there
by soft-palmed women,

In the house of brown-haired Flora,
Lachlan's daughter,

Is ì 'na banchaig
Ris na martaibh

Aig Ruairidh mór Mac
Leòid nam bratach.

'S ann 'na thaigh mór
A fhuair mi am macnas,

Danns' le sunnd air
Urlar farsaing,

An fhìdhleireachd 'gam
Chur a chadal,

A' phìobaireachd
Mo dhùsgadh maidne.

Thoir mo shoraidh, hò ó
   Hóireann ó ho bhì o,
Gu Dùn Bheagain, hì ó
   Ro hóireann ó o hao o.

milkmaid
among the cows

of Roderick Mor
MacLeod of the banners.

I have been happy
in his great house,

living it up
on the dancefloor,

fiddle-music
making me sleepy,

pibroch
my dawn chorus.

Hóireann ó ho bhì o,
Ro hóireann ó o hao o.

Say hullo for me
to Dunvegan.

English version by Robert Crawford

IAIN LOM/JOHN MACDONALD (c. 1620 – c. 1710)

Oran Cumhaidh air Cor na Rìoghachd

Mi gabhail Sraith Dhruim Uachdair,
'S beag m'aighear anns an uair so:
Tha an latha air dol gu gruamachd
   'S chan e tha buain mo sproc.

Ge duilich leam 's ge dìobhail
M'fhear cinnidh math bhith dhìth orm,
Chan usa learn an sgrìob-s'
   Thàinig air an rìoghachd bhochd.

Tha Alba dol fo chìoschain
Aig farbhalaich gun fhìrinn
Bhàrr a' chalpa dhìrich –
   'S e cuid de m' dhìobhail ghoirt.

Tha Sasannaich gar fairgneadh,
Gar creach, gar murt 's gar marbhadh;
Gun ghabh ar n-Athair fearg ruinn –
   Gur dearmad dhuinn 's gur bochd.

Mar a bha Cloinn Israel
Fo bhruid aig rìgh na h-Èiphit,
Tha sinn air a' chor cheudna:
   Chan èigh iad ruinn ach 'Seoc'.

Ar rìgh an dèidh's a chrùnadh
Mun gann a leum e ùrfhas,
Na thaisdealach bochd rùisgte
   Gun gheàrd gun chùirt gun choist;

Ga fharfhuadach as àite
Gun duine leis de chàirdean,
Mar luing air uachdar sàile,
   Gun stiùir gun ràimh gun phort.

A Lament for the State of the Country

As I travel the Strath of Drumochter,
little my joy at this season:
the day has turned out grimly
    and that does not help my gloom.

Though I feel it a hard deprivation
to be lacking my good kinsman,
no easier borne is this mishap
    that has overcome the poor land.

Scotland is under tribute
to foreigners without justice
above the right taxation –
    that is part of my sore plight.

We are plundered by the English,
despoiled, slain and murdered;
we must have caused our Father anger –
    for we are neglected and poor.

Like the Children of Israel
in bondage to the King of Egypt,
we have the same standing:
    they call us only 'Jock'.

Our king after his crowning,
barely before he was adult,
turned into a poor stripped vagrant
    without guard or parliament or court.

Expelled from his rightful position
without any of his friends with him,
like a ship on the top of the ocean
    without rudder or oar or port.

Cha tèid mi do Dhùn Èideann
O dhòirteadh fuil a' Ghreumaich,
An leòghann fearail treubhach
　　Ga cheusadh air a' chroich.

B'e siud am fìor dhuine uasal
Nach robh den linne shuarach,
Bu ro mhath rudhadh gruadhach
　　'N àm tarraing suas gu troid.

Deud chailc bu ro mhath dlùthadh
Fo mhala chaoil gun mhùgaich,
Ge tric do dhàil gam dhùsgadh
　　Cha rùisg mi chàch e nochd.

Mhic Nèill à Asaint chianail,
Nan glacainn an mo lìon thu
Bhiodh m'fhacal air do bhìnne
　　Is cha dìobrainn thu on chroich.

Thu fèin is t'athair cèile,
Fear taighe sin na Lèime,
Ged chrochta sibh le chèile
　　Cha b'èiric air mo lochd.

Craobh rùisgt' den abhall bhreugach
Gun mheas gun chliù gun cheutaidh
Bha riamh ri murt a chèile,
　　Nur fuidheall bheum is chorc.

Marbhaisg ort fèin, a dhìmheis,
Mar olc a reic thu an fhìrinn
Air son na mine Lìtich
　　Is dà thrian dith goirt.

I will go no more to Edinburgh
since Graham's blood was spilled there,
the lion valiant and mighty
 tortured on the gallows tree.

He was a nobleman truly
of no paltry lineage,
his cheek's flushing was prodigious
 when drawing up to fight.

Chalk-white teeth set closely
under a slim unfrowning eye-brow,
though often your lot kept me wakeful
 I will not make it public tonight.

Son of Niall from dismal Assynt,
if in my net I could but trap you,
I would not banish you from the gallows,
 my word would seal your doom.

You yourself and your wife's father,
that house-holder of Lemlair,
even were you hanged together
 that would not compensate my loss.

Of the perjured apple-tree a bare offshoot
without fruit or fame or decorum
you were forever murdering each other,
 the left-overs of knives and blows.

A curse on you, you disgraced one,
for wickedly have you sold justice
for the sake of a boll of Leith-meal
 with two thirds of it gone sour.

  Translated from the Gaelic by Meg Bateman

SÌLEAS NA CEAPAICH/CICELY MACDONALD
(*c.* 1660–*c.* 1729)

from *Alasdair á Gleanna Garadh*

Alasdair á Gleanna Garadh,
Thug thu 'n diugh gal air mo shùilibh;
'S beag ionghnadh mi bhith fo chreuchdaibh
'S gur tric 'gan reubadh as ùr iad;
'S beag ionghnadh mi bhith trom-osnach,
'S meud an dosgaidh th' air mo chàirdibh;
Gur tric an t-eug uainn a' gearradh
Rogha nan darag as àirde.

Chaill sinn ionann agus còmhla
Sir Dòmhnall 's a mhac 's a bhràthair;
Ciod e 'n stà dhuinn bhith 'gan gearan?
Thuit Mac Mhic Ailein 's a' bhlàr uainn;
Chaill sinn darag làidir liath-ghlas
A chumadh dìon air ar càirdean,
Capull-coille bhàrr na giùthsaich,
Seobhag sùil-ghorm lùthmhor làidir.

*   *   *

Bu tu 'n lasair dhearg gan losgadh,
'S bu tu sgoilteadh iad gu 'n sàiltibh,
Bu tu guala chur a' chatha,
Bu tu 'n laoch gun athadh làimhe,
Bu tu 'm bradan anns an fhìor-uisg,
Fìor-eun ás an eunlainn as àirde,
Bu tu 'n leòghann thar gach beathach,
Bu tu damh leathann na cràice.

Bu tu 'n loch nach faodte thaomadh,
Bu tu tobar faoilidh na slàinte,
Bu tu Beinn Nibheis thar gach aonach,
Bu tu 'chreag nach faodte theàrnadh,

from *Alasdair of Glengarry*

Alasdair of Glengarry
you brought tears to my eyes today;
no wonder that I am wounded,
and that my wounds open up again;
no wonder that my sighs are heavy,
misfortune falls heavy on my kin;
Death often cuts and takes from us
the choicest and the tallest oaks.

We lost, just about together,
Sir Donald, his son and his brother;
what good will it do us to complain?
We lost Clanranald in the battle;
we lost a strong grey oak
that would keep our friends protected,
a capercailzie in the pine-wood,
a strong, supple, blue-eyed hawk.

*   *   *

You were the red torch to burn them,
you would cleave them to their heels,
you were a hero in the battle,
a champion who never flinched;
a fresh-run salmon in the water,
an eagle in the highest flock,
lion excelling every creature,
broad-chested, strong-antlered stag.

A loch that could not be emptied,
a well liberal in health,
Ben Nevis towering over mountains,
a rock that could not be scaled;

Bu tu clach-mhullaich a' chaisteil,
Bu tu leac leathann na sràide,
Bu tu leug lòghmhar nam buadhan,
Bu tu clach uasal an fhàinne.

Bu tu 'n t-iubhar thar gach coille,
Bu tu 'n darach daingeann làidir,
Bu tu 'n cuileann 's bu tu 'n draigheann,
Bu tu 'n t-abhall molach blàthmhor;
Cha robh meur annad den chritheann,
Cha robh do dhlighe ri feàrna,
Cha robh do chàirdeas ri leamhan –
Bu tu leannan nam ban àlainn.

Bu tu cèile na mnà prìseil,
'S oil leam fhìn ga dìth an dràsd thu;
Ged nach ionann dhòmhsa 's dhìse
'S goirt a fhuair mi fhìn mo chàradh.
H-uile bean a bhios gun chèile
Guidheadh i mac Dè 'na àite,
Os e 's urra bhith ga còmhnadh
Anns gach leòn a chuireadh càs oirr'.

Guidheam t' anam a bhith sàbhailt
On a chàradh anns an ùir thu;
Guidheam sonas air na dh'fhàg thu
Ann ad àros 's ann ad dhùthaich;
'S math leam do mhac a bhith 'd àite
An saidhbhreas, am beairteas 's an cùram:
Alasdair á Gleanna Garadh,
Thug thu 'n-diugh gal air mo shùilean.

topmost stone of the castle,
broad paving-stone of the street,
the precious jewel of virtues,
the noble stone of the ring.

The yew above every wood,
the oak, steadfast and strong,
you were the holly, the blackthorn,
the apple rough-barked in bloom;
you had no twig of the aspen,
the alder made no claim on you,
there was none of the lime-tree in you,
you were the darling of lovely dames.

You were the spouse of a precious wife,
I'm sad that she has lost you now;
though she and I are different,
I too have borne a bitter fate;
let every wife who lacks a spouse
pray that God's Son takes his place,
since He can give the help she needs
in every grief that strikes her sore.

I pray that your soul may be saved,
since now you're at rest in the earth;
I pray joy for those left behind you
in your home and in your lands;
I rejoice that your son's in your place
as to wealth and riches and care;
Alexander of Glengarry,
you brought tears to my eyes today.

Translated from the Gaelic by Derick Thomson

ANON. (? early 18th century)

Thig trì nithean gun iarraidh

Thig trì nithean gun iarraidh
An t-eagal, an t-iadach 's an gaol,
'S bu bheag a' chùis mhaslaidh
Ged 'ghlacadh leo mis air a h-aon,
'S a liuthad bean uasal
A fhuaras 'sa' chiont ud robh mi,
A thug an gaol fuadain
Air ro bheagan duaise ga chionn.

Fhir a dhìreas am bealach
Beir mo shoraidh d'an ghleannan o thuath
Is innis do m' leannan,
Gur maireann mo ghaol 's gur buan
Fear eile cha ghabh mi
'S chan fhuiling mi idir a luaidh;
Gus an dèan thu ghaoil m' àicheadh,
Cha chreid mi o chàch gur fuath.

Fhir nan gorm shùilean meallach
O'n ghleannan am bitheadh an smùid,
Gam beil a' chaoin mhala
Mar chanach an t-slèibh fo dhriùchd;
Nuair rachadh tu air t' uilinn
Bhiodh fuil air fear dhìreadh nan stùc,
'S nam biodh tu ghaoil mar rium
Cha b' anaid an cèile leam thù.

Nam faicinn thu tighinn
Is fios domh gur tusa bhiodh ann,
Gun èireadh mo chridhe
Mar aiteal na grèin' thar nam beann;
'S gun tugainn mo bhriathar
Gach gaoisdean tha liath 'na mo cheann
Gum fàsadh iad buidhe
Mar dhìthein am bruthaich nan allt.

Three Things Come Without Seeking

Three things come without seeking,
jealousy, terror and love.
Nor is it shame to be counted
among those whom such agonies grieve,
since so many great ladies
have suffered the crime that I have,
being exiled by passion.
They gave but they did not receive.

You who are climbing the defile
bear my love to the glen of the north:
take this vow to my sweetheart:
'I am his while I live on the earth.
I will marry no other
nor allow such news to go forth.
Till, my dear, you've denied me,
I'll distrust the words of their mouth.'

You, of the blue eyes beguiling,
(from the glen where the mist would arise)
your eyebrows showed courteous mildness
like the moor-cotton dewed from the skies:
when you aimed as you lay on your elbow
the stag would be caught by surprise:
my love, if you lived in my dwelling,
no one could mock or despise.

My dear, if I saw you arriving
and knew that it really was you,
my heart's blood ascending
would break like the sun into view:
and I'll give you my promise
each hair that was grey would renew
its greyness to yellow
like the flowers that the waters pursue.

Cha b'ann air son beairteis
No idir ro-phailteas na sprèidh,
Cha b' fhear do shìol bhodach
Bha m' osna cho trom ad dhèidh,
Ach mhac an duin' uasail
Fhuair buaidh air an dùthaich gu lèir;
Ge do bhitheamaid falamh
'S ioma caraid a chitheadh oirnn feum.

Mur tig thus fèin tuilleadh
Gur aithne dhomh mhalairt a th'ann,
Nach eil mi cho beairteach
Ri cailin an achaidh ud thall.
Cha tugainn mo mheisneach,
Mo ghliocas is grinneas mo làimh
Air buaile chrodh ballach
Is cailin gun iùil 'nan ceann.

Ma chaidh thu orm seachad
Gur taitneach, neo-thuisleach mo chliù:
Cha d'rinn mi riut comann
'S cha d' laigh mi leat riamh ann an cùil.
Chan àraichinn arachd
Do dhuine chuir ad air a chrùn
On bha mi cho beachdail
'S gun smachdaich mi gaol nach fiù.

Bu laoghaid mo thàmailt
Nam b' airidh ni b' fheàrr a bhiodh ann,
Ach dubh chail' a' bhuachair
'Nuair ghlacas i buarach 'na làimh;
'Nuair a thig an droch earrach
'S a chaillear an nì anns a' ghleann,
Bitheas is' air an t-siulaid
Gun tuille dhe bunailteas ann.

It was not for your riches
and not for your numerous herd:
it was not for a weakling
that my heart was troubled and stirred:
but the son of a noble
who conquered a land with his sword:
we'd suffer no hunger
for many would furnish our board.

If you're never returning,
I'll know an exchange has been made,
that being more wealthy
another has suited your trade.
I'd not give my courage,
my wisdom, the love you betrayed,
for a field of bright cattle,
and a girl without sense at their head.

And though you've disowned me
I've no dark dishonour to hide:
my fame is unsullied;
I've never lain down at your side.
For a man who'd crowned monarchs
I suffer more pangs from my pride
than to rear him young bastards.
I'd strangle my love till it died.

Yet gentler the insult
if her love were higher than mine:
but a slatternly scullion
whom even the cows would disdain:
when the spring comes with tempest
and the cattle are lost in the glen
she'll be lying in child-bed,
the house without rudder or rein.

Translated from the Gaelic by Iain Crichton Smith

ALLAN RAMSAY (1684–1758)

Lucky Spence's Last Advice

Three times the carline grain'd and rifted,   *[old woman]*
Then frae the cod her pow she lifted,   *pillow; head*
In bawdy policy well gifted,
    When she now faun,   *found*
That Death na langer wad be shifted,
    She thus began:

My loving lasses, I maun leave ye,   *must*
But dinna wi' ye'r greeting grieve me,
Nor wi' your draunts and droning deave me,   *drivel; annoy*
    But bring's a gill;   *[small drink]*
For faith, my bairns, ye may believe me,
    'Tis 'gainst my will.

O black-ey'd Bess and mim-mou'd Meg,   *prim-mouthed*
O'er good to work or yet to beg;
Lay sunkots up for a sair leg,   *something*
    For whan ye fail,
Ye'r face will not be worth a feg,   *fig*
    Nor yet ye'r tail.

When e'er ye meet a fool that's fow,   *drunk*
That ye're a maiden gar him trow,   *believe*
Seem nice, but stick to him like glew;
    And whan set down,
Drive at the jango till he spew,   *[press drink on him]*
    Syne he'll sleep soun.

Whan he's asleep, then dive and catch
His ready cash, his rings or watch;
And gin he likes to light his match   *if*
    At your spunk-box,
Ne'er stand to let the fumbling wretch
    E'en take the pox.

Cleek a' ye can be hook or crook,   *catch*
Ryp ilky poutch frae nook to nook;   *[plunder every pocket]*
Be sure to truff his pocket-book,   *steal*
        Saxty pounds Scots
Is nae deaf nits: In little bouk   *is not empty nuts; bulk*
        Lie great bank-notes.

To get a mends of whinging fools,   *to be revenged*
That's frighted for repenting-stools.   *[frightened of public disgrace]*
Wha often, whan their metal cools,
        Turn sweer to pay,   *reluctant*
Gar the kirk-boxie hale the dools   *[make the Kirk fine-box triumph]*
        Anither day.

But dawt Red Coats, and let them scoup,   *dote on; [move freely]*
Free for the fou of cutty stoup;   *gill of brandy*
To gee them up, ye need na hope
        E'er to do well:
They'll rive ye'r brats and kick your doup,   *tear; clothes; arse*
        And play the Deel.

There's ae sair cross attends the craft,
That curst Correction-house, where aft
Vild Hangy's taz ye'r riggings saft   *vile hangman's whip; [back]*
        Makes black and blae,
Enough to pit a body daft;
        But what'll ye say.

Nane gathers gear withouten care.
Ilk pleasure has of pain a skare;   *each; share*
Suppose then they should tirl ye bare,   *strip*
        And gar ye fike,   *make you twitch*
E'en learn to thole; 'tis very fair   *endure*
        Ye're nibour like.

Forby, my looves, count upo' losses,   *besides*
Ye'r milk-white teeth and cheeks like roses,
Whan jet-black hair and brigs of noses,
        Faw down wi' dads   *[in lumps]*
To keep your hearts up 'neath sic crosses,
        Set up for bawds.

Wi' well-crish'd loofs I hae been canty,   *well-greased palms; cheerful*
Whan e'er the lads wad fain ha'e faun t'ye;   *[like to have fallen]*
To try the auld game Taunty Raunty,   *[Rumpy Pumpy]*
        Like coofers keen,   *fools*
They took advice of me your aunty,
        If ye were clean.

Then up I took my siller ca'   *silver caller*
And whistl'd benn whiles ane, whiles twa;   *indoors; once, twice*
Roun'd in his lug, that there was a   *whispered*
        Poor country Kate,
As halesom as the well of Spaw,
        But unka blate.   *hugely shy*

Sae whan e'er company came in,
And were upo' a merry pin,   *mood*
I slade away wi' little din   *smoothed along*
        And muckle mense,   *sense*
Left conscience judge, it was a' ane   *[let their own]*
        To Lucky Spence.

My bennison come on good doers,
Who spend their cash on bawds and whores;
May they ne'er want the wale of cures   *best*
        For a sair snout:
Foul fa' the quacks wha that fire smoors,   *smothers*
        And puts nae out.

My malison light ilka day   *curse*
On them that drink, and dinna pay,
But tak a snack and rin away;
        May't be their hap
Never to want a gonorrhœa,   *lack*
        Or rotten clap.

Lass gi'e us in anither gill,
A mutchken, Jo, let's tak our fill;   *pint*
Let Death syne registrate his bill
        Whan I want sense,
I'll slip away with better will,
        Quo' Lucky Spence.   *said*

To the Phiz an Ode

[Phiz Drinking Club]

Vides ut alta stet nive candidum
Soracte . . .   (Horace)

See how high the white snow shines
On Mount Soracte

Look up to Pentland's towring taps,
Buried beneath great wreaths of snaw,
O'er ilka cleugh, ilk scar and slap,   *every hollow; cliff; valley*
As high as ony Roman wa'.

Driving their baws frae whins or tee,   *gorse bushes*
There's no ae gowfer to be seen,   *golfer*
Nor dousser fowk wysing a jee   *more prudent; bending to one side*
The byas bouls on Tamson's green.   *bias bowls*

Then fling on coals, and ripe the ribs,
And beek the house baith butt and ben,   *warm*
That mutchken stoup it hads but dribs,   *pint mug*
Then let's get in the tappit hen.   *quart tankard*

Good claret best keeps out the cauld,
And drives away the winter soon,
It makes a man baith gash and bauld,   *wise*
And heaves his saul beyond the moon.

Leave to the gods your ilka care,
If that they think us worth their while,
They can a rowth of blessings spare,
Which will our fashious fears beguile.   *troublesome*

For what they have a mind to do,
That will they do, should we gang wood,   *mad*
If they command the storms to blaw,
Then upo' sight the hailstains thud.

But soon as e'er they cry, 'Be quiet,'
The blatt'ring winds dare nae mair move,
But cour into their caves, and wait   *cower*
The high command of supreme Jove.

Let neist day come as it thinks fit,   *next*
The present minute's only ours,
On pleasure let's imploy our wit,
And laugh at fortune's feckless power.

Be sure ye dinna quat the grip
Of ilka joy when ye are young,
Before auld age your vitals nip,
And lay ye twafald o'er a rung.   *doubled-up; stick*

Sweet youth's a blyth and heartsome time,
Then lads and lasses while it's May,
Gae pou the gowan in its prime,   *daisy*
Before it wither and decay.

Watch the saft minutes of delyte,
When Jenny speaks beneath her breath,
And kisses, laying a the wyte   *blame*
On you if she kepp ony skaith.   *comes to any harm*

Haith ye're ill bred, she'll smiling say,   *Faith*
Ye'll worry me ye greedy rook;
Syne frae your arms she'll rin away,   *then*
And hide her sell in some dark nook:

Her laugh will lead you to the place
Where lies the happiness ye want,
And plainly tells you to your face,
Nineteen nay-says are haff a grant.   *yes*

Now to her heaving bosom cling,
And sweetly toolie for a kiss.   *struggle*
Frae her fair finger whop a ring,   *steal*
As taiken of a future bliss.   *token*

These bennisons, I'm very sure,
Are of the gods indulgent grant;
Then surly carles, whisht, forbear   *old men*
To plague us with your whining cant.

ANON. (18th century)

As I was a-walking by yon green garden

As I was a walking by yon green garding
I espied an auld wife she was clawing her hole
I said you old bitchie what makes it so itchey
Begone you young Rogue I will claw it my fill.

ALASDAIR MAC MHAIGHSTIR ALASDAIR/
ALEXANDER MACDONALD (c. 1695–c. 1770)

from Òran an t-Samhraidh

Air fonn, 'Through the Wood Laddie'

Am mìos lusanach mealach,
Feurach failleanach blàth,
'S e gu gucagach duilleach,
Luachrach dìtheanach lurach,
Beachach seilleanach dearcach,
Ciùthrach dealtach trom tlàth,
'S i mar chùirneanan daoimein:
'Bhratach bhoillsgeil air làr.

*   *   *

Bidh bradan seang-mhear nam fioruisg
Gu brisg, slinn-leumnach, luath,
'Na bhuidhne tàrr-ghealach lannach,
Gu h-iteach, dearg-bhallach, earrach,
Le shoillsean airgid da earradh
'S mion-bhreac lainnireach tuar,
'S e fèin gu crom-ghobach ullamh
Ceapadh chuileag le cluain.

A' Bhealltainn bhog-bhailceach ghrianach,
Lònach, lianach mo ghràidh,
Bhainneach, fhinn-mhèagach, uachdrach,
Omhnach, loinideach, chuachach,
Ghruthach, shlamanach, mhiosrach,
Mhiodrach, mhiosganach, làn,
Uanach, mheannanach, mhaoineach,
Bhocach, mhaoiseach, làn àil.

from *Song of Summer*

To the air 'Through the Wood Laddie'

Month of plants and of honey,
warm, with grasses and shoots,
month of buds and of leafage,
rushes, flowers that are lovely,
wasps, bees and berries,
mellow mists, heavy dews,
like spangles of diamonds,
a sparkling cover for earth.

*　　*　　*

Lithe brisk fresh-water salmon,
lively, leaping the stones;
bunched, white-bellied, scaly,
fin-tail-flashing, red spot;
speckled skin's brilliant hue
lit with flashes of silver;
with curved gob at the ready,
catching insects with guile.

May, with soft showers and sunshine,
meadows, grass-fields I love,
milky, whey-white and creamy,
frothing, whisked up in pails,
time for crowdie and milk-curds,
time for firkins and kits,
lambs, goat-kids and roe-deer,
bucks, a rich time for flocks.

Translated from the Gaelic by Derick Thomson

from *Birlinn Chlann Raghnaill*

Brosnachadh Iomraidh

Gu 'n cuirt' an iùbhrach dhubh, dhealbhach,
    An àite-seòlaidh:
Sàthaibh a mach cleathan rìghne,
    Liagh-lom, còmhnard;
Ràimh mhìnlunnacha, dhealbhach,
    Shocair, aotrom,
A nì 'n t-iomramh toirteil, calma,
    Basluath caoirgheal;
Chuireas an fhairge 'na sradan
    Suas 's na speuran –
'Na teine-sionnachain a' lasadh,
    Mar fhras éibhlean.
Le buillean gailbheacha, tarbhach,
    Nan cléith troma,
Bheir air na bòcthonnan anfhach
    Lot le 'n cromadh;
Le sgionan nan ràmh geal, tana,
    Bualadh cholluinn
Air mullach nan gormchnoc gleannach,
    Garbhlach, thomach;
O! sìnibh, tàirnibh, is lùbaibh
    Anns na bacaibh
Na gallain bhas-leathann ghiùthsaich,
    Le lùths ghlac geal;
Na fuirbidhnean troma, treuna,
    Laighe suas orr',
Le 'n gairdeanan dòideach, féitheach,
    Gaoisneach, cnuacach,
Thogas 's a leagas le chéile
    Fo aon ghluasad,
A gathan liaghleobhar réidhe
    Fo bhàrr stuadhan;

from *Clanranald's Galley*

Incitement for Rowing to Sailing-place

To put the black well-fashioned yewship
    To the sailing-place
Thrust you out flexible oarbanks
    Dressed to sheer grace;
Oars smooth-shafted and shapely,
    Graceful for gripping,
Made for lusty resolute rowing,
    Palm-fast, foam-whipping;
Knocking sparks out of the water
    Towards Heaven
Like the fire-flush from a smithy
    Updriven,
Under the great measured onstrokes
    Of the oar-lunges
That confound the indrawn billows
    With their plunges,
While the shrewd blades of the white woods
    Go cleaving
The tops of the valleyed blue-hills
    Shaggily heaving.
O stretch you, pull you, and bend you
    Between the thole-pins,
Your knuckles snow with hard plying
    The pinewood fins;
All the big muscular fellows
    Along her lying
With their hairy and sinewy
    Arms keep her flying,
Raising and lowering together
    With a single motion
Their evenly dressed poles of pinewood
    Mastering the ocean.

Iorcallach garbh an tùs cléithe
 'G éigheach – 'Suas orr'!'
Iorram a dhùisgeas an spéirid
 Anns na guailnean;
Sparras a' bhìrlinn le séitrich
 Troimh gach fuar-ghleann.
A' sgoltadh nam bòcthonn a' beucaich
 Le saidh chruaidh chruim.
Dh'iomaineas beanntanan béisteil
 Roimh 'dà ghualainn.
Hùgan le cuan, nuallan gàireach,
 Heig air chnagan;
Farum le bras-ghaoir na bàirlinn
 Ris na maidean;
Ràimh 'gam pianadh, 's balgain-fhala
 Air bois gach fuirbidh.
Na suinn làidir, gharbha, thoirteil,
 Is copgheal iomradh;
Chreanaicheas gach bòrd de darach –
 Bìth is iarann;
'S lannan 'gan tilgeil le staplain
 Chnap r'a sliasaid;
Fòirne fearail a bheir tulgadh
 Dùgharra, dàicheil;
Sparras a' chaol-bhàrc le giùthsaich
 An aodann àibheis;
Nach tillear le friogh nan tonn dubhghorm
 Le lùths ghàirdean:
Siud an sgioba neartmhor, sùrdail
 Air chùl àlaich;
Phronnas na cuartagan cùl-ghlas
 Le roinn ràmhachd;
Gun sgìos, gun airteal, gun lùbadh
 Ri uchd gàbhaidh.

A Herculean planked on the fore-oar
   Roaring: 'Up, on with her!'
Makes all the thick shoulder muscles
   Glide better together,
Thrusting the birlinn with snorting
   Through each chill sea-glen;
The hard curved prow through the tide-lumps
   Drives inveighing,
On all hands sending up mountains
   Round her insistence.
Hugan, the sea says, like Stentor;
   Heig, say the thole-pins.
Rasping now, on the timbers,
   Of the shirred surges!
The oars jib; blood-blistering
   Slowly emerges
On each hard hand of the rowers
   In berserk fettle
Hurling on the trembling oakplanks,
   Caulking, and metal,
Though nailheads spring with the thunder
   Thumping her thigh.
A crew to make a right rocking
   The deeps to defy,
Working the lean ship like an auger
   Through walls of water,
The bristling wrath of blue-black billows
   No daunting matter.
They are the choice set of fellows
   To hold an oarage
Outmanœuvring the dark swirlings
   With skill and courage,
Without a point lost or tiring,
   Timely throughout,
Despite all the dire devilment
   Of the waterspout!

Translated from the Gaelic by Hugh MacDiarmid

JAMES THOMSON (1700–1748)

from *Winter. A Poem*

For, see! where *Winter* comes, himself, confest,
Striding the gloomy Blast. First Rains obscure
Drive thro' the mingling Skies, with Tempest foul;
Beat on the Mountain's Brow, and shake the Woods,
That, sounding, wave below. The dreary Plain
Lies overwhelm'd, and lost. The bellying Clouds
Combine, and deepening into Night, shut up
The Day's fair Face. The Wanderers of Heaven,
Each to his Home, retire; save those that love
To take their Pastime in the troubled Air,
And, skimming, flutter round the dimply Flood.
The Cattle, from th' untasted Fields, return,
And ask, with meaning Low, their wonted Stalls;
Or ruminate in the contiguous Shade:
Thither, the houshold, feathery, People croud,
The crested Cock, with all his female Train,
Pensive, and wet. Mean while, the Cottage-Swain
Hangs o'er th' enlivening Blaze, and, taleful, there,
Recounts his simple Frolic: Much he talks,
And much he laughs, nor recks the Storm that blows
Without, and rattles on his humble Roof.

At last, the muddy Deluge pours along,
Resistless, roaring; dreadful down it comes
From the chapt Mountain, and the mossy Wild,
Tumbling thro' Rocks abrupt, and sounding far:
Then o'er the sanded Valley, floating, spreads,
Calm, sluggish, silent; till again constrain'd,
Betwixt two meeting Hills, it bursts a Way,
Where Rocks, and Woods o'erhang the turbid Stream.
There gathering triple Force, rapid, and deep,
It boils, and wheels, and foams, and thunders thro'.

Nature! great Parent! whose directing Hand
Rolls round the Seasons of the changeful Year,
How mighty! how majestick are thy Works!
With what a pleasing Dread they swell the Soul,
That sees, astonish'd! and, astonish'd sings!
You too, ye *Winds*! that now begin to blow,
With boisterous Sweep, I raise my Voice to you.
Where are your Stores, ye viewless *Beings*! say?
Where your aerial Magazines reserv'd,
Against the Day of Tempest perilous?
In what untravel'd Country of the Air,
Hush'd in still Silence, sleep you, when 'tis calm?

Late, in the louring Sky, red, fiery, Streaks
Begin to flush about; the reeling Clouds
Stagger with dizzy Aim, as doubting yet
Which Master to obey; while rising, slow,
Sad, in the Leaden-colour'd East, the Moon
Wears a bleak Circle round her sully'd Orb.
Then issues forth the Storm, with loud Control,
And the thin Fabrick of the pillar'd Air
O'erturns, at once. Prone, on th' uncertain Main,
Descends th' Etherial Force, and plows its Waves,
With dreadful Rift: from the mid-Deep, appears,
Surge after Surge, the rising, wat'ry, War.
Whitening, the angry Billows rowl immense,
And roar their Terrors, thro' the shuddering Soul
Of feeble Man, amidst their Fury caught,
And, dash'd upon his Fate: Then, o'er the Cliff,
Where dwells the *Sea-Mew*, unconfin'd, they fly,
And, hurrying, swallow up the steril Shore.

The Mountain growls; and all its sturdy *Sons*
Stoop to the Bottom of the Rocks they shade:
Lone, on its Midnight-Side, and all aghast,
The dark, way-faring, *Stranger*, breathless, toils,
And climbs against the Blast –
Low, waves the rooted Forest, vex'd, and sheds
What of its leafy Honours yet remains.
Thus, struggling thro' the dissipated Grove,
The whirling Tempest raves along the Plain;

And, on the Cottage thacht, or lordly Dome,
Keen-fastening, shakes 'em to the solid Base.
Sleep, frighted, flies; the hollow Chimney howls,
The Windows rattle, and the Hinges creak.

Then, too, they say, thro' all the burthen'd Air,
Long Groans are heard, shrill Sounds, and distant Sighs,
That, murmur'd by the *Demon* of the Night,
Warn the devoted *Wretch* of Woe, and Death!
Wild Uproar lords it wide: the Clouds commixt,
With Stars, swift-gliding, sweep along the Sky.
All Nature reels. – But hark! the *Almighty* speaks:
Instant, the chidden Storm begins to pant,
And dies, at once, into a noiseless Calm.

from *The Castle of Indolence*

The Leper-House and the Impenitents

And here and there, on trees by lightning scathed,
Unhappy wights who loathèd life yhung;
Or in fresh gore and recent murder bathed
They weltering lay; or else, infuriate flung
Into the gloomy flood, while ravens sung
The funeral dirge, they down the torrent rolled:
These, by distempered blood to madness stung,
Had doomed themselves; whence oft, when night controlled
The world, returning hither their sad spirits howled.

Meantime a moving scene was open laid.
That lazar-house, I whilom in my lay
Depainten have, its horror deep-displayed,
And gave unnumbered wretches to the day,
Who tossing there in squalid misery lay.
Soon as of sacred light the unwonted smile
Poured on these living catacombs its ray,
Through the drear caverns stretching many a mile,
The sick up-raised their heads, and dropped their woes a while.

'O Heaven!' they cried, 'and do we once more see
Yon blessed sun, and this green earth so fair?
Are we from noisome damps of pest-house free?
And drink our souls the sweet ethereal air?
O thou, or knight or God, who holdest there
That fiend, oh keep him in eternal chains!
But what for us, the children of despair,
Brought to the brink of hell, what hope remains?
Repentance does itself but aggravate our pains.'

*   *   *

But ah! their scornèd day of grace was past:
For (horrible to tell!) a desert wild
Before them stretched, bare, comfortless, and vast;
With gibbets, bones, and carcases defiled.
There nor trim field nor lively culture smiled;
Nor waving shade was seen, nor fountain fair:
But sands abrupt on sands lay loosely piled,
Through which they floundering toiled with painful care,
Whilst Phoebus smote them sore, and fired the cloudless air.

Then, varying to a joyless land of bogs,
The saddened country a gray waste appeared,
Where nought but putrid streams and noisome fogs
For ever hung on drizzly Auster's beard;
Or else the ground, by piercing Caurus seared,
Was jagged with frost or heaped with glazèd snow:
Through these extremes a ceaseless round they steered,
By cruel fiends still hurried to and fro,
Gaunt Beggary, and Scorn, with many hell-hounds moe.

The first was with base dunghill rags yclad,
Tainting the gale in which they fluttered light;
Of morbid hue his features, sunk and sad;
His hollow eyne shook forth a sickly light;
And o'er his lank jawbone, in piteous plight,
His black rough beard was matted rank and vile;
Direful to see! a heart-appalling sight!
Meantime foul scurf and blotches him defile;
And dogs, where'er he went, still barkèd all the while.

The other was a fell despightful fiend —
Hell holds none worse in baleful bower below,
By pride, and wit, and rage, and rancour keened;
Of man, alike if good or bad, the foe:
With nose upturned, he always made a show
As if he smelt some nauseous scent; his eye
Was cold and keen, like blast from boreal snow;
And taunts he casten forth most bitterly.
Such were the twain that off drove this ungodly fry.

Even so through Brentford town, a town of mud,
An herd of bristly swine is pricked along;
The filthy beasts, that never chew the cud,
Still grunt, and squeak, and sing their troublous song,
And oft they plunge themselves the mire among;
But ay the ruthless driver goads them on,
And ay of barking dogs the bitter throng
Makes them renew their unmelodious moan;
Ne ever find they rest from their unresting fone.

DAVID MALLOCH [MALLET] (1705–1765)

On an Amorous Old Man

Still hovering round the fair at sixty-four,
Unfit to love, unable to give o'er;
A flesh-fly, that just flutters on the wing,
Awake to buzz, but not alive to sting;
Brisk where he cannot, backward where he can;
The teasing ghost of the departed man.

JEAN ADAM (1710–1765)

There's Nae Luck about the House

And are ye sure the news is true?
  And are ye sure he's weel?
Is this a time to think o' wark?
  Ye jauds, fling by your wheel.   *jades*
Is this a time to think o' wark,
  When Colin's at the door?
Rax me my cloak, I'll to the quay,   *hand*
  And see him come ashore.
    For there's nae luck about the house,
      There's nae luck at a'
    There's little pleasure in the house,
      When our gudeman's awa'.

And gie to me my bigonet,   *linen cap*
  My bishop-satin gown;
For I maun tell the baillie's wife
  That Colin's come to town.
My turkey slippers maun gae on,
  My hose o' pearl blue;
It's a' to please my ain gudeman,
  For he's baith leal and true.   *loyal*

Rise up and mak a clean fireside,
  Put on the muckle pot;   *great*
Gie little Kate her Sunday gown
  And Jock his button coat;
And mak their shoon as black as slaes,   *sloes*
  Their hose as white as snaw;
It's a' to please my ain gudeman,
  For he's been lang awa'.

Since Colin's weel, I'm weel content,
  I hae nae mair to crave;
Could I but live to mak him blest,
  I'm blest aboon the lave: *above; rest*

And will I see his face again?
    And will I hear him speak?
I'm downricht dizzy wi' the thocht,
    In troth I'm like to greet.   *cry*

There's twa fat hens upo' the bauk,   *ridge*
    They've fed this month and mair,
Mak haste and thraw their necks about,
    That Colin weel may fare;
And spread the table neat and clean,
    Gar ilka thing look braw;   *[make everything]*
For wha can tell how Colin fared
    When he was far awa'?

Sae true his heart, sae smooth his speech,
    His breath like caller air;   *fresh*
His very foot has music in't
    As he comes up the stair.
And will I see his face again?
    And will I hear him speak?
I'm downricht dizzy wi' the thocht,
    In troth I'm like to greet.
        For there's nae luck about the house,
           There's nae luck at a'
        There's little pleasure in the house,
           When our gudeman's awa'.

ANON. (18th century)

Waly, Waly

O waly, waly, up the bank,   *alas*
    And waly, waly, doun the brae,
And waly, waly, yon burn-side,   *that stream-side*
    Where I and my Love wont to gae!
I lean'd my back unto an aik,   *oak*
    I thocht it was a trustie tree;
But first it bow'd and syne it brak –   *then*
    Sae my true love did lichtlie me.   *scorn*

O waly, waly, gin love be bonnie   *if*
    A little time while it is new!
But when 'tis auld it waxeth cauld,
    And fades awa' like morning dew.
O wherefore should I busk my heid,   *dress*
    Or wherefore should I kame my hair?   *comb*
For my true Love has me forsook,
    And says he'll never lo'e me mair.

Now Arthur's Seat sall be my bed,
    The sheets sall ne'er be 'filed by me;   *defiled*
Saint Anton's well sall be my drink;
    Since my true Love has forsaken me.
Marti'mas wind when wilt thou blaw,
    And shake the green leaves aff the tree?
O gentle Death, when wilt thou come?
    For of my life I am wearie.

'Tis not the frost, that freezes fell,   *cruelly*
    Nor blawing snaw's inclemencie,
'Tis not sic cauld that makes me cry;
    But my Love's heart grown cauld to me.
When we cam in by Glasgow toun,
    We were a comely sicht to see;
My Love was clad in the black velvèt,
    And I mysel in cramasie.   *crimson*

But had I wist, before I kist,
   That love had been sae ill to win,
I had lock'd my heart in a case o' gowd,   *gold*
   And pinn'd it wi' a siller pin.
And O! if my young babe were born,
   And set upon the nurse's knee;
And I mysel were dead and gane,
   And the green grass growing over me!

Jenny Nettles

Saw ye Jenny Nettles,
Jenny Nettles, Jenny Nettles,
Saw ye Jenny Nettles
Coming frae the Market;
Bag and Baggage on her Back,
Her Fee and Bountith in her Lap;   *wages; bonus*
Bag and Baggage on her Back,
And a Babie in her Oxter.   *armpit*

I met ayont the Kairny,   *beyond*
Jenny Nettles, Jenny Nettles,
Singing till her Bairny,
Robin Rattles' Bastard;
To flee the Dool upo' the Stool,   *punishment*
And ilka ane that mocks her,   *each*
She round about seeks Robin out,
To stap it in his Oxter.   *stick*

Fy, fy! Robin Rattle,
Robin Rattle, Robin Rattle;
Fy, fy! Robin Rattle,
Use Jenny Nettles kindly:
Score out the Blame, and shun the Shame,
And without mair Debate o't,
Take hame your Wain, make Jenny fain,   *child; happy*
The leal and leesome Gate o't.   *loyal and loving way*

ROB DONN MACAOIDH/ROBERT MACKAY
(1714–1778)

Marbhrann do Chloinn Fhir Taigh Ruspainn

'Nan luighe seo gu h-ìosal
Far na thìodhlaic sinn an triùir
Bha fallain, làidir, inntinneach
Nuair dh' inntrig a' bhliadhn' ùr;
Cha deachaidh seachad fathast
Ach deich latha dhith o thùs;
Ciod fhios nach tig an teachdair-s' oirnn
Nas braise na ar dùil?

Am bliadhna thìm bha dithis diubh
Air tighinn on aon bhroinn,
Bha iad 'nan dà chomrad
O choinnich iad 'nan cloinn,
Cha d' bhris an t-aog an comann ud
Ged bu chomasach dha 'n roinn,
Ach gheàrr e snàth'nn na beath'-s' aca
Gun dàil ach latha 's oidhch'.

Aon duine 's bean on tàinig iad,
Na bràithrean seo a chuaidh,
Bha an aon bheatha thìmeil ac'
'S bha 'n aodach d' an aon chluaimh,
Mun aon uair a bhàsaich iad
'S bha 'n nàdar d' an aon bhuaidh,
Chaidh 'n aon siubhal dhaoine leo
'S chaidh 'n sìneadh san aon uaigh.

Daoine nach d' rinn briseadh iad
'S e fiosrachail do chàch,
'S cha mhò a rinn iad aon dad
Ris an can an saoghal gràs,

The Rispond Misers

Lying in their lowly state
are three we buried here,
though they were strong and healthy,
and lively at New Year;
ten days only have gone by
since then — who can be sure
that our dread Summoner is not,
unknown to us, as near?

Within one year a pair of them
had come from the one womb,
and they had been close comrades
since their childhood in one room;
their fellowship is still intact,
unsevered by the tomb —
within two days Eternity
has plucked them from Time's loom.

These brothers now departed
came from one man and wife,
their clothes were made from the one fleece,
each lived the self-same life;
their deaths came close together,
their natures were alike,
the one procession bore their dust
and laid it out of sight.

These men broke no commandments,
as far as we can trace,
nor did their deeds show anything
of what the world calls grace;

Ach ghineadh iad, is rugadh iad,
Is thogadh iad, is dh'fhàs,
Chaidh stràchd d' an t-saoghal theiris orr',
'S mu dheireadh fhuair iad bàs.

Nach eil an guth seo labhrach
Ris gach aon neach againn beò,
Gu h-àraidh ris na seann daoinibh
Nach d' ionnsaich an staid phòsd',
Nach gabh na tha 'na dhleasdanas
A dheasachadh no lòn,
Ach caomhnadh nì gu falair dhoibh
'S a' falach an cuid òir?

Cha chaith iad fèin na rinn iad,
Agus oighreachan cha dèan,
Ach ulaidhnean air shliabh ac'
Bhios a' biathadh chon is eun.
Tha iad fon aon dìteadh,
Fo nach robh 's nach bi mi fhèin,
Gur duirche, taisgte 'n t-òr ac'
Na 'n uair bha e 'n tòs sa' mhèinn.

Barail ghlic an Aird Rìgh:
Dh'fhàg e pàirt de bhuidheann gann
Gu feuchainn iochd is oileanachd
D' an dream d' an tug e meall.
Carson nach tugteadh pòrsan
Dhe 'n cuid stòrais aig gach àm
Do bhochdaibh 'n Aoin a dheònaicheadh
An còrr a chur 'na cheann?

An dèidh na rinn mi rùsgadh dhuibh –
Tha dùil agam gun lochd –
'S a liuthad focal fìrinneach
A dhìrich mi nur n-uchd,
Tha eagal orm nach èisd sibh
Gu bhith feumail don a' bhochd
Nas mò na rinn na fleasgaich ud
A sheachdain gus a-nochd.

they were conceived and brought to birth,
were nursed, and grew apace,
a swatch of life passed by them
and Death put them in their place.

Surely this sounds a warning
to each one of us alive,
especially old bachelors,
unlearned in married love:
men who will not spend on food
the cash to which they cleave,
saving for a funeral feast
the gold that they must leave.

They'll never spend what they have made,
and make no heirs besides;
their treasures on the hillsides
are food for dogs and birds;
they stand condemned – though I can plead
'not guilty' in assize –
of hoarding darklier their gold
than ever did the mines.

The High King in His providence
wisely left some men short,
to test the sense of charity
of those who have a lot;
these should surely give a part
of all the wealth they've got
to His poor folk; He's ready
to increase their meagre stock.

In spite of this straight talking –
and I feel it's only right –
and all the words of truth I've put
directly in your sight,
I fear you will not listen,
or give the poor a bite,
any more than these did
a week ago tonight.

Translated from the Gaelic by Derick Thomson

ADAM SKIRVING (1719–1803)

Johnnie Cope

Hey, Johnnie Cope, are ye wauking yet?   *awake*
Or are your drums a-beating yet?
If ye were wauking I wad wait
　　To gang to the coals i' the morning.

Cope sent a challenge frae Dunbar:
'Charlie, meet me an ye daur,   *if*
And I'll learn you the art o' war   *teach*
　　If you'll meet me i' the morning.'

When Charlie looked the letter upon
He drew his sword the scabbard from:
'Come, follow me, my merry, merry men,
　　And we'll meet Johnnie Cope i' the morning!

'Now, Johnnie, be as good's your word;
Come, let us try both fire and sword;
And dinna rin like a frighted bird,   *don't*
　　That's chased frae its nest i' the morning.'

When Johnnie Cope he heard of this,
He thought it wadna be amiss
To hae a horse in readiness
　　To flee awa' i' the morning.

Fy now, Johnnie, get up and rin;
The Highland bagpipes mak a din;
It's best to sleep in a hale skin,
　　For 'twill be a bluidy morning.

When Johnnie Cope to Dunbar came,
They speered at him, 'Where's a' your men?'   *asked*
'The deil confound me gin I ken,   *if*
　　For I left them a' i' the morning.'

'Now Johnnie, troth, ye are na blate   *timid*
To come wi' the news o' your ain defeat,
And leave your men in sic a strait
    Sae early in the morning.'

'I' faith,' quo' Johnnie, 'I got a fleg   *fright*
Wi' their claymores and philabegs;   *kilts*
If I face them again, deil break my legs!
    So I wish you a gude morning.'

IAIN MAC MHURCHAIDH/JOHN MACRAE
(d.c.1780)

Dèan Cadalan Sàmhach

Dèan cadalan sàmhach, a chuilein mo rùin,
Dèan fuireach mar thà thu, 's tu 'n dràsd an àit' ùr.
Bidh òigearan againn, làn beairteis is cliù,
'S ma bhios tu nad airidh 's leat fear-eigin dhiùbh.

Gur ann an Ameireaga tha sinn an dràsd,
Fo dhubhar na coille nach teirig gu bràth.
Nuair dh'fhalbhas an dùbhlachd 's a thionndaidheas am blàths
Bidh cnothan, bidh ùbhlan, 's bidh an siùcar a' fàs.

'S ro bheag orm fèin na daoine seo th' ann,
Le 'n còtaichean drògaid, ad mhòr air an ceann,
Le 'm briogaisean goirid, 's iad sgaoilte gu 'm bonn;
Chan fhaicear an t-osan, 's i 'bhochdainn a th' ann.

Tha sinne nar n-Innseanaich, cinnteach gu leòr;
Fo dhubhar nan craobh cha bhi h-aon againn beò;
Madaidh-allaidh is bèistean ag èigheach 's gach fròig;
Gu bheil sinn nar n-èiginn bhon là thrèig sinn Rìgh Deòrs'.

Thoir mo shoraidh le fàilte Chinn t-Sàile nam bò,
Far an d' fhuair mi greis m' àrach's mi 'm phàisde beag òg.
Bhiodh fleasgaichean donna air bonnaibh ri ceòl,
Agus nìonagan dualach 's an gruaidh mar an ròs.

An toiseach an fhoghair bu chridheil ar sùnnd,
Am fiadh anns an fhireach, 's am bradan an grùnnd;
Bhiodh luingeas an sgadain a' tighinn fo shiùil:
Bu bhòidheach an sealladh 's fir dhonn' air am bùird.

Sleep Softly

Sleep your sleep softly, my darling, my love,
just stay as you are, though the place here is new.
We'll have youngsters around us, with wealth and good name;
if you keep a look-out, you'll get one of them too.

It's in America that we are now,
in the shade of the wood that is there for all time.
When deep winter passes, and warmth comes again,
nuts and apples will grow, and sugar as well.

I have little regard for the folk we have here,
with coats made of drugget, big hats on their heads,
with their short breeches, flared at the tips,
long hose, more's the pity, are not to be seen.

We've become Indians, no doubt of that;
in the shade of the trees we will never survive;
wolves and wild beasts cry from each lair;
we are sore-pressed since we left our King George.

Say farewell but greet kindly Kintail of the cows,
where once I was reared at the time I was young.
There were brown-haired young gallants all ready to dance,
and girls with long curls and cheeks like the rose.

At onset of autumn we'd be of good cheer,
the deer in the forest, the salmon in stream;
the herring-boats came with their full spread of sail:
a fine sight they were with tanned men on their boards.

Translated from the Gaelic by Derick Thomson

DONNCHADH BÀN MAC-AN-T-SAOIR/ DUNCAN BAN MACINTYRE (1724–1812)

from *Moladh Beinn Dóbhrain*

Air fonn Pìobaireachd

Urlar

An t-urram thar gach beinn
    Aig Beinn Dóbhrain;
De na chunnaic mi fo 'n ghréin,
    'S i bu bhòidhche leam:
    Munadh fada réidh,
    Cuilidh 'm faighte féidh,
    Soilleireachd an t-sléibh
    Bha mi sònrachadh;
    Doireachan nan geug,
    Coill' anns am bi feur,
    'S foinneasach an spréidh
    Bhios a chòmhnaidh ann;
    Greadhain bu gheal céir,
    Faghaid air an déidh,
    'S laghach leam an sreud
    A bha sròineiseach.
'S aigeannach fear eutrom
    Gun mhórchuis,
Theid fasanda 'na éideadh
    Neo-spòrsail:
    Tha mhanntal uime féin,
    Caithtiche nach tréig,
    Bratach dhearg mar chéir
    Bhios mar chòmhdach air.

from *Ben Dorain*

To the Air of a Pibroch

Urlar

Honour past all bens
to Ben Dorain.
Of all beneath the sun
I adore her.

Mountain ranges clear,
Storehouse of the deer,
the radiance of the moor
I've observed there.

Leafy branchy groves,
woods where the grass grows,
inquisitive the does
that are roaming there.

Herds with white rumps race —
hunters in the chase.
O I love the grace
of these noble ones.

Spirited and delicate
and shy,
in fashionable coat
he goes by

in mantle well arrayed,
suit that will not fade,
dress of waxen-red
that he's wearing now.

'S culaidh g' a chur eug –
Duine dhèanadh teuchd,
Gunna bu mhath gleus
   An glaic òganaich;
Spor anns am biodh bearn,
Tarrann air a ceann,
Snap a bhuaileadh teann
   Ris na h-òrdaibh i;
Ochdshlisneach gun fheall,
Stoc de 'n fhiodh gun mheang,
Lotadh an damh seang
   Is a leònadh e;
'S fear a bhiodh mar cheàird
   Riutha sònraichte,
Dh'fhóghnadh dhaibh gun taing
   Le chuid seòlainean;
Gheibhte siud ri am,
Pàdraig anns a' ghleann,
Gillean is coin sheang,
   'S e toirt òrdugh dhaibh;
Peileirean 'nan deann,
Teine 'gan cur ann;
Eilid nam beann ard'
   Théid a leònadh leo.

Siubhal

'S i 'n eilid bheag bhinneach
   Bu ghuiniche sraonadh,
Le cuinnean geur biorach
   A' sireadh na gaoithe:
Gasganach speireach,
Feadh chreachainn na beinne,

Weapon that brings death,
bullet that stops breath,
expert studied youth
with his rifle there.

Flint that's notched and true,
on its head a screw,
a cock that would strike to
the hammers, it.

Eight sided, without flaw,
gun-stock would lay low
the great stag in the flow
of his own blood there.
One whose craft was dear –
Mozart of them –
would kill them with a pure
trick and stratagem.

One would find such men –
Patrick in the glen –
boys and dogs at one,
and he'd order them.

Bullets left and right,
fires creating light,
the hind on mountain height
gets its wound from them.

Siubhal

The hind that's sharp-headed
is fierce in its speeding:
how delicate, rapid,
its nostrils, wind-reading!
Light-hooved and quick limbèd,
she runs on the summit,

Le eagal roimh theine
   Cha teirinn i h-aonach;
Ged théid i 'na cabhaig,
   Cha ghearain i maothan:
Bha sìnnsireachd fallain;
'N uair shìneadh i h-anail,
'S toil-inntinn leam tannasg
   Dh' a langan a chluinntinn,
'S i 'g iarraidh a leannain
   'N am daraidh le coibhneas.
'S e damh a' chinn allaidh
Bu ghealcheireach feaman,
Gu cabarach ceannard,
   A b' fharamach raoiceadh;
'S e chòmhnaidh 'm Beinn Dóbhrain,
   'S e eòlach m' a fraoinibh.
'S ann am Beinn Dóbhrain,
   Bu mhór dhomh r' a ìnnseadh
A liuthad damh ceannard
   Tha fantainn 'san fhrìth ud;
Eilid chaol-eangach,
   'S a laoighean 'ga leantainn,
Le 'n gasgana geala,
   Ri bealach a' dìreadh,
Ri fraigh Choire Chruiteir,
   A' chuideachda phìceach.
'N uair a shìneas i h-eangan
'S a théid i 'na deannaibh,
Cha saltradh air thalamh
   Ach barra nan ìngnean:
Có b' urrainn g' a leantainn
   A dh' fhearaibh na rìoghachd?

from that uppermost limit
no gun will remove her.
You'll not see her winded,
that elegant mover.

Her forebears were healthy.
When she stopped to take breath then,
how I loved the pure wraith-like

sound of her calling,
she seeking her sweetheart
in the lust of the morning.

It's the stag, the proud roarer,
white-rumped and ferocious,
branch-antlered and noble,
would walk in the shaded
retreats of Ben Dorain,
so haughtily-headed.

O they are in Ben Dorain,
so numerous, various,
the stags that go roaring
so tall and imperious.

Hind, nimble and slender,
with her calves strung behind her
lightly ascending
the cool mountain passes
through Harper's Dell winding
on their elegant courses.

Accelerant, speedy,
when she moves her slim body
earth knows nought of this lady
but the tips of her nails.
Even light would be tardy
to the flash of her pulse.

'S arraideach faramach
 Carach air grìne,
A' chòisridh nach fhanadh
 Gnè smal air an inntinn;
 Ach caochlaideach curaideach
 Caolchasach ullamh,
 An aois cha chuir truim' orra,
 Mulad no mìghean.
'S e shlànaich an culaidh,
Feòil mhàis agus mhuineil,
Bhith tàmhachd am bunailt
 An cuilidh na frìthe;
Le àilgheas a' fuireach
Air fàsach 'nan grunnaibh;
'S i 'n àsainn a' mhuime
 Tha cumail na cìche
Ris na laoigh bhreaca bhallach
 Nach meathlaich na sianta,
Le 'n cridheacha meara
 Le bainne na cìoba;
 Gnoiseanach eangach,
Le 'n girteaga geala,
Le 'n corpanna glana
 Le fallaineachd fìoruisg;
Le faram gun ghearan
 Feadh ghleannan na mìltich.
Ged thigeadh an sneachda
Chan iarradh iad aitreabh,
'S e lag a' Choir' Altram
 Bhios aca g' an dìdean;

Dynamic, erratic,
by greenery spinning,
this troupe never static,
their minds free from sinning.

Coquettes of the body,
slim-leggèd and ready,
no age makes them tardy,
no grief nor disease.

Their coats get their shimmer —
fat flesh of their glamour —
from their local rich summer
in the store of the moor.

With pleasure abiding
in the pasture providing
— like milk for our children —
fresh grass from the heath.

Calves speckled and spotted,
unchilled by the showers,
are nursed by the rooted
gay, various grass.

Brindled, bright-hoovèd,
white-belted and vivid
as cinders quick-moving,
with the health of spring waters,
uncomplaining, belovèd —
these elegant daughters!

Though the snow should bewilder
they'll be seeking no shelter
except in the Corrie —
other dwelling disdaining.

Feadh stacan is bhacan
    Is ghlacaga dìomhair,
Le 'n leapaichean fasgach
    An taic Ais an t-Sìthein.

Among banks and steep columns
and hollows mysterious
they'd bed by the solemn
Haunt of the Fairies.

Translated from the Gaelic by Iain Crichton Smith

JEAN ELLIOT (1727–1805)

The Flowers of the Forest

I've heard the lilting at our yowe-milking,   *singing; ewe-milking*
  Lasses a-lilting before the dawn o' day;
But now they are moaning on ilka green loaning: *each pasture*
  'The Flowers of the Forest are a' wede away.'   *withered*

At buchts, in the morning, nae blythe lads are scorning;   *sheepfolds; teasing*
  The lasses are lonely, and dowie, and wae: *dismal*
Nae daffin', nae gabbin', but sighing and sabbing: *fooling*
  Ilk ane lifts her leglen, and hies her away.   *milk pail*

In hairst, at the shearing, nae youths now are jeering,   *harvest*
  The bandsters are lyart, and runkled and grey;   *grizzled; wrinkled*
At fair or at preaching, nae wooing, nae fleeching: *coaxing*
  The Flowers of the Forest are a' wede away.

At e'en, in the gloaming, nae swankies are roaming
  'Bout stacks wi' the lasses at bogle to play,   *hide-and-seek*
But ilk ane sits drearie, lamenting her dearie:
  The Flowers of the Forest are a' wede away.

Dule and wae for the order sent out lads to the Border: *grief*
  The English, for ance, by guile wan the day:
The Flowers of the Forest, that foucht aye the foremost,
  The prime o' our land are cauld in the clay.

We'll hear nae mair lilting at our yowe-milking,
  Women and bairns are heartless and wae;
Sighing and moaning on ilka green loaning:
  'The Flowers of the Forest are a' wede away.'

JAMES MACPHERSON (1736–1796)

from *Fragments of Ancient Poetry*

Collected in the Highlands of Scotland and Translated from the Gaelic or Erse Language

I sit by the mossy fountain; on the top of the hill of winds. One tree is rustling above me. Dark waves roll over the heath. The lake is troubled below. The deer descend from the hill. No hunter at a distance is seen; no whistling cow-herd is nigh. It is mid-day: but all is silent. Sad are my thoughts alone. Didst thou but appear, O my love, a wanderer on the heath! thy hair floating on the wind behind thee; thy bosom heaving on the sight; thine eyes full of tears for thy friends, whom the mist of the hill had concealed! Thee I would comfort, my love, and bring thee to thy father's house.

But is it she that there appears, like a beam of light on the heath? bright as the moon in autumn, as the sun in a summer-storm, comest thou lovely maid over rocks, over mountains to me? – She speaks: but how weak her voice! like the breeze in the reeds of the pool. Hark!

Returnest thou safe from the war? Where are thy friends, my love? I heard of thy death on the hill; I heard and mourned thee, Shilric!

Yes, my fair, I return: but I alone of my race. Thou shalt see them no more: their graves I raised on the plain. But why art thou on the desert hill? why on the heath, alone?

Alone I am, O Shilric! alone in the winter-house. With grief for thee I expired. Shilric, I am pale in the tomb.

She fleets, she sails away; as grey mist before the wind! – and, wilt thou not stay, my love? Stay and behold my tears? fair thou appearest, my love! fair thou wast, when alive!

By the mossy fountain I will sit; on the top of the hill of winds. When mid-day is silent around, converse, O my love, with me! come on the wings of the gale! on the blast of the mountain, come! Let me hear thy voice, as thou passest, when mid-day is silent around.

ROBERT FERGUSSON (1750–1774)

Caller Oysters   *fresh*

Happy the man who, free from care and strife,
In silken or in leathern purse retains
A splendid shilling. He nor hears with pain
New oysters cry'd, nor sighs for chearful ale.
    (Phillips)

Of a' the waters that can hobble   *move*
A fishin yole or salmon coble,   *yawl; [flat-bottomed boat]*
And can reward the fishers trouble,
                    Or south or north,
There's nane sae spacious and sae noble
                    As Firth o' Forth.

In her the skate and codlin sail,
The eil fou souple wags her tail,
Wi' herrin, fleuk, and mackarel,   *flounder*
                    And whitens dainty;   *young salmon trout*
Their spindle-shanks the labsters trail,
                    Wi' partans plenty.   *crabs*

Auld Reikie's sons blyth faces wear;   *[Edinburgh's]*
September's merry month is near,
That brings in Neptune's caller chere,
                    New oysters fresh;
The halesomest and nicest gear
                    Of fish or flesh.

O! then we needna gie a plack   *copper coin*
For dand'ring mountebank or quack,   *wandering*
Wha o' their drogs sae bauldly crack,   *drugs; talk up*
                    And spred sic notions,
As gar their feckless patient tak
                    Their stinkin potions.

Come prie, frail man! for gin thou art sick, *taste; if*
The oyster is a rare cathartic,
As ever doctor patient gart lick *made; swallow*
        To cure his ails;
Whether you hae the head or heart-ake,
        It ay prevails.

Ye tiplers, open a' your poses, *[hoards of money]*
Ye wha are faush'd wi' plouky noses, *troubled; pimply*
Fling owr your craig sufficient doses, *throat*
        You'll thole a hunder, *endure*
To fleg awa' your simmer roses, *[drive off]; [alcoholic complexion]*
        And naething under. *[less]*

Whan big as burns the gutters rin,
Gin ye hae catcht a droukit skin,
To Luckie Middlemist's loup in, *jump*
        And sit fu snug
O'er oysters and a dram o' gin,
        Or haddock lug. *fillet*

When auld Saunt Giles, at aught o'clock,
Gars merchant lowns their chopies lock, *tradesmen; shops*
There we adjourn wi' hearty fock
        To birle our bodles, *[spend our small change]*
And get wharewi' to crack our joke,
        And clear our noddles.

Whan Phœbus did his windocks steek, *windows; close*
How aften at that ingle cheek *fireplace; side*
Did I my frosty fingers beek, *warm*
        And taste gude fare?
I trow there was nae hame to seek
        Whan steghin there. *gorging*

While glakit fools, o'er rife o' cash, *stupid*
Pamper their weyms wi' fousom trash, *bellies; over-rich*
I think a chiel may gayly pass;
        He's no ill boden *supplied*
That gusts his gabb wi' oyster sauce, *[pleases his palate]*
        And hen weel soden. *boiled*

At Musselbrough, and eke Newhaven,
The fisher wives will get top livin,
When lads gang out on Sunday's even
   To treat their joes,   *sweethearts*
And tak of fat pandours a prieven,   *Prestonpans oysters; taste*
   Or mussel brose: *soup*

Than sometimes 'ere they flit their doup,   *shift; arse*
They'll ablins a' their siller coup   *perhaps; exchange*
For liquor clear frae cutty stoup,   *wee jug*
   To weet their wizen,   *gullet*
And swallow o'er a dainty soup,
   For fear they gizzen.   *[go thirsty]*

A' ye wha canna stand sae sicker,
Whan twice you've toom'd the big ars'd bicker,   *beaker*
Mix caller oysters wi' your liquor,   *fresh*
   And I'm your debtor,
If greedy priest or drouthy vicar   *thirsty*
   Will thole it better.   *endure*

from *Auld Reikie, a Poem*   *[Edinburgh]*

Auld Reikie! wale o' ilka town   *best; every*
That Scotland kens beneath the moon;   *knows*
Whare couthy chiels at e'ening meet   *agreeable lads*
Their bizzing craigs and mous to weet: *dry throats; mouths*
And blythly gar auld Care gae bye   *bid*
Wi' blinkit and wi' bleering eye:
O'er lang frae thee the Muse has been
Sae frisky on the simmer's green,   *summer*
Whan flowers and gowans wont to glent   *daisies; gleam*
In bonny blinks upo' the bent;   *field*
But now the leaves a yellow die,
Peel'd frae the branches, quickly fly;
And now frae nouther bush nor brier
The spreckl'd mavis greets your ear;   *thrush*
Nor bonny blackbird skims and roves
To seek his love in yonder groves.

Then, Reikie, welcome! Thou canst charm
Unfleggit by the year's alarm;   *unruffled*
Not Boreas, that sae snelly blows,   *North Wind; bitter*
Dare here pap in his angry nose: *aim*
Thanks to our dads, whase biggin stands   *building*
A shelter to surrounding lands.   *tenements*
    Now morn, with bonny purpie-smiles,   *blushes*
Kisses the air-cock o' St. Giles;
Rakin their ein, the servant lasses   *rubbing*
Early begin their lies and clashes;
Ilk tells her friend of saddest distress,   *each*
That still she brooks frae scouling mistress;
And wi' her joe in turnpike stair   *sweetheart*
She'd rather snuff the stinking air,
As be subjected to her tongue,
When justly censur'd in the wrong.
    On stair wi' tub, or pat in hand,   *pot*
The barefoot housemaids looe to stand,   *love*
That antrin fock may ken how snell   *wandering; sharp*
Auld Reikie will at morning smell:
Then, with an inundation big as
The burn that 'neath the Nore Loch Brig is,
They kindly shower Edina's roses,
To quicken and regale our noses.
Now some for this, wi' satyr's leesh,   *whip*
Ha'e gi'en auld Edinburgh a creesh: *lash*
But without souring nocht is sweet;
The morning smells that hail our street,
Prepare, and gently lead the way
To simmer canty, braw and gay;   *summer; cheerful*
Edina's sons mair eithly share   *easily*
Her spices and her dainties rare,
Than he that's never yet been call'd
Aff frae his plaidie or his fauld.   *plaid; fold*
    Now stairhead critics, senseless fools,
Censure their aim, and pride their rules,
In Luckenbooths, wi' glouring eye,
Their neighbours sma'est faults descry:
If ony loun should dander there,   *fellow; wander*
Of aukward gate, and foreign air,

They trace his steps, till they can tell
His pedigree as weel's himsell.
　　When Phœbus blinks wi' warmer ray,
And schools at noonday get the play,
Then bus'ness, weighty bus'ness comes;
The trader glours; he doubts, he hums:
The lawyers eke to Cross repair,   *also*
Their wigs to shaw, and toss an air;
While busy agent closely plies,
And a' his kittle cases tries.   *difficult*
　　Now Night, that's cunzied chief for fun,   *reckoned*
Is wi' her usual rites begun;
Thro' ilka gate the torches blaze,
And globes send out their blinking rays.
The usefu' cadie plies in street,   *messenger*
To bide the profits o' his feet:
For by thir lads Auld Reikie's fock
Ken but a sample, o' the stock
O' thieves, that nightly wad oppress,
And make baith goods and gear the less.
Near him the lazy chairman stands,   *sedan chair bearer*
And wats na how to turn his hands,   *knows*
Till some daft birky, ranting fu',   *smart alec; drunk*
Has matters somewhere else to do;
The chairman willing, gi'es his light
To deeds o' darkness and o' night:
　　It's never sax pence for a lift
That gars thir lads wi' fu'ness rift;   *makes; belch*
For they wi' better gear are paid,
And whores and culls support their trade.   *fools*
　　Near some lamp-post, wi' dowy face,   *dismal*
Wi' heavy een, and sour grimace,
Stands she that beauty lang had kend,
Whoredom her trade, and vice her end.
But see wharenow she wuns her bread,
By that which Nature ne'er decreed;
And sings sad music to the lugs,   *ears*
'Mang burachs o' damn'd whores and rogues.   *crowds*
Whane'er we reputation loss,
Fair chastity's transparent gloss!

Redemption seenil kens the name   *seldom*
But a's black misery and shame.
    Frae joyous tavern, reeling drunk,
Wi' fiery phizz, and ein half sunk,   *face*
Behad the bruiser, fae to a'   *behold*
That in the reek o' gardies fa':   *commotion of fists*
Close by his side, a feckless race
O' macaronies shew their face,   *dandies*
And think they're free frae skaith or harm,   *injury*
While pith befriends their leaders arm: *strength*
Yet fearfu' aften o' their maught,   *might*
They quatt the glory o' the faught   *quit*
To this same warrior wha led
Thae heroes to bright honour's bed;
And aft the hack o' honour shines
In bruiser's face wi' broken lines:
Of them sad tales he tells anon,
Whan ramble and whan fighting's done;
And, like Hectorian, ne'er impairs
The brag and glory o' his sairs.   *injuries*
    Whan feet in dirty gutters plash,
And fock to wale their fitstaps fash;   *choose; [take pains]*
At night the macaroni drunk,
In pools or gutters aftimes sunk:
Hegh! what a fright he now appears,
Whan he his corpse dejected rears!
Look at that head, and think if there
The pomet slaister'd up his hair!   *pomatum; greased*
The cheeks observe, where now cou'd shine
The scancing glories o' carmine?   *shining*
Ah, legs! in vain the silk-worm there
Display'd to view her eidant care;   *diligent*
For stink, instead of perfumes, grow,
And clarty odours fragrant flow.   *dirty*
    Now some to porter, some to punch,
Some to their wife, and some their wench,
Retire, while noisy ten-hours drum
Gars a' your trades gae dandring home.   *forces; wandering*
Now mony a club, jocose and free,
Gie a' to merriment and glee;

Wi' sang and glass, they fley the pow'r   [make flee]
O' care that wad harrass the hour:
For wine and Bacchus still bear down
Our thrawart fortunes wildest frown: hostile
It maks you stark, and bauld, and brave,   strong
Ev'n whan descending to the grave.
   Now some, in Pandemonium's shade,
Resume the gormandizing trade;
Whare eager looks, and glancing ein,
Forespeak a heart and stamack keen.
Gang on, my lads; it's lang sin syne
We kent auld Epicurus' line;
Save you, the board wad cease to rise;
Bedight wi' daintiths to the skies;   loaded; dainties
And salamanders cease to swill
The comforts of a burning gill.

To the Principal and Professors of the University of St Andrews, on their Superb Treat to Dr Samuel Johnson

St Andrews town may look right gawsy,   handsome
Nae grass will grow upon her cawsey,   pavement
Nor wa'-flowers of a yellow dye,
Glour dowy o'er her ruins high,   sadly
Sin Samy's head weel pang'd wi' lear,   crammed; learning
Has seen the *Alma Mater* there:
Regents, my winsome billy boys!   Professors; good lads
'Bout him you've made an unco noise;
Nae doubt for him your bells wad clink
To find him upon Eden's brink,
An' a' things nicely set in order,
Wad kep him on the Fifan border: [of Fife]
I'se warrant now frae France an' Spain,
Baith cooks and scullions mony ane
Wad gar the pats an' kettles tingle
Around the college kitchen ingle,   fire
To fleg frae a' your craigs the roup,   drive; throats; hoarseness
Wi' reeking het and crieshy soup;   hot; greasy
And snails and puddocks mony hunder   frogs; hundred
Wad beeking lie the hearth-stane under,   baking

Wi' roast and boild, an' a' kin kind,
To heat the body, cool the mind.
    But hear me lads! gin I'd been there,   *if*
How I wad trimm'd the bill o' fare!
For ne'er sic surly wight as he   *man*
Had met wi' sic respect frae me.
Mind ye what Sam, the lying loun!   *fellow*
Has in his Dictionar laid down?
That aits in England are a feast   *oats*
To cow an' horse, an' sican beast,
While in Scots ground this growth was common
To gust the gab o' man and woman.   *please; mouth*
Tak tent, ye Regents! then, an' hear   *pay attention*
My list o' gudely hamel gear,   *homely food*
Sic as ha'e often rax'd the wyme   *stretched; stomach*
O' blyther fallows mony time;
Mair hardy, souple, steive an' swank,   *sturdy; smart*
Than ever stood on Samy's shank.
    Imprimis, then, a haggis fat,   *Firstly*
Weel tottled in a seything pat,   *simmered; pot*
Wi' spice and ingans weel ca'd thro',   *onions*
Had help'd to gust the stirrah's mow,   *rude man's mouth*
And plac'd itsel in truncher clean
Before the gilpy's glowrin een.   *man's*
    Secundo, then a gude sheep's head
Whase hide was singit, never flead,   *flayed*
And four black trotters cled wi' girsle,   *gristle*
Bedown his throat had learn'd to hirsle.   *glide*
What think ye neist, o' gude fat brose   *next; [dish of oatmeal]*
To clag his ribs? a dainty dose!
And white and bloody puddins routh,
To gar the Doctor skirl, O Drouth!   *make; scream*
Whan he cou'd never houp to merit
A cordial o' reaming claret,
But thraw his nose, and brize and pegh   *puff*
O'er the contents o' sma' ale quegh: *quaich*
Then let his wisdom girn and snarl
O'er a weel-tostit girdle farl,   *cake*
An' learn, that maugre o' his wame,   *despite; belly*
Ill bairns are ay best heard at hame.

Drummond, lang syne, o' Hawthornden,
The wyliest an' best o' men,
Has gi'en you dishes ane or mae,
That wad ha' gard his grinders play,
Not to *roast beef*, old England's life,
But to the auld *east nook of Fife*,
Whare Creilian crafts cou'd weel ha'e gi'en   *[of Crail]*
Scate-rumples to ha'e clear'd his een: *skate-tails*
Than neist whan Samy's heart was faintin,
He'd lang'd for scate to mak him wanton.

    Ah! willawins, for Scotland now,   *wellaway*
Whan she maun stap ilk birky's mow   *man's mouth*
Wi' eistacks, grown as 'tware in pet   *dainties; freakish heat*
In foreign land, or green-house het,
When cog o' brose an' cutty spoon   *bowl; short-handled*
Is a' our cottar childer's boon,
Wha thro' the week, till Sunday's speal,   *rest*
Toil for pease-clods an' gude lang kail.   *pease-loaf; cabbage*
Devall then, Sirs, and never send   *leave off*
For daintiths to regale a friend,   *dainties*
Or, like a torch at baith ends burning,
Your house 'll soon grow mirk and mourning.

    What's this I hear some cynic say?
Robin, ye loun! its nae fair play;
Is there nae ither subject rife
To clap your thumb upon but Fife?
Gi'e o'er, young man, you'll meet your corning,
Than caption war, or charge o' horning;
Some canker'd surly sour-mow'd carline   *old woman*
Bred near the abbey o' Dumfarline,
Your shoulders yet may gi'e a lounder,   *blow*
An' be of verse the mal-confounder.

    Come on, ye blades! but 'ere ye tulzie,   *quarrel*
Or hack our flesh wi' sword or gulzie,   *knife*
Ne'er shaw your teeth, nor look like stink,
Nor o'er an empty bicker blink: *beaker*
What weets the wizen an' the wyme,   *throat; stomach*
Will mend your prose and heal my rhyme.

ROBERT BURNS (1759–1796)

Mary Morison

O Mary, at thy window be,
   It is the wish'd, the trysted hour;
Those smiles and glances let me see,
   That make the miser's treasure poor:
How blythly wad I bide the stoure,   *endure; struggle*
   A weary slave frae sun to sun;
Could I the rich reward secure,
   The lovely Mary Morison.

Yestreen when to the trembling string
   The dance gaed thro' the lighted ha',   *hall*
To thee my fancy took its wing,
   I sat, but neither heard nor saw:
Tho' this was fair, and that was braw,
   And yon the toast of a' the town,
I sigh'd, and said amang them a',
   'Ye are na Mary Morison.'

O Mary, canst thou wreck his peace,
   Wha for thy sake wad gladly die!
Or canst thou break that heart of his,
   Whase only faut is loving thee.
If love for love thou wilt na gie,
   At least be pity to me shown;
A thought ungentle canna be
   The thought o' Mary Morison.

Holy Willie's Prayer

And send the Godly in a pet to pray   (Pope)

ARGUMENT: Holy Willie was a rather oldish batchelor Elder in the parish of Mauchline, and much and justly famed for that polemical chattering which ends in tippling Orthodoxy, and for that Spiritualized Bawdry which refines to Liquorish Devotion. – In a Sessional process with a gentleman in Mauchline, a Mr Gavin Hamilton, Holy Willie, and his priest, father Auld, after full hearing in the Presbytry of Ayr, came off but second best; owing partly to the oratorical powers of Mr Robt Aiken, Mr Hamilton's Counsel; but chiefly to Mr Hamilton's being one of the most irreproachable and truly respectable characters in the country. – On losing his Process, the Muse overheard him at his devotions as follows –

O Thou, wha in the heavens dost dwell,
Wha, as it pleases best thysel',
Sends ane to heaven and ten to hell,
                    A' for thy glory,
And no for ony guid or ill
                    They've done afore thee!

I bless and praise thy matchless might,
Whan thousands thou hast left in night,
That I am here afore thy sight,
                    For gifts an' grace,
A burnin' an' a shinin' light,
                    To a' this place.

What was I, or my generation,
That I should get such exaltation,
I wha deserve sic just damnation,
                    For broken laws,
Five thousand years ere my creation,
                    Thro' Adam's cause.

When frae my mither's womb I fell,
Thou might ha'e plunged me in hell,
To gnash my gums, to weep and wail,
                    In burnin' lake,
Whar damned devils roar and yell,
                    Chain'd to a stake.

Yet I am here a chosen sample,
To show thy grace is great an' ample;
I'm here a pillar in thy temple,
          Strong as a rock,
A guide, a buckler, an' example
          To a' thy flock.

But yet, O Lord! confess I must,
At times I'm fash'd wi' fleshly lust   *troubled*
An' sometimes too, wi' warldly trust,
          Vile Self gets in;
But thou remembers we are dust,
          Defil'd in sin.

O Lord! yestreen, thou kens, wi' Meg –   *yesterday; knows*
Thy pardon I sincerely beg –
O may't ne'er be a living plague
          To my dishonor!
An' I'll ne'er lift a lawless leg
          Again upon her.

Besides, I farther maun avow –   *must*
Wi' Leezie's lass, three times, I trow –
But, Lord, that Friday I was fou,   *drunk*
          When I cam near her,
Or else, thou kens, thy servant true
          Wad never steer her.

Maybe thou lets this fleshly thorn
Buffet thy servant e'en and morn,
Lest he owre proud and high should turn
          That he's sae gifted:
If sae, thy han' maun e'en be borne
          Until thou lift it.

Lord, bless thy Chosen in this place,
For here thou has a chosen race!
But God confound their stubborn face
          An' blast their name,
Wha bring thy elders to disgrace
          An' open shame!

Lord mind Gaun Hamilton's deserts,
He drinks, an' swears, an' plays at carts,
Yet has sae mony takin' arts,
    Wi' great an' sma'
Frae God's ain priest the people's hearts
    He steals awa'.

An' whan we chasten'd him therefore,
Thou kens how he bred sic a splore,   *commotion*
As set the warld in a roar
    O laughin' at us;
Curse thou his basket and his store,
    Kail an' potatoes.   *cabbage*

Lord hear my earnest cry an' pray'r
Against that presbyt'ry o' Ayr;
Thy strong right hand, Lord make it bare,
    Upo' their heads,
Lord weigh it down, and dinna spare,
    For their misdeeds.

O Lord my God, that glib-tongu'd Aiken,
My very heart an' soul are quakin',
To think how we stood, sweatin', shakin',
    An' pissed wi' dread,
While Auld wi' hingin lip gaed sneakin',
    And hid his head.

Lord in the day of vengeance try him,
Lord visit them wha did employ him,
And pass not in thy mercy by 'em,
    Nor hear their prayer;
But for thy people's sake destroy 'em,
    And dinna spare.

But Lord remember me and mine
Wi' mercies temp'ral and divine,
That I for gear and grace may shine,
    Excell'd by nane,
An' a' the glory shall be thine,
    Amen, Amen.

To a Mouse
On Turning Her up in Her Nest with the Plough,
November 1785

Wee, sleeket, cowran, tim'rous *beastie*, *furtive; cowering*
O, what a panic's in thy breastie!
Thou need na start awa sae hasty,
        Wi' bickering brattle! *noisy rushing*
I wad be laith to rin an' chase thee,
        Wi' murd'ring *pattle*! *[plough-cleaning spade]*

I'm truly sorry Man's dominion
Has broken Nature's social union,
An' justifies that ill opinion,
        Which makes thee startle,
At me, thy poor, earth-born companion,
        An' *fellow-mortal*!

I doubt na, whyles, but thou may thieve; *sometimes*
What then? poor beastie, thou maun live! *must*
A *daimen-icker* in a *thrave* *ear of corn; stack of grain*
        'S a sma' request:
I'll get a blessin wi' the lave, *rest*
        An' never miss't!

Thy wee-bit *housie*, too, in ruin!
It's silly wa's the win's are strewin! *walls*
An' naething, now, to big a new ane, *build*
        O' foggage green! *rank grass*
An' bleak December's winds ensuin,
        Baith snell an' keen! *sharp*

Thou saw the fields laid bare an' wast,
An' weary Winter comin fast,
An' cozie here, beneath the blast,
        Thou thought to dwell,
Till crash! the cruel *coulter* past *ploughshare*
        Out thro' thy cell.

That wee-bit heap o' leaves an' stibble,
Has cost thee monie a weary nibble!
Now thou's turn'd out, for a' thy trouble,
    But house or hald,   *without*
To thole the Winter's sleety dribble,   *endure*
     An' *cranreuch* cauld!   *hoar-frost*

But Mousie, thou art no thy-lane,
In proving *foresight* may be vain:
The best laid schemes o' *Mice* an' *Men*,
     Gang aft agley,   *awry*
An' lea'e us nought but grief an' pain,
     For promis'd joy!

Still, thou art blest, compar'd wi' *me*!
The *present* only toucheth thee:
But Och! I *backward* cast my e'e,
     On prospects drear!
An' *forward*, tho' I canna *see*,
     I *guess* an' *fear*!

Address to the Deil

O Prince, O chief of many throned pow'rs,
That led th' embattl'd Seraphim to war
  (Milton)

O Thou, whatever title suit thee!
Auld Hornie, Satan, Nick, or Clootie!   *Cloven*
Wha in yon cavern grim an' sootie,
     Clos'd under hatches,
Spairges about the brunstane cootie,   *splurges; brimstone; tub*
     To scaud poor wretches!   *scald*

Hear me, *auld Hangie*, for a wee,   *while*
An' let poor, *damned bodies* bee;
I'm sure sma' pleasure it can gie,
     Ev'n to a *deil*,
To skelp an' scaud poor dogs like me,   *strike*
     An' hear us squeel!

Great is thy pow'r, an' great thy fame;
Far kend an' noted is thy name;
An' tho' yon *lowan heugh's* thy hame,   *blazing pit*
        Thou travels far;
An' faith! thou's neither lag nor lame,   *tardy*
        Nor blate nor scaur.   *shy; timid*

Whyles, ranging like a roaran lion,   *sometimes*
For prey, a' holes an' corners tryin;
Whyles, on the strong-wing'd tempest flyin,
        Tirlan the *kirks*;   *unroofing*
Whyles, in the human bosom pryin,
        Unseen thou lurks.

I've heard my rev'rend *Graunie* say,   *Granny*
In lanely glens ye like to stray;
Or where auld, ruin'd castles, gray,
        Nod to the moon,
Ye fright the nightly wand'rer's way,
        Wi' eldritch croon.   *unearthly singing*

When twilight did my *Graunie* summon,
To say her prayers, douse, honest woman!   *gentle*
Aft 'yont the dyke she's heard you bumman,   *humming*
        Wi' eerie drone;
Or, rustling, thro' the boortries coman,   *elder trees*
        Wi' heavy groan.

Ae dreary, windy, winter night,   *one*
The stars shot down wi' sklentan light,   *slanting*
Wi' you, *myself*, I gat a fright,
        Ayont the lough;   *beyond; loch*
Ye, like a *rass-buss*, stood in sight,   *bush of rushes*
        Wi' waving sugh.   *sigh*

The cudgel in my nieve did shake,   *fist*
Each bristl'd hair stood like a stake,
When wi' an eldritch, stoor *quaick, quaick,*   *harsh*
        Amang the springs,
Awa ye squatter'd like a *drake*,
        On whistling wings.

Let *Warlocks* grim, an' wither'd *Hags*,
Tell how wi' you on ragweed nags,   *ragwort*
They skim the muirs an' dizzy crags,
        Wi' wicked speed;
And in kirk-yards renew their leagues,
        Owre howcket dead.   *exhumed*

Thence, countra wives, wi' toil an' pain,
May plunge an' plunge the *kirn* in vain;   *churn*
For Oh! the yellow treasure's taen
        By witching skill;
An' dawtet, twal-pint *Hawkie's* gane   *petted; twelve-*
        As yell's the bill.   *dry; bull*

Thence, mystic knots mak great abuse,
On *Young-Guidmen*, fond, keen an' croose;   *bold*
When the best *wark-lume* i' the house,   *work-loom [sc. penis]*
        By cantraip wit,   *magic*
Is instant made no worth a louse,
        Just at the bit.

When thowes dissolve the snawy hoord,
An' float the jinglan icy boord,   *surface*
Then *water-kelpies* haunt the foord,   *water-horse spirits*
        By your direction,
An' nighted trav'llers are allur'd
        To their destruction.

An' aft your moss-traversing *spunkies*   *will o' the wisps*
Decoy the wight that late an' drunk is:
The bleezan, curst, mischievous monkies   *blazing*
        Delude his eyes,
Till in some miry slough he sunk is,
        Ne'er mair to rise.

When Mason's mystic *word* an' *grip*,
In storms an' tempests raise you up,
Some cock or cat, your rage maun stop,   *must*
        Or, strange to tell!
The *youngest brother* ye wad whip
        Aff straught to Hell.

Lang syne in Eden's bonie yard,
When youthfu' lovers first were pair'd,
An' all the Soul of Love they shar'd,
        The raptur'd hour,
Sweet on the fragrant, flow'ry swaird,
        In shady bow'r.

Then you, ye auld, snick-drawing dog!   *latch-lifting*
Ye cam to Paradise incog,
An' play'd on man a cursed brogue,   *trick*
        (Black be your fa'!)
An' gied the infant warld a shog,   *shake*
        'Maist ruin'd a'.

D'ye mind that day, when in a bizz,   *commotion*
Wi' reeket duds, an' reestet gizz,   *smoking clothes; cured wig*
Ye did present your smoutie phiz,   *smutty face*
        'Mang better folk,
An' sklented on the *man of Uzz*,   *aimed*
        Your spitefu' joke?

An how ye gat him i' your thrall,
An' brak him out o' house an' hal',
While scabs an' botches did him gall,   *tumours*
        Wi' bitter claw,
An' lows'd his ill-tongu'd, wicked *Scawl*   *scolding woman*
        Was warst ava?

But a' your doings to rehearse,
Your wily snares an' fechtin fierce,   *fighting*
Sin' that day Michael did you pierce,
        Down to this time,
Wad ding a *Lallan* tongue, or *Erse*,   *beat; Lowland; Gaelic*
        In Prose or Rhyme.

An' now, auld *Cloots*, I ken ye're thinkan,
A certain *Bardie's* rantin, drinkin,
Some luckless hour will send him linkan,   *walking quickly*
        To your black pit;
But faith! he'll turn a corner jinkan,   *stepping nimbly*
        An' cheat you yet.

But fare-you-weel, auld *Nickie-ben*!
O wad ye tak a thought an' men'!
Ye aiblens might – I dinna ken –   *perhaps*
        Still hae a *stake* –
I'm wae to think upo' yon den,
        Ev'n for your sake!

To a Louse
On Seeing One on a Lady's Bonnet at Church

Ha! whare ye gaun, ye crowlan ferlie!   *crawling marvel*
Your impudence protects you sairly:
I canna say but ye strunt rarely,   *strut*
        Owre *gawze* and *lace*;
Tho' faith, I fear ye dine but sparely,
        On sic a place.

Ye ugly, creepan, blastet wonner,
Detested, shunn'd, by saunt an' sinner,
How daur ye set your fit upon her,
        Sae fine a *Lady*!
Gae somewhere else and seek your dinner,
        On some poor body.

Swith, in some beggar's haffet squattle;   *shoo; whiskers; squat*
There ye may creep, and sprawl, and sprattle,   *scramble*
Wi' ither kindred, jumping cattle,
        In shoals and nations;
Whare *horn* nor *bane* ne'er daur unsettle,   *bone-comb*
        Your thick plantations.

Now haud you there, ye're out o' sight,
Below the fatt'rels, snug and tight,   *ribbon-ends*
Na faith ye yet! ye'll no be right,
        Till ye've got on it,
The vera tapmost, towrin height
        O' *Miss's bonnet*.

My sooth! right bauld ye set your nose out,
As plump an' gray as onie grozet: *gooseberry*
O for some rank, mercurial rozet,   *resin*
    Or fell, red smeddum,   *evil; [medicinal powder]*
I'd gie you sic a hearty dose o't,
    Wad dress your droddum!   *kick your arse*

I wad na been surpriz'd to spy
You on an auld wife's *flainen toy*;   *flannel cap*
Or aiblins some bit duddie boy,   *perhaps; ragged*
    On's *wylecoat*;   *short coat*
But Miss's fine *Lunardi*, fye!   *[balloon-shaped bonnet]*
    How daur ye do't?

O *Jenny* dinna toss your head,
An' set your beauties a' abroad!
Ye little ken what cursed speed
    The blastie's makin,   *beast*
Thae *winks* and *finger-ends*, I dread,
    Are notice takin!

O wad some Pow'r the giftie gie us
To see oursels as others see us!
It wad frae monie a blunder free us
    An' foolish notion:
What airs in dress an' gait wad lea'e us,
    And ev'n Devotion!

from *Love and Liberty. A Cantata*

See! the smoking bowl before us,
 Mark our jovial ragged ring!
Round and round take up the chorus,
 And in raptures let us sing.

Chorus
  A fig for those by law protected!
   Liberty's a glorious feast!
  Courts for cowards were erected,
   Churches built to please the priest.

What is title? what is treasure?
   What is reputation's care?
If we lead a life of pleasure,
   'Tis no matter *how* or *where*!

    A fig, &c.

With the ready trick and fable,
   Round we wander all the day;
And at night, in barn or stable,
   Hug our doxies on the hay.

    A fig, &c.

Does the train-attended *carriage*
   Thro' the country lighter rove?
Does the sober bed of *marriage*
   Witness brighter scenes of love?

    A fig, &c.

Life is all a *variorum*,
   We regard not how it goes;
Let them cant about *decorum*
   Who have characters to lose.

    A fig, &c.

Here's to budgets, bags and wallets!
   Here's to all the wandering train!
Here's our ragged *brats* and *callets*!   *wenches*
   One and all cry out, Amen!

    A fig for those by law protected!
      Liberty's a glorious feast!
    Courts for cowards were erected,
      Churches built to please the priest.

Second Epistle to Davie

AULD NIBOR,
I'm three times, doubly, o'er your debtor,
For your auld-farrent, frien'ly letter;   *wise*
Tho' I maun say't, I doubt ye flatter,   *must*
      Ye speak sae fair;
For my puir, silly, rhymin' clatter
      Some less maun sair.

Hale be your heart, hale be your fiddle;
Lang may your elbuck jink an' diddle,   *elbow; jerk*
Tae cheer you thro' the weary widdle   *strife*
      O' war'ly cares,
Till bairns' bairns kindly cuddle
      Your auld, gray hairs.

But DAVIE, lad, I'm red ye're glaikit;   *told; foolish*
I'm tauld the Muse ye hae negleckit;
An' gif it's sae, ye sud be licket   *punished*
      Until ye fyke;   *fuss*
Sic hauns as you sud ne'er be faikit,   *hands; excused*
      Be hain't wha like.   *whoever's spared*

For me, I'm on Parnassus brink,
Rivan the words tae gar them clink;   *wrenching; sound well*
Whyles daez't wi' love, whyles daez't wi' drink,   *sometimes*
      Wi' jads or masons;   *women*
An' whyles, but ay owre late, I think
      Braw sober lessons.

Of a' the thoughtless sons o' man,
Commen' me to the Bardie clan;
Except it be some idle plan
      O' rhymin clink,
The devil-haet, that I sud ban,   *[devil have it]*
      They never think.

Nae thought, nae view, nae scheme o' livin',
Nae cares tae gie us joy or grievin':
But just the pouchie put the nieve in,   *pocket; fist*
       An' while ought's there,
Then, hiltie, skiltie, we gae scrivin',   *[helter-skelter]; writing*
       An' fash nae mair.   *bother*

Leeze me on rhyme! it's ay a treasure,   *I'm delighted by*
My chief, amaist my only pleasure,
At hame, a-fiel, at wark or leisure,   *outdoors*
       The Muse, poor hizzie!   *housewife*
Tho' rough an' raploch be her measure,   *coarse*
       She's seldom lazy.

Haud tae the Muse, my dainty Davie:
The warl' may play you monie a shavie;   *trick*
But for the Muse, she'll never leave ye,
       Tho' e'er sae puir,
Na, even tho' limpan wi' the spavie   *rheumatism*
       Frae door tae door.

To a Haggis

Fair fa' your honest, sonsie face,   *hearty*
Great Chieftan o' the Puddin-race!
Aboon them a' ye tak your place,   *above*
       Painch, tripe, or thairm: *intestines; guts*
Weel are ye wordy of a *grace*
       As lang's my arm.

The groaning trencher there ye fill,
Your hurdies like a distant hill,   *buttocks*
Your *pin* wad help to mend a mill
       In time o' need,
While thro' your pores the dews distil
       Like amber bead.

His knife see Rustic-labour dight,   *prepare*
An' cut you up wi' ready slight,   *skill*
Trenching your gushing entrails bright
    Like onie ditch;   *any*
And then, O what a glorious sight,
    Warm-reekin, rich!   *steaming*

Then, horn for horn they stretch an' strive, *horn-spoon*
Deil tak the hindmost, on they drive,
Till a' their weel-swall'd kytes belyve *stomachs; quickly*
    Are bent like drums;
Then auld Guidman, maist like to rive,   *burst*
    Bethankit hums.

Is there that owre his French *ragout*,
Or *olio* that wad staw a sow,   *sicken*
Or *fricassee* wad mak her spew   *vomit*
    Wi' perfect sconner,   *loathing*
Looks down wi' sneering, scornfu' view
    On sic a dinner?

Poor devil! see him owre his trash,
As feckless as a wither'd rash,   *rush*
His spindle-shank a guid whip-lash,   *thin leg*
    His nieve a nit;   *fist; nut*
Thro' bluidy flood or field to dash,
    O how unfit!

But mark the Rustic, *haggis-fed*,
The trembling earth resounds his tread,
Clap in his walie nieve a blade,   *strong*
    He'll mak it whissle;
An' legs, an' arms, an' heads will sned,   *cut off*
    Like taps o' thrissle.   *tops; thistle*

Ye Pow'rs wha mak mankind your care,
An' dish them out their bill o' fare,
Auld Scotland wants nae skinking ware *thin stuff*
    That jaups in luggies;   *splashes; bowls*
But, if ye wish her gratefu' pray'r,
    Gie her a *Haggis*!

Lines Written Under the Portrait of Robert Fergusson, the Poet, in a Copy of That Author's Works Presented to a Young Lady in Edinburgh, March 19th, 1787

Curse on ungrateful man, that can be pleas'd,
And yet can starve the author of the pleasure.
O thou my elder brother in misfortune,
By far my elder brother in the muses,
With tears I pity thy unhappy fate!
Why is the bard unpitied by the world,
Yet has so keen a relish of its pleasures?

Auld Lang Syne

Should auld acquaintance be forgot
   And never brought to mind?
Should auld acquaintance be forgot,
   And auld lang syne!   *[long since]*

    For auld lang syne my jo,   *dear*
      For auld lang syne,
    We'll tak a *cup o' kindness yet,
      For auld lang syne.

And surely ye'll be your pint stowp!   *flagon*
    And surely I'll be mine!
And we'll tak a cup o' kindness yet,
    For auld lang syne.

    For auld &c.

We twa hae run about the braes,
    And pou'd the gowans fine;   *pulled; daisies*
But we've wander'd mony a weary fitt,   *foot*
    Sin auld lang syne.

    For auld &c.

* Some Sing, Kiss in place of Cup. [RB]

We twa hae paidl'd in the burn,   *paddled; stream*
    Frae morning sun till dine;   *dinner-time*
But seas between us braid hae roar'd,
    Sin auld lang syne.

    For auld &c.

And there's a hand, my trusty fiere!   *comrade*
    And gie's a hand o' thine!
And we'll tak a right gude-willie-waught,   *[hearty drink]*
    For auld lang syne.

    For auld &c.

Farewell to the Highlands

My heart's in the Highlands, my heart is not here;
My heart's in the Highlands a chasing the deer;
A chasing the wild deer, and following the roe,
My heart's in the Highlands, wherever I go.
Farewell to the Highlands, farewell to the north,
The birth place of Valour, the country of Worth,
Wherever I wander, wherever I rove,
The hills of the Highlands for ever I love.

Farewell to the mountains high cover'd with snow;
Farewell to the straths and green vallies below:
Farewell to the forests and wild hanging woods;
Farewell to the torrents and loud pouring floods.
My heart's in the Highlands, my heart is not here,
My heart's in the Highlands, a chasing the deer:
Chasing the wild deer, and following the roe,
My heart's in the Highlands, wherever I go.

John Anderson My Jo

John Anderson my jo, John,   *dear*
When we were first acquent;   *acquainted*
Your locks were like the raven,
Your bony brow was brent;   *smooth*
But now your brow is beld, John,   *bald*
Your locks are like the snaw;
But blessings on your frosty pow,   *head*
John Anderson my jo.

John Anderson my jo, John,
We clamb the hill the gither;
And mony a canty day, John,   *pleasant*
We've had wi' ane anither:
Now we maun totter down, John,   *must*
And hand in hand we'll go:
And sleep the gither at the foot,   *[together]*
John Anderson my jo.

Tam o' Shanter. A Tale

Of Brownyis and of Bogillis full is this buke.
   (Gawin Douglas)

   When chapman billies leave the street,   *[pedlar men]*
And drouthy neebors, neebors meet,   *thirsty*
As market-days are wearing late,
An' folk begin to tak the gate;   *[go home]*
While we sit bousing at the nappy,   *drinking; ale*
An' getting fou and unco happy,   *drunk; [oh so]*
We think na on the lang Scots miles,
The mosses, waters, slaps and styles,   *gaps*
That lie between us and our hame,
Whare sits our sulky sullen dame,
Gathering her brows like gathering storm,
Nursing her wrath to keep it warm.

This truth fand honest *Tam o' Shanter*, *found*
As he frae Ayr ae night did canter, *one*
(Auld Ayr wham ne'er a town surpasses;
For honest men and bonny lasses.)

O *Tam*! hadst thou but been sae wise,
As ta'en thy ain wife *Kate's* advice!
She tauld thee weel thou was a skellum, *scoundrel*
A blethering, blustering, drunken blellum; *fool*
That frae November till October,
Ae market day thou was nae sober;
That ilka melder, wi' the miller, *[whenever the meal was ground]*
Thou sat as lang as thou had siller; *silver*
That ev'ry naig was ca'd a shoe on, *nag; [shoed]*
The smith and thee gat roaring fou on; *drunk*
That at the Lord's house, ev'n on Sunday,
Thou drank wi' Kirkton Jean till Monday.
She prophesy'd that late or soon,
Thou would be found deep drown'd in Doon;
Or catch'd wi' warlocks in the mirk, *dark*
By *Alloway's* auld haunted kirk.

Ah, gentle dames! it gars me greet, *weep*
To think how mony counsels sweet,
How mony lengthen'd, sage advices,
The husband frae the wife despises!

But to our tale: Ae market night, *one*
Tam had got planted unco right; *settled*
Fast by an ingle, bleezing finely, *fireside; blazing*
Wi' reaming swats, that drank divinely; *frothing beers*
And at his elbow, Souter *Johnny*, *Cobbler*
His ancient, trusty, drouthy crony;
Tam lo'ed him like a vera brither;
They had been fou for weeks thegither.
The night drave on wi' sangs and clatter;
And ay the ale was growing better:
The landlady and *Tam* grew gracious,
Wi' favours, secret, sweet, and precious:

The Souter tauld his queerest stories;
The landlord's laugh was ready chorus:
The storm without might rair and rustle,
Tam did na mind the storm a whistle.

Care, mad to see a man sae happy,
E'en drown'd himself amang the nappy,
As bees flee hame wi' lades o' treasure,   *loads*
The minutes wing'd their way wi' pleasure:
Kings may be blest, but *Tam* was glorious,
O'er a' the ills o' life victorious!

But pleasures are like poppies spread,
You seize the flow'r, its bloom is shed:
Or like the snow falls in the river,
A moment white – then melts forever;
Or like the borealis race,
That flit ere you can point their place;
Or like the rainbow's lovely form
Evanishing amid the storm. –
Nae man can tether time nor tide;
The hour approaches Tam maun ride;   *must*
That hour, o' night's black arch the key-stane,
That dreary hour he mounts his beast in;
And sic a night he taks the road in,
As ne'er poor sinner was abroad in.

The wind blew as 'twad blawn its last;
The rattling show'rs rose on the blast;
The speedy gleams the darkness swallow'd;
Loud, deep, and lang, the thunder bellow'd:
That night, a child might understand,
The Deil had business on his hand.

Weel mounted on his gray mare, *Meg*,
A better never lifted leg,
Tam skelpit on thro' dub and mire,   *slapped; mud*
Despising wind, and rain, and fire;
Whiles holding fast his gude blue bonnet;
Whiles crooning o'er some auld Scots sonnet;

Whiles glow'ring round wi' prudent cares,
Lest bogles catch him unawares:
Kirk-Alloway was drawing nigh,
Whare ghaists and houlets nightly cry. –   *owls*

  By this time he was cross the ford,
Where in the snaw, the chapman smoor'd;   *suffocated*
And past the birks and meikle stane,   *birches; [large rock]*
Whare drunken *Charlie* brak's neck-bane;   *[broke his neck]*
And thro' the whins, and by the cairn,   *gorse*
Whare hunters fand the murder'd bairn;   *found*
And near the thorn, aboon the well,   *above*
Whare *Mungo's* mither hang'd hersel. –
Before him *Doon* pours all his floods: *[the river Doon]*
The doubling storm roars thro' the woods:
The lightnings flash from pole to pole;
Near and more near the thunders roll:
When, glimmering thro' the groaning trees,
Kirk Alloway seem'd in a bleeze;   *blaze*
Thro' ilka bore the beams were glancing;   *gap*
And loud resounded mirth and dancing. –

  Inspiring bold *John Barleycorn*!   *Whisky*
What dangers thou canst make us scorn!
Wi' tipenny, we fear nae evil;   *[cheap beer]*
Wi' usquebae we'll face the devil! –   *whisky*
The swats sae ream'd in *Tammie's* noddle,   *beers; foamed*
Fair play, he car'd na deils a boddle.   *[copper coin]*
But *Maggie* stood right sair astonish'd,
Till, by the heel and hand admonish'd,
She ventur'd forward on the light;
And, vow! *Tam* saw an unco sight!   *rare*
Warlocks and witches in a dance;
Nae cotillion brent new frae *France*,
But hornpipes, jigs, strathspeys, and reels,
Put life and mettle in their heels,
A winnock-bunker in the east,   *window-seat*
There sat auld Nick, in shape o' beast;
A towzie tyke, black, grim, and large,   *dog*
To gie them music was his charge:

He screw'd the pipes and gart them skirl,   *shriek*
Till roof and rafters a' did dirl. —   *rattle*
Coffins stood round, like open presses,   *cupboards*
That shaw'd the dead in their last dresses;
And by some devilish cantraip slight   *cunning*
Each in its cauld hand held a light. —
By which heroic *Tam* was able
To note upon the haly table,
A murderer's banes in gibbet airns;   *irons*
Twa span-lang, wee, unchristen'd bairns;   *hand-sized*
A thief, new-cutted frae a rape,   *rope*
Wi' his last gasp his gab did gape;   *mouth*
Five tomahawks, wi' blude red-rusted;
Five scymitars, wi' murder crusted;
A garter, which a babe had strangled;
A knife, a father's throat had mangled,
Whom his ain son o' life bereft,
The grey hairs yet stack to the heft;   *stuck*
Wi' mair o' horrible an' awefu',
Which ev'n to name wad be unlawfu'.

   As *Tammie* glowr'd, amaz'd, and curious,
The mirth and fun grew fast and furious;
The piper loud and louder blew;
The dancers quick and quicker flew;
They reel'd, they set, they cross'd, they cleekit,
Till ilka carlin swat and reekit,   *[every witch sweated and steamed]*
And coost her duddies to the wark,   *cast; clothes; work*
And linket at it in her sark!   *tripped; shirt*

   Now *Tam*, O *Tam*! had thae been queans,   *girls*
A' plump and strapping in their teens,
Their sarks, instead o' creeshie flannen,   *greasy flannel*
Been snaw-white seventeen hunder linnen!   *[finely woven]*
Thir breeks o' mine, my only pair,   *those*
That ance were plush, o' gude blue hair,   *once*
I wad hae gi'en them off my hurdies,   *buttocks*
For ae blink o' the bonie burdies!

But wither'd beldams, auld and droll, *old women*
Rigwoodie hags wad spean a foal, *stringy; [put a foal off its mother's milk]*
Lowping and flinging on a crummock, *leaping; crook*
I wonder didna turn thy stomach.

But *Tam* kend what was what fu' brawlie, *knew; [very well]*
There was ae winsome wench and wawlie, *one; ample*
That night enlisted in the core, *body*
(Lang after kend on *Carrick* shore;
For mony a beast to dead she shot,
And perish'd mony a bony boat,
And shook baith meikle corn and bear, *lots of; barley*
And kept the countryside in fear)
Her cutty sark, o' Paisley harn, *coarse linen*
That while a lassie she had worn, *since*
In longitude tho' sorely scanty,
It was her best, and she was vauntie. – *proud*
Ah! little kend thy reverend grannie,
That sark she coft for her wee Nannie, *bought*
Wi' twa pund Scots ('twas a' her riches)
Wad ever grac'd a dance o' witches!

But here my Muse her wing maun cour; *fold*
Sic flights are far beyond her pow'r;
To sing how Nannie lap and flang, *jumped; danced*
(A souple jade she was, and strang),
And how *Tam* stood, like ane bewitch'd,
And thought his very een enrich'd;
Ev'n Satan glowr'd, and fidg'd fu' fain, *fidgeted*
And hotch'd and blew wi' might and main: *shouted*
Till first ae caper, syne anither, *then*
Tam tint his reason a' thegither, *lost*
And roars out, 'Weel done, Cutty-sark!'
And in an instant all was dark:
And scarcely had he Maggie rallied,
When out the hellish legion sallied.

As bees bizz out wi' angry fyke, *commotion*
When plundering herds assail their byke, *hive*
As open pussie's mortal foes,
When pop! she starts before their nose;

As eager runs the market-crowd,
When 'Catch the thief!' resounds aloud;
So Maggie runs, the witches follow,
Wi' mony an eldritch skreech and hollow.   *unearthly*

Ah, *Tam*! Ah, *Tam*! thou'll get thy fairin!   *punishment*
In hell they'll roast thee like a herrin!
In vain thy *Kate* awaits thy comin!
Kate soon will be a woefu' woman!
Now, do thy speedy utmost, Meg,
And win the key-stane of the brig;
There at them thou thy tail may toss,
A running stream they dare na cross.
But ere the key-stane she could make,
The fient a tale she had to shake!   *fiend*
For Nannie, far before the rest,
Hard upon noble Maggie prest,
And flew at Tam wi' furious ettle;   *purpose*
But little wist she Maggie's mettle —
Ae spring brought off her master hale,   *safe*
But left behind her ain gray tail:
The carlin claught her by the rump,
And left poor Maggie scarce a stump.

   Now, wha this tale o' truth shall read,
Ilk man and mother's son, take heed:
Whene'er to drink you are inclin'd,
Or cutty sarks run in your mind,
Think, ye may buy the joys o'er dear,
Remember Tam o' Shanter's mare.

Ae Fond Kiss

Ae fond kiss, and then we sever;
Ae farewell and then forever!
Deep in heart-wrung tears I'll pledge thee,
Warring sighs and groans I'll wage thee.

Who shall say that fortune grieves him
While the star of hope she leaves him?
Me, nae chearfu' twinkle lights me;
Dark despair around benights me.

I'll ne'er blame my partial fancy,
Naething could resist my Nancy:
But to see her, was to love her;
Love but her, and love for ever.

Had we never lov'd sae kindly,
Had we never lov'd sae blindly,
Never met – or never parted,
We had ne'er been broken-hearted.

Fare thee weel, thou first and fairest!
Fare thee weel, thou best and dearest!
Thine be ilka joy and treasure,   *every*
Peace, Enjoyment, Love and Pleasure!

Ae fond kiss, and then we sever;
Ae fareweel, Alas! for ever!
Deep in heart-wrung tears I'll pledge thee,
Warring sighs and groans I'll wage thee.

Such a Parcel of Rogues in a Nation

Fareweel to a' our Scotish fame,
    Fareweel our ancient glory;
Fareweel even to the Scotish name,
    Sae fam'd in martial story!
Now Sark rins o'er the Solway sands,
    And Tweed rins to the ocean,
To mark whare England's province stands,
    Such a parcel of rogues in a nation!

What force or guile could not subdue,
    Thro' many warlike ages,
Is wrought now by a coward few,
    For hireling traitors' wages.

The English steel we could disdain,
   Secure in valor's station;
But English gold has been our bane,
   Such a parcel of rogues in a nation!

O would, or I had seen the day
   That treason thus could sell us,
My auld grey head had lien in clay,
   Wi' *Bruce* and loyal *Wallace*!
But pith and power, till my last hour,
   I'll mak this declaration;
We're bought and sold for English gold,
   Such a parcel of rogues in a nation!

Robert Bruce's March to Bannockburn

Scots, wha hae wi' Wallace bled,
Scots, wham Bruce has aften led,
Welcome to your gory bed
      Or to victorie!

Now's the day, and now's the hour:
See the front o' battle lour,   *glower*
See approach proud Edward's power –
      Chains and slaverie!

Wha will be a traitor knave?
Wha can fill a coward's grave?
Wha sae base as be a slave? –
      Let him turn, and flee!

Wha for Scotland's king and law
Freedom's sword will strongly draw,
Freeman stand or freeman fa',
      Let him follow me!

By Oppression's woes and pains,
By your sons in servile chains,
We will drain our dearest veins
      But they shall be free!

Lay the proud usurpers low!
Tyrants fall in every foe!
Liberty's in every blow! —
    Let us do, or die!

A Red, Red Rose

My luve is like a red, red rose,
    That's newly sprung in June:
My luve is like the melodie,
    That's sweetly play'd in tune.
As fair art thou, my bonie lass,
    So deep in luve am I,
And I will luve thee still, my dear,
    Till a' the seas gang dry.

Till a' the seas gang dry, my dear,
    And the rocks melt wi' the sun!
And I will luve thee still, my dear,
    While the sands o' life shall run.
And fare-thee-weel, my only luve,
    And fare-thee-weel a while!
And I will come again, my luve,
    Tho' it were ten-thousand mile.

Is There for Honest Poverty

Is there for honest poverty
    That hings his head, an' a' that?   *hangs*
The coward slave, we pass him by —
    We dare be poor for a' that!
      For a' that, an a' that,
        Our toils obscure, an' a' that,
      The rank is but the guinea's stamp,
      The man's the gowd for a' that.   *gold*

What tho' on hamely fare we dine,   *homely*
  Wear hodden grey, an' a' that?   *homespun*
Gie fools their silks, and knaves their wine –
  A man's a man for a' that!
    For a' that, an' a' that,
     Their tinsel show, an' a' that,
    The honest man, tho' e'er sae poor,
     Is king o' men for a' that.

Ye see yon birkie ca'd a lord,   *twit*
  Wha struts, and stares, an' a' that;
Tho' hundreds worship at his word,
  He's but a coof for a' that.   *fool*
    For a' that, an' a' that,
     His ribband, star, an' a' that,
    The man o' independent mind,
     He looks an' laughs at a' that.

A prince can mak a belted knight,
  A marquis, duke, an' a' that,
But an honest man's aboon his might –   *above*
  Gude faith, he mauna fa' that!   *[must not]*
    For a' that, an' a' that,
     Their dignities, an a' that,
    The pith o' sense an' pride o' worth
     Are higher rank than a' that.

Then let us pray that come it may –
  As come it will, for a' that –
That sense and worth, o'er a' the earth
  Shall bear the gree, an' a' that;   *degree*
    For a' that, an' a' that,
     It's comin yet for a' that,
    That man to man the world o'er,
     Shall brothers be for a' that.

Oh Wert Thou in the Cauld Blast

Oh, wert thou in the cauld blast,
　On yonder lea, on yonder lea;　　　　　　　　　　　　*pasture*
My plaidie to the angry airt,　　　　　*plaid; [direction of the wind]*
　I'd shelter thee, I'd shelter thee:
Or did misfortune's bitter storms
　Around thee blaw, around thee blaw,
Thy bield should be my bosom,　　　　　　　　　　　*shelter*
　To share it a', to share it a'.

Or were I in the wildest waste,
　Sae black and bare, sae black and bare,
The desart were a paradise,
　If thou wert there, if thou wert there.
Or were I monarch o' the globe,
　Wi' thee to reign, wi' thee to reign;
The brightest jewel in my crown,
　Wad be my queen, wad be my queen.

UILLEAM ROS/WILLIAM ROSS (1762–1790)

Òran Eile

Tha mise fo mhulad san àm,
Chan òlar leam dràm le sùnnt,
Tha durrag air ghur ann mo chàil
A dh'fhiosraich do chàch mo rùin:
Chan fhaic mi dol seachad air sràid
An cailin bu tlàithe sùil,
'S e sin a leag m' aigne gu làr
Mar dhuilleach o bhàrr nan craobh.

A ghruagach as bachlaiche cùl
Tha mise gad iùnndran mòr;
Ma thagh thu deagh àite dhut fèin
Mo bheannachd gach rè g' ad chòir;
Tha mise ri osnaich nad dhèidh
Mar ghaisgeach an dèis a leòn,
'Na laighe san àraich gun fheum
'S nach tèid anns an t-sreup nas mò.

'S e dh'fhàg mi mar iudmhail air treud,
Mar fhear nach toir spèis do mhnaoi,
Do thuras thar chuan fo bhrèid
Thug bras shileadh dheur o m' shùil.
B' fheàrr nach mothaichinn fèin
Do mhaise, do chèill, 's do chliù,
No suairceas milis do bhèil
As binne na sèis gach ciùil.

Gach anduine chluinneas mo chàs
A' cur air mo nàdur fiamh,
A' cantainn nach eil mi ach bàrd
'S nach cinnich leam dàn as fiach –
Mo sheanair ri pàigheadh a mhàil
Is m' athair ri màileid riamh;
Chuireadh iad gearrain an crann
Is ghearrainn-sa rann ro' chiad.

Another Song

Overburdened with sorrow now
I can drink no dram with joy,
a maggot broods in my mind
telling my secrets to all:
no longer I see in the street
the girl with the gentlest eyes,
and so my spirits have fallen
like leaves from the foliage of trees.

O maiden of ringletted hair,
my longing for you is deep;
if you've chosen a pleasant lot
my blessing I give for all time;
I am sighing since you are gone
like a wounded hero who lies
on the field of battle, undone,
who will enter the fray no more.

I'm a fugitive strayed from the flock,
I can give no woman my love;
your sea-voyage under your coif
brought swift-flowing tears from my eyes.
Would I had never seen
your beauty, your sense and good name,
sweet kindness that came from your lips
more melodious than music's peal.

Every ass who hears of my plight
thinks I'm fearful by nature now,
saying I'm only a bard
who can't make a decent song —
my grandfather paid up his rent
and my father carried a pack;
they would put horses in plough —
I could shape my staves just as well.

'S fad a tha m' aigne fo ghruaim,
Cha mhosgail mo chluain ri ceòl,
'M breislich mar ànrach a' chuain
Air bharraibh nan stuagh ri ceò.
'S e iùnndaran d' àbhachd uam
A chaochail air snuadh mo neòil,
Gun sùgradh, gun mhire, gun uaill,
Gun chaithream, gun bhuadh, gun treòir.

Cha dùisgear leam ealaidh air àill',
Cha chuirear leam dàn air dòigh,
Cha togar leam fonn air clàr,
Cha chluinnear leam gàir nan òg,
Cha dìrich mi bealach nan àrd
Le suigeart mar bhà mi 'n tòs,
Ach triallaim a chadal gu bràth
Do thalla nam bàrd nach beò.

My spirits have long been low,
music doesn't lift my heart,
in distress like one lost at sea
tossed on the waves in mist.
Missing your sportiveness now
has changed the fair face of my sky,
without joy or gladness or pride,
eagerness, virtue or strength.

No ode to beauty comes forth,
I can't put a poem in place,
I cannot pick out a tune,
I hear no young laughing cry,
no longer climb in the hills
with zest as at one time I did,
I must journey to final sleep
in the hall of the poets who are dead.

Translated from the Gaelic by Derick Thomson

JOANNA BAILLIE (1762–1851)

from *A Winter Day*

The fam'ly cares call next upon the wife
To quit her mean but comfortable bed.
And first she stirs the fire, and blows the flame,
Then from her heap of sticks, for winter stor'd,
An armful brings; loud crackling as they burn,
Thick fly the red sparks upward to the roof,
While slowly mounts the smoke in wreathy clouds.
On goes the seething pot with morning cheer,
For which some little wishful hearts await,
Who, peeping from the bed-clothes, spy, well pleas'd,
The cheery light that blazes on the wall,
And bawl for leave to rise. –
Their busy mother knows not where to turn,
Her morning work comes now so thick upon her.
One she must help to tye his little coat,
Unpin his cap, and seek another's shoe.
When all is o'er, out to the door they run,
With new comb'd sleeky hair, and glist'ning cheeks,
Each with some little project in his head.
One on the ice must try his new sol'd shoes:
To view his well-set trap another hies,
In hopes to find some poor unwary bird
(No worthless prize) entangled in his snare;
Whilst one, less active, with round rosy face,
Spreads out his purple fingers to the fire,
And peeps, most wishfully, into the pot.

CAROLINA OLIPHANT (LADY NAIRNE) (1766–1845)

The Heiress

I'll no be had for naething,
   I'll no be had for naething,
I tell ye, lads, that's ae thing,
   So ye needna follow me.

Oh! the change is most surprising;
   Last year I was Betsy Brown;
Now to my hand they're a' aspiring,
   The fair Eliza I am grown!
      But I'll no, etc.

Oh! the change is most surprising.
   Nane o' them e'er look'd at me;
Now my charms they're a' admiring,
   For my sake they're like to dee!
      But I'll no, etc.

The laird, the shirra, and the doctor,   *sheriff*
   And twa-three lords o' high degree;
Wi' heaps o' writers, I could mention,   *lawyers*
   Surely, sirs, it is no me!
      But I'll no, etc.

But there is ane, when I had naething,
   A' his heart he gied to me;
And sair he toiled, to mak a wee thing,
   To gie me when he cam frae sea.
      Sae I'll no, etc.

And if e'er I marry ony,
   He will be the lad for me;
For oh, he was baith gude and bonny,
   And he thocht the same o' me.

Sae I'll no be had for naething,
  I'll no be had for naething,
  I tell ye, lads, that's ae thing,
    So ye needna follow me.

Will Ye No Come Back Again?

Bonnie Charlie's now awa,
  Safely owre the friendly main;
Mony a heart will break in twa,
  Should he ne'er come back again.
    Will ye no come back again?
    Will ye no come back again?
    Better lo'ed ye canna be,
    Will ye no come back again?

Ye trusted in your Heiland men,
  They trusted you, dear Charlie;
They kent you hiding in the glen,   *knew*
  Your cleedin was but barely.   *covering*
    Will ye no, etc.

English bribes were a' in vain,
  An' e'en tho' puirer we may be;
Siller canna buy the heart
  That beats aye for thine and thee.
    Will ye no, etc.

We watched thee in the gloaming hour,   *dusk*
  We watched thee in the morning grey;
Tho' thirty thousand pounds they'd gie,
  Oh there is nane that wad betray.
    Will ye no, etc.

Sweet's the laverock's note and lang,   *lark*
  Lilting wildly up the glen;
But aye to me he sings ae sang,
  Will ye no come back again?

Will ye no come back again?
Will ye no come back again?
Better lo'ed ye canna be,
Will ye no come back again?

The Land o' the Leal

[the Afterworld]

I'm wearin' awa', John,
Like snaw-wreaths in thaw, John,
I'm wearin' awa'
    To the land o' the leal.   *loyal*
There's nae sorrow there, John,
There's neither cauld nor care, John,
The day is aye fair
    In the land o' the leal.

Our bonnie bairn's there, John,
She was baith gude and fair, John,
And, oh! we grudged her sair
    To the land o' the leal.
But sorrow's sel' wears past, John,
And joy is comin' fast, John,
The joy that's aye to last
    In the land o' the leal.

Sae dear's that joy was bought, John,
Sae free the battle fought, John,
That sinfu' man e'er brought
    To the land o' the leal.
Oh! dry your glist'nin' e'e, John,
My saul langs to be free, John,
And angels beckon me
    To the land o' the leal.

Oh! haud ye leal an' true, John,
Your day it's wearin' thro', John,
And I'll welcome you
    To the land o' the leal.

Now fare ye weel, my ain John,
This warld's cares are vain, John,
We'll meet, and we'll be fain,
    In the land o' the leal.

affectionate

JAMES HOGG (1770–1835)

from *Kilmeny*

The Thirteenth Bard's Song

Bonny Kilmeny gaed up the glen;	*went*
But it wasna to meet Duneira's men,	
Nor the rosy monk of the isle to see,	
For Kilmeny was pure as pure could be.	
It was only to hear the Yorlin sing,	*yellowhammer*
And pu' the cress-flower round the spring;	
The scarlet hypp and the hindberrye,	*rose hip; wild raspberry*
And the nut that hang frae the hazel tree;	
For Kilmeny was pure as pure could be.	
But lang may her minny look o'er the wa',	*mother*
And lang may she seek i' the green-wood shaw;	
Lang the laird of Duneira blame,	
And lang, lang greet or Kilmeny come hame!	*cry; before*
When many a day had come and fled,	
When grief grew calm, and hope was dead,	
When mess for Kilmeny's soul had been sung,	
When the bedes-man had prayed, and the dead-bell rung,	
Late, late in a gloamin when all was still,	*dusk*
When the fringe was red on the westlin hill,	
The wood was sere, the moon i' the wane,	
The reek o' the cot hung over the plain,	*smoke*
Like a little wee cloud in the world its lane;	
When the ingle lowed with an eiry leme,	*hearth; light*
Late, late in the gloamin Kilmeny came hame!	
'Kilmeny, Kilmeny, where have you been?	
Lang hae we sought baith holt and den;	
By linn, by ford, and green-wood tree,	*waterfall*
Yet you are halesome and fair to see.	

Where gat you that joup o' the lilly scheen?   *skirt*
That bonny snood of the birk sae green?   *birch*
And these roses, the fairest that ever were seen?
Kilmeny, Kilmeny, where have you been?'

   Kilmeny looked up with a lovely grace,
But nae smile was seen on Kilmeny's face;
As still was her look, and as still was her ee,   *eye*
As the stillness that lay on the emerant lea,   *emerald*
Or the mist that sleeps on a waveless sea.
For Kilmeny had been she knew not where,
And Kilmeny had seen what she could not declare;
Kilmeny had been where the cock never crew,
Where the rain never fell, and the wind never blew,
But it seemed as the harp of the sky had rung,
And the airs of heaven played round her tongue,
When she spake of the lovely forms she had seen,
And a land where sin had never been;
A land of love, and a land of light,
Withouten sun, or moon, or night:
Where the river swa'd a living stream,
And the light a pure celestial beam:
The land of vision it would seem,
A still, an everlasting dream.

Charlie is my Darling

'Twas on a Monday morning,
  Right early in the year,
That Charlie came to our town,
  The Young Chevalier.
    An' Charlie is my darling,
     My darling, my darling,
    Charlie is my darling,
     The Young Chevalier.

As Charlie he came up the gate,
   His face shone like the day;
I grat to see the lad come back
   That had been lang away.
      An' Charlie is my darling, &c.

Then ilka bonny lassie sang,
   As to the door she ran,
Our king shall hae his ain again,
   An' Charlie is the man:
      For Charlie he's my darling, &c.

Outower yon moory mountain,
   An' down the craigy glen,
Of naething else our lasses sing
   But Charlie an' his men.
      An' Charlie he's my darling, &c.

Our Highland hearts are true an' leal,   *loyal*
   An' glow without a stain;
Our Highland swords are metal keen,
   An' Charlie he's our ain.
      An' Charlie he's my darling,
        My darling, my darling;
      Charlie he's my darling,
        The young Chevalier.

The Witch O' Fife

Hurray, hurray, the jade's away,
   Like a rocket of air with her bandalet!
I'm up in the air on my bonny grey mare,
   But I see her yet, I see her yet.
I'll ring the skirts o' the gowden wain   *golden*
   Wi' curb an' bit, wi' curb an' bit;
An' catch the Bear by the frozen mane, –
   An' I see her yet, I see her yet.

Away, away, oe'r mountain an' main,
    To sing at the morning's rosy yett;   *gate*
An' water my mare at its fountain clear, —
    But I see her yet, I see her yet.
Away, thou bonny witch o' Fife,
    On foam of the air to heave an' flit,
An' little reck thou of a poet's life,
    For he sees thee yet, he sees thee yet.

SIR WALTER SCOTT (1771–1832)

Lochinvar

O, young Lochinvar is come out of the west,
Through all the wide Border his steed was the best;
And save his good broadsword he weapons had none,
He rode all unarmed, and he rode all alone.
So faithful in love, and so dauntless in war,
There never was knight like the young Lochinvar.

He stayed not for brake, and he stopped not for stone,
He swam the Eske river where ford there was none;
But ere he alighted at Netherby gate,
The bride had consented, the gallant came late:
For a laggard in love, and a dastard in war,
Was to wed the fair Ellen of brave Lochinvar.

So boldly he entered the Netherby Hall,
Among bride's-men, and kinsmen, and brothers, and all:
Then spoke the bride's father, his hand on his sword,
(For the poor craven bridegroom said never a word,)
'O come ye in peace here, or come ye in war,
Or to dance at our bridal, young Lord Lochinvar?'

'I long wooed your daughter, my suit you denied; –
Love swells like the Solway, but ebbs like its tide –
And now am I come, with this lost love of mine,
To lead but one measure, drink one cup of wine.
There are maidens in Scotland more lovely by far,
That would gladly be bride to the young Lochinvar.'

The bride kissed the goblet: the knight took it up,
He quaffed off the wine, and he threw down the cup.
She looked down to blush, and she looked up to sigh,
With a smile on her lips, and a tear in her eye.
He took her soft hand, ere her mother could bar, –
'Now tread we a measure!' said young Lochinvar.

So stately his form, and so lovely her face,
That never a hall such a galliard did grace;
While her mother did fret, and her father did fume,
And the bridegroom stood dangling his bonnet and plume;
And the bride-maidens whispered, ' 'Twere better by far,
To have matched our fair cousin with young Lochinvar.'

One touch to her hand, and one word in her ear,
When they reached the hall-door, and the charger stood near;
So light to the croupe the fair lady he swung,
So light to the saddle before her he sprung!
'She is won! we are gone, over bank, bush, and scaur;   *cliff*
They'll have fleet steeds that follow,' quoth young Lochinvar.

There was mounting 'mong Græmes of the Netherby clan;
Forsters, Fenwicks, and Musgraves, they rode and they ran:
There was racing and chasing on Cannonbie Lee,
But the lost bride of Netherby ne'er did they see.
So daring in love, and so dauntless in war,
Have ye e'er heard of gallant like young Lochinvar?

Proud Maisie

Proud Maisie is in the wood,
    Walking so early;
Sweet Robin sits on the bush,
    Singing so rarely.

'Tell me, thou bonny bird,
    When shall I marry me?' —
'When six braw gentlemen
    Kirkward shall carry ye.' —

'Who makes the bridal bed,
    Birdie, say truly?' —
'The grey-headed sexton
    That delves the grave duly.

The glow-worm o'er grave and stone
   Shall light thee steady.
The owl from the steeple sing,
   "Welcome, proud lady."'

from *The Lay of the Last Minstrel*

Canto Sixth

I

Breathes there the man, with soul so dead,
Who never to himself hath said,
   This is my own, my native land!
Whose heart hath ne'er within him burned,
As home his footsteps he hath turned,
   From wandering on a foreign strand!
If such there breathe, go, mark him well:
For him no Minstrel raptures swell;
High though his titles, proud his name,
Boundless his wealth as wish can claim;
Despite those titles, power, and pelf,
The wretch, concentred all in self,
Living, shall forfeit fair renown,
And, doubly dying, shall go down
To the vile dust, from whence he sprung,
Unwept, unhonoured and unsung.

II

O Caledonia! stern and wild,
Meet nurse for a poetic child!
Land of brown heath and shaggy wood,
Land of the mountain and the flood,
Land of my sires! what mortal hand
Can e'er untie the filial band,
That knits me to thy rugged strand!
Still as I view each well-known scene,
Think what is now, and what hath been,
Seems as, to me, of all bereft,
Sole friends thy woods and streams were left;

And thus I love them better still,
Even in extremity of ill.
By Yarrow's stream still let me stray,
Though none should guide my feeble way;
Still feel the breeze down Ettrick break,
Although it chill my withered cheek:
Still lay my head by Teviot Stone,
Though there, forgotten and alone,
The Bard may draw his parting groan.

from *The Lady of the Lake*

Canto First
The Chase

Harp of the North! that mouldering long hast hung
    On the witch-elm that shades Saint Fillan's spring,
And down the fitful breeze thy numbers flung,
    Till envious ivy did around thee cling,
Muffling with verdant ringlet every string, —
    O minstrel Harp, still must thine accents sleep?
'Mid rustling leaves and fountains murmuring,
    Still must thy sweeter sounds their silence keep,
Nor bid a warrior smile, nor teach a maid to weep?

Not thus, in ancient days of Caledon,
    Was thy voice mute amid the festal crowd,
When lay of hopeless love, or glory won,
    Aroused the fearful, or subdued the proud.
At each according pause was heard aloud
    Thine ardent symphony sublime and high!
Fair dames and crested chiefs attention bowed;
    For still the burden of thy minstrelsy
Was Knighthood's dauntless deed, and Beauty's matchless eye.

O wake once more! how rude soe'er the hand
    That ventures o'er thy magic maze to stray;
O wake once more! though scarce my skill command
    Some feeble echoing of thine earlier lay:

Though harsh and faint, and soon to die away,
    And all unworthy of thy nobler strain,
Yet if one heart throb higher at its sway,
    The wizard note has not been touched in vain.
Then silent be no more! Enchantress wake again!

I

The stag at eve had drunk his fill,
Where danced the moon on Monan's rill,
And deep his midnight lair had made
In lone Glenartney's hazel shade;
But, when the sun his beacon red
Had kindled on Benvoirlich's head,
The deep-mouthed blood-hound's heavy bay
Resounded up the rocky way,
And faint, from farther distance borne,
Were heard the clanging hoof and horn.

II

As Chief, who hears his warder call,
'To arms! the foemen storm the wall,'
The antlered monarch of the waste
Sprung from his heathery couch in haste.
But, ere his fleet career he took,
The dew-drops from his flanks he shook;
Like crested leader proud and high,
Tossed his beamed frontlet to the sky;
A moment gazed adown the dale,
A moment snuffed the tainted gale,
A moment listened to the cry,
That thickened as the chase drew nigh;
Then, as the headmost foes appeared,
With one brave bound the copse he cleared,
And, stretching forward free and far,
Sought the wild heaths of Uam-Var.

ROBERT TANNAHILL (1774–1810)

Eild

[Old age]

The rough hail rattles thro the trees,
    The sullen lift low'rs gloomy gray,   sky
The trav'ller sees the swelling storm,
    And seeks the alehouse by the way.

But, waes me! for yon widowed wretch,   woe is me
    Borne doun wi years an heavy care;
Her sapless fingers scarce can nip
    The wither'd twigs tae beet her fire.   kindle

Thus youth and vigour fends itsel;
    Its help, reciprocal, is sure,
While dowless Eild, in poortith cauld,   resourceless; poverty
    Is lanely left tae stan the stoure.   endure the storm

The Tap-Room

This warl's a tap-room owre and owre,   world's
    Whaur ilk ane tak's his caper,   each; oatcake
Some taste the sweet, some drink the sour,
    As waiter Fate sees proper;
Let mankind live, ae social core,
    An drap a' selfish quar'ling,
An whan the Landlord ca's his score,
    May ilk ane's clink be sterling.   [good money]

THOMAS CAMPBELL (1777–1841)

from *Lochiel's Warning*

Wizard

Lochiel, Lochiel! beware of the day
When the lowlands shall meet thee in battle array.
For a field of the dead rushes red on my sight,
And the clans of Culloden are scattered in fight.
They rally, they bleed, for their kingdom and crown;
Woe, woe to the riders that trample them down.
Proud Cumberland prances, insulting the slain,
And their hoof-beaten bosoms are trod to the plain.
But hark, through the fast-flashing lightning of war,
What steed to the desert flies frantic and far?
Tis thine, oh Glenullin, whose bride shall await,
Like a love-lighted watch-fire, all night at the gate.
A steed comes at morning: no rider is there;
But its bridle is red with the sign of despair.
Weep, Albin, to death and captivity led.
Oh weep, but thy tears cannot number the dead:
For a merciless sword on Culloden shall wave,
Culloden, that reeks with the blood of the brave.

To the Evening Star

Star that bringest home the bee,
And sett'st the weary labourer free,
If any star shed peace, tis thou
That send'st it from above,
Appearing when heaven's breath and brow
Are sweet as hers we love.

Come to the luxuriant skies
Whilst the landscape's odors rise,
Whilst far-off lowing herds are heard,
And songs, when toil is done,
From cottages whose smoke unstirred
Curls yellow in the sun.

Star of love's soft interviews,
Parted lovers on thee muse.
Their remembrancer in heaven
Of thrilling vows thou art,
Too delicious to be riven
By absence from the heart.

ALLAN CUNNINGHAM (1784–1842)

The Wee, Wee German Lairdie

[George I]

What the deil hae we got for a King,   *devil*
But a wee, wee German lairdie.   *little lord*
An' whan we gaed to bring him hame,   *went*
He was delving in his kail-yardie.   *cabbage-patch*
Sheughing kail an' laying leeks,   *planting*
But the hose and but the breeks,   *without*
Up his beggar duds he cleeks,   *rags; hitches*
The wee, wee German lairdie.

An' he's clapt down in our gudeman's chair,   *fastened*
The wee, wee German lairdie:
An' he's brought fouth o' foreign leeks,   *plenty*
An' dibblet them in his yardie.   *planted; wee garden*
He's pu'd the rose o' English louns,   *rascals*
An' brak the harp o' Irish clowns,
But our thistle will jag his thumbs,
The wee, wee German lairdie.

Come up amang the Highland hills,
Thou wee, wee German lairdie:
An' see how Charlie's lang-kail thrive,   *unchopped cabbages*
He dibblet in his yardie.
An' if a stock ye daur to pu',   *stalk; dare; pull*
Or haud the yoking of a pleugh,
We'll break yere sceptre o'er yere mou',   *mouth*
Thou wee bit German lairdie.

Our hills are steep, our glens are deep,
Nae fitting for a yardie;
An' our norlan' thistles winna pu',   *northern*
Thou wee, wee German lairdie.
An' we've the trenching blades o' weir,   *war*
Wad twine ye o' yere German gear: *deprive*
An' pass ye neath the claymore's shear,   *if; blade*
Thou feckless German lairdie.

The Thistle's Grown aboon the Rose

above

Full white the Bourbon lily blows,
And farer haughty England's rose.
Nor shall unsung the symbol smile,
Green Ireland, of thy lovely isle.
In Scotland grows a warlike flower,
Too rough to bloom in lady's bower;
His crest, when high the soldier bears,
And spurs his courser on the spears,
O, there it blossoms – there it blows –
The thistle's grown aboon the rose.

Bright like a steadfast star it smiles
Aboon the battle's burning files;
The mirkest cloud, the darkest night,
Shall ne'er make dim that beauteous light;
And the best blood that warms my vein
Shall flow ere it shall catch a stain.
Far has it shone on fields of fame,
From matchless Bruce till dauntless Graeme,
From swarthy Spain to Siber's snows; –
The thistle's grown aboon the rose.

What conquered ay, what nobly spared,
What firm endured, and greatly dared?
What reddened Egypt's burning sand?
What vanquished on Corunna's strand?
What pipe on green Maida blew shrill?
What dyed in blood Barossa hill?
Bade France's dearest life-blood rue
Dark Soignies and dread Waterloo?
That spirit which no terror knows; –
The thistle's grown aboon the rose.

I vow – and let men mete the grass
For his red grave who dares say less –
Men kinder at the festive board,
Men braver with the spear and sword,

Men higher famed for truth — more strong
In virtue, sovereign sense, and song,
Or maids more fair, or wives more true,
Than Scotland's, ne'er trode down the dew.
Round flies the song — the flagon flows, —
The thistle's grown aboon the rose.

WILLIAM TENNANT (1784–1848)

from *Anster Fair*   [*Anstruther, in Fife*]

Canto I

My pulse beats fire – my pericranium glows,
   Like baker's oven with poetic heat;
A thousand bright ideas, spurning prose,
   Are in a twinkling hatch'd in Fancy's seat;
Zounds! they will fly out at my ears and nose,
   If through my mouth they find not passage fleet;
I hear them buzzing deep within my noddle,
Like bees that in their hives confus'dly hum and huddle.

How now? – what's this? – my very eyes, I trow,
   Drop on my hands their base prosaic scales;
My visual orbs are purg'd from film, and lo!
   Instead of *Anster*'s turnip-bearing vales,
I see old Fairyland's mirac'lous show,
   Her trees of tinsel kiss'd by freakish gales,
Her ouphes, that cloak'd in leaf-gold skim the breeze,   *elves*
And fairies swarming thick as mites in rotten cheese.

I see the puny fair-chinn'd goblin rise
   Suddenly glorious from his mustard pot;
I see him wave his hand in seemly wise,
   And button round him tight his fulgent coat;
While *Maggie Lauder*, in a great surprise,
   Sits startled on her chair, yet fearing not;
I see him ope his dewy lips; I hear
The strange and strict command address'd to *Maggie*'s ear.

I see the *Ranter* with bagpipe on back,
   As to the fair he rides jocundly on;
I see the crowds that press with speed not slack
   Along each road that leads to *Anster* loan;   *way*

I see the suitors, that, deep-sheath'd in sack,
   Hobble and tumble, bawl and swear, and groan;
I see — but fy, thou brainish muse! what mean
These vapourings, and brags of what by thee is seen?

Go to — be cooler, and in order tell
   To all my good co-townsmen list'ning round,
How every merry incident befel,
   Whereby our loan shall ever be renown'd;
Say first, what elf or fairy could impel
   Fair *Mag*, with wit, and wealth, and beauty crown'd,
To put her suitors to such waggish test,
And give her happy bed to him that jumped best?

'Twas on a keen December night; John Frost
   Drove through mid air his chariot, icy-wheel'd,
And from the sky's crisp ceiling star-embost,
   Whiff'd off the clouds that the pure blue conceal'd;
The hornless moon amid her brilliant host
   Shone, and with silver sheeted lake and field;
'Twas cutting cold; I'm sure, each trav'ler's nose
Was pinch'd right red that night, and numb'd were all his toes.

Not so were *Maggie Lauder*'s toes, as she
   In her warm chamber at her supper sate,
(For 'twas that hour when burgesses agree
   To eat their suppers ere the night grows late).
Alone she sat, and pensive as may be
   A young fair lady, wishful of a mate;
Yet with her pearly teeth held on a picking,
Her stomach to refresh, the breast-bone of a chicken.

She thought upon her suitors that with love
   Besiege her chamber all the livelong day,
Aspiring each her virgin heart to move,
   With courtship's every troublesome essay,
Calling her, angel, sweeting, fondling, dove,
   And other nicknames in love's friv'lous way;
While she with heart more cold than new-caught herring,
Was hum'ring still the beaux, and still not one preferring.

What, what, quo' *Mag*, must thus it be my doom
   To live a spouseless never-wedded maid,
And idly toss away my body's bloom,
   Without a partner, on my joyless bed,
Giving my kisses to my pillow's plume,
   Cold, unresponsive kisses, void and dead?
Fool that I am, to live unwed so long!
More fool, since I am woo'd by such a clam'rous throng!

For e'er was heiress with much gold in chest
   And dowr'd with acres of wheat-bearing land,
By such a pack of men, in am'rous quest,
   Fawningly spaniel'd to bestow her hand?
Where'er I walk, the air that feeds my breast
   Is by the gusty sighs of lovers fann'd;
Each wind that blows wafts love-cards to my lap;
Whilst I – ah stupid *Mag*! – avoid each am'rous trap!

Then come, let me my suitors' merits weigh,
   And in the worthiest lad my spouse select:
First, there's our *Anster* merchant, Norman Ray,
   A powder'd wight with golden buttons deck'd,
That stinks with scent, and chats like popinjay,
   And struts with phiz tremendously erect;
Four brigs has he, that on the broad sea swim; –
He is a pompous fool – oh no! I'll not have him:

Next is the Master Andrew Strang, that takes
   His seat i' the Baillies' loft on Sabbath-day,
With paltry visage white as oaten cakes,
   As if no blood runs gurgling in his clay;
Heav'ns! what an awkward hunch the fellow makes,
   As to the priest he does the bow repay!
Yet he is rich – a very wealthy man, true –
But, by the holy rood, I will have none of Andrew.

Then for the Lairds – there's Melvil of Carnbee,
   A handsome gallant, and a beau of spirit;
Who can go down the dance so well as he?
   And who can fiddle with such manly merit?

– Ay, but he is too much the debauchee –
His cheeks seem sponges oozing port and claret;
In marrying him I should bestow myself ill,
And so, I'll not have you, thou fuddler Harry Melvil!

There's Cunningham of Barns, that still assails
   With verse and billet-doux my gentle heart,
A bookish Squire, and good at telling tales,
   That rhimes and whines of Cupid, flame, and dart;
But, oh! his mouth a filthy smell exhales,
   And on his nose sprouts horribly the wart;
What though there be a fund of lore and fun in him?
He has a rotten breath – I cannot think of Cunningham.

from *Papistry Storm'd*

Sang First

I sing the steir, strabush, and strife,	*stir; uproar*
Whan, bickerin' frae the towns o' Fife,	*rushing*
Great bangs of bodies, thick and rife,	*crowds*
Gaed to Sanct Androis town,	*went; St Andrews*
And, wi' John Calvin i' their heads,	
And hammers i' their hands and spades,	
Enrag'd at idols, mass, and beads,	
Dang the Cathedral down:	*smashed*
I wat the bruilzie then was dour,	*know; battle; hard*
Wi' sticks, and stanes, and bluidy clour,	*bloody lumps*
Ere Papists unto Calvin's power	
Gaif up their strangest places;	
And fearfu' the stramash and stour,	*commotion; dust*
Whan pinnacle cam doun and tow'r,	
And Virgin Maries in a shower	
Fell flat and smash't their faces;	
The capper roofs, that dazzlit heaven,	*copper*
Were frae their rafters rent and riven;	*torn*
The marble altars dash't and driven;	
The cods wi' velvet laces,	*cushions*

The siller ewers and candlesticks,
The purple stole and gowden pyx,   *golden*
And tunakyls and dalmatyks,   *[ecclesiastical vestments]*
    Cam tumblin' frae their cases;
The Devil stood bumbaz'd to see   *bamboozled*
The bonny cosy byke, whair he   *hive*
Had cuddlit monie a centurie,
    Ripp't up wi' sic disgraces!

GEORGE GORDON, LORD BYRON (1788–1824)

Lachin y Gair

Away, ye gay landscapes, ye gardens of roses!
    In you let the minions of luxury rove;
Restore me the rocks, where the snow-flake reposes,
    Though still they are sacred to freedom and love:
Yet, Caledonia, beloved are thy mountains,
    Round their white summits though elements war;
Though cataracts foam 'stead of smooth-flowing fountains,
    I sigh for the valley of dark Loch na Garr.

Ah! there my young footsteps in infancy wander'd;
    My cap was the bonnet, my cloak was the plaid;
On chieftains long perish'd my memory ponder'd,
    As daily I strode through the pine-cover'd glade;
I sought not my home till the day's dying glory
    Gave place to the rays of the bright polar star;
For fancy was cheer'd by traditional story,
    Disclosed by the natives of dark Loch na Garr.

'Shades of the dead! have I not heard your voices
    Rise on the night-rolling breath of the gale?'
Surely the soul of the hero rejoices,
    And rides on the wind, o'er his own Highland vale.
Round Loch na Garr while the stormy mist gathers,
    Winter presides in his cold icy car:
Clouds there encircle the forms of my fathers;
    They dwell in the tempests of dark Loch na Garr.

'Ill-starr'd, though brave, did no visions foreboding
    Tell you that fate had forsaken your cause?'
Ah! were you destined to die at Culloden,
    Victory crown'd not your fall with applause:
Still were you happy in death's earthly slumber,
    You rest with your clan in the caves of Braemar;
The pibroch resounds, to the piper's loud number,
    Your deeds on the echoes of dark Loch na Garr.

Years have roll'd on, Loch na Garr, since I left you,
   Years must elapse ere I tread you again:
Nature of verdure and flow'rs has bereft you,
   Yet still are you dearer than Albion's plain.
England! thy beauties are tame and domestic
   To one who has roved o'er the mountains afar:
Oh for the crags that are wild and majestic!
   The steep frowning glories of dark Loch na Garr.

She Walks in Beauty

She walks in beauty, like the night
   Of cloudless climes and starry skies;
And all that's best of dark and bright
   Meet in her aspect and her eyes:
Thus mellow'd to that tender light
   Which heaven to gaudy day denies.

One shade the more, one ray the less,
   Had half impair'd the nameless grace
Which waves in every raven tress,
   Or softly lightens o'er her face;
Where thoughts serenely sweet express
   How pure, how dear their dwelling-place.

And on that cheek, and o'er that brow,
   So soft, so calm, yet eloquent,
The smiles that win, the tints that glow,
   But tell of days in goodness spent,
A mind at peace with all below,
   A heart whose love is innocent!

So, we'll go no more a roving

So, we'll go no more a roving
   So late into the night,
Though the heart be still as loving,
   And the moon be still as bright.

For the sword outwears its sheath,
    And the soul wears out the breast,
And the heart must pause to breathe,
    And love itself have rest.

Though the night was made for loving,
    And the day returns too soon,
Yet we'll go no more a roving
    By the light of the moon.

from *Don Juan*

from *Canto II*

Alas for Juan and Haidée! They were
    So loving and so lovely; till then never,
Excepting our first parents, such a pair
    Had run the risk of being damned forever.
And Haidée, being devout as well as fair,
    Had doubtless heard about the Stygian river
And hell and purgatory, but forgot
Just in the very crisis she should not.

They look upon each other, and their eyes
    Gleam in the moonlight, and her white arm clasps
Round Juan's head, and his around hers lies
    Half buried in the tresses which it grasps.
She sits upon his knee and drinks his sighs,
    He hers, until they end in broken gasps;
And thus they form a group that's quite antique,
Half naked, loving, natural, and Greek.

And when those deep and burning moments passed,
    And Juan sunk to sleep within her arms,
She slept not, but all tenderly, though fast,
    Sustained his head upon her bosom's charms.
And now and then her eye to heaven is cast,
    And then on the pale cheek her breast now warms,
Pillowed on her o'erflowing heart, which pants
With all it granted and with all it grants.

An infant when it gazes on a light,
    A child the moment when it drains the breast,
A devotee when soars the Host in sight,
    An Arab with a stranger for a guest,
A sailor when the prize has struck in fight,
    A miser filling his most hoarded chest
Feel rapture, but not such true joy are reaping
As they who watch o'er what they love while sleeping.

For there it lies so tranquil, so beloved;
    All that it hath of life with us is living,
So gentle, stirless, helpless, and unmoved,
    And all unconscious of the joy 'tis giving.
All it hath felt, inflicted, passed, and proved,
    Hushed into depths beyond the watcher's diving,
There lies the thing we love with all its errors
And all its charms, like death without its terrors.

The lady watched her lover; and that hour
    Of love's and night's and ocean's solitude
O'erflowed her soul with their united power.
    Amidst the barren sand and rocks so rude
She and her wave-worn love had made their bower,
    Where nought upon their passion could intrude,
And all the stars that crowded the blue space
Saw nothing happier than her glowing face.

Alas, the love of women! It is known
    To be a lovely and a fearful thing,
For all of theirs upon that die is thrown,
    And if 'tis lost, life hath no more to bring
To them but mockeries of the past alone,
    And their revenge is as the tiger's spring,
Deadly and quick and crushing; yet as real
Torture is theirs, what they inflict they feel.

They are right, for man, to man so oft unjust,
    Is always so to women. One sole bond
Awaits them, treachery is all their trust.
    Taught to conceal, their bursting hearts despond
Over their idol, till some wealthier lust
    Buys them in marriage – and what rests beyond?
A thankless husband, next a faithless lover,
Then dressing, nursing, praying, and all's over.

Some take a lover, some take drams or prayers,
    Some mind their household, others dissipation,
Some run away and but exchange their cares,
    Losing the advantage of a virtuous station.
Few changes e'er can better their affairs,
    Theirs being an unnatural situation,
From the dull palace to the dirty hovel.
Some play the devil, and then write a novel.

Haidée was Nature's bride and knew not this;
    Haidée was Passion's child, born where the sun
Showers triple light and scorches even the kiss
    Of his gazelle-eyed daughters. She was one
Made but to love, to feel that she was his
    Who was her chosen. What was said or done
Elsewhere was nothing. She had nought to fear,
Hope, care, nor love beyond; her heart beat here.

And oh, that quickening of the heart, that beat!
    How much it costs us! Yet each rising throb
Is in its cause as its effect so sweet
    That Wisdom, ever on the watch to rob
Joy of its alchemy and to repeat
    Fine truths – even Conscience too – has a tough job
To make us understand each good old maxim,
So good I wonder Castlereagh don't tax 'em.

And now 'twas done; on the lone shore were plighted
   Their hearts. The stars, their nuptial torches, shed
Beauty upon the beautiful they lighted.
   Ocean their witness, and the cave their bed,
By their own feelings hallowed and united;
   Their priest was Solitude, and they were wed.
And they were happy, for to their young eyes
Each was an angel, and earth Paradise.

from *Canto X*

The lawyer and the critic but behold
   The baser sides of literature and life,
And nought remains unseen, but much untold,
   By those who scour those double vales of strife.
While common men grow ignorantly old,
   The lawyer's brief is like the surgeon's knife,
Dissecting the whole inside of a question
And with it all the process of digestion.

A legal broom's a moral chimney sweeper,
   And that's the reason he himself's so dirty.
The endless soot bestows a tint far deeper
Than can be hid by altering his shirt. He
Retains the sable stains of the dark creeper;
   At least some twenty-nine do out of thirty
In all their habits. Not so you, I own;
As Caesar wore his robe, you wear your gown.

And all our little feuds, at least all mine,
   Dear Jeffrey, once my most redoubted foe   *[Francis Jeffrey, critic]*
(As far as rhyme and criticism combine
   To make such puppets of us things below),
Are over. Here's a health to Auld Lang Syne!
   I do not know you and may never know
Your face, but you have acted on the whole
Most nobly, and I own it from my soul.

And when I use the phrase of 'Auld Lang Syne',
   'Tis not addressed to you, the more's the pity
For me, for I would rather take my wine
   With you, than aught (save Scott) in your proud city.   *[Edinburgh]*
But somehow — it may seem a schoolboy's whine,
   And yet I seek not to be grand nor witty —
But I am half a Scot by birth, and bred
A whole one, and my heart flies to my head,

As Auld Lang Syne brings Scotland, one and all,
   Scotch plaids, Scotch snoods, the blue hills, and clear streams,
The Dee, the Don, Balgounie's Brig's black wall,
   All my boy feelings, all my gentler dreams
Of what I then dreamt, clothed in their own pall,
   Like Banquo's offspring. Floating past me seems
My childhood in this childishness of mine;
I care not — 'tis a glimpse of Auld Lang Syne.

And though, as you remember, in a fit
   Of wrath and rhyme, when juvenile and curly,
I railed at Scots to show my wrath and wit,
   Which must be owned was sensitive and surly.
Yet 'tis in vain such sallies to permit;
   They cannot quench young feelings fresh and early.
I 'scotched, not killed', the Scotchman in my blood
And love the land of 'mountain and of flood'.

JANET HAMILTON (1795–1873)

Oor Location

A hunner funnels bleezin', reekin',	hundred; blazing; smoking
Coal an' ironstane charrin', smeekin';	smoking
Navvies, miners, keepers, fillers,	
Puddlers, rollers, iron millers;	
Reestit, reekit, raggit laddies,	rested; smelly
Firemen, enginemen, an' paddies;	
Boatmen, banksmen, rough an' rattlin',	
'Bout the wecht wi' colliers battlin',	weight
Sweatin', swearin', fechtin', drinkin';	fighting
Change-house bells an' gill-stoups clinkin';	ale-house; jugs
Police – ready men and willin' –	
Aye at han' whan stoups are fillin';	
Clerks an' counter-loupers plenty,	shop assistants
Wi' trim moustache and whiskers dainty –	
Chaps that winna staun at trifles!	
Min' ye, they can han'le rifles!	
'Bout the wives in oor location –	
An' the lassies' botheration –	
Some are decent, some are dandies,	
An' a gey wheen drucken randies;	fair number; drunken foul-mouthed women
Aye to neebors houses sailin',	
Greetin' bairns ahint them trailing,	crying; behind
Gaun for nouther bread nor butter,	
Juist to drink an' rin the cutter!	cary liquor from the pub
O the dreadfu' curse o' drinkin'! –	
Men are ill, but, to my thinkin',	
Leukin' through the drucken fock,	looking; folk
There's a Jenny for ilk Jock.	every
Oh the dool an' desolation,	sorrow
An' the havock in the nation	
Wrocht by dirty, drucken wives!	
Oh hoo mony bairnies lives	
Lost ilk year through their neglec'!	neglect
Like a millstane roun' the neck	

O' the strugglin', toilin' masses
Hing drucken wives an' wanton lassies.   *hang*
To see sae mony unwed mithers
Is sure a shame that taps a' ithers.   *tops*
　　An' noo I'm fairly set a-gaun;
On baith the whisky-shop and pawn
I'll speak my min' – and what for no?
Frae whence cums misery, want, an' wo,
The ruin, crime, disgrace, an' shame
That quenches a' the lichts o' hame?
Ye needna speer, the feck ot's drawn   *ask; greater part*
Oot o' the change-hoose an' the pawn.
　　Sin an' Death, as poets tell,
On ilk side the doors o' hell
Wait to ha'rl mortals in –   *drag*
Death gets a' that's catcht by sin:
There are doors where Death an' Sin
Draw their tens o' thoosan's in;
Thick an' thrang we see them gaun,
First the dram-shop, then the pawn;
Owre a' kin's o' ruination,
Drink's the King in oor location!

WILLIAM ANDERSON (1805–1866)

I'm Naebody Noo

I'm naebody noo, though in days that are gane,
Whan I'd hooses, and lands, and gear o' my ain,   *possessions*
There war mony to flatter, and mony to praise,
And wha but myself was sae prood in those days.

An' then roun' my table wad visitors thrang,
Wha laughed at my joke, and applauded my sang,
Though the tane had nae point, and the tither nae glee; *one; other*
But of course they war grand when comin frae me.

Whan I'd plenty to gie, o' my cheer and my crack, *talk*
There war plenty to come, and wi' joy to partak;
But whenever the water grew scant at the well,
I was welcome to drink all alane by mysel.

Whan I'd nae need o' aid, there were plenty to proffer,
And noo whan I want it, I ne'er get the offer;
I could greet whan I think hoo my siller decreast, *cry; silver*
In the feasting o' those who came only to feast.

The fulsome respec' to my gowd they did gie   *gold; give*
I thought a' the time was intended for me,
But whenever the end o' my money they saw,
Their friendship, like it, also flickered awa.

My advice ance was sought for by folk far and near, *once*
Sic great wisdom I had ere I tint a' my gear,   *lost*
I'm as weel able yet to gie counsel, that's true,
But I may just haud my wheest, for I'm naebody noo. *peace*

WILLIAM EDMONDSTOUNE AYTOUN (1813–1865)

from *The Execution of Montrose*

The morning dawned full darkly,
The rain came flashing down,
And the jagged streak of the levin-bolt   *lightning*
Lit up the gloomy town:
The thunder crashed across the heaven,
The fatal hour was come:
Yet aye broke in with muffled beat
The 'larum of the drum.
There was madness on the earth below
And anger in the sky,
And young and old, and rich and poor,
Came forth to see him die.

Ah, God, that ghastly gibbet.
How dismal 'tis to see
The great tall spectral skeleton,
The ladder and the tree.
Hark, hark, it is the clash of arms –
The bells begin to toll –
'He is coming, he is coming,
God's mercy on his soul.'
One last long peal of thunder:
The clouds are cleared away,
And the glorious sun once more looks down
Amidst the dazzling day.

'He is coming, he is coming!'
Like a bridegroom from his room,
Came the hero from his prison
To the scaffold and the doom.
There was glory on his forehead,
There was lustre in his eye,
And he never walked to battle
More proudly than to die:

There was colour in his visage,
Though the cheeks of all were wan,
And they marvelled as they saw him pass,
That great and goodly man.

He mounted up the scaffold,
And he turned him to the crowd;
But they dared not trust the people,
So he might not speak aloud.
But he looked upon the heavens,
And they were clear and blue,
And in the liquid ether
The eye of God shone through;
Yet a black and murky battlement
Lay resting on the hill,
As though the thunder slept within –
All else was calm and still.

The grim Geneva ministers
With anxious scowl drew near,
As you have seen the ravens flock
Around the dying deer.
He would not deign them word nor sign,
But alone he bent the knee,
And veiled his face for Christ's dear grace
Beneath the gallows-tree.
Then radiant and serene he rose,
And cast his cloak away:
For he had ta'en his latest look
Of earth and sun and day.

A beam of light fell o'er him,
Like a glory round the shriven,
And he climbed the lofty ladder
As it were the path to heaven.
Then came a flash from out the cloud,
And a stunning thunder-roll;
And no man dared to look aloft,
For fear was on every soul.

There was another heavy sound,
A hush and then a groan;
And darkness swept across the sky —
The work of death was done.

GEORGE MACDONALD (1824–1905)

Why do the houses stand

Why do the houses stand
When they that built them are gone;
When remaineth even of one
That lived there and loved and planned
Not a face, not an eye, not a hand,
Only here and there a bone?
Why do the houses stand
When they who built them are gone?
Oft in the moonlighted land
When the day is overblown,
With happy memorial moan
Sweet ghosts in a loving band
Roam through the houses that stand –
For the builders are not gone.

WILLIAM MACGONAGALL (1825–1902)

Railway Bridge of the Silvery Tay

Beautiful new railway bridge of the silvery Tay,
With your strong brick piers and buttresses in so grand array;
And your thirteen central girders, which seems to my eye,
Strong enough all windy storms to defy.

And as I gaze upon thee my heart feels gay,
Because thou art the greatest railway bridge of the present day;
And can be seen for miles away,
From north, south, east, or west, of the Tay,
On a beautiful and clear sunshiny day,
And ought to make the hearts of the Mars boys feel gay;
Because thine equal nowhere can be seen,
Only near by Dundee and the bonnie Magdalen Green.

Beautiful new railway bridge of the silvery Tay,
With your beautiful side screens along your railway;
Which will be a great protection on a windy day,
So as the railway carriages won't be blown away;
And ought to cheer the hearts of the passengers night and day,
As they are conveyed along thy beautiful railway.
And towering above the silvery Tay,
Spanning the beautiful river from shore to shore;
Upwards of two miles and more,
Which is most wonderful to be seen –
Near by Dundee and the bonnie Magdalen Green.

Thy structure, to my eye, seems strong and grand,
And the workmanship most skilfully planned;
And I hope the designers, Messrs. Barlow & Arrol, will prosper for many a day,
For erecting thee across the beautiful Tay.
And I think nobody need have the least dismay,
To cross oer thee by night or day;
Because thy strength is visible to be seen –
Near by Dundee and the bonnie Magdalen Green.

Beautiful new railway bridge of the silvery Tay,
I wish you success for many a year and day,
And I hope thousands of people will come from far and away,
Both high and low, without delay,
From the north, south, east and the west,
Because as a railway bridge thou art the best;
Thou standest unequalled to be seen –
Near by Dundee and the bonnie Magdalen Green.

And for beauty thou art most lovely to be seen,
As the train crosses o'er thee with her cloud of steam
And you look well painted with the colour of marone,
And to find thy equal there is none;
Which, without fear of contradiction, I venture to say,
Because you are the longest railway bridge of the present day;
That now crosses o'er a tidal river stream,
And the most handsome to be seen –
Near by Dundee and the bonnie Magdalen Green.

The New Yorkers boast about their Brooklyn Bridge,
But in comparison to thee it seems like a midge,
Because thou spannest the silvery Tay,
A mile and more longer I venture to say;
Besides the railways carriages are pulled across by a rope,
Therefore Brooklyn Bridge cannot with thee cope;
And as you have been opened on the 20th day of June,
I hope Her Majesty Queen Victoria will visit thee very soon;
Because thou art worthy of a visit from Duke, Lord, or Queen,
And strong and securely built, which is most worthy to be seen –
Near by Dundee and the bonnie Magdalen Green.

ALEXANDER SMITH (1830–1867)

Glasgow

Sing, Poet, 'tis a merry world;
That cottage smoke is rolled and curled
   In sport, that every moss
Is happy, every inch of soil; —
Before *me* runs a road of toil
   With my grave cut across.
Sing, trailing showers and breezy downs —
I know the tragic hearts of towns.

City! I am true son of thine;
Ne'er dwelt I where great mornings shine
   Around the bleating pens;
Ne'er by the rivulets I strayed,
And ne'er upon my childhood weighed
   The silence of the glens.
Instead of shores where ocean beats,
I hear the ebb and flow of streets.

Black Labour draws his weary waves,
Into their secret-moaning caves;
   But with the morning light,
That sea again will overflow
With a long weary sound of woe,
   Again to faint in night.
Wave am I in that sea of woes,
Which, night and morning, ebbs and flows.

I dwelt within a gloomy court,
Wherein did never sunbeam sport;
   Yet there my heart was stirr'd.
My very blood did dance and thrill,
When on my narrow window-sill,
   Spring lighted like a bird.
Poor flowers — I watched them pine for weeks,
With leaves as pale as human cheeks.

Afar, one summer, I was borne;
Through golden vapours of the morn,
   I heard the hills of sheep:
I trod with a wild ecstasy
The bright fringe of the living sea:
    And on a ruined keep
I sat, and watched an endless plain
Blacken beneath the gloom of rain.

O fair the lightly sprinkled waste,
O'er which a laughing shower has raced!
      O fair the April shoots!
O fair the woods on summer days,
While a blue hyacinthine haze
      Is dreaming round the roots!
In thee, O City! I discern
Another beauty, sad and stern.

Draw thy fierce streams of blinding ore,
Smite on a thousand anvils, roar
     Down to the harbour-bars;
Smoulder in smoky sunsets, flare
On rainy nights, when street and square
     Lie empty to the stars.
From terrace proud to alley base
I know thee as my mother's face.

When sunset bathes thee in his gold,
In wreaths of bronze thy sides are rolled,
    Thy smoke is dusky fire;
And, from the glory round thee poured,
A sunbeam like an angel's sword
    Shivers upon a spire.
Thus have I watched thee, Terror! Dream!
While the blue Night crept up the stream.

The wild Train plunges in the hills,
He shrieks across the midnight rills;
    Streams through the shifting glare,
The roar and flap of foundry fires,

That shake with light the sleeping shires;
 And on the moorlands bare,
He sees afar a crown of light
Hang o'er thee in the hollow night.

At midnight, when thy suburbs lie
As silent as a noonday sky,
 When larks with heat are mute,
I love to linger on thy bridge,
All lonely as a mountain ridge,
 Disturbed but by my foot;
While the black lazy stream beneath,
Steals from its far-off wilds of heath.

And through thy heart, as through a dream,
Flows on that black disdainful stream;
 All scornfully it flows,
Between the huddled gloom of masts,
Silent as pines unvexed by blasts –
 'Tween lamps in streaming rows.
O wondrous sight! O stream of dread!
O long dark river of the dead!

Afar, the banner of the year
Unfurls: but dimly prisoned here,
 Tis only when I greet
A dropt rose lying in my way,
A butterfly that flutters gay
 Athwart the noisy street,
I know the happy Summer smiles
Around thy suburbs, miles on miles.

'T were neither pæan now, nor dirge,
The flash and thunder of the surge
 On flat sands wide and bare;
No haunting joy or anguish dwells
In the green light of sunny dells,
 Or in the starry air.
Alike to me the desert flower,
The rainbow laughing o'er the shower.

While o'er thy walls the darkness sails,
I lean against the churchyard rails;
    Up in the midnight towers
The belfried spire, the street is dead,
I hear in silence overhead
    The clang of iron hours:
It moves me not — I know her tomb
Is yonder in the shapeless gloom.

All raptures of this mortal breath,
Solemnities of life and death,
    Dwell in thy noise alone:
Of me thou hast become a part —
Some kindred with my human heart
    Lives in thy streets of stone;
For we have been familiar more
Than galley-slave and weary oar.

The beech is dipped in wine; the shower
Is burnished; on the swinging flower
    The latest bee doth sit.
The low sun stares through dust of gold,
And o'er the darkening heath and wold
    The large ghost-moth doth flit.
In every orchard Autumn stands,
With apples in his golden hands.

But all these sights and sounds are strange;
Then wherefore from thee should I range?
    Thou hast my kith and kin:
My childhood, youth, and manhood brave;
Thou hast that unforgotten grave
    Within thy central din.
    A sacredness of love and death
Dwells in thy noise and smoky breath.

JAMES THOMSON ('B.V.') (1834–1882)

In the Room

Ceste insigne fable et tragicque comedie.
      (Rabelais)

The sun was down, and twilight grey
   Filled half the air; but in the room,
Whose curtain had been drawn all day,
   The twilight was a dusky gloom:
Which seemed at first as still as death,
   And void; but was indeed all rife
With subtle thrills, the pulse and breath
   Of multitudinous lower life.

In their abrupt and headlong way
   Bewildered flies for light had dashed
Against the curtain all the day,
   And now slept wintrily abashed;
And nimble mice slept, wearied out,
   With such a double night's uproar;
But solid beetles crawled about
   The chilly hearth and naked floor.

And so throughout the twilight hour
   That vaguely murmurous hush and rest
There brooded; and beneath its power
   Life throbbing held its throbs supprest:
Until the thin-voiced mirror sighed,
   I am all blurred with dust and damp,
So long ago the clear day died,
   So long has gleamed nor fire nor lamp.

Whereon the curtain murmured back,
   Some change is on us, good or ill;
Behind me and before is black
   As when those human things lie still:

But I have seen the darkness grow
   As grows the daylight every morn;
Have felt out there long shine and glow,
   In here long chilly dusk forlorn.

The cupboard grumbled with a groan,
   Each new day worse starvation brings:
Since *he* came here I have not known
   Or sweets or cates or wholesome things:
But now! a pinch of meal, a crust,
   Throughout the week is all I get.
I am so empty; it is just
   As when they said we were to let.

What is become, then, of our Man?
   The petulant old glass exclaimed;
If all this time he slumber can,
   He really ought to be ashamed.
I wish we had our Girl again,
   So gay and busy, bright and fair:
The girls are better than these men,
   Who only for their dull selves care.

It is so many hours ago —
   The lamp and fire were both alight —
I saw him pacing to and fro,
   Perturbing restlessly the night.
His face was pale to give one fear,
   His eyes when lifted looked too bright;
He muttered; what, I could not hear:
   Bad words though; something was not right.

The table said, He wrote so long
   That I grew weary of his weight;
The pen kept up a cricket song,
   It ran and ran at such a rate:
And in the longer pauses he
   With both his folded arms downpressed,
And stared as one who does not see,
   Or sank his head upon his breast.

The fire-grate said, I am as cold
   As if I never had a blaze;
The few dead cinders here I hold,
   I held unburned for days and days.
Last night he made them flare; but still
   What good did all his writing do?
Among my ashes curl and thrill
   Thin ghosts of all those papers too.

The table answered, Not quite all;
   He saved and folded up one sheet,
And sealed it fast, and let it fall;
   And here it lies now white and neat.
Whereon the letter's whisper came,
   My writing is closed up too well;
Outside there's not a single name,
   And who should read me I can't tell.

The mirror sneered with scornful spite
   (That ancient crack which spoiled her looks
Had marred her temper), Write and write!
   And read those stupid, worn-out books!
That's all he does, read, write, and read,
   And smoke that nasty pipe which stinks:
He never takes the slightest heed
   How any of us feels or thinks.

But Lucy fifty times a day
   Would come and smile here in my face,
Adjust a tress that curled astray,
   Or tie a ribbon with more grace:
She looked so young and fresh and fair,
   She blushed with such a charming bloom,
It did one good to see her there,
   And brightened all things in the room.

She did not sit hours stark and dumb
   As pale as moonshine by the lamp;
To lie in bed when day was come,
   And leave us curtained chill and damp.

She slept away the dreary dark,
    And rose to greet the pleasant morn;
And sang as gaily as a lark
    While busy as the flies sun-born.

And how she loved us every one;
    And dusted this and mended that,
With trills and laughs and freaks of fun,
    And tender scoldings in her chat!
And then her bird, that sang as shrill
    As she sang sweet; her darling flowers
That grew there in the window-sill,
    Where she would sit at work for hours.

It was not much she ever wrote;
    Her fingers had good work to do;
Say, once a week a pretty note;
    And very long it took her too.
And little more she read, I wis;
    Just now and then a pictured sheet,
Besides those letters she would kiss
    And croon for hours, they were so sweet.

She had her friends too, blithe young girls,
    Who whispered, babbled, laughed, caressed,
And romped and danced with dancing curls,
    And gave our life a joyous zest.
But with this dullard, glum and sour,
    Not one of all his fellow-men
Has ever passed a social hour;
    We might be in some wild beast's den.

This long tirade aroused the bed,
    Who spoke in deep and ponderous bass,
Befitting that calm life he led,
    As if firm-rooted in his place:
In broad majestic bulk alone,
    As in thrice venerable age,
He stood at once the royal throne,
    The monarch, the experienced sage:

I know what is and what has been;
  Not anything to me comes strange,
Who in so many years have seen
  And lived through every kind of change.
I know when men are good or bad,
  When well or ill, he slowly said;
When sad or glad, when sane or mad,
  And when they sleep alive or dead.

At this last word of solemn lore
  A tremor circled through the gloom,
As if a crash upon the floor
  Had jarred and shaken all the room:
For nearly all the listening things
  Were old and worn, and knew what curse
Of violent change death often brings,
  From good to bad, from bad to worse;

They get to know each other well,
  To feel at home and settled down;
Death bursts among them like a shell,
  And strews them over all the town.
The bed went on, This man who lies
  Upon me now is stark and cold;
He will not any more arise,
  And do the things he did of old.

But we shall have short peace or rest;
  For soon up here will come a rout,
And nail him in a queer long chest,
  And carry him like luggage out.
They will be muffled all in black,
  And whisper much, and sigh and weep:
But he will never more come back,
  And some one else in me must sleep.

Thereon a little phial shrilled,
  Here empty on the chair I lie:
I heard one say, as I was filled,
  With half of this a man would die.

The man there drank me with slow breath,
    And murmured, Thus ends barren strife:
O sweeter, thou cold wine of death,
    Than ever sweet warm wine of life.

One of my cousins long ago,
    A little thing, the mirror said,
Was carried to a couch to show
    Whether a man was really dead.
Two great improvements marked the case:
    He did not blur her with his breath,
His many-wrinkled, twitching face
    Was smooth old ivory: verdict, Death.

It lay, the lowest thing there, lulled
    Sweet-sleep-like in corruption's truce;
The form whose purpose was annulled,
    While all the other shapes meant use.
It lay, the *he* become now *it*,
    Unconscious of the deep disgrace,
Unanxious how its parts might flit
    Through what new forms in time and space.

It lay and preached, as dumb things do,
    More powerfully than tongues can prate;
Though life be torture through and through,
    Man is but weak to plain of fate:
The drear path crawls on drearier still
    To wounded feet and hopeless breast?
Well, he can lie down when he will,
    And straight all ends in endless rest.

And while the black night nothing saw,
    And till the cold morn came at last,
That old bed held the room in awe
    With tales of its experience vast.
It thrilled the gloom; it told such tales
    Of human sorrows and delights,
Of fever moans and infant wails,
    Of births and deaths and bridal nights.

from *The City of Dreadful Night*

II

Because he seemed to walk with an intent
    I followed him; who, shadowlike and frail,
Unswervingly though slowly onward went,
    Regardless, wrapt in thought as in a veil:
Thus step for step with lonely sounding feet
We travelled many a long dim silent street.

At length he paused: a black mass in the gloom,
    A tower that merged into the heavy sky;
Around, the huddled stones of grave and tomb:
    Some old God's-acre now corruption's sty;
He murmured to himself with dull despair,
Here Faith died, poisoned by this charnel air.

Then turning to the right went on once more,
    And travelled weary roads without suspense;
And reached at last a low wall's open door,
    Whose villa gleamed beyond the foliage dense:
He gazed, and muttered with a hard despair,
Here Love died, stabbed by its own worshipped pair.

Then turning to the right resumed his march,
    And travelled streets and lanes with wondrous strength,
Until on stooping through a narrow arch
    We stood before a squalid house at length:
He gazed, and whispered with a cold despair,
Here Hope died, starved out in its utmost lair.

When he had spoken thus, before he stirred,
    I spoke, perplexed by something in the signs
Of desolation I had seen and heard
    In this drear pilgrimage to ruined shrines:
When Faith and Love and Hope are dead indeed,
Can Life still live? By what doth it proceed?

As whom his one intense thought overpowers,
    He answered coldly, Take a watch, erase
The signs and figures of the circling hours,
    Detach the hands, remove the dial-face:
The works proceed until run down; although
Bereft of purpose, void of use, still go.

Then turning to the right paced on again,
    And traversed squares and travelled streets whose glooms
Seemed more and more familiar to my ken;
    And reached that sullen temple of the tombs;
And paused to murmur with the old despair,
Here Faith died, poisoned by this charnel air.

I ceased to follow, for the knot of doubt
    Was severed sharply with a cruel knife:
He circled thus for ever tracing out
    The series of the fraction left of Life;
Perpetual recurrence in the scope
Of but three terms, dead Faith, dead Love, dead Hope.*

XVII

How the moon triumphs through the endless nights!
    How the stars throb and glitter as they wheel
Their thick processions of supernal lights
    Around the blue vault obdurate as steel!
And men regard with passionate awe and yearning
The mighty marching and the golden burning,
    And think the heavens respond to what they feel.

Boats gliding like dark shadows of a dream,
    Are glorified from vision as they pass
The quivering moonbridge on the deep black stream;
    Cold windows kindle their dead glooms of glass
To restless crystals; cornice, dome, and column
Emerge from chaos in the splendour solemn;
    Like faëry lakes gleam lawns of dewy grass.

---

* Life divided by that persistent three $= \dfrac{LXX}{333} = .\dot{2}1\dot{0}.$ (JT)

With such a living light these dead eyes shine,
    These eyes of sightless heaven, that as we gaze
We read a pity, tremulous, divine,
    Or cold majestic scorn in their pure rays:
Fond man! they are not haughty, are not tender;
There is no heart or mind in all their splendour,
    They thread mere puppets all their marvellous maze.

If we could near them with the flight unflown,
    We should but find them worlds as sad as this,
Or suns all self-consuming like our own
    Enringed by planet worlds as much amiss:
They wax and wane through fusion and confusion;
The spheres eternal are a grand illusion,
    The empyréan is a void abyss.

XXI

Anear the centre of that northern crest
    Stands out a level upland bleak and bare,
From which the city east and south and west
    Sinks gently in long waves; and thronèd there
An Image sits, stupendous, superhuman,
The bronze colossus of a wingèd Woman,
    Upon a graded granite base foursquare.

Low-seated she leans forward massively,
    With cheek on clenched left hand, the forearm's might
Erect, its elbow on her rounded knee;
    Across a clasped book in her lap the right
Upholds a pair of compasses; she gazes
With full set eyes, but wandering in thick mazes
    Of sombre thought beholds no outward sight.

Words cannot picture her; but all men know
    That solemn sketch the pure sad artist wrought
Three centuries and threescore years ago,
    With phantasies of his peculiar thought:
The instruments of carpentry and science
Scattered about her feet, in strange alliance
    With the keen wolf-hound sleeping undistraught;

Scales, hour-glass, bell, and magic-square above;
　　The grave and solid infant perched beside,
With open winglets that might bear a dove,
　　Intent upon its tablets, heavy-eyed;
Her folded wings as of a mighty eagle,
But all too impotent to lift the regal
　　Robustness of her earth-born strength and pride;

And with those wings, and that light wreath which seems
　　To mock her grand head and the knotted frown
Of forehead charged with baleful thoughts and dreams,
　　The household bunch of keys, the housewife's gown
Voluminous, indented, and yet rigid
As if a shell of burnished metal frigid,
　　The feet thick-shod to tread all weakness down;

The comet hanging o'er the waste dark seas,
　　The massy rainbow curved in front of it
Beyond the village with the masts and trees;
　　The snaky imp, dog-headed, from the Pit,
Bearing upon its batlike leathern pinions
Her name unfolded in the sun's dominions,
　　The 'MELENCOLIA' that transcends all wit.

Thus has the artist copied her, and thus
　　Surrounded to expound her form sublime,
Her fate heroic and calamitous;
　　Fronting the dreadful mysteries of Time,
Unvanquished in defeat and desolation,
Undaunted in the hopeless conflagration
　　Of the day setting on her baffled prime.

Baffled and beaten back she works on still,
　　Weary and sick of soul she works the more,
Sustained by her indomitable will:
　　The hands shall fashion and the brain shall pore,
And all her sorrow shall be turned to labour,
Till Death the friend-foe piercing with his sabre
　　That mighty heart of hearts ends bitter war.

But as if blacker night could dawn on night,
 With tenfold gloom on moonless night unstarred,
A sense more tragic than defeat and blight,
 More desperate than strife with hope debarred,
More fatal than the adamantine Never
Encompassing her passionate endeavour,
 Dawns glooming in her tenebrous regard:

The sense that every struggle brings defeat
 Because Fate holds no prize to crown success;
That all the oracles are dumb or cheat
 Because they have no secret to express;
That none can pierce the vast black veil uncertain
Because there is no light beyond the curtain;
 That all is vanity and nothingness.

Titanic from her high throne in the north,
 That City's sombre Patroness and Queen,
In bronze sublimity she gazes forth
 Over her Capital of teen and threne,
Over the river with its isles and bridges,
The marsh and moorland, to the stern rock-ridges,
 Confronting them with a coëval mien.

The moving moon and stars from east to west
 Circle before her in the sea of air;
Shadows and gleams glide round her solemn rest.
 Her subjects often gaze up to her there:
The strong to drink new strength of iron endurance,
The weak new terrors; all, renewed assurance
 And confirmation of the old despair.

ELLEN JOHNSTON (c. 1835–1873)

The Last Sark

Gude guide me, are ye hame again, and hae ye got nae wark?   *God*
We've naething noo tae pit awa, unless your auld blue sark.   *to pawn; shirt*
My heid is rinnin roond aboot, far lichter nor a flee: *lighter than a flea*
What care some gentry if they're weel though a' the puir wad dee?   *would die*

Our merchants and mill-masters they wad never want a meal   *lack*
Though a' the banks in Scotland wad for a twalmonth fail;
For some o them hae far mair gowd than ony ane can see.   *gold*
What care some gentry if they're weel though a' the puir wad dee?

Our hoose aince bien and cosy, John, oor beds aince snug and warm,   *once; good*
Feels unco cauld and dismal noo, and empty as a barn;   *strangely cold*
The weans sit greetin in our face, and we hae nocht tae gie.   *children; crying*
What care some gentry if they're weel though a' the puir wad dee?

It is the puir man's hard-won cash that fills the rich man's purse;
I'm sure his gowden coffers they are het wi mony a curse.   *hot*
Were it no for the workin man what wad the rich man be?
What care some gentry if they're weel though a' the puir wad dee?

My head is licht, my heart is weak, my een are growing blin';
The bairn is fa'en aff my knee – oh! John, catch haud o' him,   *baby; fallen*
You ken I hinna tasted meat for days far mair than three;   *know*
Were it no for my helpless bairns I wadna care to dee.

MARION BERNSTEIN (*fl.* 1876)

Manly Sports

How brave is the hunter who nobly will dare
On horseback to follow the small timid hare;
Oh! ye soldiers who fall in defence of your flag,
What are you to the hero who brings down the stag?

Bright eyes glance admiring, soft hearts give their loves
To the knight who shoots best in 'the tourney of doves';
Nothing else with such slaughtering feats can compare,
To win manly applause, or the smiles of the fair.

A cheer for fox-hunting! Come all who can dare
Track this dangerous animal down to its lair;
'Tis first trapped, then set free for the huntsmen to follow
With horses and hounds, and with heartstirring halloo!

The brave knights on the moor when the grouse are a-drive,
Slay so many, you'd think, there'd be none left alive;
Oh! the desperate daring of slaughtering grouse,
Can only be matched in a real slaughterhouse.

The angler finds true Anglo-Saxon delight,
In trapping small fish, who so foolishly bite,
He enjoys the wild terror of creatures so weak,
And what manlier pleasures can any one seek?

ANDREW LANG (1844–1912)

Romance

My Love dwelt in a Northern land.
A grey tower in a forest green
Was hers, and far on either hand
The long wash of the waves was seen,
And leagues on leagues of yellow sand,
The woven forest boughs between.

And through the silver Northern night
The sunset slowly died away,
And herds of strange deer, lily-white,
Stole forth among the branches grey;
About the coming of the light,
They fled like ghosts before the day.

I know not if the forest green
Still girdles around that castle grey.
I know not if the boughs between
The white deer vanish ere the day.
Above my Love the grass is green,
My heart is colder than the clay.

JAMES ROBERTSON (1849–1922)

The Discovery of America
(Seen from the Ochils through the Perspective of Four Centuries)

All the mill-horses of Europe
Were plodding round and round.
All the mills were droning
The same old sound.

The drivers were dozing, the millers
Were deaf — as millers will be;
When, startling them all, without warning
Came a great shout from the sea.

It startled them all. The horses,
Lazily plodding round,
Started and stopped; and the mills dropped
Like a mantle their sound.

The millers looked over their shoulders,
The drivers opened their eyes,
A silence, deeper than deafness,
Had fallen out of the skies.

'Halloa there!' — this time distinctly
It rose from the barren sea;
And Europe, turning in wonder,
Whispered, 'What can it be?'

'Come down, come down to the shore here!'
And Europe was soon on the sand; —
It was the great Columbus
Dragging his prize to land.

ROBERT LOUIS STEVENSON (1850–1894)

The Light-Keeper

I

The brilliant kernel of the night,
The flaming lightroom circles me:
I sit within a blaze of light
Held high above the dusky sea.
Far off the surf doth break and roar
Along bleak miles of moonlit shore,
Where through the tides the tumbling wave
Falls in an avalanche of foam
And drives its churned waters home
Up many an undercliff and cave.

The clear bell chimes: the clockworks strain,
The turning lenses flash and pass,
Frame turning within glittering frame
With frosty gleam of moving glass:
Unseen by me, each dusky hour
The sea-waves welter up the tower
Or in the ebb subside again;
And ever and anon all night,
Drawn from afar by charm of light,
A sea bird beats against the pane.

And lastly when dawn ends the night
And belts the semi-orb of sea,
The tall, pale pharos in the light
Looks white and spectral as may be.
The early ebb is out: the green
Straight belt of seaweed now is seen,
That round the basement of the tower
Marks out the interspace of tide;
And watching men are heavy-eyed,
And sleepless lips are dry and sour.

The night is over like a dream:
The sea-birds cry and dip themselves:
And in the early sunlight, steam
The newly bared and dripping shelves,
Around whose verge the glassy wave
With lisping wash is heard to lave;
While, on the white tower lifted high,
The circling lenses flash and pass
With yellow light in faded glass
And sickly shine against the sky.

II

As the steady lenses circle
With a frosty gleam of glass;
And the clear bell chimes,
And the oil brims over the lip of the burner,
Quiet and still at his desk,
The lonely Light-Keeper
Holds his vigil.

Lured from far,
The bewildered seagull beats
Dully against the lantern;
Yet he stirs not, lifts not his head
From the desk where he reads,
Lifts not his eyes to see
The chill blind circle of night
Watching him through the panes.
This is his country's guardian,
The outmost sentry of peace.
This is the man
Who gives up that is lovely in living
For the means to live.

Poetry cunningly gilds
The life of the Light-Keeper,
Held on high in the blackness
In the burning kernel of night,

The seaman sees and blesses him,
The Poet, deep in a sonnet,
Numbers his inky fingers
Fitly to praise him.
Only we behold him,
Sitting, patient and stolid,
Martyr to a salary.

Requiem

Under the wide and starry sky,
Dig the grave and let me lie.
Glad did I live and gladly die,
   And I laid me down with a will.

This be the verse you grave for me:
Here he lies where he longed to be;
Home is the sailor, home from sea,
   And the hunter home from the hill.

Christmas at Sea

The sheets were frozen hard, and they cut the naked hand;
The decks were like a slide, where a seaman scarce could stand;
The wind was a nor'wester, blowing squally off the sea;
And cliffs and spouting breakers were the only things a-lee.

They heard the surf a-roaring before the break of day;
But 'twas only with the peep of light we saw how ill we lay.
We tumbled every hand on deck instanter, with a shout,
And we gave her the maintops'l, and stood by to go about.

All day we tacked and tacked between the South Head and the North;
All day we hauled the frozen sheets, and got no further forth;
All day as cold as charity, in bitter pain and dread,
For very life and nature we tacked from head to head.

We gave the South a wider berth, for there the tide-race roared;
But every tack we made we brought the North Head close aboard:
So 's we saw the cliffs and houses, and the breakers running high,
And the coastguard in his garden, with his glass against his eye.

The frost was on the village roofs as white as ocean foam;
The good red fires were burning bright in every 'longshore home;
The windows sparkled clear, and the chimneys volleyed out;
And I vow we sniffed the victuals as the vessel went about.

The bells upon the church were rung with a mighty jovial cheer;
For it 's just that I should tell you how (of all days in the year)
This day of our adversity was blessèd Christmas morn,
And the house above the coastguard's was the house where I was born.

O well I saw the pleasant room, the pleasant faces there,
My mother's silver spectacles, my father's silver hair;
And well I saw the firelight, like a flight of homely elves,
Go dancing round the china-plates that stand upon the shelves.

And well I knew the talk they had, the talk that was of me,
Of the shadow on the household and the son that went to sea;
And O the wicked fool I seemed, in every kind of way,
To be here and hauling frozen ropes on blessèd Christmas Day.

They lit the high sea-light, and the dark began to fall.
'All hands to loose topgallant sails,' I heard the captain call.
'By the Lord, she'll never stand it,' our first mate, Jackson, cried.
. . . 'It's the one way or the other, Mr Jackson,' he replied.

She staggered to her bearings, but the sails were new and good,
And the ship smelt up to windward just as though she understood.
As the winter's day was ending, in the entry of the night,
We cleared the weary headland, and passed below the light.

And they heaved a mighty breath, every soul on board but me,
As they saw her nose again pointing handsome out to sea;
But all that I could think of, in the darkness and the cold,
Was just that I was leaving home and my folks were growing old.

Untitled

The tropics vanish, and meseems that I,
From Halkerside, from topmost Allermuir,
Or steep Caerketton, dreaming gaze again.
Far set in fields and woods, the town I see
Spring gallant from the shallows of her smoke,
Cragged, spired, and turreted, her virgin fort
Beflagged. About, on seaward-drooping hills,
New folds of city glitter. Last, the Forth
Wheels ample waters set with sacred isles,
And populous Fife smokes with a score of towns.

There, on the sunny frontage of a hill,
Hard by the house of kings, repose the dead,
My dead, the ready and the strong of word.
Their works, the salt-encrusted, still survive;
The sea bombards their founded towers; the night
Thrills pierced with their strong lamps. The artificers,
One after one, here in this grated cell,
Where the rain erases and the rust consumes,
Fell upon lasting silence. Continents
And continental oceans intervene;
A sea uncharted, on a lampless isle,
Environs and confines their wandering child
In vain. The voice of generations dead
Summons me, sitting distant, to arise,
My numerous footsteps nimbly to retrace,
And, all mutation over, stretch me down
In that devoted city of the dead.

To S. C.

I heard the pulse of the besieging sea
Throb far away all night. I heard the wind
Fly crying and convulse tumultuous palms.
I rose and strolled. The isle was all bright sand,
And flailing fans and shadows of the palm;
The heaven all moon and wind and the blind vault;

The keenest planet slain, for Venus slept.
    The king, my neighbour, with his host of wives,
Slept in the precinct of the palisade;
Where single, in the wind, under the moon,
Among the slumbering cabins, blazed a fire,
Sole street-lamp and the only sentinel.
    To other lands and nights my fancy turned –
To London first, and chiefly to your house,
The many-pillared and the well-beloved.
There yearning fancy lighted; there again
In the upper room I lay, and heard far off
The unsleeping city murmur like a shell;
The muffled tramp of the Museum guard
Once more went by me; I beheld again
Lamps vainly brighten the dispeopled street;
Again I longed for the returning morn,
The awaking traffic, the bestirring birds,
The consentaneous trill of tiny song
That weaves round monumental cornices
A passing charm of beauty. Most of all,
For your light foot I wearied, and your knock
That was the glad réveillé of my day.
    Lo, now, when to your task in the great house
At morning through the portico you pass,
One moment glance, where by the pillared wall
Far-voyaging island gods, begrimed with smoke,
Sit now unworshipped, the rude monument
Of faiths forgot and races undivined:
Sit now disconsolate, remembering well
The priest, the victim, and the songful crowd,
The blaze of the blue noon, and the huge voice,
Incessant, of the breakers on the shore.
As far as these from their ancestral shrine,
So far, so foreign, your divided friends
Wander, estranged in body, not in mind.

To S. R. Crockett

On receiving a Dedication

Blows the wind today, and the sun and the rain are flying,
  Blows the wind on the moors today and now,
Where about the graves of the martyrs the whaups are crying,   *curlews*
  My heart remembers how!

Grey recumbent tombs of the dead in desert places,
  Standing-stones on the vacant wine-red moor,
Hills of sheep, and the howes of the silent vanished races,   *glens*
  And winds, austere and pure:

Be it granted me to behold you again in dying,
  Hills of home! and to hear again the call;
Hear about the graves of the martyrs the peewees crying,
  And hear no more at all.

The Lamplighter

My tea is nearly ready and the sun has left the sky;
It's time to take the window to see Leerie going by;
For every night at teatime and before you take your seat,
With lantern and with ladder he comes posting up the street.

Now Tom would be a driver and Maria go to sea,
And my papa's a banker and as rich as he can be;
But I, when I am stronger and can choose what I'm to do,
O Leerie, I'll go round at night and light the lamps with you!

For we are very lucky, with a lamp before the door,
And Leerie stops to light it as he lights so many more;
And O! before you hurry by with ladder and with light,
O Leerie, see a little child and nod to him to-night!

From a Railway Carriage

Faster than fairies, faster than witches,
Bridges and houses, hedges and ditches;
And charging along like troops in a battle,
All through the meadows the horses and cattle:
All of the sights of the hill and the plain
Fly as thick as driving rain;
And ever again, in the wink of an eye,
Painted stations whistle by.

Here is a child who clambers and scrambles,
All by himself and gathering brambles;
Here is a tramp who stands and gazes;
And there is the green for stringing the daisies!
Here is a cart run away in the road
Lumping along with man and load;
And here is a mill and there is a river:
Each a glimpse and gone for ever!

The Land of Story-Books

At evening, when the lamp is lit,
Around the fire my parents sit;
They sit at home and talk and sing,
And do not play at anything.

Now, with my little gun, I crawl
All in the dark along the wall,
And follow round the forest track
Away behind the sofa back.

There, in the night, where none can spy,
All in my hunter's camp I lie,
And play at books that I have read
Till it is time to go to bed.

These are the hills, these are the woods,
These are my starry solitudes;
And there the river by whose brink
The roaring lions come to drink.

I see the others far away
As if in firelit camp they lay,
And I, like to an Indian scout,
Around their party prowled about.

So, when my nurse comes in for me,
Home I return across the sea,
And go to bed with backward looks
At my dear land of Story-books.

To Any Reader

As from the house your mother sees
You playing round the garden trees,
So you may see, if you will look
Through the windows of this book,
Another child, far, far away,
And in another garden, play.
But do not think you can at all,
By knocking on the window, call
That child to hear you. He intent
Is all on his play-business bent.
He does not hear; he will not look,
Nor yet be lured out of this book.
For, long ago, the truth to say,
He has grown up and gone away,
And it is but a child of air
That lingers in the garden there.

JOHN DAVIDSON (1857–1909)

Thirty Bob a Week

I couldn't touch a stop and turn a screw,
    And set the blooming world a-work for me,
Like such as cut their teeth – I hope, like you –
    On the handle of a skeleton gold key;
I cut mine on a leek, which I eat it every week:
    I'm a clerk at thirty bob as you can see.

But I don't allow it's luck and all a toss;
    There's no such thing as being starred and crossed;
It's just the power of some to be a boss,
    And the bally power of others to be bossed:
I face the music, sir; you bet I ain't a cur;
    Strike me lucky if I don't believe I'm lost!

For like a mole I journey in the dark,
    A-travelling along the underground
From my Pillar'd Halls and broad Suburbean Park,
    To come the daily dull official round;
And home again at night with my pipe all alight,
    A-scheming how to count ten bob a pound.

And it's often very cold and very wet,
    And my missis stitches towels for a hunks;
And the Pillar'd Halls is half of it to let –
    Three rooms about the size of travelling trunks.
And we cough, my wife and I, to dislocate a sigh,
    When the noisy little kids are in their bunks.

But you never hear her do a growl or whine,
    For she's made of flint and roses, very odd;
And I've got to cut my meaning rather fine,
    Or I'd blubber, for I'm made of greens and sod:
So p'r'aps we are in Hell for all that I can tell,
    And lost and damn'd and served up hot to God.

I ain't blaspheming, Mr Silver-tongue;
    I'm saying things a bit beyond your art:
Of all the rummy starts you ever sprung,
    Thirty bob a week's the rummiest start!
With your science and your books and your the'ries about spooks,
    Did you ever hear of looking in your heart?

I didn't mean your pocket, Mr, no:
    I mean that having children and a wife,
With thirty bob on which to come and go,
    Isn't dancing to the tabor and the fife:
When it doesn't make you drink, by Heaven! it makes you think,
    And notice curious items about life.

I step into my heart and there I meet
    A god-almighty devil singing small,
Who would like to shout and whistle in the street,
    And squelch the passers flat against the wall;
If the whole world was a cake he had the power to take,
    He would take it, ask for more, and eat them all.

And I meet a sort of simpleton beside,
    The kind that life is always giving beans;
With thirty bob a week to keep a bride
    He fell in love and married in his teens:
At thirty bob he stuck; but he knows it isn't luck:
    He knows the seas are deeper than tureens.

And the god-almighty devil and the fool
    That meet me in the High Street on the strike,
When I walk about my heart a-gathering wool,
    Are my good and evil angels if you like.
And both of them together in every kind of weather
    Ride me like a double-seated bike.

That's rough a bit and needs its meaning curled.
    But I have a high old hot un in my mind –
A most engrugious notion of the world,
    That leaves your lightning 'rithmetic behind:
I give it at a glance when I say 'There ain't no chance,
    Nor nothing of the lucky-lottery kind.'

And it's this way that I make it out to be:
   No fathers, mothers, countries, climates – none;
No Adam was responsible for me,
   Nor society, nor systems, nary one:
A little sleeping seed, I woke – I did, indeed –
   A million years before the blooming sun.

I woke because I thought the time had come;
   Beyond my will there was no other cause;
And everywhere I found myself at home,
   Because I chose to be the thing I was;
And in whatever shape of mollusc or of ape
   I always went according to the laws.

I was the love that chose my mother out;
   I joined two lives and from the union burst;
My weakness and my strength without a doubt
   Are mine alone for ever from the first:
It's just the very same with a difference in the name
   As 'Thy will be done.' You say it if you durst!

They say it daily up and down the land
   As easy as you take a drink, it's true;
But the difficultest go to understand,
   And the difficultest job a man can do,
Is to come it brave and meek with thirty bob a week,
   And feel that that's the proper thing for you.

It's a naked child against a hungry wolf;
   It's playing bowls upon a splitting wreck;
It's walking on a string across a gulf
   With millstones fore-and-aft about your neck;
But the thing is daily done by many and many a one;
   And we fall, face forward, fighting, on the deck.

A Northern Suburb

Nature selects the longest way,
   And winds about in tortuous grooves;
A thousand years the oaks decay;
   The wrinkled glacier hardly moves.

But here the whetted fangs of change
   Daily devour the old demesne —
The busy farm, the quiet grange,
   The wayside inn, the village green.

In gaudy yellow brick and red,
   With rooting pipes, like creepers rank,
The shoddy terraces o'erspread
   Meadow, and garth, and daisied bank.

With shelves for rooms the houses crowd,
   Like draughty cupboards in a row —
Ice-chests when wintry winds are loud,
   Ovens when summer breezes blow.

Roused by the fee'd policeman's knock,
   And sad that day should come again,
Under the stars the workmen flock
   In haste to reach the workmen's train.

For here dwell those who must fulfil
   Dull tasks in uncongenial spheres,
Who toil through dread of coming ill,
   And not with hope of happier years —

The lowly folk who scarcely dare
   Conceive themselves perhaps misplaced,
Whose prize for unremitting care
   Is only not to be disgraced.

Snow

I

'Who affirms that crystals are alive?'
    I affirm it, let who will deny: —
Crystals are engendered, wax and thrive,
    Wane and wither; I have seen them die.

Trust me, masters, crystals have their day,
    Eager to attain the perfect norm,
Lit with purpose, potent to display
    Facet, angle, colour, beauty, form.

II

Water-crystals need for flower and root
    Sixty clear degrees, no less, no more;
Snow, so fickle, still in this acute
    Angle thinks, and learns no other lore:

Such its life, and such its pleasure is,
    Such its art and traffic, such its gain,
Evermore in new conjunctions this
    Admirable angle to maintain.

Crystalcraft in every flower and flake
    Snow exhibits, of the welkin free:
Crystalline are crystals for the sake,
    All and singular, of crystalry.

Yet does every crystal of the snow
    Individualize, a seedling sown
Broadcast, but instinct with power to grow
    Beautiful in beauty of its own.

Every flake with all its prongs and dints
    Burns ecstatic as a new-lit star:
Men are not more diverse, finger-prints
    More dissimilar than snow-flakes are.

Worlds of men and snow endure, increase,
    Woven of power and passion to defy
Time and travail: only races cease,
    Individual men and crystals die.

III

Jewelled shapes of snow whose feathery showers,
    Fallen or falling wither at a breath,
All afraid are they, and loth as flowers
    Beasts and men to tread the way to death.

Once I saw upon an object-glass,
    Martyred underneath a microscope,
One elaborate snow-flake slowly pass,
    Dying hard, beyond the reach of hope.

Still from shape to shape the crystal changed,
    Writhing in its agony; and still,
Less and less elaborate, arranged
    Potently the angle of its will.

Tortured to a simple final form,
    Angles six and six divergent beams,
Lo, in death it touched the perfect norm
    Verifying all its crystal dreams!

IV

Such the noble tragedy of one
    Martyred snow-flake. Who can tell the fate
Heinous and uncouth of showers undone,
    Fallen in cities! — showers that expiate

Errant lives from polar worlds adrift
    Where the great millennial snows abide;
Castaways from mountain-chains that lift
    Snowy summits in perennial pride;

Nomad snows, or snows in evil day
   Born to urban ruin, to be tossed,
Trampled, shovelled, ploughed and swept away
   Down the seething sewers: all the frost

Flowers of heaven melted up with lees,
   Offal, recrement, but every flake
Showing to the last in fixed degrees
   Perfect crystals for the crystal's sake.

V

Usefulness of snow is but a chance
   Here in temperate climes with winter sent,
Sheltering earth's prolonged hibernal trance:
   All utility is accident.

Sixty clear degrees the joyful snow,
   Practising economy of means,
Fashions endless beauty in, and so
   Glorifies the universe with scenes

Arctic and antarctic: stainless shrouds,
   Ermine woven in silvery frost, attire
Peaks in every land among the clouds
   Crowned with snows to catch the morning's fire.

from *The Crystal Palace*

Contraption, – that's the bizarre, proper slang,
Eclectic word, for this portentous toy,
The flying-machine, that gyrates stiffly, arms
A-kimbo, so to say, and baskets slung
From every elbow, skating in the air.
Irreverent, we; but Tartars from Thibet
May deem Sir Hiram the Grandest Lama, deem
His volatile machinery best, and most
Magnific, rotatory engine, meant
For penitence and prayer combined, whereby
Petitioner as well as orison

Are spun about in space: a solemn rite
Before the portal of that fane unique,
Victorian temple of commercialism,
Our very own eighth wonder of the world,
The Crystal Palace.

        So sublime! Like some
Immense crustacean's gannoid skeleton,
Unearthed, and cleansed, and polished! Were it so
Our paleontological respect
Would shield it from derision; but when a shed,
Intended for a palace, looks as like
The fossil of a giant myriapod! . . .
'Twas Isabey — sarcastic wretch! — who told
A young aspirant, studying tandem art
And medicine, that he certainly was born
To be a surgeon: 'When you try,' he said,
'To paint a boat you paint a tumour.'

                No
Idea of its purpose, and no mood
Can make your glass and iron beautiful.
Colossal ugliness may fascinate
If something be expressed; and time adopts
Ungainliest stone and brick and ruins them
To beauty; but a building lacking life,
A house that must not mellow or decay? —
'Tis nature's outcast. Moss and lichen? Stains
Of weather? From the first Nature said 'No!
Shine there unblessed, a witness of my scorn!
I love the ashlar and the well-baked clay;
My seasons can adorn them sumptuously:
But you shall stand rebuked till men ashamed,
Abhor you, and destroy you and repent!'

But come: here's crowd; here's mob; a gala day!
The walks are black with people: no one hastes;
They all pursue their purpose business-like —
The polo-ground, the cycle-track; but most
Invade the palace glumly once again.
It is 'again'; you feel it in the air —

Resigned habitués on every hand:
And yet agog; abandoned, yet concerned!
They can't tell why they come; they only know
They must shove through the holiday somehow.

In the main floor the fretful multitude
Circulates from the north nave to the south
Across the central transept – swish and tread
And murmur, like a seaboard's mingled sound.
About the sideshows eddies swirl and swing:
Distorting mirrors; waltzing-tops – wherein
Couples are wildly spun contrariwise
To your revolving platform; biographs,
Or rifle-ranges; panoramas: choose!

As stupid as it was last holiday?
They think so, – every whit! Outside, perhaps?
A spice of danger in the flying-machine?
A few who passed that whirligig, their hopes
On higher things, return disconsolate
To try the Tartar's volant oratory.
Others again, no more anticipant
Of any active business in their own
Diversion, joining stalwart folk who sought
At once the polo-ground, the cycle-track,
Accept the ineludible; while some
(Insidious anti-climax here) frequent
The water-entertainments – shallops, chutes
And rivers subterrene: – thus, passive, all,
Like savages bewitched, submit at last
To be the dupes of pleasure, sadly gay –
Victims, and not companions, of delight.

VIOLET JACOB (1863–1946)

Tam i' the Kirk

O Jean, my Jean, when the bell ca's the congregation   *calls*
   Owre valley an' hill wi' the ding frae its iron mou',   *over; sound; mouth*
When a'body's thochts is set on his ain salvation,
     Mine's set on you.

There's a reid rose lies on the Buik o' the Word afore ye   *before*
   That was growin' braw on its bush at the keek o' day,   *beautiful; break*
But the lad that pu'd yon flower i' the mornin's glory,   *pulled*
     He canna pray.

He canna pray; but there's nane i' the Kirk will heed him
   Whaur he sits sae still his lane at the side o' the wa',   *alone*
For nane but the reid rose kens what my lassie gi'ed him,   *gave*
     It an' us twa!

He canna sing for the sang that his ain hert raises,   *own*
   He canna see for the mist that's afore his een,   *eyes*
And a voice drouns the hale o' the psalms an' the paraphrases,
     Cryin' 'Jean, Jean, Jean!'

The Helpmate

I hae nae gear, nae pot nor pan,   *possessions*
   Nae lauchin' lips hae I;   *laughing*
Forbye yersel' there's ne'er a man   *except*
   Looks roond as I gang by.

And a' fowk kens nae time I've gied   *everybody knows; given*
   Tae daft strathspey and reel,
Nor idle sang nor ploy, for dreid   *play*
   O' pleasurin' the deil.

Wi' muckle care ma mither bred   *great*
   Her bairn in wisdom's way;
Come Tyesday first, when we are wed,
   A wiselike wife ye'll hae.

The best ye'll get, baith but an' ben,   *in both rooms*
   Sae mild an' douce I'll be;   *gentle*
Yer hame'll be yer haven when
   Ye're married upon me.

Ye'll find the kettle on the fire,
   The hoose pit a' tae richts,
And yer heid in the troch at the back o' the byre   *trough*
   When ye come back fu' o' nichts.   *drunk*

CHARLES MURRAY (1864–1941)

Dockens afore his Peers

(Exemption tribunal)

Nae sign o' thow yet. Ay, that's me, John Watt o' Dockenhill:	*thaw*
We've had the war throu' han' afore, at markets ower a gill.	*discussed fully*
O ay, I'll sit, birze ben a bit. Hae, Briggie, pass the snuff;	*shift along*
Ye winna hinner lang wi' me, an' speer a lot o' buff,	*won't linger; ask; nonsense*
For I've to see the saiddler yet, an' Watchie, honest stock,	*watchmaker*
To gar him sen' his 'prentice up to sort the muckle knock,	*great clock*
Syne cry upo' the banker's wife an' leave some settin' eggs,	*then*
An' tell the ferrier o' the quake that's vrang aboot the legs.	*vet; heifer; wrong*
It's yafa wedder, Mains, for Mairch, wi' snaw an' frost an' win',	*awful*
The ploos are roustin' i' the fur, an' a' the wark's ahin'.	*
Ye've grun yersel's an' ken the tyauve it is to wirk a ferm,	†
An' a' the fash we've had wi' fouk gyaun aff afore the term;	*trouble; folk; going*
We've nane to spare for sojerin', that's nae oor wark ava',	*at all*
We've rents to pey, an' beasts to feed, an' corn to sell an' saw;	*sow*
Oonless we get the seed in seen, faur will we be for meal?	*soon; where*
An' faur will London get the beef they leuk for aye at Yeel?	*always look for; Yule*
There's men aneuch in sooters' shops, an' chiels in mason's yards,	‡
An' coonter-loupers, sklaters, vrichts, an' quarrymen, an' cyaurds,	§
To fill a reg'ment in a week, withoot gyaun vera far,	
Jist shove them in ahin' the pipes, an' tell them that it's 'War';	
For gin aul' Scotland's at the bit, there's naethin' for't but list.	¶
Some mayna like it vera sair, but never heed, insist.	*may not; so much*
Bit, feich, I'm haverin' on like this, an' a' I need's a line	*babbling*
To say there's men that maun be left, an' ye've exemptit mine.	*must*
Fat said ye? Fatna fouk hae I enoo' at Dockenhill?	*what*
It's just a wastrie o' your time, to rin them throu', but still —	

* *ploughs; rusting; furrow; behind*
† *ground; know; labour; farm*
‡ *enough; shoemakers*
§ *shop assistants; slaters; carpenters; pedlars*
¶ *if; [in trouble]; to enlist*

First there's the wife — 'Pass her,' ye say. Saul! had she been a lass

Ye hadna rappit oot sae quick, young laird, to lat her pass,   *snapped out*

That may be hoo ye spak' the streen, fan ye was playin' cairds,   *yesterday*

But seein' tenants tak' at times their menners fae their lairds,

I'll tell ye this, for sense an' thrift, for skeel wi' hens an' caur,   *skill; calves*

Gin ye'd her marrow for a wife, ye woudna be the waur.   *her like; worse*

Oor maiden's neist, ye've heard o' her, new hame fae buirdin' squeel,   *

Faur she saw mair o' beuks than broth, an' noo she's never weel,

But fan she's playin' ben the hoose, there's little wird o' dwaams,   *inside; faints*

For she's the rin o' a' the tunes, strathspeys, an' sangs, an' psalms;   *knowledge*

O' 'Evan' an' 'Neander' baith, ye seen can hae aneuch,

But 'Hobble Jennie' gars me loup, an' crack my thooms, an' hooch.   †

Weel, syne we hae the kitchie deem, that milks an' mak's the maet,   *kitchen-maid*

She disna aft haud doon the deese, she's at it ear' an' late,   *[sit down on the] beach*

She cairries seed, an' braks the muck, an' gies a han' to hyow,   *hoe*

An' churns, an' bakes, an' syes the so'ens, an' fyles there's peats to rowe.   ‡

An' fan the maiden's frien's cry in, she'll mask a cup o' tay,

An' butter scones, and dicht her face, an' cairry ben the tray,   *wipe*

She's big an' brosy, reid and roch, an' swippert as she's stoot,   *well-fed; rugged; agile*

Gie her a kilt instead o' cotts, an' thon's the gran' recruit.   *petticoats*

There's Francie syne, oor auldest loon, we pat him on for grieve,   *overseer*

An', fegs, we would be in a soss, gin he should up an' leave;   *faith; mess*

He's eident, an' has lots o' can, an' cheery wi' the men,   *diligent; know-how*

An' I'm sae muckle oot aboot wi' markets till atten'.

We've twa chaps syne to wirk the horse, as sweir as sweir can be,   *lazy*

They fussle better than they ploo, they're aul' an' mairret tee,   *whistle; married too*

An' baith hae hooses on the ferm, an' Francie never kens

Foo muckle corn gyangs hame at nicht, to fatten up their hens.   *how much*

The baillie syne, a peer-hoose geet, nae better than a feel,   *cowman; poorhouse boy; fool*

He slivvers, an' has sic a mant, an' ae clog-fit as weel;   *drools; stutter; club-foot*

He's barely sense to muck the byre, an' cairry in the scull,   *cowshed; basket*

An' park the kye, an' cogue the caur, an' scutter wi' the bull.   §

Weel, that's them a' — I didna hear — the laadie i' the gig?

That's Johnnie, he's a littlan jist, for a' he leuks sae big.   *child*

* *teenage daughter; next; boarding-school*

† *dance; thumbs; whoop*

‡ *strains sowens; sometimes; barrow*

§ *take the cattle to the field; feed the calves; work awkwardly*

Fy na, he isna twenty yet — ay, weel, he's maybe near't;
Ower young to lippen wi' a gun, the crater would be fear't. *trust; creature; afraid*
He's hardly throu' his squeelin' yet, an' noo we hae a plan *schooling*
To lat him simmer i' the toon, an' learn to mizzer lan'. *summer; measure*
Fat? Gar him 'list! Oor laadie 'list? 'Twould kill his mither, that, *enlist*
To think o' Johnnie in a trench awa' in fat-ye-ca't; *what-do-you-call-it*
We would hae sic a miss at hame, gin he was hine awa', *far*
We'd raither lat ye clean the toon o' ony ither twa;
Ay, tak' the wife, the dother, deem, the baillie wi' the mant, *daughter; stutter*
Tak' Francie, an' the mairret men, but John we canna want. *married*
Fat does he dee? Ye micht as weel speir fat I dee mysel', *do; ask*
The things he hisna time to dee is easier to tell;
He dells the yard, an' wi' the scythe cuts tansies on the brae, *digs; weeds*
An' fan a ruck gyangs throu' the mull, he's thrang at wispin' strae, *
He sits aside me at the mart, an' fan a feeder's sell't
Tak's doon the wecht, an' leuks the beuk for fat it's worth fan fell't; †
He helps me to redd up the dask, he tak's a han' at loo, *clean; [card game]*
An' sorts the shalt, an' yokes the gig, an' drives me fan I'm fou. *pony; drunk*
Hoot, Mains, hae mind, I'm doon for you some sma' thing wi' the bank; ‡
Aul' Larickleys, I saw you throu', an' this is a' my thank;
An' Gutteryloan, that time ye broke, to Dockenhill ye cam' — *went broke*
'Total exemption.' Thank ye, sirs. Fat say ye till a dram?

* hayrick; busy bundling straw
† weight; looks up the book; slaughtered
‡ I'm your guarantor

MARION ANGUS (1866–1946)

Alas! Poor Queen

She was skilled in music and the dance
And the old arts of love
At the court of the poisoned rose
And the perfumed glove,
And gave her beautiful hand
To the pale Dauphin
A triple crown to win –
And she loved little dogs
   And parrots
  And red-legged partridges
And the golden fishes of the Duc de Guise
And a pigeon with a blue ruff
She had from Monsieur d'Elbœuf.

Master John Knox was no friend to her;
She spoke him soft and kind,
Her honeyed words were Satan's lure
The unwary soul to bind.
'Good sir, doth a lissome shape
And a comely face
Offend your God His Grace
Whose Wisdom maketh these
Golden fishes of the Duc de Guise?'

She rode through Liddesdale with a song;
'Ye streams sae wondrous strang,
Oh, mak' me a wrack as I come back
But spare me as I gang.'
While a hill-bird cried and cried
Like a spirit lost
By the grey storm-wind tost.

Consider the way she had to go,
Think of the hungry snare,
The net she herself had woven,
Aware or unaware,
Of the dancing feet grown still,
The blinded eyes. —
Queens should be cold and wise,
And she loved little things,
    Parrots
   And red-legged partridges
And the golden fishes of the Duc de Guise
And the pigeon with the blue ruff
She had from Monsieur d'Elbœuf.

The Blue Jacket

When there comes a flower to the stingless nettle,
  To the hazel bushes, bees,
I think I can see my little sister
  Rocking herself by the hazel trees.

Rocking her arms for very pleasure
  That every leaf so sweet can smell,
And that she has on her the warm blue jacket
  Of mine, she liked so well.

Oh to win near you, little sister!
  To hear your soft lips say —
'I'll never tak' up wi' lads or lovers,
  But a baby I maun hae.   *must have*

'A baby in a cradle rocking,
  Like a nut, in a hazel shell,
And a new blue jacket, like this o' Annie's,
  It sets me aye sae well.'   *suits*

The Doors of Sleep

Jenny come ower the hill,
Ye hae broke yer troth lang syne   *long ago*
An' ta'en yer hand frae mine,
But nichts are warm and still.

White as a flo'er in May   *flower*
Gang glimmerin' by my bed —   *go*
White flo'er sae sune tae fade
At early dawnin' day.

Come by the doors o' sleep,
Whaur ne'er a word sall fa'   *where*
O' the ring ye gi'ed awa,   *gave*
The tryst ye failed tae keep;
When nichts are clear and still,
Jenny — come ower the hill.

LEWIS SPENCE (1874–1955)

The Prows o' Reekie

[Edinburgh]

O wad this braw hie-heapit toun
Sail aff like an enchanted ship,
Drift owre the warld's seas up and doun,
And kiss wi' Venice lip to lip,
Or anchor into Naples' Bay
A misty island far astray
Or set her rock to Athens' wa',
Pillar to pillar, stane to stane,
The cruikit spell o' her backbane,   *crooked*
Yon shadow-mile o' spire and vane,
Wad ding them a', wad ding them a'!   *beat*
Cadiz wad tine the admiralty   *lose*
O' yonder emerod fair sea,   *emerald*
Gibraltar frown for frown exchange
Wi' Nigel's crags at elbuck-range,   *elbow*
The rose-red banks o' Lisbon make
Mair room in Tagus for her sake.

A hoose is but a puppet-box
To keep life's images frae knocks,
But mannikins scrieve oot their sauls   *little men; scratch*
Upon its craw-steps and its walls;   *stepped gables*
Whaur hae they writ them mair sublime
Than on yon gable-ends o' time?

RACHEL ANNAND TAYLOR (1876–1960)

The Princess of Scotland

'Who are you that so strangely woke,
   And raised a fine hand?'
Poverty wears a scarlet cloke
      In my land.

'Duchies of dreamland, emerald, rose
   Lie at your command?'
Poverty like a princess goes
      In my land.

'Wherefore the mask of silken lace
   Tied with a golden band?'
Poverty walks with wanton grace
      In my land.

'Why do you softly, richly speak
   Rhythm so sweetly-scanned?'
Poverty hath the Gaelic and Greek
      In my land.

'There's a far-off scent about you seems
   Born in Samarkand.'
Poverty hath luxurious dreams
      In my land.

'You have wounds that like passion-flowers you hide:
   I cannot understand.'
Poverty hath one name with Pride
      In my land.

'Oh! Will you draw your last sad breath
   'Mid bitter bent and sand?'
Poverty begs from none but Death
      In my land.

ANDREW YOUNG (1885–1971)

A Dead Mole

Strong-shouldered mole,
That so much lived below the ground,
Dug, fought and loved, hunted and fed,
For you to raise a mound
Was as for us to make a hole;
What wonder now that being dead
Your body lies here stout and square
Buried within the blue vault of the air?

The Stockdoves

They rose up in a twinkling cloud
And wheeled about and bowed
To settle on the trees
Perching like small clay images.

Then with a noise of sudden rain
They clattered off again
And over Ballard Down
They circled like a flying town.

Though one could sooner blast a rock
Than scatter that dense flock
That through the winter weather
Some iron rule has held together,

Yet in another month from now
Love like a spark will blow
Those birds the country over
To drop in trees, lover by lover.

A Wet Day

Breasting the thick brushwood that hid my track
Diffuse wetness of rain had stained me black;
My clinging coat I hung on a bough-knop
And sodden shapeless hat I laid on top.

With heavy hat and coat left on the bough
I felt a snake that had cast off his slough
And joined the slow black slugs that strolled abroad
Making soft shameless love on the open road.

But, turning on my steps, startled I stood
To see a dead man hanging in the wood;
By two clear feet of air he swung afloat,
One who had hanged himself in hat and coat.

HELEN B. CRUICKSHANK (1886–1975)

The Ponnage Pool

>   . . . *Sing*
> *Some simple silly sang*
> *O' willows or o' mimulus*
> *A river's banks alang.*
>   (Hugh MacDiarmid)

I mind o' the Ponnage Pule,   *remember*
The reid brae risin',   *red*
Morphie Lade.
An' the saumon that louped the dam,   *jumped*
A tree i' Martin's Den
Wi' names carved on it;
But I ken na wha I am.

Ane o' the names was mine,   *one*
An' still I own it.
Naething it kens
O' a' that mak's up me.
Less I ken o' mysel'
Than the saumon wherefore
It rins up Esk frae the sea.

I am the deep o' the pule,
The fish, the fisher,
The river in spate,
The broon o' the far peat-moss,   *moorland*
The shingle bricht wi' the flooer   *flower*
O' the yallow mim'lus,   *mimulus*
The martin fleein' across.

I mind o' the Ponnage Pule
On a shinin' mornin',
The saumon fishers
Nettin' the bonny brutes –
I' the slithery dark o' the boddom
O' Charon's Coble
Ae day I'll faddom my doobts.   *one*

EDWIN MUIR (1887–1959)

Childhood

Long time he lay upon the sunny hill,
    To his father's house below securely bound.
Far off the silent, changing sound was still,
    With the black islands lying thick around.

He saw each separate height, each vaguer hue,
    Where the massed islands rolled in mist away,
And though all ran together in his view
    He knew that unseen straits between them lay.

Often he wondered what new shores were there.
    In thought he saw the still light on the sand,
The shallow water clear in tranquil air,
    And walked through it in joy from strand to strand.

Over the sound a ship so slow would pass
    That in the black hill's gloom it seemed to lie.
The evening sound was smooth like sunken glass,
    And time seemed finished ere the ship passed by.

Grey tiny rocks slept round him where he lay,
    Moveless as they, more still as evening came,
The grasses threw straight shadows far away,
    And from the house his mother called his name.

Merlin

O Merlin in your crystal cave
Deep in the diamond of the day,
Will there ever be a singer
Whose music will smooth away
The furrow drawn by Adam's finger
Across the meadow and the wave?
Or a runner who'll outrun

Man's long shadow driving on,
Break through the gate of memory
And hang the apple on the tree?
Will your magic ever show
The sleeping bride shut in her bower,
The day wreathed in its mound of snow
And Time locked in his tower?

Scotland 1941

We were a tribe, a family, a people.
Wallace and Bruce guard now a painted field,
And all may read the folio of our fable,
Peruse the sword, the sceptre and the shield.
A simple sky roofed in that rustic day,
The busy corn-fields and the haunted holms,
The green road winding up the ferny brae.
But Knox and Melville clapped their preaching palms
And bundled all the harvesters away,
Hoodicrow Peden in the blighted corn
Hacked with his rusty beak the starving haulms.
Out of that desolation we were born.

Courage beyond the point and obdurate pride
Made us a nation, robbed us of a nation.
Defiance absolute and myriad-eyed
That could not pluck the palm plucked our damnation.
We with such courage and the bitter wit
To fell the ancient oak of loyalty,
And strip the peopled hill and the altar bare,
And crush the poet with an iron text,
How could we read our souls and learn to be?
Here a dull drove of faces harsh and vexed,
We watch our cities burning in their pit,
To salve our souls grinding dull lucre out,
We, fanatics of the frustrate and the half,
Who once set Purgatory Hill in doubt.
Now smoke and dearth and money everywhere,
Mean heirlooms of each fainter generation,
And mummied housegods in their musty niches,

Burns and Scott, sham bards of a sham nation,
And spiritual defeat wrapped warm in riches,
No pride but pride of pelf. Long since the young
Fought in great bloody battles to carve out
This towering pulpit of the Golden Calf,
Montrose, Mackail, Argyle, perverse and brave,
Twisted the stream, unhooped the ancestral hill.
Never had Dee or Don or Yarrow or Till
Huddled such thriftless honour in a grave.

Such wasted bravery idle as a song,
Such hard-won ill might prove Time's verdict wrong,
And melt to pity the annalist's iron tongue.

Scotland's Winter

Now the ice lays its smooth claws on the sill,
The sun looks from the hill
Helmed in his winter casket,
And sweeps his arctic sword across the sky.
The water at the mill
Sounds more hoarse and dull.
The miller's daughter walking by
With frozen fingers soldered to her basket
Seems to be knocking
Upon a hundred leagues of floor
With her light heels, and mocking
Percy and Douglas dead,
And Bruce on his burial bed,
Where he lies white as may
With wars and leprosy,
And all the kings before
This land was kingless,
And all the singers before
This land was songless,
This land that with its dead and living waits the Judgement Day.
But they, the powerless dead,
Listening can hear no more
Than a hard tapping on the sounding floor
A little overhead

Of common heels that do not know
Whence they come or where they go
And are content
With their poor frozen life and shallow banishment.

The Horses

Barely a twelvemonth after
The seven days war that put the world to sleep,
Late in the evening the strange horses came.
By then we had made our covenant with silence,
But in the first few days it was so still
We listened to our breathing and were afraid.
On the second day
The radios failed; we turned the knobs; no answer.
On the third day a warship passed us, heading north,
Dead bodies piled on the deck. On the sixth day
A plane plunged over us into the sea. Thereafter
Nothing. The radios dumb;
And still they stand in corners of our kitchens,
And stand, perhaps, turned on, in a million rooms
All over the world. But now if they should speak,
If on a sudden they should speak again,
If on the stroke of noon a voice should speak,
We would not listen, we would not let it bring
That old bad world that swallowed its children quick
At one great gulp. We would not have it again.
Sometimes we think of the nations lying asleep,
Curled blindly in impenetrable sorrow,
And then the thought confounds us with its strangeness.

The tractors lie about our fields; at evening
They look like dank sea-monsters couched and waiting.
We leave them where they are and let them rust:
'They'll moulder away and be like other loam.'
We make our oxen drag our rusty ploughs,
Long laid aside. We have gone back
Far past our fathers' land.
                              And then, that evening
Late in the summer the strange horses came.

We heard a distant tapping on the road,
A deepening drumming; it stopped, went on again
And at the corner changed to hollow thunder.
We saw the heads
Like a wild wave charging and were afraid.
We had sold our horses in our fathers' time
To buy new tractors. Now they were strange to us
As fabulous steeds set on an ancient shield
Or illustrations in a book of knights.
We did not dare go near them. Yet they waited,
Stubborn and shy, as if they had been sent
By an old command to find our whereabouts
And that long-lost archaic companionship.
In the first moment we had never a thought
That they were creatures to be owned and used.
Among them were some half-a-dozen colts
Dropped in some wilderness of the broken world,
Yet new as if they had come from their own Eden.
Since then they have pulled our ploughs and borne our loads,
But that free servitude still can pierce our hearts.
Our life is changed; their coming our beginning.

HUGH MACDIARMID (CHRISTOPHER MURRAY GRIEVE) (1892–1978)

The Bonnie Broukit Bairn

smudge-covered child

For Peggy

Mars is braw in crammasy,	*crimson*
Venus in a green silk goun,	
The auld mune shak's her gowden feathers,	*golden*
Their starry talk's a wheen o' blethers,	*[lot of nonsense]*
Nane for thee a thochtie sparin',	
Earth, thou bonnie broukit bairn!	
– But greet, an' in your tears ye'll droun	*weep*
The haill clanjamfrie!	*[whole rabble of them]*

The Watergaw

broken rainbow

Ae weet forenicht i' the yow-trummle	*one wet evening; [cold spell during sheep-shearing]*
I saw yon antrin thing,	*strange*
A watergaw wi' its chitterin' licht	*chattering*
Ayont the on-ding;	*beyond; downpour*
An' I thocht o' the last wild look ye gied	
Afore ye deed!	*died*

There was nae reek i' the laverock's hoose	*smoke; lark*
That nicht – an' nane i' mine;	
But I hae thocht o' that foolish licht	
Ever sin' syne;	*since then*
An' I think that mebbe at last I ken	*know*
What your look meant then.	

The Eemis Stane

wobbly

I' the how-dumb-deid o' the cauld hairst nicht   *silent depth; harvest*
The warl' like an eemis stane
Wags i' the lift: *wavers; air*
An' my eerie memories fa'
Like a yowdendrift.   *snowdrift*

Like a yowdendrift so's I couldna read
The words cut oot i' the stane
Had the fug o' fame   *moss*
An' history's hazelraw   *lichen*
No' yirdit thaim.   *buried; them*

Scunner

vexation

Your body derns   *hides*
In its graces again
As dreich grun' does   *dull ground*
In the gowden grain,   *golden*
And oot o' the daith   *death*
O' pride you rise
Wi' beauty yet
For a hauf-disguise.

The skinklan' stars   *sparkling*
Are but distant dirt.
Tho' fer owre near
You are still – whiles – girt   *sometimes*
Wi' the bonnie licht
You bood ha'e tint   *must; lost*
– And I lo'e Love
Wi' a scunner in't.

Empty Vessel

I met ayont the cairney   *beyond; cairn*
A lass wi' tousie hair   *tousled*
Singin' till a bairnie
That was nae langer there.

Wunds wi' warlds to swing   *winds*
Dinna sing sae sweet.
The licht that bends owre a' thing   *[over everything]*
Is less ta'en up wi't.

from *A Drunk Man Looks at the Thistle*

The language that but sparely floo'ers
And maistly gangs to weed;   *goes*
The thocht o' Christ and Calvary
Aye liddenin' in my heid;   *going back and forth*
And a' the dour provincial thocht
That merks the Scottish breed
– These are the thistle's characters,
To argie there's nae need.
Hoo weel my verse embodies
The thistle you can read!
– But will a Scotsman never
Frae this vile growth be freed? . . .

      *   *   *

The thistle canna vanish quite.
Inside a' licht its shape maun glint,   *must*
A spirit wi' a skeleton in't.

The world, the flesh, 'll bide in us
As in the fire the unburnt buss,   *bush*
Or as frae sire to son we gang
And coontless corpses in us thrang.   *crowd*

And e'en the glory that descends
I kenna whence on *me* depends,   *[don't know]*
And shapes itsel' to what is left
Whaur I o' me ha'e me bereft,
And still the form is mine, altho'
A force to which I ne'er could grow
Is movin' in't as 'twere a sea
That lang syne drooned the last o' me   *since*
— That drooned afore the warld began
A' that could ever come frae Man.

And as at sicna times am I,   *such*
I wad ha'e Scotland to my eye
Until I saw a timeless flame
Tak' Auchtermuchty for a name,
And kent that Ecclefechan stood   *knew*
As pairt o' an eternal mood.   *part*

         *   *   *

The stars like thistle's roses floo'er
The sterile growth o' Space ootour,   *across*
That clad in bitter blasts spreids oot
Frae me, the sustenance o' its root.

O fain I'd keep my hert entire,   *eagerly*
Fain hain the licht o' my desire,   *shield*
But ech! the shinin' streams ascend,
And leave me empty at the end.

For aince it's toomed my hert and brain,   *once; emptied*
The thistle needs maun fa' again.   *must*
— But a' its growth 'll never fill
The hole it's turned my life intill! . . .

Yet ha'e I Silence left, the croon o' a'.   *crown*

No' her, wha on the hills langsyne I saw   *long ago*
Liftin' a foreheid o' perpetual snaw.

No' her, wha in the how-dumb-deid o' nicht   *silent depth*
Kyths, like Eternity in Time's despite.   *appears*

No' her, withooten shape, wha's name is Daith,
No' Him, unkennable abies to faith   *unknowable; except*

— God whom, gin e'er He saw a man, 'ud be   *if*
E'en mair dumfooner'd at the sicht than he   *dumbfounded*

— But Him, whom nocht in man or Deity,
Or Daith or Dreid or Laneliness can touch,
Wha's deed owre often and has seen owre much.

O I ha'e Silence left,

                    — 'And weel ye micht,'
Sae Jean'll say, 'efter sic a nicht!'

At My Father's Grave

The sunlicht still on me, you row'd in clood,   *wrapped; cloud*
We look upon each ither noo like hills
Across a valley. I'm nae mair your son.
It is my mind, nae son o' yours, that looks,
And the great darkness o' your death comes up
And equals it across the way.
A livin' man upon a deid man thinks
And ony sma'er thocht's impossible.

Of John Davidson

I remember one death in my boyhood
That next to my father's, and darker, endures;
Not Queen Victoria's, but Davidson, yours,
And something in me has always stood
Since then looking down the sandslope
On your small black shape by the edge of the sea,
— A bullet-hole through a great scene's beauty,
God through the wrong end of a telescope.

On a Raised Beach

To James H. Whyte

All is lithogenesis — or lochia,
Carpolite fruit of the forbidden tree,
Stones blacker than any in the Caaba,
Cream-coloured caen-stone, chatoyant pieces,
Celadon and corbeau, bistre and beige,
Glaucous, hoar, enfouldered, cyathiform,
Making mere faculae of the sun and moon
I study you glout and gloss, but have
No cadrans to adjust you with, and turn again
From optik to haptik and like a blind man run
My fingers over you, arris by arris, burr by burr,
Slickensides, truité, rugas, foveoles,
Bringing my aesthesis in vain to bear,
An angle-titch to all your corrugations and coigns,
Hatched foraminous cavo-rilievo of the world,
Deictic, fiducial stones. Chiliad by chiliad
What bricole piled you here, stupendous cairn?
What artist poses the Earth écorché thus,
Pillar of creation engouled in me?
What eburnation augments you with men's bones,
Every energumen an Endymion yet?
All the other stones are in this haecceity it seems,
But where is the Christophanic rock that moved?
What Cabirian song from this catasta comes?

Deep conviction or preference can seldom
Find direct terms in which to express itself.
Today on this shingle shelf
I understand this pensive reluctance so well,
This not discommendable obstinacy,
These contrivances of an inexpressive critical feeling,
These stones with their resolve that Creation shall not be
Injured by iconoclasts and quacks. Nothing has stirred
Since I lay down this morning an eternity ago
But one bird. The widest open door is the least liable to intrusion,
Ubiquitous as the sunlight, unfrequented as the sun.

The inward gates of a bird are always open.
It does not know how to shut them.
That is the secret of its song,
But whether any man's are ajar is doubtful.
I look at these stones and know little about them,
But I know their gates are open too,
Always open, far longer open, than any bird's can be,
That every one of them has had its gates wide open far longer
Than all birds put together, let alone humanity,
Though through them no man can see,
No man nor anything more recently born than themselves
And that is everything else on the Earth.
I too lying here have dismissed all else.
Bread from stones is my sole and desperate dearth,
From stones, which are to the Earth as to the sunlight
Is the naked sun which is for no man's sight.
I would scorn to cry to any easier audience
Or, having cried, to lack patience to await the response.
I am no more indifferent or ill-disposed to life than death is;
I would fain accept it all completely as the soil does;
Already I feel all that can perish perishing in me
As so much has perished and all will yet perish in these stones.
I must begin with these stones as the world began.

Shall I come to a bird quicker than the world's course ran?
        To a bird, and to myself, a man?
        And what if I do, and further?
I shall only have gone a little way to go back again
And be like a fleeting deceit of development,
Iconoclasts, quacks. So these stones have dismissed
All but all of evolution, unmoved by it,
(Is there anything to come they will not likewise dismiss?)
As the essential life of mankind in the mass
Is the same as their earliest ancestors yet.

Actual physical conflict or psychological warfare
        Incidental to love or food
Brings out animal life's bolder and more brilliant patterns
        Concealed as a rule in habitude.
        There is a sudden revelation of colour,
        The protrusion of a crest,

      The expansion of an ornament,
– But no general principle can be guessed
From these flashing fragments we are seeing,
These foam-bells on the hidden currents of being.
The bodies of animals are visible substances
And must therefore have colour and shape, in the first place
Depending on chemical composition, physical structure, mode of growth,
Psychological rhythms and other factors in the case,
But their purposive function is another question.
Brilliant-hued animals hide away in the ocean deeps;
The mole has a rich sexual colouring in due season
Under the ground; nearly every beast keeps
Brighter colours inside it than outside.
What the seen shows is never anything to what it's designed to hide,
The red blood which makes the beauty of a maiden's cheek
Is as red under a gorilla's pigmented and hairy face.
Varied forms and functions though life may seem to have shown
They all come back to the likeness of stone,
So to the intervening stages we can best find a clue
In what we all came from and return to.
There are no twirly bits in this ground bass.

We must be humble. We are so easily baffled by appearances
And do not realise that these stones are one with the stars.
It makes no difference to them whether they are high or low,
Mountain peak or ocean floor, palace, or pigsty.
There are plenty of ruined buildings in the world but no ruined stones.
No visitor comes from the stars
But is the same as they are.
– Nay, it is easy to find a spontaneity here,
An adjustment to life, an ability
To ride it easily, akin to 'the buoyant
Prelapsarian naturalness of a country girl
Laughing in the sun, not passion-rent,
But sensing in the bound of her breasts vigours to come
Powered to make her one with the stream of earthlife round her,'
But not yet as my Muse is, with this ampler scope,
This more divine rhythm, wholly at one
With the earth, riding the Heavens with it, as the stones do
And all soon must.
But it is wrong to indulge in these illustrations

Instead of just accepting the stones.
It is a paltry business to try to drag down
The arduus furor of the stones to the futile imaginings of men,
To all that fears to grow roots into the common earth,
As it soon must, lest it be chilled to the core,
As it will be — and none the worse for that.
Impatience is a poor qualification for immortality.

Hot blood is of no use in dealing with eternity.
It is seldom that promises or even realisations
Can sustain a clear and searching gaze.
But an emotion chilled is an emotion controlled;
This is the road leading to certainty,
Reasoned planning for the time when reason can no longer avail.
It is essential to know the chill of all the objections
That come creeping into the mind, the battle between opposing ideas
Which gives the victory to the strongest and most universal
Over all others, and to wage it to the end
With increasing freedom, precision, and detachment
A detachment that shocks our instincts and ridicules our desires.
All else in the world cancels out, equal, capable
Of being replaced by other things (even as all the ideas
That madden men now must lose their potency in a few years
And be replaced by others — even as all the religions,
All the material sacrifices and moral restraints,
That in twenty thousand years have brought us no nearer to God
Are irrelevant to the ordered adjustments
Out of reach of perceptive understanding
Forever taking place on the Earth and in the unthinkable regions around it;
This cat's cradle of life; this reality volatile yet determined;
This instense vibration in the stones
That makes them seem immobile to us)
But the world cannot dispense with the stones.
They alone are not redundant. Nothing can replace them
Except a new creation of God.

I must get into this stone world now.
Ratchel, striae, relationships of tesserae,
    Innumerable shades of grey,
    Innumerable shapes,
And beneath them all a stupendous unity,

Infinite movement visibly defending itself
Against all the assaults of weather and water,
Simultaneously mobilised at full strength
At every point of the universal front,
  Always at the pitch of its powers,
  The foundation and end of all life.
I try them with the old Norn words – hraun
Duss, rønis, queedaruns, kollyarum;
They hvarf from me in all directions
Over the hurdifell – klett, millya, hellya, hellyina bretta,
Hellyina wheeda, hellyina grø, bakka, ayre, –
  And lay my world in kolgref.

This is no heap of broken images.
Let men find the faith that builds mountains
Before they seek the faith that moves them. Men cannot hope
To survive the fall of the mountains
Which they will no more see than they saw their rise
Unless they are more concentrated and determined,
Truer to themselves and with more to be true to,
Than these stones, and as inerrable as they are.
Their sole concern is that what can be shaken
Shall be shaken and disappear
And only the unshakable be left.
What hardihood in any man has part or parcel in the latter?
It is necessary to make a stand and maintain it forever.
These stones go through Man, straight to God, if there is one.
What have they not gone through already?
Empires, civilisations, aeons. Only in them
If in anything, can His creation confront Him.
They came so far out of the water and halted forever.
That larking dallier, the sun, has only been able to play
With superficial by-products since;
The moon moves the waters backwards and forwards,
But the stones cannot be lured an inch farther
Either on this side of eternity or the other.
Who thinks God is easier to know than they are?
Trying to reach men any more, any otherwise, than they are?
These stones will reach us long before we reach them.

Cold, undistracted, eternal and sublime.
They will stem all the torrents of vicissitude forever
With a more than Roman peace.

Death is a physical horror to me no more.
I am prepared with everything else to share
Sunshine and darkness and wind and rain
And life and death bare as these rocks though it be
In whatever order nature may decree,
But, not indifferent to the struggle yet
Nor to the ataraxia I might get
By fatalism, a deeper issue see
Than these, or suicide, here confronting me.
It is reality that is at stake.
Being and non-being with equal weapons here
Confront each other for it, non-being unseen
But always on the point, it seems, of showing clear,
Though its reserved contagion may breed
This fancy too in my still susceptible head
And then by its own hidden movement lead
Me as by aesthetic vision to the supposed
Point where by death's logic everything is recomposed,
Object and image one, from their severance freed,
As I sometimes, still wrongly, feel 'twixt this storm beach and me.
What happens to us
Is irrelevant to the world's geology
But what happens to the world's geology
Is not irrelevant to us.
We must reconcile ourselves to the stones,
Not the stones to us.
Here a man must shed the encumbrances that muffle
Contact with elemental things, the subtleties
That seem inseparable from a humane life, and go apart
Into a simple and sterner, more beautiful and more oppressive world,
Austerely intoxicating; the first draught is overpowering;
Few survive it. It fills me with a sense of perfect form,
The end seen from the beginning, as in a song.
It is no song that conveys the feeling
That there is no reason why it should ever stop,
But the kindred form I am conscious of here
Is the beginning and end of the world,

The unsearchable masterpiece, the music of the spheres,
Alpha and Omega, the Omnific Word.
These stones have the silence of supreme creative power,
The direct and undisturbed way of working
Which alone leads to greatness.
What experience has any man crystallised,
What weight of conviction accumulated,
What depth of life suddenly seen entire
In some nigh supernatural moment
And made a symbol and lived up to
With such resolution, such Spartan impassivity?
It is a frenzied and chaotic age,
Like a growth of weeds on the site of a demolished building.
How shall we set ourselves against it,
Imperturbable, inscrutable, in the world and yet not in it,
    Silent under the torments it inflicts upon us,
        With a constant centre,
With a single inspiration, foundations firm and invariable;
        By what immense exercise of will,
Inconceivable discipline, courage, and endurance,
        Self-purification and anti-humanity,
            Be ourselves without interruption,
                Adamantine and inexorable?
It will be ever increasingly necessary to find
In the interests of all mankind
Men capable of rejecting all that all other men
        Think, as a stone remains
Essential to the world, inseparable from it,
        And rejects all other life yet.
Great work cannot be combined with surrender to the crowd.
        — Nay, the truth we seek is as free
From all yet thought as a stone from humanity.
Here where there is neither haze nor hesitation
Something at least of the necessary power has entered into me.
I have still to see any manifestation of the human spirit
That is worthy of a moment's longer exemption than it gets
From petrifaction again — to get out if it can.
All is lithogenesis — or lochia;
And I can desire nothing better,
An immense familiarity with other men's imaginings
Convinces me that they cannot either

(If they could, it would instantly be granted
– The present order must continue till then)
Though, of course, I still keep an open mind,
A mind as open as the grave.
You may say that the truth cannot be crushed out,
That the weight of the whole world may be tumbled on it,
And yet, in puny, distorted, phantasmal shapes albeit,
It will braird again: it will force its way up
Through unexpectable fissures? look over this beach.
What ruderal and rupestrine growth is here?
What crop confirming any credulities?
Conjure a fescue to teach me with from this
And I will listen to you, but until then
Listen to me – Truth is not crushed;
It crushes, gorgonises all else into itself.
The trouble is to know it when you see it?
You will have no trouble with it when you do.
Do not argue with me. Argue with these stones.
Truth has no trouble in knowing itself.
This is it. The hard fact. The inoppugnable reality,
Here is something for you to digest.
Eat this and we'll see what appetite you have left
For a world hereafter.
I pledge you in the first and last crusta,
The rocks rattling in the bead-proof seas.

O we of little faith,
As romanticists viewed the philistinism of their days
As final and were prone to set over against it
Infinite longing rather than manly will –
Nay, as all thinkers and writers find
The indifference of the masses of mankind, –
So are most men with any stone yet,
Even those who juggle with lapidary's, mason's, geologist's words
    And all their knowledge of stones in vain,
Tho' these stones have far more differences in colour, shape and size
    Than most men to my eyes –
Even those who develop precise conceptions to immense distances
    Out of these bleak surfaces.
All human culture is a Goliath to fall
To the least of these pebbles withal.

A certain weight will be added yet
To the arguments of even the most foolish
And all who speak glibly may rest assured
That to better their oratory they will have the whole earth
For a Demosthenean pebble to roll in their mouths.

I am enamoured of the desert at last,
The abode of supreme serenity is necessarily a desert.
My disposition is towards spiritual issues
Made inhumanly clear; I will have nothing interposed
Between my sensitiveness and the barren but beautiful reality;
The deadly clarity of this 'seeing of a hungry man'
Only traces of a fever passing over my vision
Will vary, troubling it indeed, but troubling it only
In such a way that it becomes for a moment
Superhumanly, menacingly clear – the reflection
Of a brightness through a burning crystal.
A culture demands leisure and leisure presupposes
A self-determined rhythm of life; the capacity for solitude
Is its test; by that the desert knows us.
It is not a question of escaping from life
But the reverse – a question of acquiring the power
To exercise the loneliness, the independence, of stones,
And that only comes from knowing that our function remains
However isolated we seem fundamental to life as theirs.
　　We have lost the grounds of our being,
　　We have not built on rock.
Thinking of all the higher zones
Confronting the spirit of man I know they are bare
Of all so-called culture as any stone here;
Not so much of all literature survives
As any wisp of scriota that thrives
On a rock – (interesting though it may seem to be
As de Bary's and Schwendener's discovery
Of the dual nature of lichens, the partnership,
Symbiosis, of a particular fungus and particular alga).
These bare stones bring me straight back to reality.
　　I grasp one of them and I have in my grip
The beginning and the end of the world,
My own self, and as before I never saw

The empty hand of my brother man,
The humanity no culture has reached, the mob.
Intelligentsia, our impossible and imperative job!

'Ah!' you say, 'if only one of these stones would move
— Were it only an inch — of its own accord.
     This is the resurrection we await,
— The stone rolled away from the tomb of the Lord.
  I know there is no weight in infinite space,
     No impermeability in infinite time,
But it is as difficult to understand and have patience here
     As to know that the sublime
Is theirs no less than ours, no less confined
To men than men's to a few men, the stars of their kind.'
  (The masses too have begged bread from stones,
     From human stones, including themselves,
  And only got it, not from their fellow-men,
  But from stones such as these here — if then.)
Detached intellectuals, not one stone will move,
Not the least of them, not a fraction of an inch. It is not
     The reality of life that is hard to know.
It is nearest of all and easiest to grasp,
But you must participate in it to proclaim it.
— I lift a stone; it is the meaning of life I clasp
Which is death, for that is the meaning of death;
How else does any man yet participate
     In the life of a stone,
How else can any man yet become
Sufficiently at one with creation, sufficiently alone,
Till as the stone that covers him he lies dumb
And the stone at the mouth of his grave is not overthrown?
— Each of these stones on this raised beach,
     Every stone in the world,
Covers infinite death, beyond the reach
Of the dead it hides; and cannot be hurled
Aside yet to let any of them come forth, as love
     Once made a stone move
  (Though I do not depend on that
     My case to prove).
So let us beware of death: the stones will have
Their revenge; we have lost all approach to them,

But soon we shall become as those we have betrayed,
And they will seal us fast in our graves
As our indifference and ignorance seals them;
    But let us not be afraid to die.
No heavier and colder and quieter then,
No more motionless, do stones lie
    In death than in life to all men.
It is not more difficult in death than here
– Though slow as the stones the powers develop
To rise from the grave – to get a life worth having;
And in death – unlike life – we lose nothing that is truly ours.

Diallage of the world's debate, end of the long auxesis,
Although no ébrillade of Pegasus can here avail,
I prefer your enchorial characters – the futhorc of the future –
To the hieroglyphics of all the other forms of Nature.
Song, your apprentice encrinite, seems to sweep
The Heavens with a last entrochal movement;
And, with the same word that began it, closes
Earth's vast epanadiplosis.

The Little White Rose

To John Gawsworth

The rose of all the world is not for me.
I want for my part
Only the little white rose of Scotland
That smells sharp and sweet – and breaks the heart.

Perfect

On the Western Seaboard of South Uist
(Los muertos abren los ojos a los que viven)

I found a pigeon's skull on the machair,
All the bones pure white and dry, and chalky,
But perfect,
Without a crack or a flaw anywhere.

At the back, rising out of the beak,
Were twin domes like bubbles of thin bone,
Almost transparent, where the brain had been
That fixed the tilt of the wings.

To a Friend and Fellow-Poet*

It is with the poet as with a guinea worm
Who, to accommodate her teeming progeny
Sacrifices nearly every organ of her body, and becomes
(Her vagina obliterated in her all-else-consuming
Process of uterine expansion, and she still faced
With a grave obstetrical dilemma calling for
Most marvellous contrivance to deposit her prodigious swarm
Where they may find the food they need and have a chance in life)
Almost wholly given over to her motherly task,
Little more than one long tube close-packed with young;
Until from the ruptured bulla, the little circular sore,
You see her dauntless head protrude, and presently, slowly,
A beautiful, delicate, and pellucid tube
Is projected from her mouth, tenses and suddenly spills
Her countless brood in response to a stimulus applied
Not directly to the worm herself, but the skin of her host
With whom she has no organised connection (and that stimulus
O Poets! but cold water!) . . .The worm's whole musculocutaneous coat
Thus finally functions as a uterus, forcing the uterine tube
With its contents through her mouth. And when the prolapsed uterus ruptures
The protruded and now collapsed portion shrivels to a thread
(Alexander Blok's utter emptiness after creating a poem!)
The rapid drying of which effectually and firmly
Closes the wound for the time being . . . till, later, the stimulus being reapplied,
A fresh portion of the uterine tube protrudes, ruptures, and collapses,
Once more ejaculating another seething mass of embryos,
And so the process continues until inch by inch
The entire uterus is expelled and parturition concluded.
Is it not precisely thus we poets deliver our store,
Our whole being the instrument of our suicidal art,
And by the skin of our teeth flype ourselves into fame?

* Ruth Pitter.

Scotland Small?

Scotland small? Our multiform, our infinite Scotland *small?*
Only as a patch of hillside may be a cliché corner
To a fool who cries 'Nothing but heather!' where in September another
Sitting there and resting and gazing round
Sees not only the heather but blaeberries
With bright green leaves and leaves already turned scarlet
Hiding ripe blue berries; and amongst the sage-green leaves
Of the bog-myrtle the golden flowers of the tormentil shining;
And on the small bare places, where the little Blackface sheep
Found grazing, milkworts blue as summer skies;
And down in neglected peat-hags, not worked
Within living memory, sphagnum moss in pastel shades
Of yellow, green, and pink; sundew and butterwort
Waiting with wide-open sticky leaves for their tiny winged prey;
And nodding harebells vying in their colour
With the blue butterflies that poise themselves delicately upon them;
And stunted rowans with harsh dry leaves of glorious colour.
'Nothing but heather!' – How marvellously descriptive! And incomplete!

WILLIAM SOUTAR (1898–1943)

The Room

Into the quiet of this room
Words from the clamorous world come:
The shadows of the gesturing year
Quicken upon the stillness here.

The wandering waters do not mock
The pool within its wall of rock
But turn their healing tides and come
Even as the day into this room.

The Philosophic Taed   *Toad*

There was a taed wha thocht sae lang
On sanctity and sin;
On what was richt, and what was wrang,
And what was in atween –
That he gat naething düne.   *done*

The wind micht blaw, the snaw micht snaw,
He didna mind a wheet;
Nor kent the derk'nin frae the daw,   *dawn*
The wulfire frae the weet;   *lightning*
Nor fuggage frae his feet.   *grass*

His wife and weans frae time to time,
As they gaed by the cratur,   *creature*
Wud haut to hae a gowk at him   *stop; look*
And shak their pows, or natter: *heads*
'He's no like growing better.'

It maun be twenty year or mair   *must*
Sin thocht's been a' his trade: *since*
And naebody can tell for shair   *sure*
Whether this unco taed   *unusual*
Is dead, or thinks he's dead.

The Tryst

O luely, luely cam she in   *softly*
And luely she lay doun:
I kent her be her caller lips   *cool*
And her breists sae sma' and roun'.

A' thru the nicht we spak nae word
Nor sinder'd bane frae bane: *sundered; bone*
A' thru the nicht I heard her hert
Gang soundin' wi' my ain.

It was about the waukrife hour   *sleepless*
Whan cocks begin to craw
That she smool'd saftly thru the mirk   *slid; dark*
Afore the day wud daw.   *dawn*

Sae luely, luely, cam she in
Sae luely was she gaen
And wi' her a' my simmer days   *summer*
Like they had never been.

NORMAN CAMERON (1905–58)

Meeting my Former Self

Meeting my former self in a nostalgia
Of confident, confiding recognition,
Offering him an island in the Atlantic –
Half-way, I said, from Tenerife to England.
Great cliffs of chalk slope from the fishing-village
Up to the lighthouse. Rum sold free of duty.
Only the fishermen and lighthouse-keeper
Besides ourselves. Drinking the rum, card-playing
And walking in the wastes of stone and cactus
And meeting the mail-steamer once a fortnight.
– But these inducements pitifully withered
At his embarrassed look. Turning to welcome
A friend he had acquired since our last meeting,
Not known to me, he spoke of other matters;
And I was weeping and humiliated.

Green, Green is El Aghir

Sprawled on the crates and sacks in the rear of the truck,
I was gummy-mouthed from the sun and the dust of the track,
And the two Arab soldiers I'd taken on as hitch-hikers
At a torrid petrol-dump, had been there on their hunkers
Since early morning. I said, in a kind of French
'On m'a dit, qu'il y a une belle source d'eau fraîche,
Plus loin, à El Aghir' . . .

              It was eighty more kilometres
Until round a corner we heard a splashing of waters,
And there, in a green, dark street, was a fountain with two faces
Discharging both ways, from full-throated faucets
Into basins, thence into troughs and thence into brooks.
Our negro corporal driver slammed his brakes,
And we yelped and leapt from the truck and went at the double
To fill our bidons and bottles and drink and dabble.

Then, swollen with water, we went to an inn for wine.
The Arabs came, too, though their faith might have stood between.
'After all,' they said, 'it's a boisson,' without contrition.

Green, green is El Aghir. It has a railway-station,
And the wealth of its soil has borne many another fruit,
A mairie, a school and an elegant Salle de Fêtes.
Such blessings, as I remarked, in effect, to the waiter,
Are added unto them that have plenty of water.

ROBERT GARIOCH (ROBERT GARIOCH SUTHERLAND) (1909–1981)

The Wire

This day I saw ane endless muir   *moor*
wi sad horizon, like the sea
around some uncouth landless globe
whaur waters flauchter endlessly.   *flicker*

Heather bell and blaeberry
grow on this muir; reid burns rin   *red*
in clear daylicht; the luift is free   *sky*
frae haar, and yet there is nae sun.   *mist*

Gossamers glint in aa the airts,   *[all directions]*
criss-cross about the lang flure-heids   *flower-heads*
of girss and thristles here, and there   *gorse*
amang the purpie willow-weeds.

Bog-myrtle scent is in the air
heavy wi hinnie-sap and peat   *honey-sap*
whiles mellit like uneasy thochts   *mixed*
wi something human, shairn or sweit.   *shit; sweat*

Nou guns gaun aff, and pouther-reik   *powder-smoke*
and yappin packs of foetid dugs,   *dogs*
and blobs of cramosie, like blebs   *crimson; blisters*
of bluid squeezed frae vanilla bugs

pash suddenlike intill the licht   *knock*
that dings on this unshadowed muir   *beats*
frae ilka airt, and syne are gane   *each quarter; then*
like tourbillions of twisted stour.   *whirlwinds; dust*

The criss-cross gossamers, the while,
twang owre the heather, ticht and real;
I ken, houever jimp they seem,   *slender*
that they are spun frae strands of steel.

And they are barbed wi twisted spikes
wi scant a handsbreidth space atween,
and reinforced wi airn rods   *iron*
and hung about wi bits of tin

that hing in pairs alang the Wire,
ilkane three-cornered like a fang: *each one*
clashin thegither at a touch
they break aukwart the lairick's sang.   *awkwardly; lark*

Heich in their sentry-posts, the guairds   *high*
wha daurna sleep, on pain of daith,   *dare not*
watch throu the graticules of guns,   *sights*
cruel and persecuted, baith.

This endless muir is thrang wi folk   *thronged*
that hirple aye aa airts at aince   *limp*
wi neither purport nor content   *reason*
nor rest, in fidgan impotence.   *fidgety*

They gae in danger of the Wire
but staucher on anither mile   *stagger*
frae line to line of spider steel
to loup anither deidlie stile.   *leap*

A man trips up; the Wire gaes ding,
tins clash, the guaird lifts up his heid;
fu slaw he traverses his gun   *very slowly*
and blatters at him till he's deid.

The dugs loup on him, reivan flesh,   *tearing*
crunchin the bane as they were wud;   *mad*
swith they come and swith are gane,   *swiftly*
syne nocht is left but pools of bluid.

Bluid dreipan doun amang the roots   *dripping*
is soukit up the vampire stem   *sucked*
and suin the gaudy felloun flures   *soon; cruel flowers*
begowk the man that nourished them.   *mock*

Some pairts the Wires close in and leave
smaa space whaur men may freely gang,   *go*
and ilka step is taen in dreid;   *taken*
there flures and men maist thickly thrang.

A man gets taiglit on a barb,   *entangled*
endlang his wame the cauld fear creeps;   *[the length of his stomach]*
he daurna muve, the hert beats hard,
but beats awa. The sentry sleeps.

Aye! his virr comes back in spate,   *energy*
as some auld trout this man is slee;   *sly*
he hauds himsel still as a stane,
back comes his ain self-maistery.

Cannily he sets to wark,
warp by warp his sleeve is free,
it hings nou by a single threid:
loud clash the tins and bullets flee.

Forrit and back and in and out   *forward*
they darn in waesome figure-dance;   *woeful*
bydin still they canna thole   *staying; endure*
and ilk man warks his ain mischance.

They see the Wire, and weill they ken   *know*
whilk wey it warks. In middle-air
the glintan guns are clear in sicht,
tho nae man kens wha set them there.

Impersonal in uniform,
the guairds are neither friens nor faes;
nane ettles to propitiate   *tries*
nor fashes them wi bribes or praise.   *bothers*

Efficient and predictable,
they cairry out their orders stricht;
here naething happens unforeseen;
it is jist sae, no wrang nor richt.   *so*

On this dour mechanistic muir
wi nae land's end, and endless day,
whaur nae thing thraws a shadow, here
the truth is clear, and it is wae.   *miserable*

The crouds that thrang the danger-spots
weill ken what wey their warld's wrocht,
but aye the mair they pauchle on   *more; struggle*
to win release frae nigglin thocht.

Some pairts the pattern of the Wire   *parts*
leaves clear for fifty yairds and mair
whaur soil has crined to desert stuir   *dried up; dust*
wi scroggie bussels puir and bare.   *scraggy bushes*

Here some folk wycer nor the lave   *wiser than the rest*
or maybe suiner gien to skar   *fright*
tether theirsels wi chains to stakes,
sae they may gang, but no owre far.

Birlan in wretchedness aroun   *spinning*
their safe lives' centre, they maun dree   *must endure*
temptation sair to break their chains
for aye they ettle to gang free.   *try*

Some stark and strang stravaig their yird   *wander*
like shelties that hae never taen   *Shetland ponies*
the bit; mere smeddum drives them on,   *spirit*
their lives are short, but are their ain.

A wheen in orra ill-faur'd airts   *some; unlucky directions*
on barren stretches of the muir
gae whaur nae bluid is ever shed
to drouk the dreich unslockent stour.   *soak; bleak dry dust*

Within a pentagon of wire
they gang alane, or twae by twae,
thole the condition of their life   *endure*
and dree the weird as best they may.   *[suffer their fate]*

Alane in thon hale fremmit globe   *[all that foreign]*
thae slaw-gaun folk hae in their een   *slow-going*
some sapience, as gin their looks   *if*
reflleckit ferlies they hae seen   *wonders*

in their ain thochts, the nucleus
of man himsel is keethit there.   *revealed*
Expressed in terms of happiness
are premises of pure despair.

Thae guidlie folk are nae great men;
the best of men are unco smaa   *very small*
whan in the autumn of despair
irrelevance has dwined awa.   *faded*

Their syllogisms widdershins   *anti-clockwise*
wither the petal; syne the leaf
and stem crine in as life gaes doun   *shrink*
intill a corm of prime belief.   *core*

Wi utmaist pouer of forcy thocht
they crine their life within its core,
and what they ken wi certainty
is kent inby the bracken-spore.

And aye alane or twae by twae
they gang unhurt amang the noy   *annoyance*
of thon fell planet, and their een   *that; cruel; eyes*
lowe wi the licht of inwart joy.   *burn*

Outwartly they seem at rest,
binna the glint of hidden fires.   *except for*
Their warld shaks, but they bide still
as nodal points on dirlan wires.   *quivering*

In ither airts, whaur folk are thrang,   *crowded*
the Wire vibrates, clash gae the tins,
flures blume frae bluidie marl, dugs   *earth*
yowl throu the blatter of the guns.

I saw thon planet slawlie birl;   *turn*
I saw it as ane endless muir
in daylicht, and I saw a few
guid men bide still amang the stour.

Elegy

They are lang deid, folk that I used to ken,
their firm-set lips aa mowdert and agley,   *mouldy and awry*
sherp-tempert een rusty amang the cley:
they are baith deid, thae wycelike, bienlie men,   *sensible, agreeable*

heidmaisters, that had been in pouer for ten
or twenty year afore fate's taiglie wey   *tangled*
brocht me, a young, weill-harnit, blate and fey   *well-educated, shy and fated*
new-cleckit dominie, intill their den.   *newly-hatched schoolmaster*

Ane tellt me it was time I learnt to write –
round-haund, he meant – and saw about my hair:
I mind of him, beld-heidit, wi a kyte.   *paunch*

Ane sneerit quarterly – I cuidna square
my savings bank – and sniftert in his spite.   *sniggered*
Weill, gin they arena deid, it's time they were.   *if they aren't*

NORMAN MACCAIG (1910–1996)

Instrument and Agent

In my eye I've no apple; every object
Enters in there with hands in pockets.
I welcome them all, just as they are,
Every one equal, none a stranger.

Yet in the short journey they make
To my skull's back, each takes a look
From another, or a gesture, or
A special way of saying *Sir*.

So tree is partly girl; moon
And wit slide through the sky together;
And which is star — what's come a million
Miles or gone those inches farther?

Summer Farm

Straws like tame lightnings lie about the grass
And hang zigzag on hedges. Green as glass
The water in the horse-trough shines.
Nine ducks go wobbling by in two straight lines.

A hen stares at nothing with one eye,
Then picks it up. Out of an empty sky
A swallow falls and, flickering through
The barn, dives up again into the dizzy blue.

I lie, nor thinking, in the cool, soft grass,
Afraid of where a thought might take me — as
This grasshopper with plated face
Unfolds his legs and finds himself in space.

Self under self, a pile of selves I stand
Threaded on time, and with metaphysic hand
Lift the farm like a lid and see
Farm within farm, and in the centre, me.

Likenesses

It comes to mind,
Where there is room enough, that water goes
Between tall mountains and between small toes.

Or, if I like,
When the sun rises, his first light explores
Under high clouds and underneath low doors.

Or (doing it still)
Darkness can hide beside all that it hid
Behind a nightfall and a dropped eyelid.

Why do I add
Such notions up, unless they say what's true
In ways I don't quite see, of me and you?

Basking Shark

To stub an oar on a rock where none should be,
To have it rise with a slounge out of the sea
Is a thing that happened once (too often) to me.

But not too often – though enough. I count as gain
That once I met, on a sea tin-tacked with rain,
That roomsized monster with a matchbox brain.

He displaced more than water. He shoggled me
Centuries back – this decadent townee
Shook on a wrong branch of his family tree.

Swish up the dirt and, when it settles, a spring
Is all the clearer. I saw me, in one fling,
Emerging from the slime of everything.

So who's the monster? The thought made me grow pale
For twenty seconds while, sail after sail,
The tall fin slid away and then the tail.

Wild Oats

Every day I see from my window
pigeons, up on a roof ledge – the males
are wobbling gyroscopes of lust.

Last week a stranger joined them, a snowwhite
pouting fantail,
Mae West in the Women's Guild.
What becks, what croo-croos, what
demented pirouetting, what a lack
of moustaches to stroke.

The females – no need to be one of them
to know
exactly what they were thinking – pretended
she wasn't there
and went dowdily on with whatever
pigeons do when they're knitting.

Return to Scalpay

The ferry wades across the kyle. I drive
The car ashore
On to a trim tarred road. A car on Scalpay?
Yes, and a road where never was one before.
The ferrymen's Gaelic wonders who I am
(Not knowing I know it), this man back from the dead,
Who takes the blue-black road (no traffic jam)
From by Craig Lexie over to Bay Head.

A man bows in the North wind, shaping up
His lazybeds,
And through the salt air vagrant peat smells waver
From houses where no house should be. The sheds
At the curing station have been newly tarred.
Aunt Julia's house has vanished. The Red Well
Has been bulldozed away. But sharp and hard
The church still stands, barring the road to Hell.

A chugging prawn boat slides round Cuddy Point
Where in a gale
I spread my batwing jacket and jumped farther
Than I've jumped since. There's where I used to sail
Boats looped from rushes. On the jetty there
I caught eels, cut their heads off and watched them slew
Slow through the water. Ah – Cape Finisterre
I called that point, to show how much I knew.

While Hamish sketches, a crofter tells me that
The Scalpay folk,
Though very intelligent, are not Spinozas . . .
We walk the Out End road (no need to invoke
That troublemaker, Memory, she's everywhere)
To Laggandoan, greeted all the way –
My city eyeballs prickle; it's hard to bear
With such affection and such gaiety.

Scalpay revisited? – more than Scalpay. I
Have no defence,
For half my thought and half my blood is Scalpay,
Against that pure, hardheaded innocence
That shows love without shame, weeps without shame,
Whose every thought is hospitality –
Edinburgh, Edinburgh, you're dark years away.

Scuttering snowflakes riddling the hard wind
Are almost spent
When we reach Johann's house. She fills the doorway,
Sixty years of size and astonishment,

Then laughs and cries and laughs, as she always did
And will (Easy glum, easy glow, a friend would say) . . .
Scones, oatcakes, herrings from under a bubbling lid.
Then she comes with us to put us on our way.

Hugging my arm in her stronger one, she says,
Fancy me
Walking this road beside my darling Norman!
And what is there to say? . . .We look back and see
Her monumental against the flying sky
And I am filled with love and praise and shame
Knowing that I have been, and knowing why,
Diminished and enlarged. Are they the same?

Praise of a Collie

She was a small dog, neat and fluid —
Even her conversation was tiny:
She greeted you with *bow*, never *bow-wow*.

Her sons stood monumentally over her
But did what she told them. Each grew grizzled
Till it seemed he was his own mother's grandfather.

Once, gathering sheep on a showery day,
I remarked how dry she was. Pollóchan said, 'Ah,
It would take a very accurate drop to hit Lassie.'

She sailed in the dinghy like a proper sea-dog.
Where's a burn? — she's first on the other side.
She flowed through fences like a piece of black wind.

But suddenly she was old and sick and crippled . . .
I grieved for Pollóchan when he took her a stroll
And put his gun to the back of her head.

Intruder in a Set Scene

The way the water goes is blink blink blink.
That heap of trash was once
a swan's throne. The swans now lean their chests
against the waves that spill on Benbecula.
On the towpath a little girl
peers over the handle of the pram she's pushing.
Her mother follows her, reading a letter.

Everything is winter, everything
is a letter from another place, measuring
absence. Everything laments
the swan, drifting and dazzling on a western sealoch.

– But the little girl, five years of self-importance,
walks in her own season, not noticing
the stop-go's of water, the mouldering swan-throne,
the tears turning cold in the eyes of her mother.

Small Lochs

He's obsessed with clocks, she with politics,
He with motor cars, she with amber and jet.
There's something to be obsessed with for all of us.
Mine is lochs, the smaller the better.

I look at the big ones – Loch Ness, Loch Lomond,
Loch Shin, Loch Tay – and I bow respectfully,
But they're too grand to be invited home.
How could I treat them in the way they'd expect?

But the Dog Loch runs in eights when I go walking.
The Cat Loch purrs on the windowsill. I wade
Along Princes Street through Loch na Barrack.
In smoky bars I tell them like beads.

And don't think it's just the big ones that are lordlily named.
I met one once and when I asked what she was called
The little thing said (without blushing, mind you)
The Loch of the Corrie of the Green Waterfalls.

I know they're just H_2O in a hollow.
Yet not much time passes without me thinking of them
Dandling lilies and talking sleepily
And standing huge mountains on their watery heads.

SOMHAIRLE MACGILL-EAIN/
SORLEY MACLEAN (1911–1996)

Ban-Ghàidheal

Am faca Tu i, Iùdhaich mhóir,
ri 'n abrar Aon Mhac Dhé?
Am fac' thu 'coltas air Do thriall
ri strì an fhìon-lios chéin?

An cuallach mhiosan air a druim,
fallus searbh air mala is gruaidh;
's a' mhios chreadha trom air cùl
a cinn chrùibte bhochd thruaigh.

Chan fhaca Tu i, Mhic an t-saoir,
ri 'n abrar Rìgh na Glòir,
a miosg nan cladach carrach siar,
fo fhallus cliabh a lòin.

An t-earrach so agus so chaidh
's gach fichead earrach bho 'n an tùs
tharruing ise 'n fheamainn fhuar
chum biadh a cloinne 's duais an tùir.

'S gach fichead foghar tha air triall
chaill i samhradh buidh nam blàth;
is threabh an dubh-chosnadh an clais
tarsuinn mìnead ghil a clàir.

Agus labhair T' eaglais chaomh
mu staid chaillte a h-anama thruaigh;
agus leag an cosnadh dian
a corp gu sàmhchair dhuibh an uaigh.

A Highland Woman

Hast Thou seen her, great Jew,
who art called the One Son of God?
Hast Thou seen on Thy way the like of her
labouring in the distant vineyard?

The load of fruits on her back,
a bitter sweat on brow and cheek,
and the clay basin heavy on the back
of her bent poor wretched head.

Thou hast not seen her, Son of the carpenter,
who art called the King of Glory,
among the rugged western shores
in the sweat of her food's creel.

This Spring and last Spring
and every twenty Springs from the beginning,
she has carried the cold seaweed
for her children's food and the castle's reward.

And every twenty Autumns gone
she has lost the golden summer of her bloom,
and the Black Labour has ploughed the furrow
across the white smoothness of her forehead.

And Thy gentle church has spoken
about the lost state of her miserable soul,
and the unremitting toil has lowered
her body to a black peace in a grave.

Is thriall a tìm mar shnighe dubh
a' drùdhadh tughaidh fàrdaich bochd;
mheal ise an dubh-chosnadh cruaidh;
is glas a cadal suain an nochd.

Calbharaigh

Chan eil mo shùil air Calbharaigh
no air Betlehem an àigh
ach air cùil ghrod an Glaschu
far bheil an lobhadh fàis,
agus air seòmar an Dùn-éideann,
seòmar bochdainn 's cràidh,
far a bheil an naoidhean creuchdach
ri aonagraich gu bhàs.

Muir-tràigh

Chan eil mi strì ris a' chraoibh nach lùb rium
's cha chinn na h-ùbhlan air géig seach geug:
cha shoraidh slàn leat, cha d' rinn thu m' fhàgail:
's e tràigh a' bhàis i gun mhuir-làn 'nà déidh.

Marbh-shruth na conntraigh 'nad chom ciùrrte
nach lìon ri gealaich ùir no làin,
anns nach tig reothairt mhór an t-sùgraidh —
ach sìoladh dùbailt gu muir-tràigh.

And her time has gone like a black sludge
seeping through the thatch of a poor dwelling:
the hard Black Labour was her inheritance;
grey is her sleep tonight.

Translated from the Gaelic by the author

Calvary

My eye is not on Calvary
nor on Bethlehem the Blessed,
but on a foul-smelling backland in Glasgow,
where life rots as it grows;
and on a room in Edinburgh,
a room of poverty and pain,
where the diseased infant
writhes and wallows till death.

Translated from the Gaelic by the author

Ebb

I am not striving with the tree that will not bend for me,
and the apples will not grow on any branch;
it is not farewell to you; you have not left me.
It is the ebb of death with no floodtide after it.

Dead stream of neap in your tortured body,
which will not flow at new moon or at full,
in which the great springtide of love will not come –
but a double subsidence to lowest ebb.

Translated from the Gaelic by the author

Glac a' Bhàis

Thubhairt Nàsach air choireigin gun tug am Furair air ais do fhir na Gearmailte 'a' chòir agus an sonas bàs fhaotainn anns an àraich'.

'Na shuidhe marbh an 'Glaic a' Bhàis'
fo Dhruim Ruidhìseit,
gill' òg 's a logan sìos m' a ghruaidh
's a thuar grìsionn.

Smaoinich mi air a' chòir 's an àgh
a fhuair e bho Fhurair,
bhith tuiteam ann an raon an àir
gun éirigh tuilleadh;

air a' ghreadhnachas 's air a' chliù
nach d' fhuair e 'na aonar,
ged b' esan bu bhrònaiche snuadh
ann an glaic air laomadh

le cuileagan mu chuirp ghlas'
air gainmhich lachduinn
's i salach-bhuidhe 's làn de raip
's de sprùidhlich catha.

An robh an gille air an dream
a mhàb n h-Iùdhaich
's na Comunnaich, no air an dream
bu mhotha, dhiùbh-san

a threòraicheadh bho thoiseach àl
gun deòin gu buaireadh
agus bruaillean cuthaich gach blàir
air sgàth uachdaran?

Ge b'e a dheòin-san no a chàs,
a neoichiontas no mhìorun,
cha do nochd e toileachadh 'na bhàs
fo Dhruim Ruidhìseit.

Death Valley

Some Nazi or other has said that the Fuehrer had restored to German manhood the 'right and joy of dying in battle'.

Sitting dead in 'Death Valley'
below the Ruweisat Ridge
a boy with his forelock down about his cheek
and his face slate-grey;

I thought of the right and the joy
that he got from his Fuehrer,
of falling in the field of slaughter
to rise no more;

of the pomp and the fame
that he had, not alone,
though he was the most piteous to see
in a valley gone to seed

with flies about grey corpses
on a dun sand
dirty yellow and full of the rubbish
and fragments of battle.

Was the boy of the band
who abused the Jews
and Communists, or of the greater
band of those

led, from the beginning of generations,
unwillingly to the trial
and mad delirium of every war
for the sake of rulers?

Whatever his desire or mishap,
his innocence or malignity,
he showed no pleasure in his death
below the Ruweisat Ridge.

Translated from the Gaelic by the author

Hallaig

'Tha tìm, am fiadh, an coille Hallaig'

Tha bùird is tàirnean air an uinneig
troimh 'm faca mi an Aird an Iar
's tha mo ghaol aig Allt Hallaig
'na craoibh bheithe, 's bha i riamh

eadar an t-Inbhir 's Poll a' Bhainne,
thall 's a bhos mu Bhaile-Chùirn:
tha i 'na beithe, 'na calltuinn,
'na caorunn dhìreach sheang ùir.

Ann an Screapadal mo chinnidh,
far robh Tarmad 's Eachunn Mór,
tha 'n nigheanan 's am mic 'nan coille
ag gabhail suas ri taobh an lóin.

Uaibhreach a nochd na coilich ghiuthais
ag gairm air mullach Cnoc an Rà,
dìreach an druim ris a' ghealaich –
chan iadsan coille mo ghràidh.

Fuirichidh mi ris a' bheithe
gus an tig i mach an Càrn,
gus am bi am bearradh uile
o Bheinn na Lice f' a sgàil.

Mura tig 's ann theàrnas mi a Hallaig
a dh' ionnsaigh sàbaid nam marbh,
far a bheil an sluagh a' tathaich,
gach aon ghinealach a dh' fhalbh.

Tha iad fhathast ann a Hallaig,
Clann Ghill-Eain 's Clann MhicLeòid,
na bh' ann ri linn Mhic Ghille-Chaluim:
Chunnacas na mairbh beò.

Hallaig

'Time, the deer, is in the wood of Hallaig'

The window is nailed and boarded
through which I saw the West
and my love is at the Burn of Hallaig,
a birch tree, and she has always been

between Inver and Milk Hollow,
here and there about Baile-chuirn:
she is a birch, a hazel,
a straight, slender young rowan.

In Screapadal of my people
where Norman and Big Hector were,
their daughters and their sons are a wood
going up beside the stream.

Proud tonight the pine cocks
crowing on the top of Cnoc an Ra,
straight their backs in the moonlight –
they are not the wood I love.

I will wait for the birch wood
until it comes up by the cairn,
until the whole ridge from Beinn na Lice
will be under its shade.

If it does not, I will go down to Hallaig,
to the Sabbath of the dead,
where the people are frequenting,
every single generation gone.

They are still in Hallaig,
MacLeans and MacLeods,
all who were there in the time of Mac Gille Chaluim
the dead have been seen alive.

Na fir 'nan laighe air an lianaig
aig ceann gach taighe a bh' ann,
na h-igheanan 'nan coille bheithe,
dìreach an druim, crom an ceann.

Eadar an Leac is na Feàrnaibh
tha 'n rathad mór fo chóinnich chiùin,
's na h-igheanan 'nam badan sàmhach
a' dol a Chlachan mar o thùs.

Agus a' tilleadh ás a' Chlachan,
á Suidhisnis 's á tìr nam beò;
a chuile té òg uallach
gun bhristeadh cridhe an sgeòil.

O Allt na Feàrnaibh gus an fhaoilinn
tha soilleir an dìomhaireachd nam beann
chan eil ach coimhthional nan nighean
ag cumail na coiseachd gun cheann.

A' tilleadh a Hallaig anns an fheasgar,
anns a' chamhanaich bhalbh bheò,
a' lìonadh nan leathadan casa,
an gàireachdaich 'nam chluais 'na ceò,

's am bòidhche 'na sgleò air mo chridhe
mun tig an ciaradh air na caoil,
's nuair theàrnas grian air cùl Dhùn Cana
thig peileir dian á gunna Ghaoil;

's buailear am fiadh a tha 'na thuaineal
a' snòtach nan làraichean feòir;
thig reothadh air a shùil 'sa' choille:
chan fhaighear lorg air fhuil ri m' bheò.

The men lying on the green
at the end of every house that was,
the girls a wood of birches,
straight their backs, bent their heads.

Between the Leac and Fearns
the road is under mild moss
and the girls in silent bands
go to Clachan as in the beginning,

and return from Clachan
from Suisnish and the land of the living;
each one young and light-stepping,
without the heartbreak of the tale.

From the Burn of Fearns to the raised beach
that is clear in the mystery of the hills,
there is only the congregation of the girls
keeping up the endless walk,

coming back to Hallaig in the evening,
in the dumb living twilight,
filling the steep slopes,
their laughter a mist in my ears,

and their beauty a film on my heart
before the dimness comes on the kyles,
and when the sun goes down behind Dun Cana
a vehement bullet will come from the gun of Love;

and will strike the deer that goes dizzily,
sniffing at the grass-grown ruined homes;
his eye will freeze in the wood,
his blood will not be traced while I live.

Translated from the Gaelic by the author

RUTHVEN TODD (1914–1978)

Of Moulds and Mushrooms

Agrippina, well aware of Claudius' greed
For Caesar's mushroom, knew also that it looked
Like death-cap or destroying angel, so a god
Made room on earth for Nero, whose joke,
'Food of the gods', allowed for deadly poison.

Some still, with unreasoning fear, disgust,
Kick or switch down the mushrooms by their path,
Leaving the amanita rudely shattered, gills
Like fallen feathers scattered, veil and volva
Broken, and all this symmetry destroyed.

The lack of chlorophyll suggests the parasite
Which guilty man so readily despises.
These are strange fruit of the thin mycelium,
That webs this world beneath the surface,
And which can persist in its invisibility

Breaking down discard of leaves and timber,
Which otherwise would overtop the wood
Extinguishing everything, so that the seed
May sprout to nourishment, and the cycle
Of death, decay and rebirth still go on.

And I, aesthetic and somewhat botanical,
Would note and praise the diversity
Of shapes, variety of colours of the fungi,
Ball, club, shelf, parasol, cup and horn,
And the suave velvet of the different moulds.

I would recall the fungi in their settings:
Fly-agaric, scarlet with wrinkled creamy warts,
In birch woods of Dumbartonshire, but lemon-
Yellow in New England, toxic they said to flies,
But intoxicant for the Kamchatka tribesman.

Near Selkirk once I found a monstrous puff ball,
Far bigger than my younger brother's head,
A gleaming baldpate beckoning me across the field
To find and greet poor Yorick's vegetable skull,
Solitary underneath the well-clipped hazel hedge.

Where anciently the monks had had their abbey,
Beside my Essex farmhouse, clustered blewits
Were palely violet below the dark-fruited sloes,
And the old gnarled oaks within the woods
Were sometimes richly shelved with beefsteaks;

And I, in a strictly rationed world,
Welcomed and ate these, and others that I found,
Spongy cèpe, chanterelle and honeycombed morel,
Grey oyster-mushroom and tall dignified parasol,
Which I again met later on a Chilmark lawn.

Brown-purple trumpets of the cornucopia
Stand clear against the brilliance of the moss
Under a clump of beech-trees at Gay Head,
While vast fairy-rings, some centuries of age,
Manacle the cropped grass of the South Downs.

The wooden ships of England knew dry-rot,
Pepys gathering toadstools bigger than his fists,
So that ten oaks were cut for each one used,
And the white-rimmed tawniness rioted again
Among the bombed buildings that I sometime knew.

Fungi have made their share of history:
St Anthony's fire, from ergot in the rye,
Swept savagely through medieval France,
Rotting potatoes drove the Irishman abroad,
And French grapes grown on North American stock.

A mouldering cantaloup from a Peoria supermarket
Supplanted the culture Fleming kept for years,
And others now sample soil, remove and scan
The moulds that, in their destructiveness,
Aid ailing man by driving out his enemies.

But I, walking in fields or through the woods,
Welcome the vermilion russula, the sulphur
Polyporus, or inky shaggy-cap upon a heap of dung,
Without questioning their usefulness to me.
The ecology of my appreciation seems to need

Clavaria's coral branches on a damp dark bank,
Odorous stink-horns prodding through the grass,
And petalled dry geasters studding a sandy road.
These many-fangled fruits make bright
My sundry places where no flowers can bloom.

SYDNEY GOODSIR SMITH (1915–1975)

from *Armageddon in Albyn*

VII. The War in Fife

Gurlie an gray the snell Fife shore,   *stormy; bitterly cold*
Frae the peat-green sea the cauld haar drives,   *mist*
The weet wind sings on the wire, and war
Looks faur frae the land o Fife.

In ilka house tashed by the faem   *every; stained*
Tuim beds tell o anither life,   *empty*
The windae's blind wi the scuddan rain,
While war taks toll o the land o Fife.

By the 'Crusoe', backs tae the rain-straikit waa,
Auld jersied men staun hauf the day,
The fishing killt by trawlers, nou
They drink the rents the tourists pay.

But anither race has come, the pits
Breed a raucle fowk nae geck beguiles,   *fearless folk; trick*
Deep in the yerth nae haar affects   *earth*
The second war in the land o Fife.

Thae are the banded future; here
Dwine the auld defeated race;   *dwindle*
Unseen throu the cauld an seepan haar
Destroyers slip at a snail's pace.

A foghorn booms athort the Forth,   *across*
Drumlie lament for a sundered life,   *troubled*
The root an flouer that aince were kith
Made strangers in the land o Fife.

The haar is chill, near in til the shore,
Nae maws screich owre the yalla freith,   *gulls; yellow firth*
The wireless frae a sweyan door
Ennobles horror, fire, an daith.

The foreign war tuims mony a bed
But yet seems faur awa —
Twa hunner years o Union's bled
The veins mair white nor ony war.   *than any*

A third war cracks; lyart an loon   *[old and young]*
Thegither curse the lang stouthrife,   *robbery*
Mirk ower Scotland hings its rule   *gloom*
Like the snell haar hings ower Fife.

The Grace of God and the Meth-Drinker

There ye gang, ye daft   *go*
And doitit dotterel, ye saft   *raving idiot*
Crazed outland skalrag saul   *homeless vagabond*
In your bits and ends o winnockie duds   *holed clothes*
Your fyled and fozie-fousome clouts   *fouled and musty*
As fou's a fish, crackt and craftie-drunk   *intoxicated*
Wi bleerit reid-rimmed
Ee and slaveran crozie mou   *eye; wheedling mouth*
Dwaiblan owre the causie like a ship   *staggering; street*
Storm-toss't i' the Bay of Biscay O
At-sea indeed and hauf-seas-owre
Up-til-the-thrapple's-pap   *[up to your neck]*
Or up-til-the-crosstrees-sunk —
   Wha kens? Wha racks?   *knows; cares*
Hidderie-hetterie stouteran in a dozie dwaum   *back and forth; stumbling; stupor*
O' ramsh reid-biddie — Christ!   *fiery; red wine with meths*
     The stink
O' jake ahint him, a mephitic
Rouk o miserie, like some unco exotic   *reek; strange*
Perfume o the Orient no juist sae easilie tholit   *tolerated*

By the bleak barbarians o the Wast
But subtil, acrid, jaggan the nebstrous *jabbing the nostrils*
Wi'n owrehailan ugsome guff, maist delicat, *supremely horrible smell*
Like in scent til the streel o a randie gib . . . *piss; tomcat*
      O-hone-a-ree!

His toothless gums, his lips, bricht cramasie *red*
A schene-bricht slash o bluid
A schene like the leaman gleid o rubies *shining fire*
Throu the gray-white stibble
O' his blank unrazit chafts, a hangman's *cheeks*
Heid, droolie wi gob, the bricht een
Sichtless, cannie, blythe, and slee – *sly*
      Unkennan.

Ay,
   Puir gangrel! *outcast*
      There
– But for the undeemous glorie and grace *inexplicable*
O' a mercifu omnipotent majestic God
Superne eterne and sceptred in the firmament *[on high]*
Whartil the praises o the leal rise *faithful*
Like incense aye about Your throne,
Ayebydan, thochtless, and eternallie hauf-drunk *everlasting*
Wi nectar, Athole-brose, ambrosia – nae jake for *[whisky with honey and oatmeal]*
   You –
      God there! –
But for the 'bunesaid unsocht grace, unprayed-for, *aforesaid*
Undeserved
      Gangs,
        Unregenerate,
          Me.

DEÒRSA MAC IAIN DEÒRSA/
GEORGE CAMPBELL HAY (1915–1984)

Bisearta

Chì mi rè geàrd na h-oidhche
dreòs air chrith 'na fhroidhneas thall air fàire,
a' clapail le a sgiathaibh,
a' sgapadh 's a' ciaradh rionnagan na h-àird' ud.

Shaoileadh tu gun cluinnte,
ge cian, o 'bhuillsgein ochanaich no caoineadh,
ràn corruich no gàir fuatha,
comhart chon cuthaich uaidh no ulfhairt fhaolchon,
gun ruigeadh drannd an fhòirneirt
o'n fhùirneis òmair iomall fhéin an t-saoghail;
ach sud a' dol an leud e
ri oir an speur an tosdachd olc is aognaidh.

C' ainm nochd a th' orra,
na sràidean bochda anns an sgeith gach uinneag
a lasraichean 's a deatach,
a sradagan is sgreadail a luchd thuinidh,
is taigh air thaigh 'ga reubadh
am broinn a chéile am brùchdadh toit a' tuiteam?
Is có an nochd tha 'g atach
am Bàs a theachd gu grad 'nan cainntibh uile,
no a' spàirn measg chlach is shailthean
air bhàinidh a' gairm air cobhair, is nach cluinnear?
Cò an nochd a phàidheas
sean chìs àbhaisteach na fala cumant?

Uair dearg mar lod na h-àraich,
uair bàn mar ghile thràighte an eagail éitigh,
a' dìreadh 's uair a' teàrnadh,
a' sìneadh le sitheadh àrd 's a' call a mheudachd,
a' fannachadh car aitil
's ag at mar anail dhiabhail air dhéinead,
an t-Olc 'na chridhe 's 'na chuisle,

Bizerta

I see during the night guard
a blaze flickering, fringing the skyline over yonder,
beating with its wings
and scattering and dimming the stars of that airt.   *area*

You would think that there would be heard
from its midst, though far away, wailing and lamentation,
the roar of rage and the yell of hate,
the barking of the dogs from it or the howling of wolves,
that the snarl of violence would reach
from yon amber furnace the very edge of the world;
but yonder it spreads
along the rim of the sky in evil ghastly silence.

What is their name tonight,
the poor streets where every window spews
its flame and smoke,
its sparks and the screaming of its inmates,
while house upon house is rent
and collapses in a gust of smoke?
And who tonight are beseeching
Death to come quickly in all their tongues,
or are struggling among stones and beams,
crying in frenzy for help, and are not heard?
Who tonight is paying
the old accustomed tax of common blood?

Now red like a battlefield puddle,
now pale like the drained whiteness of foul fear,
climbing and sinking,
reaching and darting up and shrinking in size,
growing faint for a moment
and swelling like the breath of a devil in intensity,
I see Evil as a pulse

chì mi 'na bhuillean a' sìoladh 's a' leum e.
Tha 'n dreòs 'na oillt air fàire,
'na fhàinne ròis is òir am bun nan speuran,
a' breugnachadh 's ag àicheadh
le shoillse sèimhe àrsaidh àrd nan reultan.

and a heart declining and leaping in throbs.
The blaze, a horror on the skyline,
a ring of rose and gold at the foot of the sky,
belies and denies
with its light the ancient high tranquillity of the stars.

Translated from the Gaelic by the author

W. S. GRAHAM (1918–1986)

Malcolm Mooney's Land

1

Today, Tuesday, I decided to move on
Although the wind was veering. Better to move
Than have them at my heels, poor friends
I buried earlier under the printed snow.
From wherever it is I urge these words
To find their subtle vents, the northern dazzle
Of silence cranes to watch. Footprint on foot
Print, word on word and each on a fool's errand.
Malcolm Mooney's Land. Elizabeth
Was in my thoughts all morning and the boy.
Wherever I speak from or in what particular
Voice, this is always a record of me in you.
I can record at least out there to the west
The grinding bergs and, listen, further off
Where we are going, the glacier calves
Making its sudden momentary thunder.
This is as good a night, a place as any.

2

From the rimed bag of sleep, Wednesday,
My words crackle in the early air.
Thistles of ice about my chin,
My dreams, my breath a ruff of crystals.
The new ice falls from canvas walls.
O benign creature with the small ear-hole,
Submerger under silence, lead
Me where the unblubbered monster goes
Listening and makes his play.
Make my impediment mean no ill
And be itself a way.

A fox was here last night (Maybe Nansen's,
Reading my instruments.) the prints
All round the tent and not a sound.
Not that I'd have him call my name.
Anyhow how should he know? Enough
Voices are with me here and more
The further I go. Yesterday
I heard the telephone ringing deep
Down in a blue crevasse.
I did not answer it and could
Hardly bear to pass.

Landlice, always my good bedfellows,
Ride with me in my sweaty seams.
Come bonny friendly beasts, brother
To the grammarsow and the word-louse,
Bite me your presence, keep me awake
In the cold with work to do, to remember
To put down something to take back.
I have reached the edge of earshot here
And by the laws of distance
My words go through the smoking air
Changing their tune on silence.

3

My friend who loves owls
Has been with me all day
Walking at my ear
And speaking of old summers
When to speak was easy.
His eyes are almost gone
Which made him hear well.
Under our feet the great
Glacier drove its keel.
What is to read there
Scored out in the dark?

Later the north-west distance
Thickened towards us.
The blizzard grew and proved
Too filled with other voices
High and desperate
For me to hear him more.
I turned to see him go
Becoming shapeless into
The shrill swerving snow.

4

Today, Friday, holds the white
Paper up too close to see
Me here in a white-out in this tent of a place
And why is it there has to be
Some place to find, however momentarily
To speak from, some distance to listen to?

Out at the far-off edge I hear
Colliding voices, drifted, yes
To find me through the slowly opening leads.
Tomorrow I'll try the rafted ice.
Have I not been trying to use the obstacle
Of language well? It freezes round us all.

5

Why did you choose this place
For us to meet? Sit
With me between this word
And this, my furry queen.
Yet not mistake this
For the real thing. Here
In Malcolm Mooney's Land
I have heard many
Approachers in the distance
Shouting. Early hunters
Skittering across the ice

Full of enthusiasm
And making fly and,
Within the ear, the yelling
Spear steepening to
The real prey, the right
Prey of the moment.
The honking choir in fear
Leave the tilting floe
And enter the sliding water.
Above the bergs the foolish
Voices are lighting lamps
And all their sounds make
This diary of a place
Writing us both in.

Come and sit. Or is
It right to stay here
While, outside the tent
The bearded blinded go
Calming their children
Into the ovens of frost?
And what's the news? What
Brought you here through
The spring leads opening?

Elizabeth, you and the boy
Have been with me often
Especially on those last
Stages. Tell him a story.
Tell him I came across
An old sulphur bear
Sawing his log of sleep
Loud beneath the snow.
He puffed the powdered light
Up on to this page
And here his reek fell
In splinters among
These words. He snored well.
Elizabeth, my furry
Pelted queen of Malcolm

Mooney's Land, I made
You here beside me
For a moment out
Of the correct fatigue.

I have made myself alone now.
Outside the tent endless
Drifting hummock crests.
Words drifting on words.
The real unabstract snow.

Loch Thom

1

Just for the sake of recovering
I walked backward from fifty-six
Quick years of age wanting to see,
And managed not to trip or stumble
To find Loch Thom and turned round
To see the stretch of my childhood
Before me. Here is the loch. The same
Long-beaked cry curls across
The heather-edges of the water held
Between the hills a boyhood's walk
Up from Greenock. It is the morning.

And I am here with my mammy's
Bramble jam scones in my pocket.
The Firth is miles and I have come
Back to find Loch Thom maybe
In this light does not recognize me.

This is a lonely freshwater loch.
No farms on the edge. Only
Heather grouse-moor stretching
Down to Greenock and One Hope
Street or stretching away across
Into the blue moors of Ayrshire.

2

And almost I am back again
Wading the heather down to the edge
To sit. The minnows go by in shoals
Like iron-filings in the shallows.
My mother is dead. My father is dead
And all the trout I used to know
Leaping from their sad rings are dead.

3

I drop my crumbs into the shallow
Weed for the minnows and pinheads.
You see that I will have to rise
And turn round and get back where
My running age will slow for a moment
To let me on. It is a colder
Stretch of water than I remember.

The curlew's cry travelling still
Kills me fairly. In front of me
The grouse flurry and settle. GOBACK
GOBACK GOBACK FAREWELL LOCH THOM.

ELMA MITCHELL (1919–)

The Passenger Opposite

British Rail

Everything falls asleep with sleep
    – The wariness, the will –
It's hard to loathe a sleeping face
Lapsed back into a state of grace,
    Naked, relaxed and still.

Even the hair is childish now,
    Rumpled and damp and young,
The teeth unclenched, the hands let loose,
Both smile and frown gone out of use,
    No message from the tongue.

The mouth has slackened, and the chin
    Given up its thrust and drive,
The eyes have left their sentry box,
The ears have closed their subtle locks,
    Content to be alive

Just breathing; and the eyelashes
    Are delicate, and long,
They stoop, and soothe the fretted cheek
Which knows no words nor need to speak,
    No scope for going wrong.

This is the sleep of train, and plane,
    Of hammock, bunk and pram,
Deck-chair and hospital and cot,
Of slaked desire, of world-forgot,
    Of I-Am-That-I-Am.

And if the shoulder's tapped, or shouts
   Disturb the rhythmic bliss,
Will the face resurrect its fears,
Its irritations and its years
   Or smile, and shape a kiss?

Here is my stop. I must get out
   And cannot answer this.

EDWIN MORGAN (1920–   )

Message Clear

```
    am              i
                            if
 i am                   he
      he r          o
       h     ur   t
      the re           and
       he     re      and
      he re
  a               n   d
      the r                 e
          r                 ife
                   i n
           s     ion and
 i                     d    i e
   am   e res   ect
   am   e res   ection
                   o           f
      the                      life
                   o           f
    m    e             n
          sur e
       the               d    i e
 i        s
          s    e t    and
 i am the    sur         d
    a   t   res    t
                   o         life
 i am he r                   e
 i a            ct
 i       r   u      n
 i  m   e  e     t
 i           t            i e
 i        s    t    and
 i am th          o      th
 i am   r            a
```

```
i am the  su      n
i am the  s         on
i am the  e   rect on        e if
i am    re      n     t
i am      s         a       fe
i am      s   e   n     t
i    he e               d
i    t e  s     t
i       re          a d
  a   th re          a d
  a      s    t on       e
  a   t  re          a d
  a   th r       on       e
i          resurrect
                     a       life
i am               i n      life
i am      resurrection
i am the resurrection and
i am
i am the resurrection and the life
```

King Billy

Grey over Riddrie the clouds piled up,
dragged their rain through the cemetery trees.
The gates shone cold. Wind rose
flaring the hissing leaves, the branches
swung, heavy, across the lamps.
Gravestones huddled in drizzling shadow,
flickering streetlight scanned the requiescats,
a name and an urn, a date, a dove
picked out, lost, half regained.
What is this dripping wreath, blown from its grave
red, white, blue, and gold
'To Our Leader of Thirty years Ago' —

Bareheaded, in dark suits, with flutes
and drums, they brought him here, in procession
seriously, King Billy of Brigton, dead,
from Bridgeton Cross; a memory of violence,

brooding days of empty bellies,
billiard smoke and a sour pint,
boots or fists, famous sherrickings,   *beatings up*
the word, the scuffle, the flash, the shout,
bloody crumpling in the close,
bricks for papish windows, get
the Conks next time, the Conks ambush
the Billy Boys, the Billy Boys the Conks till
Sillitoe scuffs the razors down the stank —   *drain*
No, but it isn't the violence they remember
but the legend of a violent man
born poor, gang-leader in the bad times
of idleness and boredom, lost in better days,
a bouncer in a betting club,
quiet man at last, dying
alone in Bridgeton in a box bed.
So a thousand people stopped the traffic
for the hearse of a folk hero and the flutes
threw 'Onward Christian Soldiers' to the winds
from unironic lips, the mourners kept
in step, and there were some who wept.

Go from the grave. The shrill flutes
are silent, the march dispersed.
Deplore what is to be deplored,
and then find out the rest.

The Loch Ness Monster's Song

Sssnnnwhuffffll?
Hnwhuffl hhnnwfl hnfl hfl?
Gdroblboblhobngbl gbl gl g g g g glbgl.
Drublhaflablhaflubhafgabhaflhafl fl fl —
gm grawwwww grf grawf awfgm graw gm.
Hovoplodok-doplodovok-plovodokot-doplodokosh?
Splgraw fok fok splgrafhatchgabrlgabrl fok splfok!
Zgra kra gka fok!
Grof grawff gahf?
Gombl mbl bl —
blm plm,

blm plm,
blm plm,
blp.

The First Men on Mercury

— We come in peace from the third planet.
Would you take us to your leader?

— Bawr stretter! Bawr. Bawr. Stretterhawl?

— This is a little plastic model
of the solar system, with working parts.
You are here and we are there and we
are now here with you, is this clear?

— Gawl horrop. Bawr. Abawrhannahanna!

— Where we come from is blue and white
with brown, you see we call the brown
here 'land', the blue is 'sea', and the white
is 'clouds' over land and sea, we live
on the surface of the brown land,
all round is sea and clouds. We are 'men'.
Men come —

— Glawp men! Gawrbenner menko. Menhawl?

— Men come in peace from the third planet
which we call 'earth'. We are earthmen.
Take us earthmen to your leader.

— Thmen? Thmen? Bawr. Bawrhossop.
Yuleeda tan hanna. Harrabost yuleeda.

— I am the yuleeda. You see my hands,
we carry no benner, we come in peace.
The spaceways are all stretterhawn.

– Glawn peacemen all horrabhanna tantko!
Tan come at'mstrossop. Glawp yuleeda!

– Atoms are peacegawl in our harraban.
Menbat worrabost from tan hannahanna.

– You men we know bawrhossoptant. Bawr.
We know yuleeda. Go strawg backspetter quick.

– We cantantabawr, tantingko backspetter now!

– Banghapper now! Yes, third planet back.
Yuleeda will go back blue, white, brown
nowhanna! There is no more talk.

– Gawl han fasthapper?

– No. You must go back to your planet.
Go back in peace, take what you have gained
but quickly.

– Stretterworra gawl, gawl . . .

– Of course, but nothing is ever the same,
now is it? You'll remember Mercury.

Cinquevalli

Cinquevalli is falling, falling.
The shining trapeze kicks and flirts free,
solo performer at last.
The sawdust puffs up with a thump,
settles on a tangle of broken limbs.
St Petersburg screams and leans.
His pulse flickers with the gas-jets. He lives.

Cinquevalli has a therapy.
In his hospital bed, in his hospital chair
he holds a ball, lightly, lets it roll round his hand,
or grips it tight, gauging its weight and resistance,

begins to balance it, to feel its life attached to his
by will and knowledge, invisible strings
that only he can see. He throws it
from hand to hand, always different,
always the same, always
different, always the
same.
His muscles learn to think, his arms grow very strong.

Cinquevalli in sepia
looks at me from an old postcard: bundle of enigmas.
Half faun, half military man; almond eyes, curly hair,
conventional moustache; tights, and a tunic loaded
with embroideries, tassels, chains, fringes; hand on hip
with a large signet-ring winking at the camera
but a bull neck and shoulders and a cannon-ball
at his elbow as he stands by the posing pedestal;
half reluctant, half truculent,
half handsome, half absurd,
but let me see you forget him: not to be done.

Cinquevalli is a juggler.
In a thousand theatres, in every continent,
he is the best, the greatest. After eight years perfecting
he can balance one billiard ball on another billiard ball
on top of a cue on top of a third billiard ball
in a wine-glass held in his mouth. To those
who say the balls are waxed, or flattened,
he patiently explains the trick will only work
because the spheres are absolutely true.
There is no deception in him. He is true.

Cinquevalli is juggling with a bowler,
a walking-stick, a cigar, and a coin.
Who foresees? How to please.
The last time round, the bowler
flies to his head, the stick sticks in his hand,
the cigar jumps into his mouth, the coin
lands on his foot – ah, but
is kicked into his eye

and held there as the miraculous monocle
without which the portrait would be incomplete.

Cinquevalli is practising.
He sits in his dressing-room talking to some friends,
at the same time writing a letter with one hand
and with the other juggling four balls.
His friends think of demons, but
'You could all do this,' he says,
sealing the letter with a billiard ball.

Cinquevalli is on the high wire in Odessa.
The roof cracks, he is falling, falling
into the audience, a woman breaks his fall,
he cracks her like a flea, but lives.

Cinquevalli broods in his armchair in Brixton Road.
He reads in the paper about the shells whining
at Passchendaele, imagines the mud and the dead.
He goes to the window and wonders through that dark evening
what is happening in Poland where he was born.
His neighbours call him a German spy.
'Kestner, Paul Kestner, that's his name!'
'Keep Kestner out of the British music-hall!'
He frowns; it is cold; his fingers seem stiff and old.

Cinquevalli tosses up a plate of soup
and twirls it on his forefinger; not a drop spills.
He laughs, and well may he laugh
who can do that. The astonished table
breathe again, laugh too, think the world
a spinning thing that spills, for a moment, no drop.

Cinquevalli's coffin sways through Brixton
only a few months before the Armistice.
Like some trick they cannot get off the ground
it seems to burden the shuffling bearers, all their arms
cross-juggle that displaced person, that man
of balance, of strength, of delights and marvels,
in his unsteady box at last into the earth.

The Coin

We brushed the dirt off, held it to the light.
The obverse showed us *Scotland*, and the head
of a red deer; the antler-glint had fled
but the fine cut could still be felt. All right:
we turned it over, read easily *One Pound*,
but then the shock of Latin, like a gloss,
Respublica Scotorum, sent across
such ages as we guessed but never found
at the worn edge where once the date had been
and where as many fingers had gripped hard
as hopes their silent race had lost or gained.
The marshy scurf crept up to our machine,
sucked at our boots. Yet nothing seemed ill-starred.
And least of all the realm the coin contained.

RUARAIDH MACTHÒMAIS/DERICK THOMSON
(1921–   )

Clann-Nighean an Sgadain

An gàire mar chraiteachan salainn
ga fhroiseadh bho 'm beul,
an sàl 's am picil air an teanga,
's na miaran cruinne, goirid a dheanadh giullachd,
no a thogadh leanabh gu socair, cuimir,
seasgair, fallain,
gun mhearachd,
's na sùilean cho domhainn ri fèath.

B'e bun-os-cionn na h-eachdraidh a dh'fhàg iad
'nan tràillean aig ciùrairean cutach,
thall 's a-bhos air Galldachd 's an Sasainn.
Bu shaillte an duais a thàrr iad
ás na mìltean bharaillean ud,
gaoth na mara geur air an craiceann,
is eallach a' bhochdainn 'nan ciste,
is mara b'e an gàire
shaoileadh tu gu robh an teud briste.

Ach bha craiteachan uaille air an cridhe,
ga chumail fallain,
is bheireadh cutag an teanga
slisinn á fanaid nan Gall –
agus bha obair rompa fhathast
nuair gheibheadh iad dhachaigh,
ged nach biodh maoin ac':
air oidhche robach gheamhraidh,
ma bha siud an dàn dhaibh,
dheanadh iad daoine.

The Herring Girls

Their laughter like a sprinkling of salt
showered from their lips,
brine and pickle on their tongues,
and the stubby short fingers that could handle fish,
or lift a child gently, neatly,
safely, wholesomely,
unerringly,
and the eyes that were as deep as a calm.

The topsy-turvy of history had made them
slaves to short-arsed curers,
here and there in the Lowlands, in England.
Salt the reward they won
from those thousands of barrels,
the sea-wind sharp on their skins,
and the burden of poverty in their kists,
and were it not for their laughter
you might think the harp-string was broken.

But there was a sprinkling of pride on their hearts,
keeping them sound,
and their tongues' gutting-knife
would tear a strip from the Lowlanders' mockery –
and there was work awaiting them
when they got home,
though they had no wealth:
on a wild winter's night,
if that were their lot,
they would make men.

Translated from the Gaelic by the author

GEORGE MACKAY BROWN (1921–1996)

Kirkyard

A silent conquering army,
The island dead,
Column on column, each with a stone banner
Raised over his head.

A green wave full of fish
Drifted far
In wavering westering ebb-drawn shoals beyond
Sinker or star.

A labyrinth of celled
And waxen pain.
Yet I come to the honeycomb often, to sip the finished
Fragrance of men.

Hamnavoe Market

They drove to the Market with ringing pockets.

Folster found a girl
Who put lipstick wounds on his face and throat,
Small and diagonal, like red doves.

Johnston stood beside the barrel.
All day he stood there.
He woke in a ditch, his mouth full of ashes.

Grieve bought a balloon and a goldfish.
He swung through the air.
He fired shotguns, rolled pennies, ate sweet fog from a stick.

Heddle was at the Market also.
I know nothing of his activities.
He is and always was a quiet man.

Garson went three rounds with a negro boxer,
And received thirty shillings,
Much applause, and an eye loaded with thunder.

Where did they find Flett?
They found him in a brazen circle,
All flame and blood, a new Salvationist.

A gypsy saw in the hand of Halcro
Great strolling herds, harvests, a proud woman.
He wintered in the poorhouse.

They drove home from the Market under the stars
Except for Johnston
Who lay in a ditch, his mouth full of dying fires.

Taxman

Seven scythes leaned at the wall.
Beard upon golden beard
The last barley load
Swayed through the yard.
The girls uncorked the ale.
Fiddle and feet moved together.
Then between stubble and heather
A horseman rode.

IAN HAMILTON FINLAY (1925–   )

Evening – Sail

THE BOAT'S BLUEPRINT

water

THE CLOUD'S ANCHOR

s w a l l o w

ALASTAIR REID (1926–   )

Scotland

It was a day peculiar to this piece of the planet,
when larks rose on long thin strings of singing
and the air shifted with the shimmer of actual angels.
Greenness entered the body. The grasses
shivered with presences, and sunlight
stayed like a halo on hair and heather and hills.
Walking into town, I saw, in a radiant raincoat,
the woman from the fish-shop. 'What a day it is!'
cried I, like a sunstruck madman.
And what did she have to say for it?
Her brow grew bleak, her ancestors raged in their graves
as she spoke with their ancient misery:
'We'll pay for it, we'll pay for it, we'll pay for it!'

IAIN MAC A' GHOBHAINN/IAIN CRICHTON SMITH (1928–1998)

The Clearances

The thistles climb the thatch. Forever
this sharp scale in our poems,
as also the waste music of the sea.

The stars shine over Sutherland
in a cold ceilidh of their own,
as, in the morning, the silver cane

cropped among corn. We will remember this.
Though hate is evil we cannot
but hope your courtier's heels in hell

are burning: that to hear
the thatch sizzling in tanged smoke
your hot ears slowly learn.

Old Woman

And she, being old, fed from a mashed plate
as an old mare might droop across a fence
to the dull pastures of its ignorance.
Her husband held her upright while he prayed

to God who is all-forgiving to send down
some angel somewhere who might land perhaps
in his foreign wings among the gradual crops.
She munched, half dead, blindly searching the spoon.

Outside, the grass was raging. There I sat
imprisoned in my pity and my shame
that men and women having suffered time
should sit in such a place, in such a state

and wished to be away, yes, to be far away
with athletes, heroes, Greek or Roman men
who pushed their bitter spears into a vein
and would not spend an hour with such decay.

'Pray God,' he said, 'we ask you, God,' he said.
The bowed back was quiet. I saw the teeth
tighten their grip around a delicate death.
And nothing moved within the knotted head

but only a few poor veins as one might see
vague wishless seaweed floating on a tide
of all the salty waters where had died
too many waves to mark two more or three.

Two Girls Singing

It neither was the words nor yet the tune.
Any tune would have done and any words.
Any listener or no listener at all.

As nightingales in rocks or a child crooning
in its own world of strange awakening
or larks for no reason but themselves.

So on the bus through late November running
by yellow lights tormented, darkness falling,
the two girls sang for miles and miles together

and it wasn't the words or tune. It was the singing.
It was the human sweetness in that yellow,
the unpredicted voices of our kind.

Contrasts

Against your black I set the dainty deer
stepping in mosses and in water where
there are miles of moorland under miles of air.

Against your psalms I set the various seas
slopping against the mussels fixed in place,
slums on the ancient rocks in salty rows.

Against your bible I set the plateau
from which I see the people down below
in their random kingdoms moving to and fro.

Against your will I set the changing tones
of water swarming over lucid stones
and salmon bubbling in repeated suns.

Against your death I let the tide come in
with its weight of water and its lack of sin,
the opulent millions of a rising moon.

The Herring Girls

The herring girls,
where did they go to
with their necklaces of salt?
They would come home with presents,
small yellow rings,
sweets,
dresses of water.
Where did they go
with their long skirts,
they who never had a rose
or shadow of poetry,
were they drowned in time
sinking deeper and deeper
till nothing was seen
but their wet rings?

Sgialachdan Gàidhlig

1
Iasgair ann am bòtannan móra,
a leannan
's a mhàthair.

2
Sgialachd
mu dheidhinn bodach
is ròn.

3
Té
a' leughadh a' Bhìobaill airson seachd bliadhna
a' feitheamh ri seòladair.

4
Melódeon.
Cruach mhònach.
Cailleach-oidhche.

5
Croit.
Dà bhràthair.
Truinnsear le buntàta.

6
Té á Glaschu
le mini
ann an eaglais.

7
An cuan
is an drifter
an Golden Rose.

Gaelic Stories

1
A fisherman in wellingtons
and his sweetheart
and his mother.

2
A story
about an old man
and a seal.

3
A woman
reading a Bible for seven years
waiting for a sailor.

4
A melodeon.
A peat stack.
An owl.

5
A croft.
Two brothers.
A plate with potatoes.

6
A girl from Glasgow
wearing a mini
in church.

7
The sea
and a drifter,
the Golden Rose.

8
Fear a bha 'n Astràilia
a' tilleadh dhachaigh
air oidhche bainnse.

9
'Romance'
eadar càis
is bainne.

10
Glaschu
ann an saoghal de naidhlon
is de neon.

11
Dà bhoireannach
a' còmhradh
ann an taigh dubh.

12
Uilebhiast
ag éirigh ás a' chuan
'An gabh thu copan tea?'

13
Comadaidh
ann an cidsin
le geansaidhean.

14
Còmhradh
eadar lof is
mulachag.

15
Còmhradh
eadar bòtann
is sgadan.

8
A man who was in Australia
coming home
on a wedding night.

9
A romance
between cheese
and milk.

10
Glasgow
in a world of nylons
and of neon.

11
Two women
talking
in a black house.

12
A monster
rising from the sea,
'Will you take tea?'

13
A comedy
in a kitchen,
with jerseys.

14
A conversation
between a loaf and
cheese.

15
A conversation
between a wellington
and a herring.

16
Còmhradh
eadar ìm ùr
is copan.

17
Còmhradh
eadar Yarmouth
is Garrabost.

18
Gealach
chruaidh àrd
os cionn boglaich.

Na h-Eilthirich

A liuthad soitheach a dh'fhàg ar dùthaich
le sgiathan geala a' toirt Chanada orra.
Tha iad mar neapaigearan 'nar cuimhne
's an sàl mar dheòirean
's anns na crainn aca seòladairean a' seinn
mar eòin air gheugan.
Muir a' Mhàigh ud gu gorm a' ruith,
gealach air an oidhche, grian air an latha,
ach a' ghealach mar mheas buidhe,
mar thruinnsear air balla,
ris an tog iad an làmhan,
neo mar mhagnet airgeadach
le gathan goirte
a' sruthadh do'n chridhe.

16
A conversation
between fresh butter
and a cup.

17
A conversation
between Yarmouth
and Garrabost.

18
A moon
hard and high
above a marsh.

Translated from the Gaelic by the author

The Exiles

The many ships that left our country
with white wings for Canada.
They are like handkerchiefs in our memories
and the brine like tears
and in their masts sailors singing
like birds on branches.
That sea of May running in such blue,
a moon at night, a sun at daytime,
and the moon like a yellow fruit,
like a plate on a wall
to which they raise their hands
like a silver magnet
with piercing rays
streaming into the heart.

Translated from the Gaelic by the author

STEWART CONN (1936–   )

Todd

My father's white uncle became
Arthritic and testamental in
Lyrical stages. He held cardinal sin
Was misuse of horses, then any game

Won on the sabbath. A Clydesdale
To him was not bells and sugar or declension
From paddock, but primal extension
Of rock and soil. Thundered nail

Turned to sacred bolt. And each night
In the stable he would slaver and slave
At cracked hooves, or else save
Bowls of porridge for just the right

Beast. I remember I lied
To him once, about oats: then I felt
The brand of his loving tongue, the belt
Of his own horsey breath. But he died,

When the mechanised tractor came to pass.
Now I think of him neighing to some saint
In a simple heaven or, beyond complaint,
Leaning across a fence and munching grass.

Under the Ice

Like Coleridge, I waltz
on ice. And watch my shadow
on the water below. Knowing that
if the ice were not there
I'd drown. Half willing it.

In my cord jacket
and neat cravat, I keep
returning to the one spot.
How long, to cut
a perfect circle out?

Something in me
rejects the notion.
The arc is never complete.
My figures-of-eight
almost, not quite, meet.

Was Raeburn's skating parson
a man of God, poised
impeccably on the brink;
or his bland stare
no more than a decorous front?

If I could keep my cool
like that. Gazing straight ahead,
not at my feet. Giving
no sign of knowing
how deep the water, how thin the ice.

Behind that, the other
question: whether the real you
pirouettes in space,
or beckons from under the ice
for me to come through.

AONGHAS MACNEACAIL (1942–   )

tha gàidhlig beò

mar chuimhneachan air caitlín maude

cuireamaid an dàrna taobh
obair an là an-diugh
dèan dannsa ri
port-a-beul na gaoithe

'tha gàidhlig beò'
a dh'aindeoin gach saighead
's i streap nan sìthean
fiùran daraich fo h-achlais
a sùilean dùbhlanach
a' sìneadh gu fàire fad' as
's i sireadh na fàire fad' as
lasair-bhuan leugach 'na broilleach

'n aire nach gabh i sùrdag ro bhras

ach dèan dannsa dèan dannsa
's e obair th'ann a bhith dannsa

gaelic is alive

in memoriam caitlín maude

let's put aside
today's work
and dance to
the wind's port-a-beul

'gaelic is alive'
despite all arrows
she climbs the hillside
sapling of oak in her arms
her defiant eyes
reaching the far-off horizon
she aims for the far-off horizon
a bright lasting star in her breast

defend her from too bold a leap

but be dancing be dancing
it is work to be dancing

Translated from the Gaelic by the author

DOUGLAS DUNN (1942–   )

Landscape with One Figure

Shipyard cranes have come down again
To drink at the river, turning their long necks
And saying to their reflections on the Clyde,
'How noble we are.'

The fields are waiting for them to come over.
Trees gesticulate into the rain,
The nerves of grasses quiver at their tips.
Come over and join us in the wet grass!

The wings of gulls in the distance wave
Like handkerchiefs after departing emigrants.
A tug sniffs up the river, looking like itself.
Waves fall from their small heights on river mud.

If I could sleep standing, I would wait here
For ever, become a landmark, something fixed
For tug crews or seabound passengers to point at,
An example of being a part of a place.

St Kilda's Parliament: 1879–1979

The photographer revisits his picture

On either side of a rock-paved lane,
Two files of men are standing barefooted,
Bearded, waistcoated, each with a tam-o'-shanter
On his head, and most with a set half-smile
That comes from their companionship with rock,
With soft mists, with rain, with roaring gales,
And from a diet of solan goose and eggs,
A diet of dulse and sloke and sea-tangle,
And ignorance of what a pig, a bee, a rat,
Or rabbit look like, although they remember

The three apples brought here by a traveller
Five years ago, and have discussed them since.
And there are several dogs doing nothing
Who seem contemptuous of my camera,
And a woman who might not believe it
If she were told of the populous mainland.
A man sits on a bank by the door of his house,
Staring out to sea and at a small craft
Bobbing there, the little boat that brought me here,
Whose carpentry was slowly shaped by waves,
By a history of these northern waters.
Wise men or simpletons – it is hard to tell –
But in that way they almost look alike.
You also see how each is individual,
Proud of his shyness and of his small life
On this outcast of the Hebrides
With his eyes full of weather and seabirds,
Fish, and whatever morsel he grows here.
Clear, too, is manhood, and how each man looks
Secure in the love of a woman who
Also knows the wisdom of the sun rising,
Of weather in the eyes like landmarks.
Fifty years before depopulation –
Before the boats came at their own request
To ease them from their dying babies –
It was easy, even then, to imagine
St Kilda return to its naked self,
Its archaeology of hazelraw
And footprints stratified beneath the lichen.
See, how simple it all is, these toes
Playfully clutching the edge of a boulder.
It is a remote democracy, where men,
In manacles of place, outstare a sea
That rattles back its manacles of salt,
The moody jailer of the wild Atlantic.
    Traveller, tourist with your mind set on
Romantic Staffas and materials for
Winter conversations, if you should go there,
Landing at sunrise on its difficult shores,
On St Kilda you will surely hear Gaelic
Spoken softly like a poetry of ghosts

By those who never were contorted by
Hierarchies of cuisine and literacy.
You need only look at the faces of these men
Standing there like everybody's ancestors,
This flick of time I shuttered on a face.
Look at their sly, assuring mockery.
They are aware of what we are up to
With our internal explorations, our
Designs of affluence and education.
They know us so well, and are not jealous,
Whose be-all and end-all was an eternal
Casual husbandry upon a toehold
Of Europe, which, when failing, was not their fault.
You can see they have already prophesied
A day when survivors look across the stern
Of a departing vessel for the last time
At their gannet-shrouded cliffs, and the farewells
Of the St Kilda mouse and St Kilda wren
As they fall into the texts of specialists,
Ornithological visitors at the prow
Of a sullenly managed boat from the future.
They pose for ever outside their parliament,
Looking at me, as if they have grown from
Affection scattered across my own eyes.
And it is because of this that I, who took
This photograph in a year of many events –
The Zulu massacres, Tchaikovsky's opera –
Return to tell you this, and that after
My many photographs of distressed cities,
My portraits of successive elegants,
Of the emaciated dead, the lost empires,
Exploded fleets, and of the writhing flesh
Of dead civilians and commercial copulations,
That after so much of that larger franchise
It is to this island that I return.
Here I whittle time, like a dry stick,
From sunrise to sunset, among the groans
And sighings of a tongue I cannot speak,
Outside a parliament, looking at them,
As they, too, must always look at me

Looking through my apparatus at them
Looking. Benevolent, or malign? But who,
At this late stage, could tell, or think it worth it?
For I was there, and am, and I forget.

War Blinded

For more than sixty years he has been blind
Behind that wall, these trees, with terrible
Longevity wheeled in the sun and wind
On pathways of the soldiers' hospital.

For half that time his story's troubled me –
That showroom by the ferry, where I saw
His basketwork, a touch-turned filigree
His fingers coaxed from charitable straw;

Or how he felt when young, enlisting at
Recruiting tables on the football pitch,
To end up slumped across a parapet,
His eye-blood running in a molten ditch;

Or how the light looked when I saw two men,
One blind, one in a wheelchair, in that park,
Their dignity, which I have not forgotten,
Which helps me struggle with this lesser dark.

That war's too old for me to understand
How he might think, nursed now in wards of want,
Remembering that day when his right hand
Gripped on the shoulder of the man in front.

Land Love

We stood here in the coupledom of us.
I showed her this – a pool with leaping trout,
Split-second saints drawn in a rippled nimbus.

We heard the night-boys in the fir trees shout.
Dusk was an insect-hovered dark water,
The calling of lost children, stars coming out.

With all the feelings of a widower
Who does not live there now, I dream my place.
I go by the soft paths, alone with her.

Dusk is a listening, a whispered grace
Voiced on a bank, a time that is all ears
For the snapped twig, the strange wind on your face.

She waits at the door of the hemisphere
In her harvest dress, in the remote
Local August that is everywhere and here.

What rustles in the leaves, if it is not
What I asked for, an opening of doors
To a half-heard religious anecdote?

Monogamous swans on the darkened mirrors
Picture the private grace of man and wife
In its white poise, its sleepy portraitures.

Night is its Dog Star, its eyelet of grief
A high, lit echo of the starry sheaves.
A puff of hedge-dust loosens in the leaves.
Such love that lingers on the fields of life!

TOM LEONARD (1944–)

from *Unrelated Incidents*

this is thi
six a clock
news thi
man said n
thi reason
a talk wia
BBC accent
iz coz yi
widny wahnt
mi ti talk
aboot thi
trooth wia
voice lik
wanna yoo
scruff. if
a toktaboot
thi trooth
lik wanna yoo
scruff yi
widny thingk
it wuz troo.
jist wanna yoo
scruff tokn.
thirza right
way ti spell
ana right way
ti tok it. this
is me tokn yir
right way a
spellin. this
is ma trooth.
yooz doant no
thi trooth

yirsellz cawz
yi canny talk
right. this is
the six a clock
nyooz. belt up.

Jist ti Let Yi No

from the American of Carlos Williams

ahv drank
thi speshlz
that wurrin
thi frij

n thit
yiwurr probbli
hodn back
furthi pahrti

awright
they wur great
thaht stroang
thaht cawld

Fathers and Sons

I remember being ashamed of my father
when he whispered the words out loud
reading the newspaper.

'Don't you find
the use of phonetic urban dialect
rather constrictive?'
asks a member of the audience.

The poetry reading is over.
I will go home to my children.

LIZ LOCHHEAD (1947–   )

Something I'm Not

familiar with, the tune
of their talking, comes tumbling before them
down the stairs which (oh I forgot) it was my turn
to do again this week.
My neighbour and my neighbour's child. I nod, we're not
on speaking terms exactly.

I don't know much about her. Her dinners smell
different. Her husband's a busdriver,
so I believe.
She carries home her groceries in Grandfare bags
though I've seen her once or twice around the corner
at Shastri's for spices and such.
(I always shop there – he's open till all hours
making good). How does she feel?
Her children grow up with foreign accents,
swearing in fluent Glaswegian. Her face
is sullen. Her coat is drab plaid, hides
but for a hint at the hem, her sari's
gold embroidered gorgeousness. She has
a jewel in her nostril.
The golden hands with the almond nails
that push the pram turn blue
in the city's cold climate.

Neckties

Paisleys squirm with spermatozoa.
All yang, no yin. Liberties are peacocks.
Old school types still hide behind their prison bars.
Red braces, jacquards, watermarked brocades
are the most fun a chap can have
in a sober suit.

You know about knots,
could tie, I bet, a bowtie properly
in the dark with your eyes shut, but
we've a diagram hung up
beside the mirror in our bedroom.
Left over right, et cetera . . .
The half or double Windsor,
even that extra fancy one it takes
an extra long tie to pull off successfully.
You know the times a simple schoolboy four-in-hand
will be what's wanted.

I didn't used to be married.
Once neckties were coiled occasional serpents
on the dressing-table by my bed
beside the car-keys and the teetering
temporary leaning towers of change.
They were dangerous nooses on the backs of chairs
or funny fishes in the debris on the floor.
I should have known better.

Picture me away from you
cruising the high streets
under the watchful eyes of shopboys
fingering their limp silks
wondering what would please you.
Watch out, someday I'll bring you back a naked lady,
a painted kipper, maybe a bootlace
dangling from a silver dollar
and matching collarpoints.
You could get away with anything
you're that goodlooking.
Did you like that screenprinted slimjim from Covent Garden?

Once I got a beauty in a Cancer Shop
and a sort of forties effort in Oxfam for a song.
Not bad for one dull town.
The dead man's gravy stain wasn't the size of sixpence
and you can hide it behind your crocodile tie pin.

FRANK KUPPNER (1951–   )

from *An Old Guidebook to Prague*

Architecture is when the sun shines on a façade daily
But some parts of it nonetheless remain in permanent shadow;
Ah, those little valleys in the lower cathedral roofing,
Where only two people walk each century.

A little swarm of people has gathered in the square,
As if uncertain in which direction to move next;
The moment's sun cools them in a black rectangle;
A shower of back windows is open in the town beyond.

Such tiny skylights in the roof of the castle;
So inconspicuous only the tenth look notices them;
They seem to have been burrowed out from the inside;
I see a patch of sun beside so many sleeping faces.

A man in uniform is walking alone up an oblique sidestreet;
He seems to look at the window beside him, grown from the street below;
At the foot of this, in sunlight, beyond walkers and two parked cars,
A lady lugging a heavy bag has just emerged into tiny view.

Though forty-five years later I can see them both
There is no possibility of their seeing each other;
They may have been intense lovers a year or two before;
It's more likely they will never meet throughout their lives.

Or they may pass each other at intervals of years,
In queues, in passport offices, in trams,
And never for one moment notice each other,
Or ever feel a long gap widening.

JOHN BURNSIDE (1955–   )

Dundee

The streets are waiting for a snow
that never falls:
too close to the water,
too muffled in the afterwarmth of jute,
the houses on Roseangle
opt for miraculous frosts
and the feeling of space that comes
in the gleam of day
when you step outside for the milk
or the morning post
and it seems as if a closeness in the mind
had opened and flowered:
the corners sudden and tender, the light immense,
the one who stands here proven after all.

Autobiography

It was late on a winter's evening:
travelling home from work on a crowded train
and stopping from time to time at a quiet station
to wait amidst the nothing that was there
between the darkness and the platform lamps,

and I'll never know quite who it was, when a single
thread of my being stood up and opened the door,
the night air chilling his skin and the smell of water
finding its own dark level in his lungs,
the entire train groaning and throbbing as it drew

away from the empty platform, leaving
only this stain of blood-heat on the snow:
a not-quite-human creature, all regret
and muted terror seeping from his throat
like old smoke, or the heat of eucalyptus.

CAROL ANN DUFFY (1955–   )

Warming Her Pearls

for Judith Radstone

Next to my own skin, her pearls. My mistress
bids me wear them, warm them, until evening,
when I'll brush her hair. At six, I place them
round her cool, white throat. All day I think of her,

resting in the Yellow Room, contemplating silk
or taffeta, which gown tonight? She fans herself
whilst I work willingly, my slow heat entering
each pearl. Slack on my neck, her rope.

She's beautiful. I dream about her
in my attic bed; picture her dancing
with tall men, puzzled by my faint, persistent scent
beneath her French perfume, her milky stones.

I dust her shoulders with a rabbit's foot,
watch the soft blush seep through her skin
like an indolent sigh. In her looking-glass
my red lips part as though I want to speak.

Full moon. Her carriage brings her home. I see
her every movement in my head . . .Undressing,
taking off her jewels, her slim hand reaching
for the case, slipping naked into bed, the way

she always does . . .And I lie here awake,
knowing the pearls are cooling even now
in the room where my mistress sleeps. All night
I feel their absence and I burn.

Words, Wide Night

Somewhere on the other side of this wide night
and the distance between us, I am thinking of you.
The room is turning slowly away from the moon.

This is pleasurable. Or shall I cross that out and say
it is sad? In one of the tenses I singing
an impossible song of desire that you cannot hear.

La lala la. See? I close my eyes and imagine
the dark hills I would have to cross
to reach you. For I am in love with you and this

is what it is like or what it is like in words.

Prayer

Some days, although we cannot pray, a prayer
utters itself. So, a woman will lift
her head from the sieve of her hands and stare
at the minims sung by a tree, a sudden gift.

Some nights, although we are faithless, the truth
enters our hearts, that small familiar pain;
then a man will stand stock-still, hearing his youth
in the distant Latin chanting of a train.

Pray for us now. Grade I piano scales
console the lodger looking out across
a Midlands town. Then dusk, and someone calls
a child's name as though they named their loss.

Darkness outside. Inside, the radio's prayer —
Rockall. Malin. Dogger. Finisterre.

ROBIN ROBERTSON (1955–   )

Aberdeen

The grey sea turns in its sleep
disturbing seagulls from the green rock.

We watched the long collapse, the black drop
and frothing of the toppled wave; looked out
on the dark that goes to Norway.

We lay all night in an open boat, that rocked
by the harbour wall – listening to the tyres creak
at the stone quay, trying to keep time –
till the night-fishers came in their arc, their lap
of light: the fat slap of waves, the water's
sway, the water mullioned with light.

The sifting rain, italic rain; the smirr
that drifted down for days; the sleet.
Your hair full of hail, as if sewn there.
In the damp sheets we left each other sea-gifts,
watermarks: long lost now in all these years
of the rip-tide's swell and trawl.

All night the feeding storm banked up
the streets and houses. In the morning
the sky was yellow, the frost ringing.

The grey sea turns in its sleep
disturbing seagulls from the green rock.

MEG BATEMAN (1959–)

Aotromachd

B' e d' aotromachd a rinn mo thàladh,
aotromachd do chainnte 's do ghàire,
aotromachd do lethchinn nam làmhan,
d' aotromachd lurach ùr mhàlda;
agus 's e aotromachd do phòige
a tha a' cur trasg air mo bheòil-sa,
is 's e aotromachd do ghlaic mum chuairt-sa
a leigeas seachad leis an t-sruth mi.

Lightness

It was your lightness that drew me,
the lightness of your talk and your laughter,
the lightness of your cheek in my hands,
your sweet gentle modest lightness;
and it is the lightness of your kiss
that is starving my mouth,
and the lightness of your embrace
that will let me go adrift.

Translated from the Gaelic by the author

W. N. HERBERT (1961–   )

The Socialist Manifesto for East Balgillo

I thi hovie an thi howd o sleep,	*swelling; swaying*
whaur Dundee dovirs oan thi rink	*where; half-sleeps*
o ma frore-thocht lyk a Michael-	
angelo oan skates, inna sowff o	*murmur*
faain, Eh gae back intae mains	*falling; farmlands*
oan mains o gorse an Pict-banes	
whaur thi doozie-land's a roidit	*flame (as of a candle); roughly made*
rist, and Sandy Hole Gaelic's pirn's	*
unspoolan i thi prisk guschet	*ancient corner of land*
o aa thocht's birth's biforrows,	*befores*
an therr, whaur garrons o thi speak	*horses, either elderly or sturdy; language*
ur growein back lyk a lizard's tail	
an aa'uts baists ur scarts an jenny-	*hermaphrodites*
wullocks, an aathin's lyk pellack,	*flesh of a porpoise*
thi peltin-pyock o aa 'feel'osophy,	*shabby garment*
Eh pense o naethin, lat naethin be,	*think*
see thi mense o Scoatlan lyk Mozart's	*meek*
gartillin concerto, hiz piana spaldit	*great; sprawled*
assa smokie, and innuts paums	*smoked fish; palms*
a gaitherin o chestnuts lyk shut een.	

* *[stringed instrument]; [variety of language spoken in Broughty Ferry]; spool's*

Coco-de-Mer — [Molucca bean]

Dinna bathir wi thi braiggil o wir lends	*dangerously unstable article; our loins*
that maks a cothaman o gravy	*surfeit*
i thi cot, but famine in wir crullit herts —	*cowering*
let gae oan thi dumbswaul, be	*silent sea-swell*
brankie i thi breakirs, an flocht,	*ready for fun; float*
flocht lyk thi crospunk intae Lewis —	*Molucca bean*
thi lucky-bean tae thi haunds o thi misk.	*coarse grassland*

KATHLEEN JAMIE (1962–   )

The Queen of Sheba

Scotland, you have invoked her name
just once too often
in your Presbyterian living rooms.
She's heard, yea
even unto heathenish Arabia
your vixen's bark of poverty, come down
the family like a lang neb, a thrawn streak,   nose; stubborn
a wally dug you never liked   [china dog]
but can't get shot of.

She's had enough. She's come.
Whit, tae this dump? Yes!
She rides first camel
of a swaying caravan
from her desert sands
to the peat and bracken
of the Pentland hills
across the fitba pitch
to the thin mirage
of the swings and chute; scattered with glass.

Breathe that streamy musk
on the Curriehill Road, not mutton-shanks
boiled for broth, nor the chlorine stink
of the swimming pool where skinny girls
accuse each other of verrucas.
In her bathhouses women bear
warm pot-bellied terracotta pitchers
on their laughing hips.
All that she desires, whatever she asks
She will make the bottled dreams
of your wee lasses
look like *sweeties*.

Spangles scarcely cover
her gorgeous breasts, hanging gardens,
jewels, frankincense; more voluptuous
even than Vi-next-door, whose
high-heeled slippers
keeked from dressing gowns
like little hooves, wee tails
of pink fur stuffed in the cleavage of her toes;
more audacious even than Currie Liz
who led the gala floats
through the Wimpey scheme
in a ruby-red Lotus Elan
before the Boys' Brigade band
and the Brownies' borrowed coal-truck;
hair piled like candy-floss;
who lifted her hands from the neat wheel
to tinkle her fingers
at her tricks
        among the Masons and the elders and the police.

The cool black skin
of the Bible couldn't hold her,
nor the atlas green
on the kitchen table,
you stuck with thumbs
and split to fruity hemispheres –
yellow Yemen, Red Sea, *Ethiopia*. Stick in
with the homework and you'll be
cliver like yer faither,
but no too cliver,
no *above yersel*.

See her lead those great soft camels
widdershins round the kirk-yaird,
smiling
as she eats
avocados with apostle spoons
she'll teach us how. But first

she wants to strip the willow
she desires the keys
              to the National Library
she is beckoning
      the lasses
      in the awestruck crowd . . .

Yes, we'd like to
        clap the camels,
to smell the spice,
admire her hairy legs and
bonny wicked smile, we want to take
PhDs in Persian, be vice
to her president: we want
to help her
        ask some Difficult Questions

she's shouting for our wisest man
to test her mettle:

        Scour Scotland for a Solomon!

Sure enough: from the back of the crowd
someone growls:
                whae do you think y'ur?

and a thousand laughing girls and she
draw our hot breath
            and shout:
THE QUEEN OF SHEBA!

Flower-sellers, Budapest

In the gardens
of their mild southern crofts, their
end-of-the-line hillside vineyards,
where figs turn blue, and peppers dry
strung from the eaves,

old women move among flowers,
each with a worn knife, a sliver
crooked in the first finger
of her right hand –
each, like her neighbours,
drawing the blade
onto the callus of her thumb,
so flowers, creamy dahlias,
fall into their arms; the stems'
spittle wiped on their pinafores.

Then, when they have enough,
the old women
foregather at the station
to await the slow, busy little train
that will take them to the city,
where families drift between mass
and lunch; and they hunker   *squat*
at bus depots, termini
scented with chrysanthemums,
to pull from plastic buckets
yellows, spicy russets,
the petally nub of each flower
tight as a bee;
and from their pockets, pink ribbon
strictly for the flowers.

We must buy some,
– though they will soon wither –
from this thin-faced
widow in a headscarf, this mother
perhaps, of married daughters
down at the border –
or *this* old woman, sat
among pigeons and lottery kiosks,
who reaches towards us to proffer
the morning's fresh blooms;
or the woman there who calls 'Flowers!'
in several languages –
one for each invasion:

We must buy some,
because only when the flowers are dispersed
will the old women head for home,
each with her neighbours,
back where they came, with their
empty buckets and thick aprons
on a late morning train.

St Bride's

So this is women's work: folding
and unfolding, be it linen or a selkie-   *[seal]*
skin tucked behind a rock. Consider

the hare in jizzen: her leverets' ears   *childbed*
flat as the mizzen of a ship
entering a bottle. A thread's trick;

adders uncoil into Spring. Feathers
of sunlight, glanced from a butterknife
quiver on the ceiling,

and a last sharp twist for the shoulders
delivers my daughter, the placenta
following, like a fist of purple kelp.

DON PATERSON (1963–)

A Private Bottling

So I will go, then. I would rather grieve over your absence than over you.
    (Antonio Porchia)

Back in the same room that an hour ago
we had led, lamp by lamp, into the darkness
I sit down and turn the radio on low
as the last girl on the planet still awake
reads a dedication to the ships
and puts on a recording of the ocean.

I carefully arrange a chain of nips
in a big fairy-ring; in each square glass
the tincture of a failed geography,
its dwindled burns and woodlands, whin-fires, heather,
the sklent of its wind and its salty rain,
the love-worn habits of its working-folk,
the waveform of their speech, and by extension
how they sing, make love, or take a joke.

So I have a good nose for this sort of thing.

Then I will suffer kiss after fierce kiss
letting their gold tongues slide along my tongue
as each gives up, in turn, its little song
of the patient years in glass and sherry-oak,
the shy negotiations with the sea,
air and earth, the trick of how the peat-smoke
was shut inside it, like a black thought.

Tonight I toast her with the extinct malts
of Ardlussa, Ladyburn and Dalintober
and an ancient pledge of passionate indifference:
Ochon o do dhóigh mé mo chlairsach ar a shon,
wishing her health, as I might wish her weather.

When the circle is closed and I have drunk myself sober
I will tilt the blinds a few degrees, and watch
the dawn grow in a glass of liver-salts,
wait for the birds, the milk-float's sweet nothings,
then slip back to the bed where she lies curled,
replace the live egg of her burning ass
gently, in the cold nest of my lap,
as dead to her as she is to the world.

*　　*　　*

Here we are again; it is precisely
twelve, fifteen, thirty years down the road
and one turn higher up the spiral chamber
that separates the burnt ale and dark grains
of what I know, from what I can remember.
Now each glass holds its micro-episode
in permanent suspension, like a movie-frame
on acetate, until it plays again,
revivified by a suave connoisseurship
that deepens in the silence and the dark
to something like an infinite sensitivity.
This is no romantic fantasy: my father
used to know a man who'd taste the sea,
then leave his nets strung out along the bay
because there were no fish in it that day.
Everything is in everything else. It is a matter
of attunement, as once, through the hiss and backwash,
I steered the dial into the voice of God
slightly to the left of Hilversum,
half-drowned by some big, blurry waltz
the way some stars obscure their dwarf companions
for centuries, till someone thinks to look.

In the same way, I can isolate the feints
of feminine effluvia, carrion, shite,
those rogues and toxins only introduced
to give the composition a little weight
as rough harmonics do the violin-note
or Pluto, Cheiron and the lesser saints
might do to our lives, for all you know.

(By Christ, you would recognise their absence
as anyone would testify, having sunk
a glass of *North British*, run off a patent still
in some sleet-hammered satellite of Edinburgh:
a bleak spirit, no amount of caramel
could sweeten or disguise, its after-effect
somewhere between a blanket-bath and a sad wank.
There is, no doubt, a bar in Lothian
where it is sworn upon and swallowed neat
by furloughed riggers and the Special Police,
men who hate the company of women.)

O whiskies of Long Island and Provence!
This little number catches at the throat
but is all sweetness in the finish: my tongue trips
first through burning brake-fluid, then nicotine,
pastis, *Diorissimo* and wet grass;
another is silk sleeves and lip-service
with a kick like a smacked puss in a train-station;
another, the light charge and the trace of zinc
tap-water picks up at the moon's eclipse.
You will know the time I mean by this.

Because your singular absence, in your absence,
has bred hard, tonight I take the waters
with the whole clan: our faceless ushers, bridesmaids,
our four Shelties, three now ghosts of ghosts;
our douce sons and our lovely loudmouthed daughters
who will, by this late hour, be fully grown,
perhaps with unborn children of their own.
So finally, let me propose a toast:
not to love, or life, or real feeling,
but to their sentimental residue;
to your sweet memory, but not to you.

The sun will close its circle in the sky
before I close my own, and drain the purely
offertory glass that tastes of nothing
but silence, burnt dust on the valves, and whisky.

The Chartres of Gowrie

for T.H.

Late August, say the records, when the gowk-storm   *spring storm*
shook itself out from a wisp of cloud
and sent them flying, their coats over their heads.
When every back was turned, the thunder-egg
thumped down in an empty barley-field.

No witness, then, and so we must imagine
everything, from the tiny crystal-stack,
its tingling light-code, the clear ripple of tines,
the shell snapping awake, the black rock
blooming through its heart like boiling tar,

to the great organ at dawn thundering away
half-a-mile up in the roof, still driving
each stone limb to its own extremity
and still unmanned, though if we find this hard
we may posit the autistic elder brother

of Maurice Duruflé or Messiaen.
Whatever, the reality is this:
at Errol, Grange, Longforgan, and St Madoes
they stand dumb in their doorframes, all agog
at the black ship moored in the sea of corn.

Biographical Notes

ST COLUMBA (521–597)

Born at Garton, Co. Donegal, into the warrior aristocracy of Ireland, he studied at the Irish centres of monastic learning, Magh Bile, Clonard and Glasnevin, and in 546 founded the monastery at Derry. Exiled in 563 for involvement in the Battle of Cuildreimhne, he found haven, with twelve disciples, on the Hebridean island of Iona: the monastery he founded there was the mother church of Celtic Christianity in Scotland. As well as writing hymns, he is credited with having transcribed over 300 books.

ANEIRIN (fl. 6th–7th century)

'Aneirin' is the name given to the author of the manuscript in the Brythonic language, the form of primitive Welsh once current throughout Britain south of the Forth. The chief work in Brythonic, Y Gododdin, describes the annihilation of British heroes at the Battle of Cattraeth (Catterick, Yorkshire).

MUGRÓN, ABBOT OF IONA (d. 980)

Mugrón, whose name means 'seal-slave', was Abbot of Iona at a time when the monastery there was recovering the prestige it had largely lost to Kells in Ireland. 'Cros Chríst' is an example of a common form of incantatory Gaelic devotional verse, the lorica ('breastplate').

EARL ROGNVALD KALI (ST RONALD OF ORKNEY) (d. 1158)

Rognvald Kali was a Norwegian nobleman with a claim, through his uncle St Magnus of Orkney, to the earldom of Orkney. He duly conquered the Northern Isles in 1136, and built the cathedral at Kirkwall, the finest surviving Viking monument, in his uncle's honour. He employed many poets at his court, with one of whom, the Icelander Hall Thorarinsson, he is said to have composed the Hattalykill, the 'Key of Metres', which demonstrated every metre of Norse poetry. Rognvald Kali was murdered in Caithness in 1158. His relics were removed to his cathedral in Kirkwall where they remain today.

GUILLAUME LE CLERC (d. 1238)

'Guillaume le Clerc' was the pen-name of a Frenchman living and working in Scotland at the end of the twelfth century; William Malveisin, a native of the lower Seine, and Bishop of St Andrews from 1202 until his death in 1238, has been proposed as a viable candidate.

MUIREADHACH ALBANACH Ó DÁLAIGH (fl. 1200–1224)

One of the earliest named practitioners of strictly metrical Gaelic verse, Muireadhach Ó Dálaigh was poet to the king of Tír Conaill in Ireland until he murdered the king's steward, and was forced to flee to Scotland. He is reputed to be the progenitor of the famous bardic family of MacMhuirich, which can be traced, in poems and other records, through six centuries.

JOHN BARBOUR (c. 1320–1395)

Barbour was Archdeacon of Aberdeen, and attached as Auditor to the court of Robert II. He wrote two long poems that are now lost: *The Brut* (a history of the Britons) and *The Stewartis Original*, which invented a pedigree for the Stewart dynasty. *The Bruce* was written by royal request, around 1375, to relate Robert I's exploits in freeing Scotland from English domination.

JAMES I (1394–1437)

James I was captured at sea by the English while travelling to France as a boy in 1406, and was held in England until 1424. During his imprisonment he fell in love with Henry V's cousin, Lady Joan Beaufort, for whom he is reputed to have written *The Kingis Quair*, which, though written in Scots, shows the influence of Chaucer's dream visions. On his return to Scotland, his policies of restraining the powers of the nobility led to his murder in Perth by Sir Robert Stewart.

ROBERT HENRYSON (c. 1420–c. 1490)

Little is known about his life, except that he was a schoolmaster in Dunfermline, and that he was dead by 1508 when Dunbar writes of him in his 'Lament for the Makars'. External evidence and the content of his poems suggest that he studied law in Glasgow and in Rome. His output was small. Aside from his *Testament of Cresseid*, which takes up her story where Chaucer's *Troylus and Cryseyde* leaves it, and the *Fables*, drawn from Aesop and the thirteenth-century *Roman de Renart*, each with its suspiciously complacent 'moralitas', and the witty version of the story of Orpheus and Eurydice, there are only the Scottish pastoral of 'Robene and Makyne' and a few short morality pieces; but the distinction of this slender *œuvre* puts him in the front rank of Scottish poets of any period.

BLIND HARRY (c. 1450–1493)

'Blind Hary', mentioned in Dunbar's 'Lament for the Makars', described himself as 'unlearned', though his work shows familiarity with contemporary scholarship. He seems to have lived as a professional poet, receiving patronage from James IV. His *Wallace*, in twelve books of heroic couplets, glorifies the exploits of Sir William Wallace (1272–1305) in his campaigns against the English.

AITHBHREAC INGHEAN CORCADAIL (fl. 1460s)

Highly developed conventions of praise and lament informed the eulogies and elegies of professional Gaelic bards; but Aithbhreac Inghean Corcadail's lament for her husband, chief of the MacNeills on the island of Gigha, strikes a more personal note. 'A Phaidrín do dhúisg mo dhéar' comes down to us from the Book of the Dean of Lismore.

WILLIAM DUNBAR (c. 1460–c. 1520)

Born in East Lothian, Dunbar was enrolled at the University of St Andrews between 1477 and 1479. His poem 'How Dunbar was desyred to be ane Freir' describes how he trained as a Franciscan novice, travelling to England and Picardy before leaving the order. He served at the court of King James IV, first as an ambassador and then, from 1500, as court poet. The 'Golden Age' of James's reign and its literature, of which Dunbar is the brilliant central figure, ended with the death of the king at the Battle of Flodden in 1513; thereafter Dunbar's poetry began to embrace spiritual subjects more often than secular ones, and the natural melancholy of his temperament is increasingly apparent.

GAVIN DOUGLAS (c. 1474–1522)

Son of the 5th Earl of Angus, Douglas was born in Tantallon Castle, East Lothian. Educated for the priesthood at St Andrews, in 1503 he became Provost of St Giles in Edinburgh, and in 1515 Bishop of Dunkeld. He enjoyed the patronage of James IV, but was involved in intrigue during the long upheavals after the Battle of Flodden (1513), and was exiled in 1521 to England, where he died suddenly of the plague. His only surviving original poem is the courtly allegory *The Palice of Honour*, but each of the thirteen books of his famous translation of the Aeneid, the *Eneados*, has an original prologue.

SIR DAVID LINDSAY (1490–1555)

Last of the great 'makars' of the late Middle Ages, Lindsay was born into an aristocratic family and as a youth was made companion to the future King James V. In the 1530s and 1540s he was an influential diplomat. His verse is principally satirical, rebuking social abuses in the medieval manner, but from an increasingly Protestant standpoint. Lindsay's best-known work is *Ane Satyre of the Thrie Estaits* (1540), which combines the form of morality drama with topical concerns.

GEORGE BUCHANAN (1506–1582)

Born near Killearn in Stirlingshire, Buchanan was educated at the local grammar school, where he showed such aptitude that he was sent at the age of fourteen to the University of Paris. In 1537, James V recalled him to act as tutor to one of his sons, but his satirical writings led to his condemnation as a heretic and to his arrest (at Coimbra in Portugal) and imprisonment for six years by the Inquisition. On his release, despite his leanings towards Protestantism he was made Classical tutor to the teenage Queen Mary, but turned against her in a scurrilous pamphlet after the murder of her husband, Darnley. Author of a monumental twenty-volume history of Scotland, *Rerum scoticarum historia*, he was one of the foremost scholars of the Scottish Reformation and one of the finest Latinists of his day.

JAMES (d.1553), JOHN (d.1556), and ROBERT (d.1557) WEDDERBURN

The three sons of a prosperous Dundee merchant were all educated at St Leonard's College in St Andrews, where they first encountered the ideas of the Reformation. All three were ultimately banished from Scotland for their beliefs. Together they were responsible for the compilation of sacred and secular songs and ballads known as *The Gude and Godlie Ballatis*, published in 1567, after their deaths.

ALEXANDER SCOTT (c. 1513–1583)

Trained as a musician, he became organist at the Augustinian Priory of Inchmahome in the Firth of Forth in 1548, and was associated with the court of Mary, Queen of Scots, though he may subsequently have favoured Protestantism. He became a considerable landowner in Perthshire, Fife and around Edinburgh. His love poems in the courtly tradition, collected in the Bannatyne MS, are predominantly bitter – the result, it is said, of his wife's leaving him.

SIR THOMAS MAITLAND (1522–c. 1572)

Younger brother of the poet and anthologist Sir Richard Maitland of Lethington (who compiled the Maitland Manuscripts, an important source of early Scots texts), he was born in what is now East Lothian. The full title of his 'Satyr' gives the following description of Neil Laing: 'who was a priest and one of the Pope's knights about the time of the Reformation'.

MRS MACGREGOR OF GLENSTRAE (*fl.* 1570)

Having failed in his attempt to preserve his clan's independence, MacGregor of Glenstrae was beheaded at Balloch Castle, Taymouth, in 1570 by members of the Clan Campbell. The lament attributed to his widow, Marion Campbell, combines elements of classic bardic syllabic verse with the looser qualities of folksong. By 1604, Glenstrae was forfeited and the MacGregor clan outlawed.

MARY, QUEEN OF SCOTS (1542–1587)

She was born at Linlithgow, the daughter of James V and Mary of Guise-Lorraine, and succeeded to the Scottish throne on the death of her father when she was only six days old. In her minority, factions led by her mother (as regent) and the reformers vied for power. In 1558 she married Francis, the Dauphin of France, but he died in 1561, shortly after his accession. That year she returned to Scotland and claimed the kingdom. She pursued a conciliatory religious policy, but her second marriage, to her cousin Henry, Lord Darnley, his murder, and her subsequent marriage to the Earl of Bothwell outraged the nobility, who overthrew her in 1567 and imprisoned her in Lochleven Castle. Abdicating in favour of her son, James VI, she then escaped, but after defeat at the Battle of Langside was compelled to take refuge in England. Perceived there as a potential focus for Catholic dissent, she was kept in detention and eventually executed in 1587 for her part in the Babington plot.

NIALL MÓR MACMHUIRICH (*c.* 1550–c. 1615)

Perhaps born in Kintyre, he was one of the many generations of his family to inherit bardic office. Among the few surviving poems ascribed to him, the lyric 'Soraidh slan don oidhche a-réir' is in the *dánta grádha* or courtly mode of bardic verse.

ALEXANDER MONTGOMERIE (*c.* 1555–1598)

Born at Hessilhead Castle near Beith, Ayrshire, he became a leading member of the 'Castalian' of poets at the court of James VI, founded by the king himself in 1583. Montgomerie's adherence to Catholicism led eventually (in 1597) to his banishment for treason, and he died in exile. His long poem 'The Cherrie and the Slae' is an allegorical complaint for his faith.

ALEXANDER HUME (*c.* 1556–1609)

Son of the fifth Lord Polwarth, he was born on the family estate in the Borders, and educated at the University of St Andrews and in France. He spent some years at the court of James VI before becoming a minister of the Reformed Church. It was at court that he wrote his one great poem, 'Of the Day Estivall', his comtemplation of the sights and sounds of a midsummer's day, and other 'Sacred Songs'.

WILLIAM FOWLER (1560–1612)

After studying at St Andrews, Fowler operated as a spy for the Protestant cause in Paris before returning in 1584 to become a minister in Hawick. He enjoyed the patronage of James VI, and was secretary to Queen Anne in London when he died. An *aficionado* of Italian poetry, he translated Petrarch, and his sonnet sequence *The Tarantula of Love* is modelled after Castiglione.

MARK ALEXANDER BOYD (1563–1601)

Born in Penkill in Ayrshire, Boyd studied law in Paris, Orleans, Bourges and Italy. He fought in the French civil war in the army of Henry III, and alternated his studies with a career as a soldier. His wanderings in Europe are recounted in his letters, written in Latin and published in 1592. Boyd wrote Latin poetry after the model of Ovid; his single poem in Scots is one of the dialect's finest love poems.

SIR ROBERT AYTOUN (1570–1638)

Born at Kinaldie, Fife, and educated at nearby St Andrews, he later studied law in Paris, returning in 1603 to become a member of the court of James VI. He followed the king to London, became secretary to the queen, and was knighted in 1612. He is buried in Westminster Abbey. He wrote poetry in English in the Metaphysical manner, as well as Latin poems for state occasions and a number of songs: he has been credited with a version of 'Auld Lang Syne'.

WILLIAM DRUMMOND OF HAWTHORNDEN (1585–1649)

The son of a gentleman-usher to James VI, he was born in the family house of Hawthornden near Edinburgh. Educated at the newly-founded University of Edinburgh, he became laird on his father's death in 1610, and thereafter led a retiring life, much of it in his substantial library. Ben Jonson visited him in 1618 and kept a record of their conversations. Drummond wrote in English, but harking back to the Petrarchan tradition rather than in the Metaphysical mode prevailing in his own day. His death is said to have been hastened by grief at the execution of Charles I.

ARTHUR JOHNSTON (1587–1641)

Johnston was educated at King's College, Aberdeen, where he was made Lord Rector in 1637 after a long stay on the Continent. He compiled (with Sir John Scott of Scotstarvit) the *Delitiae Poetarum Scotorum*, a collection of poems in Latin by thirty-seven Scottish poets. The best of his own Latin verse is rooted in the everyday life of his native Donside.

JAMES GRAHAM, MARQUIS OF MONTROSE (1612–1650)

Educated at the University of St Andrews, he was one of the first to sign the National Covenant (in 1638) against the Anglican church policy of Charles I, but he fought on the side of the king against Parliament in the Civil War, and his Highland and Irish army won several victories before defeat at Philiphaugh in 1645. He spent the next five years in Europe, trying to raise support for the Royalist cause. When he returned to Scotland, his attempt to raise the Highlanders for Charles II ended in defeat at the Battle of Carbisdale in 1650, and he was executed in Edinburgh that spring. Only fragments of his poetry have survived.

FRANCIS SEMPILL (c. 1616–1682)

He was born in Beltrees in Renfrewshire, the son of Robert Sempill, who had written the poem ('The Life and Death of Habbie Simson, the Piper of Kilbarchan') which patented in Scots the 'Standard Habbie' stanza so often used by Ramsay, Fergusson and Burns. Francis Sempill studied law, and was latterly appointed Sheriff-Depute of Renfrewshire; during his lifetime he enjoyed a reputation as a light-hearted poet and wit.

MÀIRI NIGHEAN ALASDAIR RUAIDH / MARY MACLEOD (c. 1616–c. 1706)

Born in Rodel, on Harris, she was employed for very many years as a nurse to the MacLeods of Dunvegan on Skye, though she is said to have been banished at some point. Famed for her poems in praise of clan chiefs, she stands with Iain Lom at the watershed between classical Gaelic poetry and the more individualistic verse of the eighteenth century, using stressed versification in place of syllabics and employing a more colloquial diction.

IAIN LOM / JOHN MACDONALD (c. 1624–c. 1710)

Born into a family closely related to the chiefs of the Macdonalds of Keppoch, he is said to have trained as a priest at the Catholic seminary at Valladolid in Spain, and throughout his life was devoted to his clan, his church and the house of Stewart. A typical early poem gloats over the defeat of the Campbells by Montrose and the Macdonalds at the Battle of Inverlochy in 1645. At the Restoration, Charles II reputedly awarded Iain Lom a pension as his poet in Scotland. He continued to make vituperative poems in the Stewart or Jacobite cause, against William and Mary, and against the Act of Union, until his death and burial in Brae Lochaber. His work is a remarkable document of sixty years of Highland history, and he extended the imaginative range of poetry in Gaelic.

SÌLEAS NA CEAPAICH / CICELY MACDONALD (c. 1660–c. 1729)

She was born in Glen Roy, the daughter of Gilleasbuig Mac Mhic Raghnaill, chief of the MacDonalds of Keppoch. She married Alexander Gordon, and lived most of her life in Banffshire where he was a factor to the Duke of Gordon. Like many Gaelic poets of her day, she poured scorn on the Act of Union, and made several pro-Jacobite songs. The Glengarry elegy is a formal lament, but it is informed by her own grief at the death of her husband, who died the year before Glengarry, in 1720.

ALLAN RAMSAY (1684–1758)

He was born in Leadhills, Lanarkshire, son of the factor to the Earl of Hopetoun. In 1700, he was apprenticed to a wig-maker in Edinburgh. Later he became a bookseller, founded the first circulating library in Britain, and, in 1736, opened a playhouse in Edinburgh, though this was closed by the Licensing Act of the following year. Ramsay wrote poems in both English and Scots (the best of the latter being mock-elegies for certain Edinburgh personalities), and a verse drama, *The Gentle Shepherd* (1725), with lively scenes of peasant dialogue. He also did important work as an editor of literature in Scots, producing a two-volume anthology of early poetry, *The Ever Green* (1724), largely taken from the Bannatyne MS, and five volumes of traditional songs and ballads, *The Tea-Table Miscellany* (1724–37).

ALASDAIR MAC MHAIGHSTIR ALASDAIR / ALEXANDER MACDONALD (c. 1695–c. 1770)

A native of Moidart and son of an Episcopalian minister, Alasdair Mac Mhaighstir Alasdair taught for the Society for the Propagation of Christian Knowledge at Ardnamurchan, where he remained until the Jacobite rising of 1745, in which he fought in Clanranald's regiment. In 1741 he produced a Gaelic–English dictionary, and in 1751 published his poems as *Ais-Eiridh na Sean-Chánoin Albannaich* ('Resurrection of the Ancient Scottish Tongue'). He eventually converted to Catholicism. His range as a poet was broad, encompassing political satire, robust love poetry and nature poems like 'Òran an t-Samhraidh' ('Song of Summer'), which is evidently influenced by James Thomson's *Seasons*. 'Birlinn Chlann Raghnaill' ('Clanranald's Galley') is the outstanding single poem of the eighteenth-century Gaelic revival.

JAMES THOMSON (1700–1748)

Born in Ednam, Roxburghshire, Thomson was educated at Jedburgh School and studied for the ministry at Edinburgh University, but he abandoned his studies to seek his fortune in London as a writer. 'Winter' (1726) was the first of the four poems printed together as *The Seasons* in 1730, and substantially revised in 1744. He wrote several verse plays and the masque *Alfred* (which contained the song 'Rule, Britannia'), and won considerable patronage:

a pension from the Prince of Wales and the sinecure of Surveyor-General of the Leeward Islands. The Spenserian *The Castle of Indolence* was published a few weeks before his death.

DAVID MALLOCH [MALLET] (1705–1765)

Born in Perthshire, the son of a schoolmaster, he served as a tutor to various families, settling in London and embarking, through his friendship with James Thomson, on a literary career. He changed his surname, either to disguise his Scottish origins or in response to being satirized as 'Moloch'. Though his several plays and long poem *An Excursion* are forgotten now, he earned notoriety in his day for his attacks on Alexander Pope.

JEAN ADAM (1710–1765)

Born in Greenock, the daughter of a shipmaster, she was orphaned at an early age and became a governess, later establishing a school for girls in Greenock. She died in a Glasgow poorhouse. She published only one collection of poems, but 'There's Nae Luck about the House' became well known after David Herd included it in his collection of 1776.

ROB DONN MACAOIDH / ROBERT MACKAY (1714–1778)

Born in Strathmore in Sutherland, he stayed in that district for most of his life (though he served in the Sutherland Highlanders for a time in the 1760s); and it is the life of an isolated Highland community that informs his poems. Though he could not read or write, he was familiar with the works of Pope, and his poems are fairly sophisticated. A Protestant, he was none the less firmly attached to the Jacobite cause.

ADAM SKIRVING (1719–1803)

An occasional songwriter, Skirving was a farmer near Prestonpans in East Lothian, where in 1745 Jacobite forces defeated the government army under Sir John Cope; Skirving may well have witnessed the battle.

IAIN MAC MHURCHAIDH / JOHN MACRAE (d. c. 1780)

A native of Kintail in Ross-shire, he emigrated to North Carolina in 1774, and fought on the side of the rebels in the American War of Independence. He was taken prisoner in 1776 and died in captivity. 'Dèan Cadalan Sàmhach' is a nostalgic lullaby addressed to the poet's daughter.

DONNCHADH BAN MAC-AN-T-SAOIR/DUNCAN BAN MACINTYRE (1724–1812)

Born in Glen Orchy, on the border between Argyll and Perthshire, MacIntyre worked as a gamekeeper and forester. He did not read or write, but his intricate poems and songs were copied down and published in 1768. 'Moladh Beinn Dobhrain', composed in praise of Ben Dorain, the mountain dominating Glen Orchy, is the summit of his achievement in nature poetry, its elaborate rhyming structure resembling the patterning of the pibroch. He lived latterly in Edinburgh where he kept a whisky shop with his wife, Màiri. A granite monument to the poet stands at the head of Loch Awe.

JEAN ELLIOT (1727–1805)

Jean Elliot was the daughter of Sir Gilbert Elliot of Minto. The lament for the dead of the Battle of Flodden (1513), 'The Flowers of the Forest', existed in traditional form before it was reworked and preserved by the songwriters of the eighteenth century. Jean Elliot's version has proved the most durable; it is her only surviving composition.

JAMES MACPHERSON (1736–1796)

Born at Ruthven, Inverness-shire, the son of a farmer, he was educated at Aberdeen and Edinburgh Universities. In 1758 he published his epic, *The Highlander*. Encouraged by Hugh Blair and John Home, Macpherson then began to pursue his interest in collecting Gaelic poetry, and in 1760 published *Fragments of Ancient Poetry Collected in the Highlands of Scotland and Translated from the Gaelic or Erse Language*, with an introduction by Blair speculating that great epic poetry relating to the third-century hero Fingal (Finn Mac Cumhail), as told by his son Ossian, was still extant in parts of the Highlands. After further fieldwork, Macpherson duly published *Fingal: an Ancient Epic Poem* as by Ossian. The poem was a sensational success, though it eventually emerged that while Macpherson did collect and translate materials from authentic sources, these were only parts of a patchwork devised and substantially composed by him. Moving to London, he subsequently became a wealthy man with interests in the East India Company. He is buried in Westminster Abbey.

ROBERT FERGUSSON (1750–1774)

Born in Edinburgh, he was schooled there, in Dundee, and at the University of St Andrews, from which he had to withdraw in 1768 on the death of his father, taking a position as clerk in the Commissary Office. Though he had many friends in Edinburgh's literary and tavern societies, illness (probably syphilis) and severe depression forced him out of his employment, and a fall downstairs was the pretext for his confinement in the Edinburgh Bedlam, where he died at the age of twenty-four. More than half of Fergusson's *œuvre* is in literary English; but there are also thirty-three poems in Scots vernacular. His work is generally urban and comic in spirit, but with an ambition and breadth of expression (especially in the long piece *Auld Reikie*) that revived the literary potential of Scots, and so helped to make possible the achievement of his admirer Burns.

ROBERT BURNS (1759–1796)

Burns was one of seven children born to a cotter or tenant farmer near Alloway in Ayrshire. Though the family was poor he received a thorough education, and began to write verses while still at school. On his father's death in 1784, he and his brother Gilbert took on the ailing farm at Mossgiel, near Mauchline. In 1785, the servant girl Elizabeth Paton bore his first child; in 1786, he made Jean Armour pregnant with twins. When the latter's father forbade her to marry him, he took up with another girl, Mary Campbell, who died soon after. This was the turbulent background to the publication of *Poems, Chiefly in the Scottish Dialect* in 1786. The book was an immediate success in Edinburgh, where Burns duly travelled to be lionized (in the words of Henry Mackenzie) as 'a Heaven-taught ploughman'; but he found no patron. It was during his twenty-one months in the capital that he was asked to help in the collection of old Scottish songs, a project he was to pursue with wonderful energy, recording, adapting, or composing anew over 200 vernacular lyrics. In 1788 he finally married Jean Armour and settled back in the south-west, first as a farmer, then as an exciseman in the town of Dumfries, where he died of rheumatic heart disease.

UILLEAM ROS / WILLIAM ROSS (1762–1790)

He was born in Strath on the Isle of Skye, but his family later settled in Gairloch in Wester Ross. While visiting Stornoway as a travelling packman he fell in love with Marion Ross, for whom most of his melancholy love poetry was composed. In 1786 he was appointed parish schoolmaster in Gairloch, but he died young and heartbroken, probably suffering from tuberculosis. Ros made poems in praise of clan chiefs, whisky, the Jacobite cause and the seasons, but it was the love poems that influenced (for example) Somhairle MacGill-Eain (Sorley MacLean).

JOANNA BAILLIE (1762–1851)

Born in Bothwell, Lanarkshire, the daughter of a minister who claimed descent from William Wallace, she moved to London with her family in 1784. She became known there as a dramatist, and her plays were admired by her friend Walter Scott, though they proved more successful on the page than in performance. She is remembered now rather for a handful of lyrics in *Fugitive Verses* (1790) which catch the tone of Lowland Scots folksong.

CAROLINA OLIPHANT (LADY NAIRNE) (1766–1845)

Daughter of a Perthshire Jacobite, she married her cousin William Nairne, who was subsequently restored to his estates and peerage; in later life she travelled widely in Europe and Ireland. A keen student of the songs of Burns, she composed songs of her own to traditional airs (publishing as 'Mrs Bogan of Bogan'), many of them demonstrating her sentimental attachment to the Jacobite cause, and attaining lasting popularity.

JAMES HOGG (1770–1835)

Born on a farm in the Ettrick Forest, Hogg worked as a shepherd while developing an interest in writing and in the Border ballads, which he helped to collect. A meeting with Walter Scott led to a lifelong friendship. In 1810 he moved to Edinburgh, and his fortunes changed when, with the publication of his poem-sequence *The Queen's Wake* (1813), the Duke of Buccleuch gave him a farm in Yarrow rent-free for life. His most famous work is his third novel, *The Private Memoirs and Confessions of a Justified Sinner* (1824).

SIR WALTER SCOTT (1771–1832)

Born in Edinburgh, Scott studied law and moved to live in the Borders when he was made Sheriff-Depute of Selkirkshire in 1799. There he completed *The Minstrelsy of the Scottish Border*, a collection of the best Border ballads. A series of long narrative poems followed, including *The Lay of the Last Minstrel, Marmion* and *The Lady of the Lake*, which were phenomenally successful. When public taste began to prefer Byron's verse romances, Scott turned to prose fiction, effectively inventing the historical novel in the anonymous Waverley series (called after the title of the first of them, in 1814), which themselves featured many songs and ballads. The immense earnings generated by these books caused him to overreach himself, particularly in the building of his grand house, Abbotsford, on the Tweed near Melrose; and when his publisher crashed in 1825 he heroically dedicated the last years of his life to working off the debt – amounting to £120,000 – for which he took responsibility.

ROBERT TANNAHILL (1774–1810)

A weaver from Paisley, he composed a number of songs to traditional tunes. His poems were printed in 1807, but recognition eluded him and depression caused him to drown himself in a canal. He became celebrated after his death as Paisley's own 'bard'.

THOMAS CAMPBELL (1777–1841)

Campbell was born in Glasgow and educated at the University there. In 1803, failing to make headway in his law studies at Edinburgh, he moved to London and began to produce the ballads and martial poems which became fixtures in the Victorian schoolroom.

ALLAN CUNNINGHAM (1784–1842)

Born in Dalswinton, Dumfriesshire, he was apprenticed as a stonemason, but through his father's friendship with Robert Burns he turned to a literary career, collecting (and inventing) ballads for Robert Cromek's *Remains of Nithsdale and Galloway Song*. In 1811 he moved to London, working as a parliamentary reporter, and wrote sentimental Jacobite and sea songs which became popular.

WILLIAM TENNANT (1784–1848)

He was born in Anstruther, Fife, and educated at the University of St Andrews, where in 1834, after a career spent as a schoolmaster, he was appointed Professor of Oriental Languages. His *Synopsis of Chaldic and Syriac Grammar* (1840) was a standard textbook for many years. Tennant wrote two verse dramas, *Cardinal Beaton* and *John Balliol*, and an epic poem, *The Thane of Fife*. *Anster Fair*, a comic poem in English about a country festival, and *Papistry Storm'd*, a lively account in Scots of the destruction of St Andrews Cathedral, have lasted better than his other works.

GEORGE GORDON, LORD BYRON (1788–1824)

Born in London, he was taken to Aberdeen at the age of four so that his mother could be near her relatives, and he attended Aberdeen Grammar School. In 1798 he succeeded to the family title, and soon after left Scotland for good. After Harrow and Trinity College, Cambridge, he travelled widely, and composed *Childe Harold's Pilgrimage* (1812), the first of the series of Romantic narrative poems that eclipsed those of Scott in the public taste and made him the most celebrated poet of his day. Sexual scandal drove him from London to the Continent; having taken up the Greek cause against the Turks, he died of rheumatic fever at Missolonghi.

JANET HAMILTON (1795–1873)

Born in Carshill in Lanarkshire, she was the daughter of a shoemaker. Though her childhood was poor, and though she married at thirteen and raised a large family, she had a sound education; and her reading of Ramsay and Burns inspired her to write poems and songs. Though derivative in style and comic in spirit, these reflect the hardships of the mining community in which she lived. In later life she went blind.

WILLIAM ANDERSON (1805–1866)

Born in Edinburgh, he was the son of the supervisor of excise at Oban. From 1831 he was a working journalist, first on the *Aberdeen Journal* and later as chief sub-editor on the *Glasgow Daily Mail*, Scotland's first daily newspaper.

WILLIAM EDMONDSTOUNE AYTOUN (1813–1865)

He was born in Edinburgh, where he studied law at the University. While practising at the bar, he worked on the staff of *Blackwood's Magazine*. A versatile writer, he was known for his satirical prose and for his romantic ballads of Scottish history, the latter collected in *Lays of the Scottish Cavaliers and Other Poems* (1849), which was a bestseller.

GEORGE MACDONALD (1824–1905)

Born in Huntly, Aberdeenshire, the son of a farmer, he was educated at King's College, Aberdeen, and at Highbury Theological College in London. After a spell as a Congregationalist minister, he turned to journalism and lecturing. His first published works were poems of an other-worldly cast; later, he found success with novels of the Aberdeenshire countryside, fantasy novels (notably *Lilith*, 1895), and fairy-tales for children.

WILLIAM MACGONAGALL (1825–1902)

Probably born in Ireland, before his father (an Irish weaver) settled his family in Dundee. He was over fifty when his first collection of poems was published, containing 'Railway Bridge of the Silvery Tay'; their distinctively wayward metrics and tortured rhymes caught the imagination of a half-mocking public, and MacGonagall, with the connivance of his audiences, grew convinced that he was a genuine 'tragedian'. A later poem laments the collapse of the Tay Bridge.

ALEXANDER SMITH (1830–1867)

Born in Kilmarnock, Ayrshire, the son of a pattern designer, he worked in Glasgow until he was appointed Secretary to the University of Edinburgh in 1854. A precocious poet, he allied himself to the 'Spasmodic' school, with their overheated imagery; *City Poems* (1857), which included 'Glasgow', revealed a more substantial talent. *A Summer in Skye* (1865) is one of the best of Scottish travel books.

JAMES THOMSON ('B.V.') (1834–1882)

Thomson was born in Port Glasgow, the son of a merchant seaman, but at the age of six he was removed to London, where he attended an institution for Scottish orphans. An alcoholic, he was 'discharged with disgrace' from his first post as an army schoolmaster, and thereafter lived in a succession of rented rooms, with an irregular income from freelance journalism. He never published under his own name, preferring the pseudonym 'B.V.' ('Bysshe', from Shelley's middle name, and 'Vanolis', an anagram of the name of the German poet Novalis).

ELLEN JOHNSTON (c. 1835–1873)

Born in Hamilton, she published poems on industrial life under the pseudonym 'Factory Girl'. She is known to have received £50 from the Royal Bounty Fund, but she died destitute at the Barony Poorhouse in Glasgow.

MARION BERNSTEIN (*fl.* 1876)

Little is known of the life of the Paisley poet Marion Bernstein. Poems from her collection *Mirren's Musings* (1876) were included by Tom Leonard in his anthology *Radical Renfrew* (1989). In the preface to her book, Bernstein alludes to a physical affliction which rendered her bedbound through the years of its composition.

ANDREW LANG (1844–1912)

Born in Selkirk, the son of the Sheriff-Clerk of Selkirkshire, he was educated at the University of St Andrews and at Oxford before settling in London, where he became a highly successful journalist, a prolific critic and an influential anthropologist. He wrote and collected fairy-stories in a celebrated series of 'coloured' books.

JAMES ROBERTSON (1849–1922)

Born in Milnathort, Kinross, Robertson was educated at Edinburgh University and taught for nearly forty years at the Edinburgh Ladies College. He invented the pseudonym 'Hugh Haliburton' for a series of pastoral poems, written in Scots, which became highly popular. He produced useful editions of Scottish poets for schools.

ROBERT LOUIS STEVENSON (1850–1894)

Born in Edinburgh, the son of a lighthouse engineer, he studied law at the University there. His writing career began with travel books, and continued with a series of adventure, mystery and children's novels through the 1880s, including *Treasure Island*, *Kidnapped* and

The Master of Ballantrae. His poems were collected in *A Child's Garden of Verses* (1885) and *Underwoods* (1887). Always frail, he left Britain for his health in 1888, and settled in Samoa, where he died suddenly of a cerebral haemorrhage.

JOHN DAVIDSON (1857–1909)

Born in Barrhead, Renfrewshire, the son of a minister, Davidson held various teaching posts until he moved to London in 1890. Though he had written plays and fiction, his preferred forms by this time were the ballad and the dramatic monologue. W. B. Yeats praised his *In a Music Hall and Other Poems* (1891), but sales of subsequent volumes failed to support him financially; the onset of illness and the strain of debt drove him to kill himself by drowning off Penzance, Cornwall.

VIOLET JACOB (1863–1946)

She was born Violet Kennedy-Erskine, the daughter of the 18th Laird of Dun. She married an army officer and spent some years in India, before returning to her native north-east, which supplied the accent and subject-matter of her poems, short stories and novels.

CHARLES MURRAY (1864–1941)

Born in Alford, Aberdeenshire, he trained as an engineer and later emigrated to South Africa. He served in the Boer War and then in the government of South Africa, becoming Secretary of Public Works in 1912. From this great distance he wrote poems in the dialect of his native north-east. They were criticized by Hugh MacDiarmid for their sentimentality, but were highly popular, and at their best were more vigorous and worldly than his detractors allowed.

MARION ANGUS (1866–1946)

Brought up in Arbroath, where her father was a minister, she moved on his death to Aberdeen to look after her sister and invalid mother. She did not start writing poetry, influenced by her reading of the Border ballads, until she was in her fifties.

LEWIS SPENCE (1874–1955)

Born in Broughty Ferry near Dundee, he gave up a career in dentistry to pursue his interest in world mythologies, becoming an authority on Central and South America and Celtic Britain. In poetry, he was one of the first Scottish poets of the twentieth century to use archaic Scots vocabulary, earning the approval of Hugh MacDiarmid, though the two later quarrelled. In politics, he was one of the founder-members of the National Party of Scotland in 1928, and wrote many articles on the issue of Scottish independence.

RACHEL ANNAND TAYLOR (1876–1960)

Born in Aberdeen and educated at the University there, she later lived in Dundee and London. Her own poetry has a Pre-Raphaelite quality, but she wrote a study of Dunbar (1931) which assisted the revival of interest in the early Scots 'makars'.

ANDREW YOUNG (1885–1971)

Born in Elgin, Young was educated in Edinburgh and became a minister of the United Free Church before moving to Sussex and taking orders in the Church of England.

HELEN B. CRUICKSHANK (1886–1975)

Born near Montrose in the north-east, Cruickshank worked as a civil servant in Edinburgh. She was secretary of Scottish PEN and befriended (among other poets) Hugh MacDiarmid, whom she helped to support in the 1930s.

EDWIN MUIR (1887–1959)

Muir was born on his father's rented farm on Deerness, Orkney, and brought up on the neighbouring island of Wyre. His peaceful childhood gained symbolic significance when the family moved to Glasgow in 1901; his poems return obsessively to the myth of Eden and the Fall enacted in his early life. In 1919 he married Willa Anderson, with whom he collaborated on translations (notably of Kafka). In 1921 they left for Europe, and it was in Dresden, at the age of thirty-five, that Muir began to write poetry. After the Second World War Muir held British Council posts in Prague and Rome, and later retired to a cottage in Cambridgeshire.

HUGH MACDIARMID (Christopher Murray Grieve) (1892–1978)

Christopher Grieve was born in Langholm, Dumfriesshire, the son of a postman, and educated at Langholm Academy. After war service, he settled in Montrose, where he worked as a journalist and edited the *Scottish Chapbook* (1922–3), which promoted the idea of writing in the Scots language and printed his own Scots lyrics over his pseudonym. These lyrics were collected in *Sangschaw* (1925) and *Penny Wheep* (1926); 1926 also saw the publication of *A Drunk Man Looks at the Thistle*, his bold, abundant, 3,000-line poem in a Scots diction 'synthesized' from the various dialects of Lowland Scotland: 'designed to show that Braid Scots [which he later preferred to call "Lallans"] can be effectively applied to all manner of subjects and measures'. In 1928 he was a founder-member of the National Party of Scotland (from which he was subsequently expelled for his communism); in 1934 he joined the Communist Party (from which he was expelled for his nationalism). In 1933 he moved with his second wife to the Shetland island of Whalsay. He stopped writing poetry in Scots around this time, but his ambition and outspokenness continued to express themselves as forcefully in English.

WILLIAM SOUTAR (1898–1943)

Born in Perth, the son of a joiner, Soutar served in the Royal Navy during the First World War, when he first showed signs of the condition – spondylitis – that was to render him bedridden from 1930 onwards. His first collection of poems in Scots, in 1933, were 'bairn-rhymes' for children; he wrote to Hugh MacDiarmid of his belief 'that if the Doric is to come back alive, it will come first on a cock-horse'; in 1935 he published *Poems in Scots*, though he later turned to verse in English. Through his wide circle of friends he maintained an interest in Scottish nationalism. In the last year of his life he kept a diary, published as *Diaries of a Dying Man* in 1954.

NORMAN CAMERON (1905–1958)

Cameron was educated at Fettes College, Edinburgh, and Oxford University, where he befriended Robert Graves; he later lived with Graves (and Laura Riding) in Majorca. He worked as an advertising copywriter, and in the Second World War as a political officer in North Africa.

ROBERT GARIOCH (1909–1981)

Born Robert Garioch Sutherland in Edinburgh, he was educated at the University there and taught at schools in Edinburgh, London and Kent. In the Second World War he served in North Africa, and was a prisoner-of-war in Italy and Germany for three years. He wrote in Scots, and his best-known poems are pithy pieces concerned, often satirically, with his native city; 'The Wire' is a more sombre long poem born out of his wartime experience.

NORMAN MACCAIG (1910–1996)

Born in Edinburgh, MacCaig was educated at the Royal High School and at Edinburgh University, where he read Classics. He was a conscientious objector during the Second World War. He worked as a schoolteacher in Edinburgh from 1934 to 1970, and thereafter at the University of Stirling, where he was Reader in Poetry. Many of his poems reflect his affection for the area around Lochinver in Sutherland, where he spent his summers.

SOMHAIRLE MACGILL-EAIN/SORLEY MACLEAN (1911–1996)

Born on the island of Raasay, he went to school on Skye and studied English at Edinburgh University. His career as a schoolteacher – latterly as headmaster at Plockton in Wester Ross – was interrupted by the Second World War, during which he served with the Signal Corps in North Africa and was severely wounded at the Battle of El Alamein in 1943. In the same year he published *Dàin do Eimhir agus Dàin Eile*, a mixture of love poems and political poems which is the most prominent landmark in the revival of Gaelic literature in the twentieth century.

RUTHVEN TODD (1914–1978)

Born in Edinburgh of American parents, he was educated at Fettes College and the Edinburgh School of Art. He worked as a labourer on Mull and as a journalist before moving to London, where he began to edit the poems of William Blake and to write adventure novels (as 'R. T. Campbell'), and then to New York State, where he became a successful small-press publisher.

SYDNEY GOODSIR SMITH (1915–1975)

Born in Wellington, New Zealand, of Scottish parents, Sydney Goodsir Smith went to live in Edinburgh at the age of twelve when his father was appointed to a Chair of Medicine at the University. By 1940, he was writing poetry in Scots. Exuberant and bawdy, much of his work features aspects of his adopted city, in the spirit of his literary forebear Robert Fergusson. He also wrote a nationalist play in verse, *The Wallace* (1960).

DEÒRSA MAC IAIN DEÒRSA/GEORGE CAMPBELL HAY (1915–1984)

Born in Renfrewshire, the son of the novelist John Macdougall Hay, he studied Modern Languages at Oxford University. He served in North Africa in the Second World War. His first two collections were in Gaelic, though he was not a native speaker; he later wrote in Scots and in English, and translated European poetry into all three languages.

W. S. GRAHAM (1918–1986)

Born in Greenock, Graham trained as a structural engineer while studying literature and philosophy at night classes; he then studied at Newbattle Abbey, near Edinburgh. After 1943 he lived at Madron and Mevagissey in Cornwall, where poetry was his main employment. He published his first book in 1942, and was associated with neo-Romantic models – Dylan Thomas and George Barker – until his breakthrough in 1955 with the wholly individual *The Nightfishing*.

ELMA MITCHELL (1919–   )

Elma Mitchell was born in Airdrie, but has spent most of her life in England. A professional librarian, she has lived latterly in Somerset, working as a freelance writer and translator.

EDWIN MORGAN (1920–   )

Born in Glasgow, he attended and subsequently taught at Glasgow University, becoming Professor of English in 1975. After the breakthrough of his collection *The Second Life* (1968), his poetry has embraced scientific imagery and a technological vocabulary, and his exuberant experimentalism has sometimes taken 'concrete' form. Morgan is a skilful and prolific translator from many languages of poems ranging from the 'Altus Prosator' and *Beowulf* to those of Mayakovsky and Lorca, sometimes into Scots.

RUARAIDH MACTHÒMAIS/DERICK THOMSON (1921–   )

Born on the island of Lewis, he was educated in Stornoway and at the Universities of Aberdeen and Cambridge. He held the chair of Celtic Studies at Glasgow from 1963 to 1991, and has written extensively on Gaelic and Highland culture. He writes his poetry in Gaelic, translating it himself into English.

GEORGE MACKAY BROWN (1921–1996)

He was born in Stromness, Orkney, where, after attending the University of Edinburgh, he returned to spend the rest of his life. The communal life of Orkney, from prehistory to the present day, provided the material, not only for his poems, but for novels, short stories and plays.

IAN HAMILTON FINLAY (1925–   )

Born in Nassau, in the Bahamas, he was sent to boarding school in Scotland; he took various unskilled jobs until, after attending Glasgow School of Art, he settled in Perthshire. In the 1960s he became a prominent figure in the international movement of 'concrete' poetry, and there is a strong visual element in his own work – which is sometimes indivisible from sculpture. Since 1966 he has lived in Lanarkshire in a farm cottage with a four-acre garden ('Little Sparta'), where his works are installed.

ALASTAIR REID (1926–   )

Reid was born in Whithorn, Wigtonshire. After serving in the Royal Navy and studying at the University of St Andrews, he has spent most of his life in America; he was for many years a staff writer for the *New Yorker*.

IAIN MAC A' GHOBHAINN/IAIN CRICHTON SMITH (1928–1998)

Born and brought up on the island of Lewis, he studied at the University of Aberdeen and was a schoolteacher in Clydebank and Oban until 1977, when he retired to write – novels, short stories and plays, as well as verse. He published poetry in English and Gaelic, and made several translations from one to the other, including his acclaimed version of Duncan Ban MacIntyre's 'Ben Dorain'.

STEWART CONN (1936–   )

Born in Glasgow, Conn studied at Glasgow University and after national service worked as a producer with BBC radio, in which capacity he has encouraged many young Scottish writers. As well as verse, he has written the successful play *The Burning* (1972), about James VI.

AONGHAS MACNEACAIL (1942–   )

Born at Uig, Isle of Skye, he studied at Glasgow University. A well-known campaigner for Gaelic, he has written for radio and television, and has authored several collections of poetry in Gaelic and English, including *Oideachadh Ceart / A Proper Schooling* (1996).

DOUGLAS DUNN (1942–   )

Born at Inchinnan, Renfrewshire, Dunn studied at the Scottish School of Librarianship and at the University of Hull, where he fell under the influence of the University Librarian, Philip Larkin, and composed his first book, *Terry Street*, about that city. Other notable volumes include *Elegies* (1985), a series of poems about the death of his first wife. Since his return to Scotland in the 1980s, he has concerned himself increasingly with Scottish subjects. He edited *The Faber Book of Twentieth-Century Scottish Poetry* (1992), and teaches at the University of St Andrews.

TOM LEONARD (1944–   )

Born in Glasgow, Leonard studied at Glasgow University. As well as his poems in Scots, which use phonetic misspellings to render working-class Glaswegian speech, he has written humorous poems in English and an innovative biography, *Places of the Mind* (1991), of James Thomson ('B.V.').

LIZ LOCHHEAD (1947–   )

Born in Motherwell, she attended Glasgow School of Art and was an art teacher for a decade before becoming a full-time writer, most notably of plays and monologues for the theatre.

FRANK KUPPNER (1951–   )

Born in Glasgow and educated at Glasgow University, Kuppner is an offbeat writer in verse and fictional prose. He has specialized in long sequence-poems composed in numbered free-verse quatrains.

JOHN BURNSIDE (1955–   )

Born in Dunfermline, he was brought up in Corby, Northamptonshire, and educated at Cambridge College of Arts and Technology. He has worked as a computer analyst. In addition to his volumes of verse, he has published novels and short stories. He lives in Fife.

CAROL ANN DUFFY (1955–   )

Born in Glasgow, she was brought up in Staffordshire and graduated in philosophy from the University of Liverpool. An early interest in the theatre developed into her continuing preoccupation with verse monologue, which she has used to lyrical and satirical effect.

ROBIN ROBERTSON (1955–   )

Born in Aberdeen and brought up in the north-east, he has worked in London as a publisher, of Scottish authors in particular. He was over forty when his first collection, *A Painted Field*, was published in 1997.

MEG BATEMAN (1959–   )

Born in Edinburgh, Meg Bateman learned Gaelic at Aberdeen University and on South Uist. She has since taught in the Celtic Studies Department at Aberdeen University and at Sabhal Mór Ostaig on Skye.

W. N. HERBERT (1961–   )

Born in Dundee and educated at Oxford University, he has held various teaching posts and writer's residencies in Scotland and England, and has published poetry in both English and Scots, as well as a critical book on Hugh MacDiarmid.

KATHLEEN JAMIE (1962–   )

Born in Johnstone, Renfrewshire, Kathleen Jamie grew up near Edinburgh and studied philosophy at Edinburgh University. She has written in verse and prose about her travels, especially in the East, and lives in Fife where she teaches at St Andrews University.

DON PATERSON (1963–   )

Born in Dundee in 1963, Don Paterson left school at sixteen. A professional jazz musician, he also works as an editor. He lives in Edinburgh.

Index of Poets

Index of First Lines

Acknowledgements

ANEIRIN: from 'The Gododdin', translated by Joseph P. Clancy, from *The Triumph Tree: Scotland's Earliest Poetry, AD 550–1350*, edited by T. O. Clancy (Canongate Books, 1998), reprinted by permission of the publisher; MARION ANGUS: 'Alas! Poor Queen', 'The Blue Jacket' and 'The Doors of Sleep' from *The Turn of the Day* (Faber and Faber, 1931), reprinted by permission of the publisher; ANONYMOUS: 'The Dream of the Rood', reprinted by permission of the translator, Robert Crawford; 'A Ughdar so Oiséan'/'The Author of this is Ossian' from *The Book of the Dean of Lismore* (1542), translated by Derick Thomson in *An Introduction to Gaelic Poetry* by Derick Thomson (Victor Gollancz, 1977), reprinted by permission of Derick Thomson; 'Arann', translated by Thomas Owen Clancy, from *The Triumph Tree: Scotland's Earliest Poetry, AD 550–1350*, edited by T. O. Clancy (Canongate Books, 1998), reprinted by permission of Canongate Books and Cork University Press; 'Thig trì nithean gun iarraidh'/'Three things come without seeking', translated by Iain Crichton Smith, from *Collected Poems* by Iain Crichton Smith (Carcanet Press, 1992), reprinted by permission of the publisher; MEG BATEMAN: 'Aotromachd'/'Lightness' from *Lightness and Other Poems* (Polygon, 1997), reprinted by permission of the publisher; GEORGE MACKAY BROWN: 'Kirkyard', 'Hamnavoe Market' and 'Taxman' from *Selected Poems 1954–1983* (John Murray, 1991), reprinted by permission of the publisher; GEORGE BUCHANAN: 'Ad Henricum Scotorum Regem'/'To Henry Darnley, King of Scots', reprinted by permission of the translator, Robert Crawford; JOHN BURNSIDE: 'Dundee' from *The Myth of the Twin* (Jonathan Cape, 1994), reprinted by permission of The Random House Archive and Library; 'Autobiography' from *The Times Literary Supplement* (15 January 1999), reprinted by permission of the author; NORMAN CAMERON: 'Meeting my Former Self' and 'Green, Green is El Aghir' from *Norman Cameron: Collected Poems and Selected Translations*, edited by Warren Hope and Jonathan Barker (Anvil Press Poetry, 1990), reprinted by permission of the publisher; SÌLEAS NA CEAPAICH: from 'Alasdair of Glengarry', translated by Derick Thomson, from *Gaelic Poetry in the Eighteenth Century*, edited by Derick Thomson (Association for Scottish Literary Studies, 1993), reprinted by permission of Derick Thomson; GUILLAUME LE CLERC: from 'Fergus', reprinted by permission of the translator, Mick Imlah; ST COLUMBA: 'Altus Prosator'/'The Maker on High', translated by Edwin Morgan, from *Collected Translations* by Edwin Morgan (Carcanet Press, 1996), reprinted by permission of the publisher; STEWART CONN: 'Todd' and 'Under the Ice' from *Stolen Light: Selected Poems* (Bloodaxe Books, 1999), reprinted by permission of the publisher; AITHBHREAC INGHEAN CORCADAIL: 'A phaidrín do dhúsig mo dhéar'/'O rosary that recalled my tear', translated by Derick Thomson, from *An Introduction to Gaelic Poetry* by Derick Thomson (Victor Gollancz, 1977), reprinted by permission of Derick

Thomson; HELEN B. CRUICKSHANK: 'The Ponnage Pool' from *Collected Poems* (Reprographia, 1971); MUIREADHACH ALBANACH Ó DÁLAIGH: 'M'anam do sgar riomsa a-raoir'/ 'Elegy on Mael Mhedha, his Wife', translated by Thomas Owen Clancy, from *The Triumph Tree: Scotland's Earliest Poetry, AD 550–1350*, edited by T. O. Clancy (Canongate Books, 1998), reprinted by permission of the publisher; WILLIAM DRUMMOND: 'Polemo-Middinia inter Vitarvam et Nebernam'/'The Midden-Battle between Lady Scotstarvit and the Mistress of Newbarns', translated by Allan H. MacLaine, from *Christis Kirk Tradition: Scots Poems of Folk Festivity* (Association for Scottish Literary Studies, 1996), reprinted by permission of Allan H. MacLaine; CAROL ANN DUFFY: 'Warming Her Pearls' from *Selling Manhattan* (Anvil Press Poetry, 1987), 'Words, Wide Night' from *The Other Country* (Anvil Press Poetry, 1990) and 'Prayer' from *Mean Time* (Anvil Press Poetry, 1993), reprinted by permission of the publisher; DOUGLAS DUNN: 'Landscape with One Figure', 'St Kilda's Parliament: 1879–1979', 'War Blinded' and 'Land Love' from *Selected Poems 1964–1983* (Faber and Faber, 1986), reprinted by permission of the publisher; IAN HAMILTON FINLAY: 'Evening – Sail', reprinted by permission of the author; 'The Boat's Blueprint' and 'The Cloud's Anchor' from *Ian Hamilton Finlay: A Visual Primer* by Yves Abrioux (Reaktion Books, 1992), reprinted by permission of the author and publisher; ROBERT GARIOCH: 'Elegy' and 'The Wire' from *Complete Poetical Works*, edited by Robin Fulton (Macdonald Publishers, 1983), reprinted by permission of The Saltire Society; W. S. GRAHAM: 'Malcolm Mooney's Land' and 'Loch Thom' from *Collected Poems 1942–1977* (Faber and Faber, 1979), © The Estate of W. S. Graham, reprinted by permission of Margaret Snow, Literary Executor for W. S. Graham Estate; GEORGE CAMPBELL HAY: 'Bisearta'/'Bizerta' from *Modern Scottish Gaelic Poems*, edited by D. Macaulay (Southside, 1976), reprinted by permission of Canongate Books; W. N. HERBERT: 'The Socialist Manifesto for East Balgillo' from *Forked Tongue* (Bloodaxe Books, 1994), reprinted by permission of the publisher; 'Coco-de-Mer' from *Sharawaggi* (Polygon, 1990), reprinted by permission of the publisher; VIOLET JACOB: 'Tam i' the Kirk' and 'The Helpmate' from *The Scottish Poems of Violet Jacob* (Oliver & Boyd, 1944); KATHLEEN JAMIE: 'The Queen of Sheba' from *The Queen of Sheba* (Bloodaxe Books, 1994), reprinted by permission of the publisher; 'Flower-sellers, Budapest' and 'St Bride's' from *Jizzen* (Picador, 1999), reprinted by permission of Macmillan Publishers Ltd; ARTHUR JOHNSTON: from 'Ad Robertum Baronium'/'To Robert Baron', reprinted by permission of the translator, Robert Crawford; EARL ROGNVALD KALI: 'The Attributes of a Gentleman' (newly translated for this volume by Paul Bibire), reprinted by permission; FRANK KUPPNER: from 'An Old Guidebook to Prague' from *The Intelligent Observation of Naked Women* (Carcanet Press, 1987), reprinted by permission of the publisher; TOM LEONARD: lines from 'Unrelated Incidents', 'Jist ti Let Yi No' and 'Fathers and Sons' from *Intimate Voices: Selected Work 1965–1983* (Galloping Dog Press, 1984; Vintage, 1985), © Tom Leonard, reprinted by permission of the author; LIZ LOCHHEAD: 'Something I'm Not' from *Dreaming Frankenstein and Collected Poems* (Polygon, 1984), reprinted by permission of the publisher: 'Neckties' from *Bagpipe Muzak* (Penguin Books, 1991); NORMAN MACCAIG: 'Instrument and Agent', 'Summer Farm', 'Likenesses', 'Basking Shark', 'Wild Oats', 'Return to Scalpay', 'Praise of a Collie', 'Intruder in a Set Scene' and 'Small Lochs' from *Collected Poems* (Chatto & Windus, 1990), reprinted by permission of The Random House Archive and Library; HUGH MACDIARMID: 'The Bonnie Broukit Bairn', 'The Watergaw', 'The Eemis Stane', 'Scunner', 'Empty Vessel', from 'A Drunk Man Looks at the Thistle', 'At

My Father's grave', 'Of John Davison', 'On a Raised Beach', 'The Little White Rose', 'Perfect', 'To a Friend and Fellow-Poet' and 'Scotland Small?' from *Complete Poems 1920–1976*, two volumes, edited by M. Grieve and W. R. Aitken (Martin Brian & O'Keeffe, 1978), reprinted by permission of Carcanet Press; ALEXANDER MACDONALD: from 'Song of Summer', translated by Derick Thomson, from *Gaelic Poetry in the Eighteenth Century*, edited by Derick Thomson (Association for Scottish Literary Studies, 1993), reprinted by permission of Derick Thomson; from 'Birlinn Chlann Raghnaill'/'Clanranald's Galley', translated by Hugh MacDiarmid, from *Complete Poems I* by Hugh MacDiarmid (Carcarnet Press, 1993), reprinted by permission of the publisher; JOHN MACDONALD: 'Oran Cumhaidh air cor na Rìoghachd'/'A Lament for the State of the Country', translated by Meg Bateman, from *The Harp's Cry: An Anthology of 17th Century Gaelic Poetry*, edited by Colm ú'Baoill (Birlinn, 1994), reprinted by permission of the publisher; MRS MACGREGOR OF GLENSTRAE: 'Cumha Ghriogair MhicGhriogair Ghlinn Sréith'/'Lament for MacGregor of Glenstrae', translated by Iain Crichton Smith, from *Collected Poems* by Iain Crichton Smith (Carcanet Press, 1992), reprinted by permission of the publisher; DUNCAN BAN MACINTYRE: from 'Moladh Beinn Dobhrain'/'Ben Dorain', translated by Iain Crichton Smith, from *Collected Poems* by Iain Crichton Smith (Carcanet Press, 1992), reprinted by permission of the publisher; ROBERT MACKAY: 'The Rispond Misers', translated by Derick Thomson, from *Gaelic Poetry in the Eighteenth Century*, edited by Derick Thomson (Association for Scottish Literary Studies, 1993), reprinted by permission of Derick Thomson; SORLEY MACLEAN: 'Ban-Ghaidheal'/'A Highland Woman', 'Calbharaigh'/'Calvary', 'Muir-tràigh'/'Ebb', 'Glac a' Bhàis'/'Death Valley' and 'Hallaig' from *Collected Poems in Gaelic and English* (Carcanet Press, 1989), reprinted by permission of the publisher; NIALL MÓR MACMHUIRICH: 'Farewell for ever to last night', translated by Derick Thomson, from *An Introduction to Gaelic Poetry* by Derick Thomson (Victor Gollancz, 1977), reprinted by permission of Derick Thomson; AONGHAS MACNEACAIL: 'tha gàidhlig beo'/'gaelic is alive', from *an seachnadh agus dàin eile/the avoiding and other poems* (Macdonald, 1986), reprinted by permission of the Saltire Society; JOHN MACRAE: 'Sleep Softly', translated by Derick Thomson, from *Gaelic Poetry in the Eighteenth Century*, edited by Derick Thomson (Association for Scottish Literary Studies, 1993), reprinted by permission of Derick Thomson; MARY, QUEEN OF SCOTS: 'Poem, Composed on the Morning of her Execution', translated by Agnes Strickland, from *The Paradise of Women: Writings by Englishwomen of the Renaissance*, edited by Betty Travitsky (Columbia University Press, 1989); ELMA MITCHELL: 'The Passenger Opposite' from *People Etcetera: Poems New and Selected* (Peterloo Poets, 1987), reprinted by permission of the publisher; EDWIN MORGAN: 'King Billy', 'Message Clear', 'The Loch Ness Monster's Song', 'The First Men on Mercury', 'Cinquevalli' and 'The Coin' from *Collected Poems* (Carcanet Press, 1990), reprinted by permission of the publisher; MUGRÓN: 'Cros Críst'/'Christ's Cross', translated by Thomas Owen Clancy, from *The Triumph Tree: Scotland's Earliest Poetry, AD 550–1350*, edited by T. O. Clancy (Canongate Books, 1998), reprinted by permission of the publisher; EDWIN MUIR: 'Childhood', 'Merlin', 'Scotland 1941', 'Scotland's Winter' and 'The Horses' from *The Complete Poems of Edwin Muir*, edited by P. H. Butter (Association for Scottish Literary Studies, 1991), reprinted by permission of Faber and Faber Ltd; CHARLES MURRAY: 'Dockens afore his Peers' from *Hamewith and Other Poems* (Constable, 1927) reprinted by permission of Colin Milton on behalf of the Charles Murray Memorial Fund; DON PATERSON: 'The

Chartres of Gowrie' and 'A Private Bottling' from *God's Gift to Women* (Faber and Faber, 1997), reprinted by permission of the publisher; ALASTAIR REID: 'Scotland' from *Weathering: Poems and Translations* (Canongate Books, 1978), © Alastair Reid, reprinted by permission of the author; ROBIN ROBERTSON: 'Aberdeen' from *A Painted Field* (Picador, 1997), reprinted by permission of Macmillan Publishers Ltd; WILLIAM ROSS: 'Oran Eile'/ 'Another Song', translated by Derick Thomson, from *Gaelic Poetry in the Eighteenth Century*, edited by Derick Thomson (Association for Scottish Literary Studies, 1993), reprinted by permission of the translator; IAIN CRICHTON SMITH: 'The Clearances', 'Old Woman', 'Two Girls Singing', 'Contrasts', 'The Herring Girls', 'Gaelic Stories' and 'Na h-Eilthirich'/'The Exiles' from *Collected Poems* (Carcanet, 1992), reprinted by permission of the publisher; SYDNEY GOODSIR SMITH: 'The War in Fife', Part VII of 'Armageddon in Albyn' from *Collected Poems* (Calder Publications, 1975), reprinted by permission of the publisher; WILLIAM SOUTAR: 'The Room', 'The Philosophic Taed' and 'The Tryst' from *Poems of William Soutar, A New Selection*, edited by W. R. Aitken (Scottish Academic Press, 1988), reprinted by permission of the publisher; LEWIS SPENCE: 'The Prows O'Reekie' from *The Collected Poems of Lewis Spence* (Serif Books, 1953); RACHEL ANNAND TAYLOR: 'The Princess of Scotland' from *The Faber Book of Twentieth-Century Scottish Poetry*, edited by Douglas Dunn (Faber and Faber, 1993), reprinted by permission of Louise G. Annand and Dr Walter J. D. Annand; DERICK THOMSON: 'Clann-Nighean an Sgadain'/'The Herring Girls' from *Plundering the Harp: Collected Poems 1940–1980* (Macdonald Publishers, 1982), reprinted by permission of the author; RUTHVEN TODD: 'Of Moulds and Mushrooms' from *Garland for the Winter Solstice* (Dent, 1961), reprinted by permission of David Higham Associates; ANDREW YOUNG: 'A Dead Mole', 'The Stockdoves' and 'A Wet Day' from *Selected Poems*, edited by Edward Lowbury and Alison Young (Carcanet Press, 1998), reprinted by permission of the publisher.

Penguin apologize for any errors or omissions in the above list and would be grateful to be notified of any corrections that should be incorporated in the next edition or reprint of this volume.